Who Were the Progressives?

HISTORIANS AT WORK

Advisory Editor
Edward Countryman, Southern Methodist University

How Did American Slavery Begin?
Edward Countryman, Southern Methodist University

What Caused the Pueblo Revolt of 1680?
David J. Weber, Southern Methodist University

What Did the Declaration Declare?
Joseph J. Ellis, Mount Holyoke College

What Did the Constitution Mean to Early Americans?
Edward Countryman, Southern Methodist University

Whose Right to Bear Arms Did the Second Amendment Protect?
Saul Cornell, The Ohio State University

What Were the Causes of the Civil War?
Bruce Levine, University of California, Santa Cruz
(forthcoming)

When Did Southern Segregation Begin?
John David Smith, North Carolina State University

Does the Frontier Experience Make America Exceptional?
Richard W. Etulain, University of New Mexico

Who Were the Progressives?
Glenda Elizabeth Gilmore, Yale University

What Did the Internment of Japanese Americans Mean?
Alice Yang Murray, University of California, Santa Cruz

Who Were the Progressives?

Readings Selected and Introduced by

Glenda Elizabeth Gilmore
Yale University

Selections by

Richard Hofstadter

Elizabeth Sanders

Robert H. Wiebe

Richard L. McCormick

Shelton Stromquist

James J. Connolly

Maureen A. Flanagan

Glenda Elizabeth Gilmore

Bedford / St. Martin's   *Boston* ♦ *New York*

For Bedford / St. Martin's

Publisher for History: Patricia A. Rossi
Developmental Editors: Gretchen Boger, Sarah Barrash
Editorial Assistant: Julie Mooza
Editorial Assistant, Publishing Services: Maria Teresa Burwell
Senior Production Supervisor: Dennis J. Conroy
Production Associate: Christie Gross
Marketing Manager: Jenna Bookin Barry
Project Management: Books By Design, Inc.
Text Design: Claire Seng-Niemoeller
Cover Design: Zenobia Rivetna
Cover Photo: Vaccine Queue © Lewis W. Hine/Getty Images.
Composition: Stratford Publishing Services, Inc.
Printing and Binding: Haddon Craftsmen, an RR Donnelley & Sons Company

President: Charles H. Christensen
Editorial Director: Joan E. Feinberg
Director of Marketing: Karen R. Melton
Director of Editing, Design, and Production: Marcia Cohen
Manager, Publishing Services: Emily Berleth

Library of Congress Control Number: 2001096412

Copyright © 2002 by Bedford/St. Martin's

Manufactured in the United States of America.

7   6   5   4   3   2
f   e   d   c   b   a

For information, write: Bedford/St. Martin's, 75 Arlington Street, Boston, MA 02116 (617-399-4000)

ISBN: 0-312-18930-3 (paperback)
       0-312-29436-0 (hardcover)

Acknowledgments

JAMES J. CONNOLLY. "The Dimensions of Progressivism." From *The Triumph of Ethnic Progressivism: Urban Political Culture in Boston, 1900–1925.* Copyright © 1998 by the President and Fellows of Harvard College. Reprinted by permission of Harvard University Press.
MAUREEN A. FLANAGAN. "Gender and Urban Political Reform: The City Club and the Woman's City Club of Chicago in the Progressive Era." From *The American Historical Review,* Volume 95, No. 4, October 1990. Copyright © 1990. Reprinted by permission.

Acknowledgments and copyrights are continued at the back of the book on page 266, which constitutes an extension of the copyright page.

Foreword

The short, inexpensive, and tightly focused books in the Historians at Work series set out to show students what historians do by turning closed specialist debate into an open discussion about important and interesting historical problems. These volumes invite students to confront the issues historians grapple with while providing enough support so that students can form their own opinions and join the debate. The books convey the intellectual excitement of "doing history" that should be at the core of any undergraduate study of the discipline. Each volume starts with a contemporary historical question that is posed in the book's title. The question focuses on either an important historical document (the Declaration of Independence, the Emancipation Proclamation) or a major problem or event (the beginnings of American slavery, the Pueblo Revolt of 1680) in American history. An introduction supplies the basic historical context students need and then traces the ongoing debate among historians, showing both how old questions have yielded new answers and how new questions have arisen. Following this two-part introduction are four to eight interpretive selections by top scholars, many reprinted in their entirety from journals and books, including endnotes. Each selection is either a very recent piece or a classic argument that is still in play and is headed by a question that relates it to the book's core problem. Volumes that focus on a document reprint it in the opening materials so that students can read arguments alongside the evidence and reasoning on which they rest.

One purpose of these books is to show students that they *can* engage with sophisticated writing and arguments. To help them do so, each selection includes apparatus that provides context for engaged reading and critical thinking. An informative headnote introduces the angle of inquiry that the reading explores and closes with Questions for a Closer Reading, which invite students to probe the selection's assumptions, evidence, and argument. Suggestions for Further Reading conclude each book, pointing interested students toward relevant materials for extended study.

Historical discourse is rarely a matter of simple opposition. These volumes show how ideas develop and how answers change, as minor themes turn into major considerations. The Historians at Work volumes bring together thoughtful statements in an ongoing conversation about topics that continue to engender debate, drawing students into the historical discussion with enough context and support to participate themselves. These books aim to show how serious scholars have made sense of the past and why what they do is both enjoyable and worthwhile.

EDWARD COUNTRYMAN

Preface

This book results from my own discontents with Progressive Era synthesis. The selections I have chosen highlight how historical thinking in the second half of the twentieth century has reshaped the way we see the beginning of that century. This volume introduces students to the period 1890–1920 by asking, "Who were the Progressives?" Beginning with Richard Hofstadter's old-stock middle-class reformers and moving through a vibrant debate on how others in society participated in the Progressive Era, *Who Were the Progressives?* introduces the broad diversity of Progressive reformers.

So that students can grasp the historical arguments and the stakes behind identifying which groups participated in Progressivism, the Introduction turns first to a description of the Progressive Era. It portrays not only the changing material circumstances of Americans resulting from urbanization, migration, and the changing nature of work, but also the processes by which the Progressives imagined creating a smoothly functioning and democratic society in an industrial world. It questions who took part in those imaginings and finally examines the solutions that they implemented. The Introduction goes on to point out how Progressive Era thinking changed over time and how historians have seen the period since. Suggestions on how to read and question the historical essays come at the end of the Introduction.

In the course of creating this volume, I realized how difficult it is to do everything well in a small space. I wanted to include articles that represented the geographic diversity of Progressivism — North and South, East and West, urban and rural — but the collection ultimately slights rural settings and the West to portray in greater detail Progressivism in cities in the Midwest, East, and South. I wanted to include working-class, immigrant, and African American viewpoints and be sure that women and gender figured into the book. To accomplish these goals within a reasonable number of pages, an article on Progressivism and imperialism had to be cut, and the collection does not include an article on Progressives as conservationists. Even with these regrettable cuts, I burst the seams of the Historians at

Work format with inclusions; I thank Edward Countryman for generously allowing me to do that.

Who Were the Progressives? departs from the format of the questions and selections of other Historians at Work volumes. Because historians take such contrasting views of who the Progressives were, two examples of these divergent views are grouped under a single question in each of four sections. Questions for a Closer Reading prompt students to do close reading, but focus on getting students to compare arguments among the articles and thereby take the place of the Making Connections questions that appear in other volumes. Headnotes provide background information on the author and selection. Suggestions for Further Reading point students to additional scholarly topics and works related to Progressivism.

Acknowledgments

This is a short book with a long history. Just how long is made clear by the fact that I began work on it while teaching Gretchen Boger here at Yale. Katherine E. Kurzman, then at Bedford/St. Martin's, encouraged me to explore the issue of Progressivism in the Historians at Work series. My ex-student, Boger, went on to work with Kurzman at Bedford/St. Martin's, to win promotion, and to become my editor. We enjoyed a successful working relationship, and after some years, she joined the Peace Corps. Meanwhile, I was still sorting out answers to the question "Who were the Progressives?"

The reviewers who read two earlier versions of the book almost deserve coeditor billing. I have never been through a more thorough review process—Bedford/St. Martin's sends out detailed questionnaires to seven or eight readers—nor a more helpful one. I paid an enormous amount of attention to their criticisms and suggestions, right up until the last moment. Some remained anonymous, but I want especially to thank those who did not: Alan Dawley, The College of New Jersey; Sarah Deutsch, University of Arizona; Robert Mangrum, Howard Payne University; Kimberly Porter, University of North Dakota; and Daniel Rodgers, Princeton University. I responded to their reviews by changing the final version to incorporate their suggestions, so none of them saw the book you hold in your hands. But they can surely see their influence spread over its pages.

My second editor at Bedford/St. Martin's, Sarah Barrash, raced against two deadlines, her wedding and our publication date, and worked with me over Memorial Day to make both of them with time to spare. She has been industrious and patient as she came fresh to the project, inspiring me to get a second wind and to enjoy finishing the book. She knew just how to handle my frustrations.

Karen Leathem stepped forward to edit each incarnation of the book long after other friends would have let me know they did not care any longer who the Progressives were. Katherine Charron surveyed the literature and located articles for me. Adriane Smith and Jed Shugerman read and commented on drafts, as did Jacquelyn Hall and Jon Butler. Robert Johnston, who is about to publish an important book on Progressivism, offered invaluable comments on every draft and very patiently suggested yet another article to replace the one that had most recently fallen out of favor. I drafted the introduction while I was a visiting scholar at the University of Melbourne in Melbourne, Australia, where I became interested in the period in Australian history. In conversations with other historians and graduate students, I came to appreciate the international themes of Progressivism and social change.

As *Who Were the Progressives?* inched forward, life leapt forward. I gained a husband who hung the moon and a fine new family in Australia and America. Miles grew big and I grew happy, and we've all grown closer together. I thank Ben Kiernan for making all of this, and everything else, possible.

GLENDA ELIZABETH GILMORE

A Note for Students

Every piece of written history starts when somebody becomes curious and asks questions. The very first problem is who, or what, to study. A historian might ask an old question yet again, after deciding that existing answers are not good enough. But brand-new questions can emerge about old, familiar topics, particularly in light of new findings or directions in research, such as the rise of women's history in the late 1970s.

In one sense history is all that happened in the past. In another it is the universe of potential evidence that the past has bequeathed. But written history does not exist until a historian collects and probes that evidence *(research)*, makes sense of it *(interpretation)*, and shows to others what he or she has seen so that they can see it too *(writing)*. Good history begins with respecting people's complexity, not with any kind of preordained certainty. It might well mean using modern techniques that were unknown at the time, such as Freudian psychology or statistical assessment by computer. But good historians always approach the past on its own terms, taking careful stock of the period's cultural norms and people's assumptions or expectations, no matter how different from contemporary attitudes. Even a few decades can offer a surprisingly large gap to bridge, as each generation discovers when it evaluates the accomplishments of those who have come before.

To write history well requires three qualities. One is the courage to try to understand people whom we never can meet—unless our subject is very recent—and to explain events that no one can re-create. The second quality is the humility to realize that we can never entirely appreciate either the people or the events under study. However much evidence is compiled and however smart the questions posed, the past remains too large to contain. It will always continue to surprise.

The third quality historians need is the curiosity that turns sterile facts into clues about a world that once was just as alive, passionate, frightening, and exciting as our own, yet in different ways. Today we know how past events "turned out." But the people taking part had no such knowledge. Good history recaptures those people's fears, hopes, frustrations, failures, and achievements; it tells about people who faced the predicaments and choices that still confront us in the twenty-first century.

All the essays collected in this volume bear on a single, shared problem that the authors agree is important, however differently they may choose to respond to it. On its own, each essay reveals a fine mind coming to grips with a worthwhile question. Taken together, the essays give a sense of just how complex the human situation can be. That point—that human situations are complex—applies just as much to life today as to the lives led in the past. History has no absolute "lessons" to teach; it follows no invariable "laws." But knowing about another time might be of some help as we struggle to live within our own.

EDWARD COUNTRYMAN

Contents

Who Were the Progressives?

PART ONE

Introduction

*Responding to the Challenges
of the Progressive Era*

Responding to the Challenges of the Progressive Era

An Overview of the Progressive Era

During the years 1890 to 1920, people in the United States thought that they lived in a time of unparalleled change. Industrialization, technological advances, migration, and urbanization threatened to overturn tradition everywhere, from the neighborhood to the White House. As people crowded into cities, monopolists cornered industries, municipal politicians proved corrupt, children toiled ten hours a day in factories, and workers struck. Americans debated what was going wrong and why. And they argued about how to fix those problems.

How someone defined the wrongs and what remedies he or she prescribed to right them depended to a large extent on that person's position in society. For example, the rapid migration of Italian immigrants to the Northeast that posed problems for white, native-born New Englanders offered opportunities and challenges to the immigrants themselves. And, of course, whether a solution is "progressive" or not depends on who is "reforming" whom. In other words, the native New Englanders might have considered it a reform to require an English literacy test to register to vote, but Italian immigrants might have considered such a test an infringement on their rights. One group's progressive reform might become another group's repressive burden. One group's attempts to introduce order into society might depend on controlling another group's behavior.

That is why it is so important for historians to know who participated in Progressive reform and how their participation shaped reform. Did workers find a voice—either through direct action or electoral politics—in Progressivism? What sorts of issues did women take up, and how effective were they in resolving them? What was the relationship between urban Progressives and rural Progressives? Did businessmen introduce reform to foreclose radical intervention in the economic system, or did concerned citizens impose legislative restrictions on the economy that businessmen found onerous? How much power did immigrants have to participate in

American life, even as they tried to hold onto the culture of their home-lands? In sum, what groups of people participated in devising solutions for Progressive Era problems, and whose behavior did those solutions aim to control? Historians cannot agree on the answers to these questions. Asking, "Who were the Progressives?" provokes answers that contradict one another, as you will discover in reading this volume.

Despite their different circumstances, most Americans during the period 1890 to 1920 took progress—the simple idea that life would get better and better—to be a given. They believed that modern civilization had reached a point at which most of the ills that had plagued society for millennia could be eradicated, provided, of course, everyone put his or her shoulder to the wheel and pushed together. They were certain that change, reform, and progress characterized their times, but they were reluctant to compress their complicated political movements into a single strand of thought called "Progressivism." Historians since have searched for a unifying explanation for the changes that Americans initiated at the turn of the twentieth century. Yet they too have failed to force Progressivism into any single model, just as they have failed to confine the answer to the question "Who were the Progressives?" to any single group, race, sex, or class of people.

At the turn of the century, America was replete with promise, even as the society and individuals in it faced dramatic change. Incredible problems came to public attention on a daily basis, but it seemed as if people actually relished dissecting some newly discovered festering cancer on the body politic. The main cure for society's ills, they thought, consisted of exposure to the light and air of public opinion. When journalists uncovered problems, the public responded by buying more newspapers and magazines. In 1906 Republican President Theodore Roosevelt nicknamed crusading journalists "muckrakers," deploring the apparent tendency to focus on the lowest, rather than the most uplifted, aspects of life. Reporters were, Roosevelt scolded, like "the Man with the Muck-rake, . . . constantly refus[ing] to see aught that is lofty and fix[ing] his eyes with solemn intentness only on that which is vile and debasing."[1] The public took up the handle with alacrity, reckoning that muckraking was just the sort of thing the press should do. Whether the problem *du jour* was contaminated milk, tuberculosis running rampant in tenements, or a city official on the take, people stood ready to uncover the cause of the trouble, to cure it, and to throw in several ounces of prevention for good measure. As historian Daniel Rodgers points out, Progressives were not people overwhelmed by their problems; rather, "It would be more accurate to say that they swam in a sudden abundance of solutions."[2] Average men and women felt that they had the knowledge close at hand to improve life forever.

Those problems for which they devised solutions sprang principally from the industrialization of the United States and its participation in an emerging world economy. Industrialization began in England in the eighteenth century and progressed in the United States throughout the nineteenth century. Industry grew rapidly, consuming not only raw materials but enormous numbers of workers as well. It reordered the landscape of the world. Most directly, it required that people move to manufacturing centers, which produced rapid urbanization and vast migrations of people from farm to city and from Europe to the United States, South America, and Australia. Moreover, industrialization reordered the relationship of people to their work. Before industrialization, farmers had been involved in local trading circles and artisans had worked in intimate relationships with their masters. After industrialization, most men worked for wages, often never setting eyes on the owners of the company. Industrialization's by-products—urbanization, migration, and wage work—combined to produce real misery along with real opportunity for change.

The industrial revolution touched the lives of most people in the United States, Europe, and Australia, even of those inhabitants who lived far away from the steel mills of Pittsburgh, the foundries of Glasgow, or the coal mines of Gippsland, Australia. Wherever farmers depended on growing a crop for market, the tentacles of the global economy wound round them. For example, an African American family farming cotton in Eufaula, Alabama, found the price of their bales set not just by their greedy white landowner down the road, but also by Mobile factoring agents, New York railroadmen, and British textile-mill owners. The Swedish-speaking family growing wheat in Red Cloud, Nebraska, in 1910 found themselves far from home, but among their own countrypeople, as 20 percent of Sweden's population had emigrated in one generation.[3] The African Americans and the Swedes sold their crops on a world market, and both families depended on the consumer products of an industrialized economy. When they laid the crops by, they could dream of and sometimes purchase plowshares, shoes, and phonographs from the Sears and Roebuck catalog. The railroads that brought those long-awaited packages from Chicago took away the farmers' cotton, their wheat, and, often, their sons and daughters.

In all regions of the United States, great cities grew to serve as manufacturing and distribution centers. The youngest daughter of the cotton farming family in Eufaula might board the smoky segregated railroad car—the Jim Crow car, they called it—bound for Atlanta to search for work as a domestic servant.[4] Atlanta's population exploded from 65,533 in 1890 to 200,616 by 1920. The middle son of the Swedish farming family might hop a freight loading grain in Red Cloud in 1920 to travel to the stockyards of Omaha, raw and swollen from population growth from 140,452 to 191,601 in the past thirty years. Down the middle of Atlanta and Omaha ran cords of steel, the tracks, cutting a huge slash that reminded everyone that what the railroads gave, they also took away. In 1890, one in three Americans lived in cities, but in 1920 one of every two persons lived in cities, albeit most of them in urban areas we would consider small today.[5]

With such rapid growth, urban areas burst at their seams. Reformers pronounced them "congested," an apt description of streets, housing, and all too often the sunken chests of impoverished city dwellers.[6] In Atlanta the young black woman from Eufaula might find housing in rudely cut alleys behind more substantial dwellings, with no running water and an outhouse—her own if she had good fortune, but more likely one shared with neighbors. Her house would be a three-room wooden structure, one room opening off another, lending the name "shotgun shack," as the floor plan afforded a clear shot from the front porch to the back steps. Once a week, she would awaken to hear the night soil wagon driver dredging out sewage from the shallow troughs that lay behind the alley outhouses. Most major cities had limited sewer systems until after the turn of the century. In Omaha, the Swedish stockyard worker would have frozen to death in an Atlanta-style shotgun shack, but he could find similarly crowded and unhealthy accommodation with a cheap bed in a "railroad" flat, the midwestern version of a shotgun shack. Both newcomers to the city would be lucky if they escaped tuberculosis, typhoid fever, or syphilis—even luckier if all their children lived through infancy. After a few years of struggling in Atlanta and Omaha, the African American woman might move on to New York and the Swede to Chicago, where both would be astonished by the numbers of fresh immigrants they would find.

After industrialization and urbanization, the inpouring of immigrants to America figured as a third catalyst for Progressive reformers. During the Progressive Era, the United States opened its borders to the greatest number of people it would ever admit. The fifteen million new Americans who produced this demographic bulge came primarily from southern and eastern Europe beginning in the late nineteenth century, and many spoke languages that were new to the United States.[7] It was in urban areas that immigrants were the most visible as a group; indeed, most immigrants settled in cities of more than 50,000 population.[8]

Southern African Americans also poured into northern cities in increasing numbers after 1910, an exodus that historians call "The Great Migration." For African Americans, 80 percent of whom lived in the South, the promise of Reconstruction had set as the Progressive Era dawned. Agriculture fell into a depression in the mid-1890s, and many black and white southerners fell into debt through the sharecropping and tenancy systems. African Americans found most industrial jobs foreclosed to them in the

South.[9] By 1895, Mississippi and Louisiana had already stolen the right to vote from their black citizens. Southern states passed new laws to use literacy tests, registration restrictions, and poll taxes, among other devices, to keep African Americans from voting. In 1896, Homer Plessy, a New Orleanian who was one-eighth black, tested the streetcar company's rule of separating black from white passengers. Plessy had full faith that the federal government, under the Fourteenth Amendment that granted citizenship to ex-slaves, would uphold equal access to public accommodation as a key right of citizenship. Instead, the U.S. Supreme Court upheld the doctrine of "separate but equal" in public places. After the Supreme Court's decision in *Plessy v. Ferguson,* the federal government did little to protect African Americans.[10] White southerners upheld these measures with frequent lynchings of African Americans and wholesale massacres of urban African Americans in southern cities, including New Orleans, Wilmington (North Carolina), and Tulsa (Oklahoma).

In response to disfranchisement, agricultural poverty, brutal intimidation, and exclusion from industrial jobs in the South, African Americans moved to urban industrial areas in greater numbers after 1900. The migrant stream increased markedly again after 1910, and Philadelphia, New York, Chicago, and Detroit became favored destinations for black families seeking to start new lives, hoping to work in factories and to send their children to integrated schools. Between 1915 and 1930, one and a half million African Americans moved from the states of the old Confederacy to the North, usually settling in urban areas.[11] In one decade, Chicago gained 65,355 African Americans and New York 60,758.[12] African Americans escaped the terror of lynching, sharecropping's debt peonage, and the imposition of segregation by law when they left the South. However, in the North they often encountered discrimination in housing and employment, and they competed with European immigrants for the lowest-paying jobs.[13]

It was in urban areas, whether in regional cities such as Atlanta, Omaha, St. Louis, or Galveston, or in those cities of more than a million population in 1900 such as Chicago and New York, that all Americans most often encountered the pressing problems that inspired Progressive solutions. Vast numbers of newcomers, including European immigrants, southern African Americans, and rural whites, faced housing shortages, irregular work opportunities at low wages, sickness from the epidemics that erupted from urban filth, and danger from industrial accidents. They also encountered a new social setting, far from Eufaula or Red Cloud but even farther from Warsaw or Bologna. At work they might feel themselves to be anonymous cogs in a fast-moving machine, separated from family, church, and even from the very core of the identity that had fit them so well back home. But in their neighborhoods, they created communities that incorporated familiar traditions and nurtured their families.

In the city, danger and pleasure blended in confusing ways, and many Progressive Era solutions focused on directing city dwellers toward activities that middle-class reformers saw as moral, virtuous activities. Sometimes the native-born newcomers arrived straight from the farm; sometimes they had stopped in a mid-sized regional city. The Young Men's and Young Women's Christian Associations (YMCA, YWCA) tried to orient newcomers to urban life and protect them from the moral dangers of the city. The numbers of young women living by themselves or in boarding houses—women "adrift"—caused alarm.[14] These women generally lived in poverty because women customarily and legally earned less than men did, a form of discrimination that most Progressives justified because women were expected to live in households headed by male wage earners. Now, cities teemed with working women living outside the "protection" of a male head of household. Moreover, with young unaccompanied women spending leisure time on the streets, it seemed to many that a sexual revolution was at hand, as girls escaped their fathers' control.[15]

Native-born white urbanites saw cause for alarm in these masses of newcomers—immigrants, rural whites, and southern African Americans—and worried about incorporating them into civic life. Deprived of a fair chance at education in the South and confined in unhealthy neighborhoods in the North, African Americans often found themselves restricted to the most base jobs in urban areas. The same was true for recent immigrants, and Progressives thought it a pressing necessity to teach the children of these immigrants English, to improve the housing into which most immigrants were crowded, and to mold immigrant men into American voters. Nothing less than democracy was at stake, as Progressives believed that a large foreign population in the midst of American life could cause nothing but trouble if it remained "foreign," following the still-feudal ways of European countries.

Not all could agree on how to incorporate European immigrants into American society. Some Progressives believed that the absorption of immigrants required them to forsake their language and obliterate their cultural differences. Others simply hoped that a mythical process of assimilation would take place in the "melting pot" of American culture. A few could envision an approach we might call "multicultural" today, in which more seasoned Americans could be taught to appreciate new immigrants' culture, even as immigrants accepted the best of American life.[16] Some native-born American reformers saw immigrants' cultural differences as foreign institutions that might subvert democracy or corrupt the municipal polity.

In the name of Americanization, groups of young social activists, mostly college-educated white women, moved to ethnic neighborhoods to live and work among the immigrants. In settlement houses, Progressives taught immigrants to be Americans through English-language classes, job-skills training, civics classes, girls' and boys' clubs, and playing basketball and baseball. As they learned together, settlement house workers came to understand immigrant culture to be a source of strength for the urban newcomers. Jane Addams, founder of the most famous settlement house, Hull House in Chicago, commented on the cultural resources among her varied ethnic constituency: "Our American citizenship might be built without disturbing these foundations which were laid of old time."[17] From this grassroots location sprang much of the Progressive reform agenda that would eventually occupy even the president, Congress, and the courts.

In this new industrial and urban age, most often people moved to find work, whether in the Chicago stockyards, in a New York garment factory, or in a mining camp in the Rockies. Wherever they found wage work, they found trouble. For both sides, the employee–employer relationship seemed strange and new. The system that we know so well today—one in which a person works for a company for wages—was by no means a foregone conclusion in the 1890s. Other alternatives existed, as the goals of an early labor movement, the Knights of Labor, remind us. The Knights, with a membership of 700,000 in 1885, argued that the employee should earn a rightful share of an employer's profits and that there could be a high degree of cooperation between the two. But federal and state power always lay on the side of the employer's private property rights, and after a series of bloody strikes in the 1880s, the Knights' membership dwindled.[18]

Thereafter, it was the American Federation of Labor (AFL) that became the leading labor organization in the country, growing from a membership of 238,000 in 1891 to 1,562,000 in 1910 to 4,078,000 in 1920. Unlike the Knights, the AFL accepted the wage-labor system and sought to ameliorate it, not to overturn it.[19] Therefore, AFL leaders worked for higher wages, an eight-hour working day, better working conditions, and the abolition of child labor. But what they did not pursue is as important as what they supported. AFL leaders largely eschewed protective legislation to dictate working conditions for men and did not espouse profit sharing or cooperative schemes. The AFL organized skilled workers, those who would be the most difficult for employers to replace. Despite an initiative begun in 1914 to recruit women, skilled workers were most often men. With some exceptions in the coal fields, other mining endeavors, and stockyards, AFL members were exclusively white as well. The AFL succeeded where others had failed, but its success came at a cost of liberty and opportunity. It accepted the wage-labor system, set limited and concrete goals, and gained the support of non-union Progressives. A period of overall prosperity, when gold discoveries increased the money supply and new markets opened as a result of imperialism, caused wages to rise among skilled workers and the AFL grew.

Alongside the AFL's membership increase, radical alternatives to the wage-labor system persisted throughout the Progressive Era. The Industrial Workers of the World tried to organize everyone—skilled and unskilled, male and female, white and black—into "one big union." The IWW members, or the Wobblies as they were known, believed, as the Knights had, that the workers deserved a share of the goods that they produced, but by 1905 they had lost all faith in the harmony that the Knights hoped for between producer and employer. They felt that since employers used violence to break strikes, Wobblies were entitled to use violence against capitalists. The Preamble of the IWW constitution put the adversarial relationship between labor and capital curtly: "The working class and the employing class have nothing in common. Instead of the conservative A.F.L. motto, 'A fair day's wage for a fair day's work,' we must inscribe on our banner the revolutionary watchword, 'Abolition of the wage system.' "[20] The IWW managed occasionally to organize the toughest industries among the least organized workers—for example, mining in the West, lumber in the South, and largely unorganized textile mills with predominately female workforces in New England. But during World War I, widespread fear of treason and the shock waves spreading from the Bolshevik revolution in Russia caused increased persecution of IWW leaders on the grounds that they were Socialists or Bolsheviks.[21]

To others, socialism itself seemed to offer solutions to the problems caused by industrialism because it called for a fairer distribution of wealth through state intervention. Many Socialists saw themselves as Progressives too, and they had support from a broad range of reformers. In 1917, 70,000 Americans were Socialist party members, and 600,000 voted for the Socialist candidate in the presidential election of 1916. Across the country, Socialists held elected municipal and statewide offices.[22] But as with the IWW, the United States' entry into World War I in 1917 created an atmosphere of crisis that worked against the Socialists, and the party itself disavowed the conflict. Eugene V. Debs, the presidential candidate of the Socialist party, spent WWI in federal prison in Atlanta for violating the Espionage Law passed in 1917 and amended in 1918. His incarceration did not mean that Debs was a spy; rather, the federal government accused him of disloyalty and inciting insubordination, since he and his party did not support the war.[23] While in prison, Debs received 920,000 votes for President of the United States. When the war ended, several Socialists were expelled from the offices to which they had been legitimately elected.[24]

After 1920, Socialists never garnered the voter support that they had in the decade 1910–20.

Faced with industrialization's consequences—urbanization, migration, and a wage system that stripped workers of power—the Progressives argued that the times called for reform rather than radicalism. Instead of turning to radical alternatives such as anarchism or socialism, Progressives sought to reshape the system that rapid industrialization had so haphazardly imposed on them. If we can reserve judgment on what the Progressives hoped to gain by their reforms, we should give them the credit they are due for their civic imagination. In this time when problems loomed so large, the Progressives re-imagined profound ways to reform society. Very few imagined an alternative to wage labor, in other words, an alternative to capitalism.[25] But Progressives did turn their attention to redrawing the boundaries of what was public and what was private, what men should do and what women should do, what government should do and what it should not do, who should decide public issues and who should give those decision makers advice. Rarely have citizens rethought their society and its limits so creatively, so completely, and so peacefully.

In redrawing the boundaries of the public and the private, Progressives challenged a tradition in the United States that centered civic rights in the independence of male household heads. The political philosophy of liberalism, widely accepted in the United States since the American Revolution, assumed that democracy depended on maximizing individual choices, provided the individual was white and male. To fashion this philosophy of individual rights, Americans had drawn on ideas of classical liberalism that asserted that all men had natural rights that no government could usurp and that a "noninterventionist state" could best protect.[26] This set of beliefs meant that the best government was one that intervened least into daily life and left men free to make myriad choices to suit themselves, without regard to their neighbors. Translated into practical, everyday terms, it meant, for example, that many Americans believed in 1890 that a man should decide for himself whether his children went to work or to school. It meant that legislators should not mandate an eight-hour work day, because such laws would limit a man's right to choose his working hours. It meant that men should earn a family wage in order to provide for their dependents but that their wives and children should not, thus remaining dependent. In urban areas, it meant that private property was sacrosanct, impervious to regulation by a city government. In rural areas, it meant that a man should be free to let his cows roam and to expect his neighbors to fence their crops if they did not want them trampled by his herd. A dairyman could set his own standards of purity for milk, but a mother had no guarantee that the milk she bought from him would be fit to drink.

This maximization of individual rights came at the expense of group interests.[27] For example, the children of any coming generation might grow up ignorant, retarding the growth and competitiveness of society. Without legislation for an eight-hour work day, employers could, and did, make ten- or twelve-hour days the norm, withholding jobs from all others who did not want to work twelve hours a day by accommodating the right of the hypothetical man who did. The family wage meant that women and children earned pittances compared to the male household head; it also caused them to remain his dependents, guaranteeing his individual right to choose for all in his household, while condemning women without male "protection" to a life of poverty. If a man's home was his castle, he might crowd boarders into unhealthy tenements. If one man's cows could roam unfenced, another man's crops could be trampled with impunity. If one man sold impure milk, another man's children might die. In 1890, the proper function of government included little regulation of these parts of life, leaving those decisions to individuals, which meant that many areas we think of today as matters of public concern belonged then to the private sphere.

Progressives began to envision things differently, and they built on limited existing municipal and state regulations and on the reform program first advocated by the Populist party in the 1890s.[28] Farmers had flocked to the Populist party as a way to redress the imbalance between themselves and big business, but their political party had foundered after 1896 with the defeat of William Jennings Bryan. Many Populist reforms—reorganization of the currency, railroad regulation, antimonopoly legislation, and the eight-hour day—remained on the Progressive agenda. But perhaps the most important contribution the Populists made to Progressivism was the recognition of a collectivity of interests among people. The Populists realized that farmers and workers must unite cooperatively to stand up to the concentration of power that business exercised over them. And they realized that unbridled individualism sometimes hurt groups of people.

Progressives searched for ways to articulate the public good in the face of a system that upheld individual rights. It might be as simple as bringing to bear municipal pressure to get a landlord to clean up germ-ridden privies or as difficult as implementing compulsory school attendance laws, but Progressives determined that what was good for the individual might be bad for groups of individuals. Government, they argued, should exist to balance individual rights with community well-being. For example, government should have the authority to regulate child labor because all citizens had an interest in having an educated electorate and a productive workforce twenty years hence. "Do not grind the seed corn," one southern Progressive begged when he argued for legislation against child labor.[29] Your children were no longer your children; they represented the seed of future civilization.

The Social Gospel, which emerged in American Protestant thinking as a response to Social Darwinism's "survival of the fittest" doctrine, helped Progressives bridge the gap between individual rights and collective responsibility. Social Gospelers recognized the community's responsibilities, and they argued that the best way to rationalize the new industrial chaos was through cooperation and caring, just as Jesus had advocated. The individual must act on his or her convictions. Liberal Protestant Progressive thought redefined the individual's relationship to other people and to God in ways that made men and women turn away from saving their own souls before a "judgmental God" as they might have before 1890 and toward helping their neighbors.[30]

Along with a change in the individual's relationship with God, Progressives experienced a change in men's and women's relationships with each other within and outside the household. Re-imagining male head of household rights and community interests necessitated a wider public role for women. In the nineteenth century, few thought that women had a place in the public sphere, in economic, civic, or political matters. Although the reality always belied the theoretical construction of public and private spheres—for example, poor single women worked in factories as early as the 1830s—most Americans vested natural rights only in men, who theoretically represented women's interests. In fact, woman suffragists in the nineteenth century failed to convince many that women should vote on the basis that they, too, had natural rights. But in the 1910s, they began to convince people that women needed the vote to protect the home. Industrial capitalism's consequences—bad housing, contaminated food, and the like—meant that the public sphere had invaded the private sphere; the unregulated economy threatened the home. Women deserved the vote because they must now enter politics to guard the private sphere.[31]

Securing decent housing, buying uncontaminated food, supporting compulsory education, fighting germs, and regulating prostitution—problems that for centuries had been resolved within households or patriarchal local networks—became problems that communities shared. Even as some women continued to fight for the vote on the basis of natural rights, suffragists and nonsuffragists alike argued that women must take a role in "municipal housekeeping": cleaning up the city, government, and bureaucracy. This role would take them into settlement houses, schools, voluntary associations, and city government well before they won the vote through the Nineteenth Amendment to the Constitution in 1920.

Women won the right to vote nationally only at the end of the Progressive Era, but they were key to Progressive reform. Their role went beyond the actual work that women assumed in municipal housekeeping; they contributed to Progressivism's intellectual and organizational framework as well. Women reformers played a key role in naming the conditions that had become problems created by industrial capitalism in the first place. Women reformers redefined what might be "considered good and right in public life," and condemned its wrongs.[32] Moreover, women's organizations became foundation stones for Progressive solutions because they so often became the units through which Progressives actually delivered help to citizens. For example, women's groups ran settlement houses, administered branches of the Associated Charities, organized cleanup days, and built and maintained urban playgrounds.[33]

In this new, feminized public sphere, many tried to rethink the sort of governmental system that would recognize community interests in a constitutional structure originally designed to maximize individual rights. Herbert Croly, who in 1909 had detailed *The Promise of American Life,* by 1914 argued for extensive government regulation of the economy in his work *Progressive Democracy.*[34] His co-editor at the *New Republic,* Walter Lippmann, put it more plaintively when he bemoaned that the industrialized world was no longer ordered by kinship, neighborhood ties, and male authority. "We," Lippmann complained, "are unsettled to the very roots of our being. . . . There are no precedents to guide us, no wisdom that wasn't made for a simpler age."[35] If he went it alone, Lippmann implied, the individual simply could not measure up to the task of solving the society's problems. Progressive thinkers, of whom Croly was one of the most articulate, criticized the constitutional basis of individual rights and called for, as he put it, "a genuinely popular system of representative government," one in which democracy better represented group interests.[36] Croly and other Progressives did not argue that all citizens were equal in material circumstances, nor that the government should attempt to make them equal; rather, they argued that the function of government was to represent groups of citizens—what today we might call "interest groups"—fairly.[37] The task that lay ahead of the Progressives was to balance "pure democracy" with recognition of a "democratic community on a national scale."[38]

The solution, as Croly articulated it, was to tap into something he called "public opinion." "Public opinion requires to be aroused, elicited, informed, developed, concentrated and brought to an understanding of its own dominant purpose," Croly argued. To Croly, this meant instituting a different sort of President, one who appointed public administrators who could "scientific[ally] analyze" problems, put those analyses before the public, and discern what the public wanted to do about them.[39] To other readers, the taskmasters that Croly wanted to loose upon public opinion—the arousers, the elicitors, the informers, the developers, and the clarifiers—suggested structural transformations in government itself.

As Progressives tried to arouse public opinion more effectively, they argued that America needed both more and less democracy. It needed more democracy to let the people's voices be heard. But it needed less democracy when it came to carrying out the public's wishes; there, specialists and experts could serve best. Progressives pushed on two fronts: to use voting to measure educated public opinion and to identify citizens who could serve that public through specialized knowledge. In many places, reformers enacted "reforms" that restricted voting rights to the literate, or to those who could pay poll taxes. The white supremacists who restricted African American voting in the South from 1890 to 1906 saw themselves as Progressives.[40]

Working at the municipal level, in many places Progressives abolished the ward system of city government that had tended to elect neighborhood patronage machines and substituted at-large elections, that is, elections where candidates stood citywide. In some states, they enabled people to vote for actual legislation without going through the state legislature, a mechanism known as the initiative. Some states adopted the referendum also, which allowed people to vote directly on bills passed by or referred to them by the legislature. Some gave voters the ability to recall public officials and to elect members of the judiciary. With the Seventeenth Amendment, Progressives changed the U.S. Constitution to provide for the direct election of Senators.[41]

Most advocates of more democracy worked to add women to the voting rolls. Although women could not vote in national elections until November 1920, women in some places could vote on a statewide basis earlier. In some cities, women cast ballots for selected public offices, such as school boards. It is helpful to think of the process that occurred between 1910 and 1920, in the words of historian Victoria Bissell Brown, as "the gradual accretion of women's voting rights in the United States." Women effectively melded the expansion of the private sphere and the language of collective rights to argue for woman suffrage as a Progressive democratic measure. Jane Addams put it clearly when she said, "Personal ambition . . . is certainly too archaic to accomplish anything now. Our thoughts, at least for this generation, cannot be too much directed from mutual relationships and responsibilities."[42]

Those "mutual relationships and responsibilities" did not include white women fighting for black women's right to campaign for woman suffrage, nor did white women support black women when southern white registrars denied them the right to vote after the passage of the Nineteenth Amendment in 1920. When Ida B. Wells-Barnett, an African American woman who headed Chicago's Alpha Suffrage Club, arrived in Washington, D.C., in 1913 for a march sponsored by the National American Woman Suffrage Association, march organizers told her to walk in the back of the parade with the other black women. Wells-Barnett refused, broke back in line, and marched with the predominately white Chicago delegation. In 1920, officials of the National Women's Party refused to intervene when black women in the South reported that they had been denied registration because of their color. Black women, even in the South, insisted on their rights, and the Nineteenth Amendment that granted women the right to vote became a disruption for white Southerners' strategies for disfranchising all African Americans.[43]

"Mutual relationships and responsibilities" required education—at least for all whites. As historian Leon Fink points out, "For Progressives . . . democracy depended on the self-cultivation of the citizen as active student." An educational revolution, given voice by John Dewey, transformed education from a passive affair in which students memorized lessons into "learning by doing." Students had to do more than master facts; they had to learn how to think. The Progressives faced a conundrum, however: while the new educational policy meant to democratize, more than ever much educational policy was to be directed by experts.[44]

The educational revolution taught America that it needed more democracy while promoting a potentially undemocratic reliance on planning and management as a response to a highly complicated, technically advanced world. One example was the problem of what to do with Atlanta's sewage. A ward politician was perfectly qualified to let a contract to the driver of the night soil wagon, and the driver was perfectly qualified to go and shovel out outhouse troughs. But if Atlanta wanted a sewer system, and it certainly did, it had to hire experts to design it, others to build it, and yet others to manage it. As city management grew more and more complex, some cities adopted the Staunton, Virginia, plan, which put the actual affairs of the city in the hands of a hired, not an elected, city manager.[45]

Just as these dramas of expert intervention played out at the local level, so too did they operate at the national level. Progressives believed that the federal government needed to take a more active role in protecting interest groups. For example, President Theodore Roosevelt pushed for a bill that would create a Children's Bureau in the federal government, a measure that sprang from the work of settlement house women and would ensure that experts on child welfare helped to shape federal policy.[46] Roosevelt's successor, President William Howard Taft, was lukewarm about the growth of the federal government and only reluctantly supported a measure to finance that growth: the imposition of a federal income tax. The measure passed Congress in 1909 and became the Sixteenth Amendment to the Constitution when ratified in 1913.[47] In 1912, when some Republicans splintered into the Progressive Party, headed by Theodore Roosevelt, one of the major issues prompting the split was the role the federal government should take in solving problems. Woodrow Wilson, the Democrat, won the election because of the split, and he advocated a "New Freedom" to counteract Roosevelt's "New Nationalism."

Whereas Roosevelt boosted the growth of the federal government to make it a more equal partner with capitalism, Wilson argued that government did not need to grow to enormous proportions to regulate the economy. Wilson's New Freedom sounded to some as if it might serve as a revival of individual rights, but his freedom to experiment was short lived. As war broke out in Europe in 1914, Wilson presided over a country increasingly divided on America's involvement in that war. After the United States entered the war in April 1917, Wilson used Progressive organizational methods to build the largest federal system in the country's history thus far to lead the nation through World War I.[48] Many Progressives watched in horror as their reform tools served wartime aims.[49]

Despite their recognition that government had responsibilities to groups in society as well as to individuals, Progressives never imagined that the federal government would emerge as the major provider of social welfare.[50] Voluntary associations would do much of the work of improving society, they thought. For example, the forerunner of the United Way, the Associated Charities, was active in the Progressive Era, and the National Association for the Advancement of Colored People (NAACP) was founded in 1910. In voluntary associations, men and women would join together in groups, some nationwide, some local, to resolve the challenges facing their communities. The varied resolutions they proposed to meet those challenges are apparent in the articles in this volume.

As we examine questions of democracy, efficiency, and Americanization, we may see Progressivism as a mirror for our times. One hundred years ago, men and women looked with dismay at the problems that industrial capitalism had wrought. They doubted their ability to harness technology and deplored the lack of meaning in industrial work. They tried to create livable spaces, to control diseases for which they knew no cures, and to tame a sexual revolution. They worried about the breakdown of kinship networks and the nuclear, male-headed family. We can learn a great deal from the solutions they forged and take comfort in their optimism. They did not completely solve the problems they tackled, but they began their tasks full of faith in the ability of people to remake their world. In the end, that faith in human action may be a more valuable lesson for us than any of the solutions they enacted.

Historians Ask, "Who Were the Progressives?"

As you read the selections in this book, the authors will argue about who the Progressives were, what sorts of conditions Progressives identified as problems, and how Progressives imagined reform. If you think you will find a single answer to the question "Who were the Progressives?" these selections will only frustrate you. Remember that you are studying something on which historians *cannot* agree; thus it is a perfect way to see for yourself how historians work. To understand how these historians could take such widely divergent stands, you should understand the historiography of the Progressive Era, or how its history has changed as people have written about it.

The first historians who wrote about the Progressive Era, such as Charles Beard and Frederick Jackson Turner, lived through the period. They were themselves called Progressives. The Progressive historians saw the period as a watershed in American history, the first time when the American people gained a real voice in their democracy. This volume does not include any selections from those Progressive historians, but it does include work from people who disagreed with them, whom historians have called the counter-Progressives, such as Richard Hofstadter.

Hofstadter, writing in 1954, concluded that Progressivism was not a popular revolution; rather, it was a time of careful reordering. The white middle class guided its reforms. Writing a little more than ten years after Hofstadter, Robert H. Wiebe also identified the Progressive reform impulse as coming from middle-class men who sought to organize their world to make it more manageable. However, Hofstadter and Wiebe disagreed on what sort of middle class initiated the reform movement. Hofstadter saw a crisis among the old middle class that had held power in small, well-established towns. Industrialization and urbanization had made these people superfluous and had undercut their traditional authority over their neighbors. They took up the reins of reform to regain cultural and political authority. Wiebe saw the middle-class Progressives differently. To him, they were a new, recently urbanized group trying to bring organization to chaos, for the purpose of fostering a smoother-running economy.

Both Hofstadter and Wiebe found the Progressives to be white, middle-class men who deplored the chaos that resulted from industrialization and urbanization and who imposed order on what seemed to them a strange new world. Hofstadter and Wiebe argue that these middle-class reforms enabled the United States to absorb millions of immigrants, become a world leader, and prosper as never before. Scores of historians followed Wiebe's thinking, finding middle-class organizers as the driving force in Progressivism and earning themselves the name "organizational" historians.

But if all of the Progressives were middle-class organizers, Progressivism could be seen simply as a way to impose social control over the growing working classes, immigrants, and unsatisfied farmers. It might not be as progressive as Hofstadter and Wiebe portrayed it; certainly, it was not the popular force for change that Beard and Turner described. Did the Progressives simply tinker with the rusty mechanism of capitalism to preserve the status quo? Some historians—Gabriel Kolko, for example—have argued that middle-class Progressive reform of the sort Hofstadter and Wiebe describe took the wind out of the sails of the real forces for change, such as the Socialists and the IWW. Kolko's argument underscores the importance of finding out who the Progressives were.[51]

In the 1970s and 1980s revisionist historians began to find more diversity among the Progressives than the organizational historians had. They found women reformers, working-class political organizations, African Americans operating settlement houses, and urban immigrant associations working for better government. Today, most historians concede that the Progressive Era brought together broad coalitions of people to effect reform. However, they still argue about which groups had *agency*, in other words, which groups' actions counted in identifying problems and enacting solutions to them.[52] In the 1980s and 1990s, a group of historians we might call the neo-Progressives began to assert that the urban working class, through electoral politics and through direct action such as strikes, had a great deal of influence in determining the Progressive agenda. Historians who argue for working-class agency are called the *neo*-Progressives because they recapture the popular basis of change for which Beard and Turner argued. Shelton Stromquist introduces his article in this volume with a good overview of the emergence of the neo-Progressives, and he argues for the agency of urban workers.

Others argue that, in harmony with the efforts of the neo-Progressives to move the focus away from white middle-class men, women were leaders in Progressive reform and that gender mattered in the diagnosis and solution of problems. Historians were slow to recognize women's influence on Progressive Era politics. When historians posed the question "Who were the Progressives?" they simply could not come up with satisfactory answers because they overlooked the role women played in Progressivism.[53]

Maureen A. Flanagan and I look at Progressive reform in two vastly different settings—Chicago and North Carolina—to conclude that Progressives included women and that gender mattered in political reform. James
J. Connolly completes the circle by arguing that recent immigrants used
their ethnicity as a base around which to organize for Progressive reform.
Connolly's ethnic Progressives alter the kind of Progressivism that the
white middle class had in store for them, an argument similar to the one I
make about African American women in North Carolina.

You will read one article that does not fit neatly with this historiography.
So far all the articles mentioned agree on one thing: Progressivism originated among those who lived in cities and towns. Elizabeth Sanders argues
the opposite case. She traces the major national legislation of the Progressive Era to the farmers' revolt of the 1890s, known as the Populist Movement. In a stunning analysis of legislation, Sanders draws parallels between
agrarian complaints and urban remedies, as she credits the Populists with
inspiring reform that far outlived their original political organization.
Sanders's argument is the most recently written, suggesting that we may
be struggling with the question "Who were the Progressives?" for decades
to come.

The following are a few methods that might help you sort out the arguments you will read. First, note when the article was written. Where does it
fit in the historiography I outlined? Is this historian arguing generally or
specifically with another historian? Imagine the authors serving on a jury
together, charged with reaching a single answer to the question "Who were
the Progressives?" Where would you find points of agreement? How would
you characterize their disagreements?

Second, look at the kinds of sources the authors are using. Are their
sources national or local in scope? Do they represent a broad spectrum of
people or do they focus on one class, race, or gender? Do the sources
allow you to hear debates among different groups of Progressives?

Third, assess the author's claims, keeping the sources in mind. How
much does the author generalize about the nature of Progressivism from
his or her case study? Does the author's evidence back that generalization?
Does the author claim to have identified the only group of Progressives, or
the group that led all Progressive reform? How does that claim fit with the
others in this volume?

These articles are yours to use, to accept, or to reject. Each offers an
explanation to one of the most important questions in a democracy: How
does peaceful social change occur? As you evaluate them, think about your
own theories of change, reform, and revolution. In 1920, the United States
was quite a different place than it had been in 1890. Who bore responsibility for that change is the central question of this book.

Notes

1. Quoted in John Milton Cooper, *Pivotal Decades* (New York: W. W. Norton, 1990), 88.

2. Daniel Rodgers, *Atlantic Crossings: Social Politics in a Progressive Age* (Cambridge: Harvard University Press, 1998), 6–7.

3. Rodgers, *Atlantic Crossings*, 49.

4. Tera Hunter, *To 'Joy My Freedom: Southern Black Women's Lives and Labors after the Civil War* (Cambridge: Harvard University Press, 1997).

5. Steven J. Diner, *A Very Different Age: Americans of the Progressive Era* (New York: Hill and Wang, 1998), 5.

6. In 1907, Florence Kelley organized the Committee on Congestion of the Population to address overcrowding and lack of city planning in New York. Rodgers, *Atlantic Crossings*, 181.

7. Diner, *A Very Different Age*, 77.

8. Richard W. Abrams and Lawrence W. Levine, *The Shaping of Twentieth Century America* (Boston: Little, Brown, 1965), 295.

9. Glenda Elizabeth Gilmore, *Gender and Jim Crow: Women and the Politics of White Supremacy in North Carolina, 1896–1920* (Chapel Hill: University of North Carolina Press, 1996), 25.

10. Gilmore, *Gender and Jim Crow*; J. Morgan Kousser, *The Shaping of Southern Politics: Suffrage Restriction and the Establishment of the One Party South* (New Haven: Yale University Press, 1974); Edward Ayers, *The Promise of the New South: Life after Reconstruction* (New York: Oxford University Press, 1992); William Link, *The Paradox of Southern Progressivism* (Chapel Hill: University of North Carolina Press, 1992).

11. Leon F. Litwack, *Trouble in Mind: Black Southerners in the Age of Jim Crow* (New York: Knopf, 1998), 487.

12. Diner, *A Very Different Age*, 151.

13. William J. Collins, "When the Tide Turned: Immigration and the Delay of the Great Migration," *Journal of Economic History*, 57 (September 1997): 607–32.

14. Joanne Meyerowitz, "Sexual Geography and Gender Economy: The Furnished-Room Districts of Chicago, 1890–1930," *Gender and History*, 2 (Autumn 1990): 186–202. See also, Mary E. Odem, *Delinquent Daughters: Protecting and Policing Adolescent Female Sexuality in the United States, 1885–1920* (Chapel Hill: University of North Carolina Press, 1995).

15. James McGovern, "The American Woman's Pre–World War I Freedom in Manners and Morals," *Journal of American History*, 55 (September 1968): 315–33, and Kathy Peiss, *Cheap Amusements: Working Women and Leisure in Turn-of-the-Century New York* (Philadelphia: Temple University Press, 1986).

16. Milton M. Gordon, "Assimilation in America," in Abrams and Levine, *The Shaping of Twentieth Century America*, 296–315; James J. Connolly, *The Triumph of Ethnic Progressivism: Urban Political Culture in Boston, 1900–1925* (Cambridge: Harvard University Press, 1998).

17. Jane Addams, *Twenty Years in Hull House*, quoted in Gordon, "Assimilation in America," 309. See also, Hilda Satt Polacheck, *I Came a Stranger: The Story of a Hull House Girl*, Dena J. Polacheck Epstein, ed. (Urbana: University of Illinois Press, 1989).

18. Leon Fink, *Workingmen's Democracy: The Knights of Labor and American Politics* (Urbana: University of Illinois Press, 1983); Kim Voss, *The Making of American*

Exceptionalism: The Knights of Labor and Class Formation in the Nineteenth Century (Ithaca, N.Y.: Cornell University Press, 1993).

19. On the American Federation of Labor and Progressivism, see Julie Greene, "The Making of Labor's Democracy: William Jennings Bryan, The American Federation of Labor, and Progressive Era Politics," *Nebraska History*, 77 (3–4, 1996): 149–58. On connections between Progressivism and labor, see George Leidenberger, "'The Public Is the Labor Union': Working-Class Progressivism in Turn-of-the-Century Chicago," *Labor History*, 36 (Spring 1995): 187–210.

20. "Preamble, Constitution of the IWW," at http://www.iww.org.

21. On the IWW, see Melvyn Dubfosky, *We Shall Be All: A History of the Industrial Workers of the World* (Urbana: University of Illinois Press, 1998); Charles H. McCormick, *Seeing Reds: Federal Surveillance of Radicals in the Pittsburgh Mill District, 1917–1921* (Pittsburgh: University of Pittsburgh Press, 1997); Howard Kimeldorf, *Battling for American Labor: Wobblies, Craftworkers, and the Making of the Union Movement* (Berkeley: University of California Press, 1999).

22. David M. Kennedy, *Over Here: The First World War and American Society* (New York: Oxford University Press, 1980), 26.

23. Nick Salvatore, *Eugene V. Debs: Citizen and Socialist* (Chicago: University of Illinois Press, 1982).

24. See, for example, Sally M. Miller, *Victor Berger and the Promise of Constructive Socialism, 1910–1920* (Westport, Conn.: Greenwood Press, 1973).

25. Christopher Lasch, *The True and Only Heaven: Progress and Its Critics* (New York: W. W. Norton, 1991).

26. James Kloppenberg, *Uncertain Victory: Social Democracy and Progressivism in European and American Thought, 1870–1920* (New York: Oxford University Press, 1986), 299.

27. See Eldon J. Eisenach, *The Lost Promise of Progressivism* (Lawrence: University Press of Kansas, 1994); Colin Gordon, "Still Searching for Progressivism," *Reviews in American History*, 23 (December 1995): 669–74.

28. On the nineteenth-century precursors of Progressive Era legislation, see William J. Novak, *The People's Welfare: Law and Regulation in Nineteenth-Century America* (Chapel Hill: University of North Carolina Press, 1996). On the Populists, see Lawrence Goodwyn, *The Populist Moment: A Short History of the Agrarian Revolt in America* (New York: Oxford University Press, 1978).

29. "Do Not Grind the Seed Corn," pamphlet in the North Carolina Collection, Wilson Library, University of North Carolina at Chapel Hill.

30. Richard Wrightman Fox, "The Culture of Liberal Protestant Progressivism, 1875–1925," *Journal of Interdisciplinary History*, XXIII (Winter 1993): 639–60. See also Robert M. Crunden, *Ministers of Reform: The Progressives' Achievement in American Civilization, 1889–1920* (New York: Basic Books, 1982); Richard Hofstadter, *Social Darwinism in American Thought* (Boston: Beacon Press, 1955).

31. Robyn Muncy, *Creating a Female Dominion in American Reform, 1890–1935* (New York: Oxford University Press, 1991). On the creation of social work as a feminized profession and its links to Progressivism, see Ellen Fitzpatrick, *Endless Reform: Women Social Scientists and Progressive Reform* (New York: Oxford University Press, 1990; Daniel J. Walkowitz, "The Making of a Feminine Professional Identity, Social Workers in the 1920s," *American Historical Review*, 95 (October 1990): 1051–75. For an extension of this topic to the New Deal, see Linda Gordon, *Pitied*

but Not Entitled: Single Mothers and the History of Welfare (Cambridge: Harvard University Press, 1994).

32. Kathryn Kish Sklar, *Florence Kelley and the Nation's Work: The Rise of Women's Political Culture, 1830–1900* (New Haven: Yale University Press, 1995), xv.

33. Sklar, *Florence Kelley and the Nation's Work,* xiv.

34. Edward A. Stettner, *Shaping Modern Liberalism: Herbert Croly and Progressive Thought* (Lawrence: University Press of Kansas, 1993), 5.

35. Walter Lippmann, *Drift and Mastery: An Attempt to Diagnose the Current Unrest* (New York: Mitchell Kennerley, 1914), quoted in Kloppenberg, *Uncertain Victory,* 298.

36. Herbert Croly, *Progressive Democracy,* 1914. Reprint edition. (New Brunswick, N.J.: Transaction Publishers, 1998). See in this edition, Sidney A. Pearson Jr., "Introduction," for a detailed analysis of Croly's constitutional reinterpretation.

37. Pearson, "Introduction," xiv.

38. Pearson, "Introduction," xxx.

39. Pearson, "Introduction," xxxix. For an overview of ways that the Progressives tried to harness public opinion, see Kevin Mattson, *Creating a Democratic Public: The Struggle for Urban Participatory Democracy during the Progressive Era* (University Park: The Pennsylvania State University Press, 1998); Elizabeth Sanders, *Roots of Reform: Farmers, Workers, and the American State, 1877–1917* (Chicago: University of Chicago Press, 1999); Elisabeth S. Clemens, *The People's Lobby: Organizational Innovation and the Rise of Interest Group Politics in the United States, 1890–1925* (Chicago: University of Chicago Press, 1997).

40. J. Morgan Kousser, *The Shaping of Southern Politics and the Establishment of the One Party South, 1880–1910* (New Haven: Yale University Press, 1974); Alexander Keyssar, *The Right to Vote: The Contested History of Democracy in the United States* (New York: Basic Books, 2000).

41. See, for example, Pamela Tyler, *Silk Stockings and Ballot Boxes: Women and Politics in New Orleans, 1920–1963* (Athens: University of Georgia Press, 1996).

42. For work on women's politics before the Progressive Era, see Michael L. Goldberg, *An Army of Women: Gender and Politics in Gilded Age Kansas* (Baltimore: Johns Hopkins University Press, 1997); Rebecca Edwards, *Angels in the Machinery: Gender in American Party Politics from the Civil War to the Progressive Era* (New York: Oxford University Press, 1997). For the Progressive Era, there is extensive work on woman suffrage. Some of the most recent include: Melanie Gustafson, "Partisan Women in the Progressive Era: The Struggle for Inclusion in American Political Parties," *Journal of Women's History,* 9 (Summer 1997): 8–30; Victoria Bissell Brown, "Jane Addams, Progressivism, and Woman Suffrage: An Introduction to Why Women Should Vote," in Marjorie Spruill Wheeler, ed., *One Woman, One Vote: Rediscovering the Woman Suffrage Movement* (Troutdale, Ore.: New Sage Press, 1995), 187–8, Addams quoted, 190.

43. On black women and ballots, see Rosalyn Terborg-Penn, *African American Women in the Struggle for the Vote, 1850–1920* (Bloomington: Indiana University Press, 1998); Gilmore, *Gender and Jim Crow,* chapter 8; Debra Gray White, *Too Heavy a Load: Black Women in Defense of Themselves, 1894–1994* (New York: W. W. Norton, 1999), 87–141.

44. Leon Fink, "Progressive Reformers, Social Scientists, and the Search for a Democratic Public," *Progressive Intellectuals and the Dilemmas of Democratic Commitment*

(Cambridge: Harvard University Press, 1997), 18. See also Julie A. Reuben, "Beyond Politics: Community Civics and the Redefinition of Citizenship in the Progressive Era," *History of Education Quarterly*, 37 (Winter 1997): 399–420.

45. C. Vann Woodward, *Origins of the New South, 1877–1913* (Baton Rouge: Louisiana State University Press, 1951), 388–9.

46. For women's contributions in child welfare, see Molly Ladd-Taylor, *Mother-Work: Women, Child Welfare, and the State, 1890–1930* (Urbana: University of Illinois Press, 1994); Muncy, *Creating a Female Dominion.*

47. Diner, *A Very Different Age*, 217.

48. For biographical coverage of both Theodore Roosevelt and Woodrow Wilson and their programs, see John Milton Cooper, *The Warrior and the Priest: Woodrow Wilson and Theodore Roosevelt* (Cambridge: Belknap Press of Harvard University Press, 1983).

49. Kennedy, *Over Here.*

50. Rodgers, *Atlantic Crossings*, 22–4.

51. Gabriel Kolko, *The Triumph of Conservatism* (New York: The Free Press, 1963). See also James Weinstein, *The Corporate Ideal in the Liberal State* (Boston: Beacon Press, 1968); Sklar, *The Corporate Reconstruction of American Capitalism.* For a recent review of the literature, see Philip Gullis, "The Limits of Progressivism: Louis Brandeis, Democracy and the Corporation," *Journal of American Studies*, 3, no. 3 (1996): 381–404.

52. For reconceptualizations of Progressivism, see Peter G. Filene, "An Obituary for the Progressive Movement," *American Quarterly*, 22 (Spring 1970): 20–34; Filene, "Narrating Progressivism: Unitarians v. Pluralists v. Students," *Journal of American History*, 79 (March 1993): 1546–62; Rodgers, "In Search of Progressivism."

53. Anne Firor Scott, "A Historian's Odyssey," in Scott, *Making the Invisible Woman Visible* (Urbana: University of Illinois Press, 1984), xv, xviii–xix; Daniel Rodgers, "In Search of Progressivism," *Reviews in American History*, 10 (December 1982): 113–32.

PART TWO

Some Current Questions

The selections that follow deal with some of the issues about the American Progressive Era that now interest historians. Other selections could have been chosen, but these show the current state of the conversation. Each selection is preceded by a headnote that introduces both its specific subject and its author. After the headnote come Questions for a Closer Reading. The headnote and the questions offer signposts that will allow you to understand more readily what the author is saying. Unless otherwise noted, the selections are uncut and include the original notes. The notes are also signposts for further exploration. If an issue that the author raises intrigues you, use the notes to follow it up. You may find that you need to reread some of the material presented because no historical source yields all that is within it to a person content to read it just once.

1. Do we find the roots of Progressivism in the cities or on the farms?

Richard Hofstadter

From *The Status Revolution and Progressive Leaders*

Richard Hofstadter was one of America's leading historians when he died in 1970 after serving as the DeWitt Clinton Professor of American History at Columbia University. *The Age of Reform,* from which this selection is taken, won the Pulitzer Prize for History in 1956.

Hofstadter begins his argument by nodding to the Populist contribution to Progressivism—and then proceeds to ignore it. He recognizes that Populism contributed to the spirit of reform, but labels the Populists as "rural and provincial." He argues that the leaders of Progressivism were urban, middle-class men who were "almost pathetically respectable," having sprung from "civic leaders of an earlier era" in small towns and mid-sized cities. This group and their children became appalled by the corruption, greed, and growth they saw around them as the nineteenth century drew to a close. Whereas Hofstadter's group of elites had been able to manage change around them in the past, they now saw themselves losing power in the new industrial society of big industry, big capital, and big politics. They became Progressives, Hofstadter thinks, because they were determined to influence this new world with the values they had learned in their old world.

Questions for a Closer Reading

1. Imagine that you are a Hofstadter Progressive placing a personal ad. How might you describe yourself? Be sure to explain to your potential callers what a Mugwump is.

2. What does Hofstadter mean by the "status revolution"? Can you think of any other group in American society that experienced a similar status revolution at another time? If so, how did that group react? Is the concept of status revolution a useful one for thinking about social change?

3. Imagine that you are a Presbyterian minister's son, living in North Carolina in 1880. Your girlfriend has jilted you, and you have just dropped out of the University of Virginia Law School because you hated studying law. Now you are living at home with your mom and dad. Your dad is making you study law at home so that you can take the bar exam, but you don't want to be a lawyer; you want to change the world. Based on Hofstadter's description of the Mugwumps' criticisms of American society, write a journal entry describing what's wrong with America and what you propose to do about it. In case you recognize this description, remember that in 1880 you don't know that you will go on to be President Thomas Woodrow Wilson; you are just Tommy Wilson, law school dropout.

4. Glance over Hofstadter's endnotes. What kinds of sources is he using (newspapers, letters, published works, magazine articles, census data, etc.)? Do his sources allow him to hear from all Americans? How might using these particular sources shape his argument? Where does Hofstadter locate his argument geographically?

5. Look at Hofstadter's introductory paragraphs and find examples of how he limits his argument about the origins of Progressivism in the old-stock middle class. How does he acknowledge the fact that Populists contributed to Progressive reform? How then does he dismiss the Populists as unimportant to the leadership of Progressivism?

The Status Revolution
and Progressive Leaders

Populism* had been overwhelmingly rural and provincial. The ferment of the Progressive era was urban, middle-class, and nation-wide. Above all, Progressivism differed from Populism in the fact that the middle classes of the cities not only joined the trend toward protest but took over its leadership. While Bryan's old followers still kept their interest in certain reforms, they now found themselves in the company of large numbers who had hitherto violently opposed them. As the demand for reform spread from the farmers to the middle class and from the Populist Party into the major parties, it became more powerful and more highly regarded. It had been possible for their enemies to brand the Populists as wild anarchists, especially since there were millions of Americans who had never laid eyes on either a Populist or an anarchist. But it was impossible to popularize such a distorted image of the Progressives, who flourished in every section of the country, everywhere visibly, palpably, almost patheti-cally respectable.

William Allen White recalled in his *Autobiography,* perhaps with some exaggeration, the atmosphere of the Greenback and Populist conventions he had seen, first as a boy, then as a young reporter. As a solid middle-class citizen of the Middle West, he had concluded that "those agrarian move-ments too often appealed to the ne'er-do-wells, the misfits—farmers who

---

*In 1892, the Populist party sprang from the Farmers' Alliance, which provided a home for agrarian reformers in the 1880s and 1890s, to challenge the Republican and Democratic parties. Among other reforms, the Populists supported the regulation of monopolies, nation-alization of railroads and telephone and telegraph companies, increasing the money supply by using silver as well as gold as a standard, legislation for the eight-hour work day, and a graduated national income tax. By 1896, the Democrats had persuaded former Populist William Jennings Bryan to run for president on the Democratic ticket. With this preemptive strike, the Democratic party absorbed much of the Populist strength—and added many of their goals to its platform. The Populist party never recovered.

Richard Hofstadter, "The Status Revolution and Progressive Leaders," from *The Age of Reform: From Bryan to F.D.R.* (New York: Knopf, 1955), 131–48.

had failed, lawyers and doctors who were not orthodox, teachers who could not make the grade, and neurotics full of hates and ebullient, evanescent enthusiasms." Years later, when he surveyed the membership of the Bull Moose movement of 1912, he found it "in the main and in its heart of hearts *petit bourgeois*": "a movement of little businessmen, professional men, well-to-do farmers, skilled artisans from the upper brackets of organized labor . . . the successful middle-class country-town citizens, the farmer whose barn was painted, the well-paid railroad engineer, and the country editor."[1]

White saw himself as a case in point. In the nineties he had been, in his own words, "a child of the governing classes," and "a stouthearted young reactionary," who rallied with other young Kansas Republicans against the Populists and won a national reputation with his fierce anti-Populist diatribe: "What's the Matter with Kansas?" In the Progressive era he became one of the outstanding publicists of reform, a friend and associate of the famous muckrakers, and an enthusiastic Bull Mooser. His change of heart was also experienced by a large portion of that comfortable society of which he was a typical and honored spokesman, a society that had branded the Populists and Bryan as madmen and then appropriated so much of the Populist program, as White said of its political leaders, that they "caught the Populists in swimming and stole all of their clothing except the frayed underdrawers of free silver."[2]

Clearly, the need for political and economic reform was now felt more widely in the country at large. Another, more obscure process, traceable to the flexibility and opportunism of the American party system, was also at work: successful resistance to reform demands required a partial incorporation of the reform program. As Bryan Democracy had taken over much of the spirit and some of the program of Populism, Theodore Roosevelt, in turn, persistently blunted Bryan's appeal by appropriating Bryan's issues in modified form. In this way Progressivism became nationwide and bipartisan, encompassing Democrats and Republicans, country and city, East, West, and South. A working coalition was forged between the old Bryan country and the new reform movement in the cities, without which the broad diffusion and strength of Progressivism would have been impossible. Its spirit spread so widely that by the time of the three-cornered presidential contest of 1912 President Taft, who was put in the position of the "conservative" candidate, got less than half the combined popular vote of the "Progressives," Wilson and Roosevelt.

 After 1900 Populism and Progressivism merge, though a close student may find in the Progressive era two broad strains of thought, one influenced chiefly by the Populist inheritance, the other mainly a product of urban life. Certainly Progressivism was characterized by a fresh, more intimate and sympathetic concern with urban problems—labor and social welfare, municipal reform, the interest of the consumer. However, those achievements of the age that had a nationwide import and required Congressional action, such as tariff and financial legislation, railroad and trust regulation, and the like, were dependent upon the votes of the Senators from the agrarian regions and were shaped in such a way as would meet their demands.

While too sharp a distinction between Populist and Progressive thinking would distort reality, the growth of middle-class reform sentiment, the contributions of professionals and educated men, made Progressive thought more informed, more moderate, more complex than Populist thought had been. Progressivism, moreover, as the product of a more prosperous era, was less rancorous. With the exception of a few internally controversial issues of a highly pragmatic sort, the Populists had tended to be of one mind on most broad social issues, and that mind was rather narrow and predictable. The Progressives were more likely to be aware of the complexities of social issues and more divided among themselves. Indeed, the characteristic Progressive was often of two minds on many issues. Concerning the great corporations, the Progressives felt that they were a menace to society and that they were all too often manipulated by unscrupulous men; on the other hand, many Progressives were quite aware that the newer organization of industry and finance was a product of social evolution which had its beneficent side and that it was here to stay. Concerning immigrants, they frequently shared Populist prejudices and the Populist horror of ethnic mixture, but they were somewhat more disposed to discipline their feelings with a sense of some obligation to the immigrant and the recognition that his Americanization was a practical problem that must be met with a humane and constructive program. As for labor, while they felt, perhaps more acutely than most Populists of the nineties, that the growth of union power posed a distinct problem, even a threat, to them, they also saw that labor organization had arisen in response to a real need among the urban masses that must in some way be satisfied. As for the bosses, the machines, the corruptions of city life, they too found in these things grave evils; but they were ready, perhaps all too ready, to admit that the existence of such evils was in large measure their own fault. Like the Populists the Progressives were full of indignation, but their indignation was more qualified by a sense of responsibility, often even of guilt, and it was supported by a greater capacity to organize, legislate, and administer. But lest all this seem unfair to the Populists, it should be added that the Progressives did not, as a rule, have the daring or the originative force of the Populists of the 1890s, and that a great deal of Progressive political effort was spent enacting proposals that the Populists had outlined fifteen or even twenty years earlier.

Curiously, the Progressive revolt—even when we have made allowance for the brief panic of 1907 and the downward turn in business in 1913—took place almost entirely during a period of sustained and general prosperity. The middle class, most of which had been content to accept the conservative leadership of Hanna and McKinley during the period of crisis in the mid-nineties, rallied to the support of Progressive leaders in both parties during the period of well-being that followed. This fact is a challenge to the historian. Why did the middle classes undergo this remarkable awakening at all, and why during this period of general prosperity in which most of them seem to have shared? What was the place of economic discontents in the Progressive movement? To what extent did reform originate in other considerations?

Of course Progressivism had the adherence of a heterogeneous public whose various segments responded to various needs. But I am concerned here with a large and strategic section of Progressive leadership, upon whose contributions the movement was politically and intellectually as well as financially dependent, and whose members did much to formulate its ideals. It is my thesis that men of this sort, who might be designated broadly as the Mugwump type,* were Progressives not because of economic deprivations but primarily because they were victims of an upheaval in status that took place in the United States during the closing decades of the nineteenth and the early years of the twentieth century. Progressivism, in short, was to a very considerable extent led by men who suffered from the events of their time not through a shrinkage in their means but through the changed pattern in the distribution of deference and power.

Up to about 1870 the United States was a nation with a rather broad diffusion of wealth, status, and power, in which the man of moderate means, especially in the many small communities, could command much deference and exert much influence. The small merchant or manufacturer, the distinguished lawyer, editor, or preacher, was a person of local eminence in an age in which local eminence mattered a great deal. In the absence of very many nationwide sources of power and prestige, the pillars of the local communities were men of great importance in their own right. What

---

*Mugwump was the name given to reform Republicans who opposed the nomination of James G. Blaine for president in 1884. They opposed corruption and patronage in party politics and endorsed the Democratic party's presidential candidate, Grover Cleveland.

Henry Adams remembered about his own bailiwick was, on the whole, true of the country at large: "Down to 1850, and even later, New England society was still directed by the professions. Lawyers, physicians, professors, merchants were classes, and acted not as individuals, but as though they were clergymen and each profession were a church."[3]

In the post–Civil War period all this was changed. The rapid development of the big cities, the building of a great industrial plant, the construction of the railroads, the emergence of the corporation as the dominant form of enterprise, transformed the old society and revolutionized the distribution of power and prestige. During the 1840s there were not twenty millionaires in the entire country; by 1910 there were probably more than twenty millionaires sitting in the United States Senate.[4] By the late 1880s this process had gone far enough to become the subject of frequent, anxious comment in the press. In 1891 the *Forum* published a much-discussed article on "The Coming Billionaire," by Thomas G. Shearman, who estimated that there were 120 men in the United States each of whom was worth over ten million dollars.[5] In 1892 the *New York Tribune,* inspired by growing popular criticism of the wealthy, published a list of 4,047 reputed millionaires, and in the following year a statistician of the Census Bureau published a study of the concentration of wealth in which he estimated that 9 per cent of the families of the nation owned 71 per cent of the wealth.[6]

The newly rich, the grandiosely or corruptly rich, the masters of great corporations, were bypassing the men of the Mugwump type—the old gentry, the merchants of long standing, the small manufacturers, the established professional men, the civic leaders of an earlier era. In a score of cities and hundreds of towns, particularly in the East but also in the nation at large, the old-family, college-educated class that had deep ancestral roots in local communities and often owned family businesses, that had traditions of political leadership, belonged to the patriotic societies and the best clubs, staffed the governing boards of philanthropic and cultural institutions, and led the movements for civic betterment, were being overshadowed and edged aside in the making of basic political and economic decisions. In their personal careers, as in their community activities, they found themselves checked, hampered, and overridden by the agents of the new corporations, the corrupters of legislatures, the buyers of franchises, the allies of the political bosses. In this uneven struggle they found themselves limited by their own scruples, their regard for reputation, their social standing itself. To be sure, the America they knew did not lack opportunities, but it did seem to lack opportunities of the highest sort for men of the highest standards. In a strictly economic sense these men were not growing poorer as a class, but their wealth and power were being dwarfed by comparison with the new eminences of wealth and power. They were less important, and they knew it.

Against the tide of new wealth the less affluent and aristocratic local gentry had almost no protection at all. The richer and better-established among them found it still possible, of course, to trade on their inherited money and position, and their presence as window-dressing was an asset for any kind of enterprise, in business or elsewhere, to which they would lend their sponsorship. Often indeed the new men sought to marry into their circles, or to buy from them social position much as they bought from the bosses legislation and franchises. But at best the gentry could only make a static defense of themselves, holding their own in absolute terms while relatively losing ground year by year. Even this much they could do only in the localities over which they had long presided and in which they were well known. And when everyone could see that the arena of prestige, like the market for commodities, had been widened to embrace the entire nation, eminence in mere localities ceased to be as important and satisfying as once it had been. To face the insolence of the local boss or traction magnate in a town where one's family had long been prominent was galling enough;[7] it was still harder to bear at a time when every fortune, every career, every reputation, seemed smaller and less significant because it was measured against the Vanderbilts, Harrimans, Goulds, Carnegies, Rockefellers, and Morgans.[8]

The first reaction of the Mugwump type to the conditions of the status revolution was quite different from that later to be displayed by their successors among the Progressives. All through the seventies, eighties, and nineties men from the upper ranks of business and professional life had expressed their distaste for machine politics, corruption, and the cruder forms of business intervention in political affairs. Such men were commonly Republicans, but independent enough to bolt if they felt their principles betrayed. They made their first organized appearance in the ill-fated Liberal Republican movement of 1872, but their most important moment came in 1884, when their bolt from the Republican Party after the nomination of James G. Blaine was widely believed to have helped tip the scales to Cleveland in a close election.

While men of the Mugwump type flourished during those decades, most conspicuously about Boston, a center of seasoned wealth and seasoned conscience, where some of the most noteworthy names in Massachusetts were among them,[9] they were also prominent in a metropolis like New York and could be found in some strength in such Midwestern cities as Indianapolis and Chicago. None the less, one senses among them the prominence of the cultural ideals and traditions of New England, and beyond these of old England. Protestant and Anglo-Saxon for the most part, they were very frequently of New England ancestry; and even when they were not, they tended to look to New England's history for literary, cultural, and political models and for examples of moral idealism. Their conception of statecraft was set by the high example of the Founding Fathers, or by the great debating statesmen of the silver age, Webster, Sumner, Everett, Clay, and Calhoun. Their ideal leader was a well-to-do, well-educated, high-minded citizen, rich enough to be free from motives of what they often called "crass materialism," whose family roots were deep not only in American history but in his local community. Such a person, they thought, would be just the sort to put the national interest, as well as the interests of civic improvement, above personal motives or political opportunism. And such a person was just the sort, as Henry Adams never grew tired of complaining, for whom American political life was least likely to find a place. To be sure, men of the Mugwump type could and did find places in big industry, in the great corporations, and they were sought out to add respectability to many forms of enterprise. But they tended to have positions in which the initiative was not their own, or in which they could not feel themselves acting in harmony with their highest ideals. They no longer called the tune, no longer commanded their old deference. They were expropriated, not so much economically as morally.

They imagined themselves to have been ousted almost entirely by new men of the crudest sort. While in truth the great business leaders of the Gilded Age were typically men who started from comfortable or privileged beginnings in life,[10] the Mugwump mind was most concerned with the newness and the rawness of the corporate magnates, and Mugwumps and reformers alike found satisfaction in a bitter caricature of the great businessman. One need only turn to the social novels of the "realists" who wrote about businessmen at the turn of the century—William Dean Howells, H. H. Boyesen, Henry Blake Fuller, and Robert Herrick, among others—to see the portrait of the captain of industry that dominated the Mugwump imagination. The industrialists were held to be uneducated and uncultivated, irresponsible, rootless and corrupt, devoid of refinement or of any sense of noblesse. "If our civilization is destroyed, as Macaulay predicted," wrote Henry Demarest Lloyd in an assessment of the robber barons, "it will not be by his barbarians from below. Our barbarians come from above. Our great money-makers have sprung in one generation into seats of power kings do not know. *The forces and the wealth are new, and have been the opportunity of new men. Without restraints of culture, experience, the pride, or even the inherited caution of class or rank,* these men, intoxicated, think they are the wave instead of the float, and that they have created the business which has created them. To them science is but a never-ending repertoire of investments stored up by nature for the syndicates, government but a fountain of franchises, the nations but customers in squads, and a million the unit of a new arithmetic of wealth written for them. They claim a power without control, exercised through forms which make it secret, anonymous, and perpetual. The possibilities of its gratification have been widening before them without interruption since they began, and even at a thousand millions they will feel no satiation and will see no place to stop."[11]

Unlike Lloyd, however, the typical Mugwump was a conservative in his economic and political views. He disdained, to be sure, the most unscrupulous of the new men of wealth, as he did the opportunistic, boodling, tariff-mongering politicians who served them. But the most serious abuses of the unfolding economic order of the Gilded Age he either resolutely ignored or accepted complacently as an inevitable result of the struggle for existence or the improvidence and laziness of the masses.[12] As a rule, he was dogmatically committed to the prevailing theoretical economics of *laissez faire.* His economic program did not go much beyond tariff reform and sound money—both principles more easily acceptable to a group whose wealth was based more upon mercantile activities and the professions than upon manufacturing and new enterprises—and his political program rested upon the foundations of honest and efficient government and civil-service reform. He was a "liberal" in the classic sense. Tariff reform, he thought, would be the sovereign remedy for the huge business combinations that were arising. His pre-eminent journalist and philosopher was E. L. Godkin, the honorable old free-trading editor of the *Nation* and the New York *Evening Post.* His favorite statesman was Grover Cleveland, who described the tariff as the "mother of trusts." He imagined that most of the economic ills that were remediable at all could be remedied by free trade, just as he believed that the essence of government lay in honest dealing by honest and competent men.

Lord Bryce spoke of the Mugwump movement as being "made more important by the intelligence and social position of the men who composed it than by its voting power."[13] It was in fact intellect and social position, among other things, that insulated the Mugwump from the sources of voting power. If he was critical of the predatory capitalists and their political allies, he was even more contemptuously opposed to the "radical" agrarian movements and the "demagogues" who led them, to the city workers when, led by "walking delegates," they rebelled against their employers, and to the urban immigrants and the "unscrupulous bosses" who introduced them to the mysteries of American civic life. He was an impeccable constitutionalist, but the fortunes of American politics had made him an equally firm aristocrat. He had his doubts, now that the returns were in, about the beneficence of universal suffrage.[14] The last thing he would have dreamed of was to appeal to the masses against the plutocracy, and to appeal to them against the local bosses was usually fruitless. The Mugwump was shut off from the people as much by his social reserve and his amateurism as by his candidly conservative views. In so far as he sought popular support, he sought it on aristocratic terms.

One of the changes that made Progressivism possible around the turn of the century was the end of this insulation of the Mugwump type from mass support. For reasons that it is in good part the task of these pages to explore, the old barriers melted away. How the Mugwump found a following is a complex story, but it must be said at once that this was impossible until the Mugwump type itself had been somewhat transformed. The sons and successors of the Mugwumps had to challenge their fathers' ideas, modify their doctrinaire commitment to *laissez faire*, replace their aristocratic preferences with a startling revival of enthusiasm for popular government, and develop greater flexibility in dealing with the demands of the discontented before they could launch the movement that came to dominate the political life of the Progressive era.

But if the philosophy and the spirit were new, the social type and the social grievance were much the same. The Mugwump had broadened his base. One need not be surprised, for instance, to find among the Progressive leaders in both major parties a large number of well-to-do men whose personal situation is reminiscent of the Mugwumps of an earlier generation. As Professor George Mowry has remarked, "few reform movements in American history have had the support of more wealthy men."[15] Such men as George W. Perkins and Frank Munsey, who may perhaps be accused of joining the Progressive movement primarily to blunt its edge, can be left out of account, and such wealthy reformers as Charles R. Crane, Rudolph Spreckels, E. A. Filene, the Pinchots, and William Kent may be dismissed as exceptional. Still, in examining the lives and backgrounds of the reformers of the era, one is impressed by the number of those who had considerably more than moderate means, and particularly by those who had inherited their money. As yet no study has been made of reform leaders in both major parties, but the systematic information available on leaders of the Progressive Party of 1912 is suggestive. Alfred D. Chandler, Jr., surveying the backgrounds and careers of 260 Progressive Party leaders throughout the country, has noted how overwhelmingly urban and middle-class they were. Almost entirely native-born Protestants, they had an extraordinarily high representation of professional men and college graduates. The rest were businessmen, proprietors of fairly large enterprises. None was a farmer, only one was a labor-union leader, and the white-collar classes and salaried managers of large industrial or transportation enterprises were completely unrepresented. Not surprisingly, the chief previous political experience of most of them was in local politics. But on the whole, as Chandler observes, they "had had little experience with any kind of institutional discipline. In this sense, though they lived in the city, they were in no way typical men of the city. With very rare exceptions, all these men had been and continued to be their own bosses. As lawyers, businessmen, and professional men, they worked for themselves and had done so for most of their lives. As individualists, unacquainted with institutional discipline or control, the Progressive leaders represented, in spite of their thoroughly urban backgrounds, the ideas of the older, more rural America."[16] From the only other comparable study, George Mowry's survey of the California Progressives, substantially the same conclusions emerge. The average California Progressive was "in the jargon of his day, 'well fixed.' He was more often than not a Mason,* and almost invariably a member of his town's chamber of commerce. . . . He apparently had been, at least until 1900, a conservative Republican, satisfied with McKinley and his Republican predecessors."[17]

While some of the wealthier reformers were self-made men, like John P. Altgeld, Hazen Pingree, the Mayor of Detroit and Governor of Michigan, and Samuel ("Golden Rule") Jones, the crusading Mayor of Toledo, more were men of the second and third generation of wealth or (notably Tom Johnson and Joseph Fels) men who had been declassed for a time and had recouped their fortunes. Progressive ideology, at any rate, distinguished consistently between "responsible" and "irresponsible" wealth—a distinction that seems intimately related to the antagonism of those who had had money long enough to make temperate and judicious use of it for those who were rioting with newfound means.

A gifted contemporary of the Progressives, Walter Weyl, observed in his penetrating and now all but forgotten book *The New Democracy* that this distinction between types of wealth could often be seen in American cities: "As wealth accumulates, moreover, a cleavage of sentiment widens between the men who are getting rich and the men who *are* rich. The old Cincinnati distinction between the 'stick-'ems' (the actual pork-packers) and the rich 'stuck-'ems' is today reflected in the difference between the retired millionaires of New York and the millionaires, in process or hope, of Cleveland, Portland, Los Angeles, or Denver. The gilt-edged millionaire bondholder of a standard railroad has only a partial sympathy with timber thieves, though his own fortune may have originated a few generations ago in railroad-wrecking or the slave and Jamaica rum trade; while the cul-

---

*Mason refers to a member of the Free and Accepted Masons, an international secret fraternal society that often included leading citizens.

tured descendants of cotton manufacturers resent the advent into their society of the man who had made his 'pile' in the recent buying or selling of franchises. Once wealth is sanctified by hoary age . . . it tends to turn quite naturally against new and evil ways of wealth getting, the expedients of prospective social climbers. The old wealth is not a loyal ally in the battle for the plutocracy; it inclines, if not to democratic, at least to mildly reformatory, programs . . . the battle between the plutocracy and the democracy, which furiously wages in the cities where wealth is being actually fought for, becomes somewhat gentler in those cities where bodies of accumulated wealth exercise a moderating influence. Inheritance works in the same direction. Once wealth is separated from its original accumulator, it slackens its advocacy of its method of accumulation."[18]

Weyl realized, moreover, that so far as a great part of the dissenting public was concerned, the central grievance against the American plutocracy was not that it despoiled them economically but that it overshadowed them, that in the still competitive arena of prestige derived from conspicuous consumption and the style of life, the new plutocracy had set standards of such extravagance and such notoriety that everyone else felt humbled by comparison. Not only was this true of the nation as a whole in respect to the plutocracy, but there was an inner plutocracy in every community and every profession that aroused the same vague resentment: "The most curious factor," he found, in the almost universal American antagonism toward the plutocracy, was "that an increasing bitterness is felt by a majority which is not worse but better off than before. This majority suffers not an absolute decline but a relatively slower growth. It objects that the plutocracy grows too fast; that in growing so rapidly it squeezes its growing neighbors. Growth is right and proper, but there is, it is alleged, a rate of growth which is positively immoral. . . . To a considerable extent the plutocracy is hated not for what it does but for what it is. . . . It is the mere existence of a plutocracy, the mere 'being' of our wealthy contemporaries, that is the main offense. Our over-moneyed neighbors cause a relative deflation of our personalities. Of course, in the consumption of wealth, as in its production, there exist 'non-competitive groups,' and a two-thousand-dollar-a-year-man need not spend like a Gould or a Guggenheim. Everywhere, however, we meet the millionaire's good and evil works, and we seem to resent the one as much as the other. Our jogging horses are passed by their high-power automobiles. We are obliged to take their dust.

"By setting the pace for a frantic competitive consumption, our infinite gradations in wealth (with which gradations the plutocracy is inevitably associated) increase the general social friction and produce an acute social irritation. . . . We are developing new types of destitutes—the automobile-less, the yachtless, the Newport-cottageless. The subtlest of luxuries become necessities, and their loss is bitterly resented. The discontent of today reaches very high in the social scale. . . .

"For this reason the plutocracy is charged with having ended our old-time equality. . . . Our industrial development (of which the trust is but one phase) has been towards a sharpening of the angle of progression. Our eminences have become higher and more dazzling; the goal has been raised and narrowed. Although lawyers, doctors, engineers, architects, and professional men, generally, make larger salaries than ever before, the earning of one hundred thousand dollars a year by one lawyer impoverishes by comparison the thousands of lawyers who scrape along on a thousand a year. The widening of the competitive field has widened the variation and has sharpened the contrast between success and failure, with resulting inequality and discontent."[19]

Notes

1. *Autobiography,* pp. 482–3.
2. Quoted by Kenneth Hechler: *Insurgency* (New York, 1940), pp. 21–2.
3. *The Education of Henry Adams* (New York, Modern Library ed., 1931), p. 32; cf. Tocqueville: *Democracy in America* (New York, 1912), Vol. I, pp. 40–1.
4. Sidney Ratner: *American Taxation* (New York, 1942), pp. 136, 275.
5. Thomas G. Shearman: "The Coming Billionaire," *Forum,* Vol. X (January 1891), pp. 546–57; cf. the same author's "The Owners of the United States," ibid., Vol. VIII (November 1889), pp. 262–73.
6. Ratner, op. cit., p. 220. Sidney Ratner has published the *Tribune's* list and one compiled in 1902 by the *New York World Almanac,* together with a valuable introductory essay in his *New Light on the History of Great American Fortunes* (New York, 1953). The *Tribune's* list was compiled chiefly to prove to the critics of the tariff that an overwhelming majority of the great fortunes had been made in businesses that were not beneficiaries of tariff protection. For an analysis of the *Tribune's* list, see G. P. Watkins: "The Growth of Large Fortunes," *Publications of the American Economic Association,* third series, Vol. VIII (1907), pp. 141–7. Out of the alarm of the period over the concentration of wealth arose the first American studies of national wealth and income. For a review of these studies, see C. L. Merwin: "American Studies of the Distribution of Wealth and Income by Size," in *Studies in Income and Wealth,* Vol. III (New York, 1939), pp. 3–84.
7. In the West and South it was more often the absentee railroad or industrial corporation that was resented. In more recent times, such local resentments have frequently taken a more harmful and less constructive form than the similar resentments of the Progressive era. Seymour M. Lipset and Reinhard Bendix have pointed out that in small American cities dependent for their livelihood upon large national corporations, the local upper classes, who are upper class only in their own community, resent their economic weakness and their loss of power to the outsiders. "The small industrialist and business man of the nation is caught in a struggle between big unionism and big industry, and he feels threatened. This experience of the discrepancy between local prominence and the decline of local

economic power provides a fertile ground for an ideology which attacks both big business and big unionism." "Social Status and Social Structure," *British Journal of Sociology,* Vol. II (June 1951), p. 233.

8. It may be significant that the era of the status revolution was also one in which great numbers of patriotic societies were founded. Of 105 patriotic orders founded between 1783 and 1900, 34 originated before 1870 and 71 between 1870 and 1900. A high proportion of American patriotic societies is based upon descent and length of family residence in the United States, often specifically requiring family participation in some such national event as the American Revolution. The increase of patriotic and genealogical societies during the status revolution suggests that many old-family Americans, who were losing status in the present, may have found satisfying compensation in turning to family glories of the past. Of course, a large proportion of these orders were founded during the nationalistic outbursts of the nineties; but these too may have had their subtle psychological relation to status changes. Note the disdain of men like Theodore Roosevelt for the lack of patriotism and aggressive nationalism among men of great wealth. On the founding of patriotic societies, see Wallace E. Davies: *A History of American Veterans' and Hereditary Patriotic Societies, 1783–1900,* unpublished doctoral dissertation, Harvard University, 1944, Vol. II, pp. 441 ff.

9. Notably Charles Francis Adams, Jr., Edward Atkinson, Moorfield Storey, Leverett Saltonstall, William Everett, Josiah Quincy, Thomas Wentworth Higginson.

10. See William Miller: "American Historians and the Business Elite," *Journal of Economic History,* Vol. IX (November 1949), pp. 184–208; "The Recruitment of the American Business Elite," *Quarterly Journal of Economics,* Vol. LXIV (May 1950), pp. 242–53. C. Wright Mills: "The American Business Elite: a Collective Portrait," *Journal of Economic History,* Vol. V (Supplemental issue, 1945), pp. 20–44. Frances W. Gregory and Irene D. Neu: "The American Industrial Elite in the 1870's," in William Miller, ed.: *Men in Business* (Cambridge, 1952), pp. 193–211.

11. Henry Demarest Lloyd: *Wealth against Commonwealth* (New York, 1894, ed. 1899), pp. 510–11; italics added. For some characteristic expressions on the plutocracy by other writers, see the lengthy quotations in Lloyd's article: "Plutocracy," in W. D. P. Bliss, ed.: *Encyclopedia of Social Reform* (New York, 1897), pp. 1012–16.

12. For a cross-section of the views of this school, see Alan P. Grimes: *The Political Liberalism of the New York* NATION, *1865–1932* (Chapel Hill, 1953), chapter ii.

13. *The American Commonwealth,* Vol. II, p. 45; see pp. 45–50 for a brief characterization of the Mugwump type.

14. Grimes, op. cit., chapter iii.

15. George Mowry: *Theodore Roosevelt and the Progressive Movement* (Madison, 1946), p. 10.

16. Alfred D. Chandler, Jr.: "The Origins of Progressive Leadership," in Elting Morison, ed.: *The Letters of Theodore Roosevelt,* Vol. VIII (Cambridge, 1954), pp. 1462–5. Chandler found the 260 leaders distributed as follows: business, 95; lawyers, 75; editors, 36; other professional (college professors, authors, social workers, and a scattering of others), 55. Chandler also found significant regional variations. In the cities of the Northeast and the old Northwest, the role of the intellectuals and professionals was large, while the businessmen were chiefly those who managed old, established enterprises. In the South, however, a rising social elite of aggressive new businessmen took part. In the West and the rural areas, editors and lawyers dominated party leadership, while the businessmen tended to be

from businesses of modest size, like cattle, real estate, lumber, publishing, small manufacturing.

17. George Mowry: *The California Progressives* (Berkeley, 1951), pp. 88–9; see generally chapter iv, which contains an illuminating brief account of 47 Progressive leaders. Three fourths of these were college-educated. There were 17 lawyers, 14 journalists, 11 independent businessmen and real-estate operators, 3 doctors, 3 bankers. Of the ideology of this group Mowry observed that they were opposed chiefly to "the impersonal, concentrated, and supposedly privileged property represented by the behemoth corporation. Looking backward to an older America [they] sought to recapture and reaffirm the older individualistic values in all the strata of political, economic, and social life." Ibid., p. 89.

18. Walter Weyl: *The New Democracy* (New York, 1914), pp. 242–3.

19. Ibid., pp. 244–8.

Elizabeth Sanders

Agrarian Politics and Parties after 1896

Elizabeth Sanders is a political scientist rather than a historian. She is Professor of Government at Cornell University. Sanders bases her argument on evidence that both political scientists and historians use: economic data and voting patterns.

This selection is part of *Roots of Reform: Farmers, Workers, and The American State, 1877–1917,* in which Sanders argues that the leaders of Progressivism were rural people, who built on the Populist agenda. Thus she argues against every other selection in this volume, all of which find the roots of Progressivism in the cities. She traces the evolution of that movement from the Populists to the Farmer's Union, and she follows William Jennings Bryan, the Populist leader turned Democrat, through his subsequent long career.

Sanders is interested in the political behavior of people in the "periphery," which she defines as the "vast area long characterized by its agrarian and extraction-based economic system."[1] The periphery cut a crescent across the nation with one tip in coastal North Carolina in the east to Texas in the south to another tip in the west where the Great Plains meet the Rocky Mountains. Following it from east to west, we note that the crescent produces cotton, wheat, and wool, and extracts minerals. Sanders finds that the periphery greatly influenced Progressive Era national legislation.

Sanders is clearly arguing with Hofstadter's vision of the Progressives. Moreover, she is disputing Robert Wiebe, whose article you will also read. Pay close attention to the methods she uses to construct a tight argument.

Questions for a Closer Reading

1. Imagine that you are Richard Hofstadter defending your-self against Sanders's argument that rural representatives took the lead in Progressive Era reform. What are the major differences between you and Sanders? How would you attack her argument? After reading Sanders, how might you have qualified your argument to strengthen it?

2. What evidence does Sanders use to argue for continuity between the Populists and the Progressives? What role did the direct primary play in strengthening that continu-ity? What other factors came into play? How does she use William Jennings Bryan to make the case for continuity?

3. Sanders relies heavily on national legislation and legisla-tors to prove that the roots of Progressivism are in rural reform. Give three examples. Can you think of any limita-tions to using national legislation as evidence?

4. Sanders asks, "Who Were the 'Progressives'?" "One way," she tells us, to "avoid the quagmire of ideological labels is to focus on what people *did* during this period, as opposed to what they said or what they (presumably) were *thinking*."[1] Evaluate this statement by comparing Sanders and Hofstadter. Is historians' best evidence what people *did* as opposed to what they were *thinking*? What sort of evidence tells you what people did; what sort tells you what they were thinking? Do you risk losing anything by relying only on what people actually did?

5. Compare Hofstadter's and Sanders's evidence. What sources are they using? How might sources affect a histo-rian's ability to generalize about findings? Defend either Sanders's or Hofstadter's ability to make an argument about the nature of Progressivism *nationally*.

Note

1. Elizabeth Sanders, *Roots of Reform: Farmers, Workers, and the American State, 1877–1917* (Chicago: University of Chicago Press, 1999), 19.

Agrarian Politics and Parties after 1896

The American farmer is the most learned farmer in all the world about politics.

> —Rep. William H. Murray of Oklahoma,
> *Congressional Record,* 63rd Congress,
> 2nd session (1914)

It is a widely accepted view that 1896 marked the end of agrarian-led reform. With the Populist dissenters vanquished, the two major parties are said to have become sectional vehicles of elite dominance. In a tacit bargain, the plantation elite controlled the South, and the industrial and financial elite dominated the North. Competition and voter turnout declined sharply; most congressional seats became safe regional sinecures.[1] Within the southern Populist heartland, the restoration of elite hegemony began with the passage, in state after state, of new constitutions and electoral laws that made it all but impossible for African Americans to vote. Populists generally resisted the imposition of electoral restrictions but without enough force to block them. Frustrated after their own electoral defeats at the hands of a manipulated black vote, a minority of southern Populists were beguiled by the Bourbon Democrats'* argument that if only the electoral process could be "purified"—by the elimination of the black franchise—white southerners could divide among themselves without fear of corruption or loss of white social supremacy.[2]

---

*Bourbon Democrats were the southern white men of the Democratic party who came into power after the end of Reconstruction in the 1870s. Also called the "Redeemers," they tried where possible to replace African American officeholders with white men, keep black voting to a minimum, and provide only minimal state services to whites and blacks.

Elizabeth Sanders, "Agrarian Politics and Parties after 1896," from *Roots of Reform: Farmers, Workers, and the American State, 1877–1917* (Chicago: University of Chicago Press, 1999), 148–72.

The results òf the Bourbon electoral coup are well-known. Registration requirements, poll taxes, literacy tests, and new ballot forms proved devastating to the poor-white electorate as well as the black. The new institution of the white primary, offered as a sop by the Bourbons, was not a "purified" arena in which class politics could thrive: it gave rise to a politics characterized by short-term and personalistic, rather than programmatic, factions and to a new breed of racist demagogues.[3] In spite of these developments, the South was washed by a new reform tide in the first decade of the twentieth century, but in both South and North, reform, in the conventional telling, was now very much an urban, middle- and upper-class phenomenon.[4] Agrarian radicalism had presumably died at the polls in 1896 or been buried under a mound of suffrage restrictions.

The problem with this account is that it ignores the continuity across the 1896 divide and the fact that most of the national legislative fruits of the Progressive Era had their unmistakable origins in the agrarian movements of the 1870s, 1880s, and 1890s. Given the indisputable facts of suffrage restriction and resurgent racism, how can we explain the apparent afterlife of populism? One might, of course, deny the paradox and interpret the national legislation of 1909–17 as a conscious program of the bourgeoisie,[5] but this interpretation is difficult to sustain empirically, as the evidence set out below will demonstrate.

The alternative approach, followed here, distinguishes intrastate and national political processes and argues that the decline of interparty competition and voter turnout and the tragedy of racist politics within the South did not destroy the agrarian impulse in national politics. That impulse retained significant organizational and institutional support in the agrarian areas, and its rationale in the national political economy was not significantly undermined after 1896, despite the improvement in farm prices and currency volume. There were, in particular, four factors that sustained the agrarian reform program in national politics after 1896: a new wave of farmer organization; the direct primary; the national Democratic Party leadership of William Jennings Bryan; and most fundamentally, regional political economy.

The Farm Organization Revival

Even as the Farmers' Alliance consumed itself in politics in the 1890s, the older Grange* began a modest revival. By 1900 it had a dues-paying mem-

---

*The National Grange was a farmers' movement active in the 1870s and 1880s. It focused on educational and social programs, but also lobbied state legislatures for legislation favorable to farmers. The Grange shared many members and goals with the Farmers' Alliance.

bership of almost 190,000.[6] Another source puts the Progressive Era peak at about 300,000 in 1917.[7] Writing of the Grange revival in western Washington, Marilyn Watkins observes that the farm organization became a vibrant focus of rural life, combining social, political, and educational activities in a manner very reminiscent of the Farmers' Alliance. Like the FA, the western Grange joined farm men and women in a relatively gender-egalitarian association and sought alliances with labor organizations on issues of both state and national politics (including railroad regulation, money, taxation, the eight-hour day, workmen's compensation, the power of the judiciary, and the direct primary, referendum and recall).[8]

A few years after the Grange began its slow revival, a new farm organization began to take root in the old Farmers' Alliance territory. The years from 1896 to 1900 were marked by a bottoming out of cotton prices and a profound demoralization in the heartland of the old Alliance. In 1902, the price trend turned up, and with that shot of optimism Newt Gresham, a former Allianceman and Populist of very modest means, convinced a few of his neighbors in Rains County, Texas, that the time was right to rebuild a general farmers' organization.[9] Ten charter members—three Populists, one Socialist, one independent, and five Democrats (including Gresham, who had been a Populist and became a Bryan Democrat)—organized the Farmers' Educational and Cooperative Union of America, known as the Farmers' Union (FU), to assist farmers "in marketing and obtaining better prices for their products" and to encourage fraternal and cooperative activities. Some of the early organizers combined hopes of benefiting farmers as a class with a strong dose of self-interest. Gresham, for example, was a man of proven idealism, living more or less off the charity of his friends. The fees collected from organizing must have been quite welcome. In fact, disputes over the handling of fee money eventually led to the dismissal of most of the founders. But the eager enrollment of Texas farmers in the new organization in Rains, a hardscrabble county of small farmers and high tenancy, amazed the early organizers. Soon the tiny post office at Point, Texas, was swamped with inquiries. The desire for a farmers' organization had sprouted again, almost overnight, in the old Alliance soil.[10]

The first state organization was formed in 1904, and the revival spread rapidly from Texas through the Southwest and Southeast. A national organization took shape in 1905, with Charles Barrett of Georgia elected its first president in 1906. The national secretary claimed 935,837 active members in 1907, and Barrett referred to "a membership approaching three million" at the 1908 convention, but there are no accurate membership records.[11] Carl C. Taylor, dividing national dues collected by sixteen cents (the per-member share to national headquarters), derives a much more modest figure of around 130,000 in 1908 and about 136,000 in 1915–19. But, as he reports, the large female membership paid no dues, and given the casualness about national contributions, actual adherents were probably at least four times that number.[12]

A range of 500,000 to 900,000 would yield an organization with a more modest penetration than the 1870s Grange or the 1880s Alliance but comparable in absolute size to the Knights of Labor in the mid-1880s and the AFL in 1900–1901. Structurally, there were about 20,000 locals in twenty-nine states, stretching from the Pacific Coast through the Midwest and South. Growers of cash crops (cotton, tobacco, wheat) were the main adherents. In 1912, three-quarters of the national dues were collected from the twelve states of the cotton belt, the biggest contributors being North Carolina (which had the largest and most militant organization), Texas, Arkansas, Alabama, and Tennessee. However, the wheat regions of the Midwest and West would loom largest after 1915 as the southern cooperative movement ran into the same problems that had stymied the Farmers' Alliance.[13]

Reflecting the established racism of the time and place, the FU was committed to a racially exclusive membership centered on white farmers (both male and female) and farm laborers. In response, black farmers formed their own organization.[14] In addition to farmers, the FU admitted mechanics, schoolteachers, ministers, and doctors, along with newspaper editors who took a pledge to "support the principles of the Order." Bankers, merchants, lawyers, and speculators were excluded.[15] The FU devoted most of its energies to cooperatives, collective control of marketing, and campaigns to withhold crops for a better price. The Texas organization alone built 323 cooperative warehouses between 1905 and 1908, and a 1913 report on agricultural cooperation counted 1,600 FU warehouses in the cotton states at the end of the decade. The FU Jobbing Association in Kansas City, Kansas, was described by *Literary Digest* as "the largest cooperative institution in the world." Throughout the South, Midwest, and West, the FU sponsored a great variety of cooperative enterprises, though the familiar problems of inadequate funds, inexpert management, and the opposition of private business had thrown many of the southern warehouses into bankruptcy by 1916.[16]

It is important to remember that the Farmers' Union was hardly "new." Many of its organizers and members had been active Alliance members and/or Populists, and its goals and methods, as well as its image of farmers as a proud but oppressed class suffering great injustice, were clear links to the old FA. However, chastened by the failure of the Alliance, and with a membership probably less representative of tenants and more of landowners, the FU was more cautious and less radical than the old Alliance.[17]

more an organized interest group than a movement (and in this respect it had more in common with the AFL than had the Alliance). Nevertheless, its political agenda was probably the broadest and most "progressive" of any grass-roots organization of this era. There was scarcely a radical reform (in the Progressive Era context)—from nationalizing essential natural resources to outlawing child labor—that the FU did not advocate between 1911 and 1915. The organization clearly manifested an agrarian republican ideology of Greenback/Jeffersonian lineage, with some surprising twists.[18]

The national FU leadership was determined to avoid the party politics that had ended the old Alliance. At the same time, political collective action was seen as essential to the improvement of the farmers' lot, particularly after the cooperatives began to fail. "The Ballot is the deadliest weapon known to modern history," Barrett proclaimed. "The only way to impress your purpose is to shoot them in the neck with your ballot." Trying to solve the farmer's problems without political action would be like "trying to turn over the earth with a toothpick."[19]

To that end, the national and state organizations, from the earliest years, passed resolutions advocating legislation and maintained state and national committees to lobby for their agenda, which centered on facilitation of cooperation, antitrust investigations, railroad regulation, public control of banking and currency, government-supplied credit for farmers, lower tariffs, aid for agricultural and industrial education and public schools generally, direct election of the president and the Supreme Court, and the outlawing of commodity speculation.[20] Like the Alliance, the FU frequently attempted to make common cause with labor unions. FU publications displayed a printers' union label, and officials of the FU and the AFL attended each other's conventions as fraternal delegates.[21] In Texas, trade unionists were "conspicuous by their appearance on the program of all open meetings" of the state FU, and AFL and FU members were urged to buy products carrying each other's labels. The Texas FU passed resolutions opposing convict labor in competition with free labor and advocating an eight-hour day,[22] and workers achieved significant legislative gains in the reform administration of a Democratic governor backed by former Populists, the Texas Federation of Labor, and the FU.[23] Worth R. Miller describes the formation of the Farmers' Union as a critical step in the return of the Populists to the Texas Democratic Party, the strengthening of the Democratic reform wing, and the instigation of a new reform era in that state.[24]

As a result of its organization, legislative advocacy, and close ties with southern members of Congress, the FU acquired substantial political influence as the organizational voice of the periphery farmers in the Progressive Era. State officials and congressmen in the South and (later) the

Midwest and West "naturally tried to win Union support by offering to do the farmers' bidding in legislation and government administration."[25] The FU was certainly less frightening to the political and economic elites of its time than the Alliance and the Populist Party had been, but that is a measure not only of the FU's caution but also of the extent to which agrarian positions of the 1890s had been absorbed into a regional ideology. This difference may also reflect the emergence of other, more radical manifestations of collective action by dissenting farmers, such as the Socialist tenant farmers' unions of the Southwest and various "direct action" episodes in the South.[26]

The Direct Primary

In response to the popular demand that control of party nominations be wrested from conservative party bosses, the direct primary swept the southern, midwestern, and mountain states in the first decade and a half of the twentieth century and was part and parcel of the progressive movement for political reform. In the South, which invented it (in South Carolina in 1896), the reputation of the primary is much less salutary than in Wisconsin, which touched off the midwestern electoral reform wave in 1903. In the states of the old Confederacy, this intraparty opening occurred for white men only. It excluded African Americans from what was, in most cases, the only significant election, and the contention that the organization that conducted this election (the Democratic Party) was a private and exclusive association of white citizens reigned until the Supreme Court struck down the white primary in 1944.[27]

Further, as every student of southern politics has learned from V. O. Key, the gathering of almost all political contestation into one socioeconomically diverse party produced factionalized, personalistic, and demagogic politics as individual candidates attempted to distinguish themselves to a confused electorate. Even when a genuine reformer won, the absence of a permanent legislative organization pledged to a program made it extremely difficult to carry reform through the legislature.[28]

On the other hand, southern Democrats, already compelled to adopt major Populist platform stances in order to compete, were also forced to grant the Populist constituency a voice in nominations via the institution of the primary, and the primary did provide a mechanism through which the interests of low-income whites could be pressed. The use of these intraparty elections for the nomination of U.S. senators, a process that the southern states pioneered years before the constitutional amendment for direct election, also introduced an element of popular democracy into the conservative upper chamber. Had the direct primary not also been marked by (or encouraged) race-baiting, the reforms won by poor white farmers might have made primary elections a source of some economic advantage for black citizens as well. But the racist demagoguery that accompanied the rise of Democratic primary politics was an undeniable evil. The best that can be said of the institution by those who stress its constructive aspects is that "the Negro . . . fared the same—no better, no worse"—with the inauguration of primary elections.[29]

The advantage for poor whites lay in the fact that the primary broke the control of the plantation-county Bourbons over the Democratic Party nominating process. To win nomination, a candidate would have to appeal to the masses, and the numerous poor-white voters of the southern hill country and pine flats—where sympathetic local registrars often winked at registration requirements—saw their influence in the party greatly enhanced. The first victor of the new system in Mississippi was James K. Vardaman, who as "a champion of the farmer against the 'predatory' corporate interests" excoriated banks and railroads. As governor, he ended the viciously inhumane system by which state convicts, mostly black, were leased to plantation owners and private industries, increased public school appropriations by almost 20 percent, expanded state regulation of banks, railroads, insurance companies, and monopolies, and improved conditions in state asylums.[30] Elected to the U.S. Senate in 1907 (by a vote highly and inversely correlated with county wealth),[31] Vardaman became one of the leading progressives in that body, a consistent supporter of legislation on behalf of low-income farmers and workers. The Vardaman pattern, combining support for radical economic reform with scurrilously racist rhetoric, was repeated with the election of Theodore Bilbo, who would go on to become one of the strongest Senate supporters of the New Deal.[32] Thus did the direct primary achieve its mixed legacy within the South even as it linked the region's agrarian politics with national progressive reform.

Bryan

> *In 1896, when we nominated the grandest and truest man the world ever knew—William Jennings Bryan—for President, we stole all the Populists had; we stole their platform, we stole their candidate, we stole them out lock, stock and barrel. . . . Populists—why I used to hate them; but I did not know as much then as I do now.*
> —GOVERNOR JEFF DAVIS of Arkansas, 1905

The ideological and organizational leader of the transformed Democratic Party from 1897 through at least 1912 was William Jennings Bryan. Whatever Bryan was in his early political career in the 1890s—perhaps, as his critics charge, an ordinary left-of-center silver Democrat with a flair for oratory—such a superficial description hardly fit him during the period from 1896 to 1915 (the year in which Bryan effectively ended his political career by resigning his cabinet seat to protest administration policies he believed would lead the country into war). At some point after receiving the nomination of the Populist and silver Democratic Parties, Bryan became, heart and soul, a populist. He was committed to the farmer-labor alliance, to a great expansion of government regulatory functions, and to the democratization of wealth and political power; he opposed militarism at home and abroad; and in all his stands, political principle was cast in the strong moral tones of nineteenth-century republicanism.[33] In his remarkable career, including three presidential races, Bryan's electoral base was periphery farmers. He himself never found a formula with which to win the labor vote of the core and diverse regions, but that was not for lack of trying.

In the 1900 campaign, Bryan played down the monetary issue and stressed opposition to trusts and imperialism and support for labor. The Democratic platform that bore his imprint "condemned two practices inimical to labor's well-being, the injunction and the blacklist; pandered to its fears by opposing Asian immigration; underscored the contradiction between militarism and labor's self-interest; called for a federal 'labor bureau'; and carried Bryan's own pet proposal for avoiding strikes and lockouts, a plan of voluntary arbitration."[34]

None of these propositions, however, could counter the Republicans' "full dinner pail" and Spanish American War victory. The Republican convention had proclaimed, in Chauncey Depew's words, "gold and glory—gold, the standard which . . . had given us the first rank among commercial nations and the glory of our arms, which has made us a world power."[35] Northern intellectuals drawn to Bryan's anti-imperialism were offended by his economic radicalism and his collaboration with Tammany Hall (whose Irish leader, a gold Democrat in 1896, had come over to Bryan for his anticolonialism). Many western silver Republicans, on the other hand, were too nationalistic to stay with Bryan on the imperialism issue. The GOP again funded a propaganda blitz to warn workers of the dangers of a devalued dollar and cuts in the protective tariff, and the northeastern press reported business contracts contingent on McKinley's reelection and attacked Bryan for stirring up class resentments. Though Tammany's endorsement improved Bryan's vote in New York, and anti-imperialism had a similar effect in Massachusetts, McKinley still swept the core and diverse states and took from Bryan's column six states, all west of the Mississippi, that he had carried in 1896.[36]

Though Bryan remained the most influential national Democrat, his demoralized party turned elsewhere in 1904. He had led a progressive reform party twice and lost. Shortly after the 1900 defeat, northern conservative Democrats (centered in New York) and disgruntled southern Bourbons alienated by the party's economic radicalism were emboldened to seek reinstatement. They promised success if the party returned to its pre-1896 "moderation" under their leadership. Emerging victorious out of the internecine party warfare of 1901–4, the conservative "reorganizers" succeeded in nominating the New York gold Democrat Judge Alton B. Parker. However, Bryan attended the convention as the leader of the progressive wing and obtained appointment to the platform committee. There he countered every conservative proposal with a progressive plank of his own, advocating nationalization of railroads and the telegraph, a government-issued currency, an income-tax amendment to the constitution, a strong antitrust plank, anti-imperialism, electoral reform, and several labor planks. Though the convention had seemed stacked against him, Bryan rallied his troops and, by the force of his personality and his standing with the mass of Democratic voters, succeeded in foiling the reorganizers' plan to adopt a conservative platform. He took to the hustings in support of state and local progressive Democrats, attacked Roosevelt for his militarism, and propounded his own progressive program. When Parker lost overwhelmingly, "the Commoner" was ready to pick up the pieces and reconstitute the party. Abandoning its outreach to the "plutocracy," the Democratic Party, under Bryan's leadership, returned to the basics of the farmer–labor alliance and the populist creed.[37]

By 1905 progressive reform was coming into bloom in state and city politics across the West, Midwest, and South, with tentative buds in the Northeast, and even the White House colored in remarkable new hues. Bryan, like a devoted gardener, encouraged all this growth, advertising it in his paper, the *Commoner,* and fighting for the cause in Nebraska, on the Chautauqua circuit,* and on the hustings as he campaigned for progressive state and local candidates around the country. He praised Roosevelt's efforts in peacemaking abroad, and in antitrust, railroad regulation, and meat inspection at home, but he criticized the president for not going far enough.[38] Indeed, Roosevelt's progressive transformation may be read as a

---

*The Chautauqua circuit was the route generally followed by speakers, both famous and lesser known, who traveled across the country lecturing on topics of interest. Generally held in the open air or under tents, the Chautauqua lectures drew enormous numbers of people in towns outside of major urban areas. Begun at Lake Chautauqua as summer entertainment, the Chautauqua circuit spread adult education across the nation.

response not only to the small progressive wing of the GOP but also to the massive support for Bryan's agrarian progressivism in the interior of the country.

Bryan and his hinterland constituents had few serious disagreements on policy; in the case of the southern Democrats' defense of white supremacy, the absence of conflict points to a serious contradiction in the reformer's democratic creed. Indeed, Bryan's greatest flaw as a champion of the disadvantaged stemmed from his compromises with racism within the farmer–labor coalition that he hoped to lead to power. Though he courted black votes, strongly condemned lynching, and advocated equal "citizenship" rights in education and voting, Bryan did little, if anything, to put these ideals into practice and seldom challenged the prejudices of the southern Democrats. Likewise, he took the Gompers/AFL line on Chinese exclusion.[39] On the "woman question," however, the Nebraskan's stand was far more advanced than that of most of his troops, and his public advocacy of government ownership of railroads and telephone and telegraph companies caused great distress for conservative elements in the party.[40]

As one of the many reform enterprises in which he participated, Bryan was one of the fathers of the constitution of the new state of Oklahoma in 1907, advising on its construction and strongly endorsing the resulting document. Not surprisingly for a state soon to host the nation's strongest Socialist Party, the new platform was described in the *Outlook* as "the most radical organic law ever adopted in the Union." It had extensive provisions for direct democracy via the initiative and referendum and contained provisions for the election of administrative and judicial officials, advanced labor and antitrust sections, and authorization for state and city governments to engage in any enterprise they might wish to undertake.[41] When, in the following year, Bryan supervised the drafting of the Democratic Party platform, he combined elements of the Oklahoma constitution, the Nebraska state party platform, and labor planks endorsed by the AFL.[42]

Even after his third defeat in 1908, agrarian and labor reformers rallied around the program Bryan had championed for years, and conservatives in the party were forced to endorse ideas they had long opposed. It was the pull of Bryan's leadership, his de facto control of the party's nomination, and the desire to tap into his mass following that transformed the prim, conservative governor of New Jersey (who had been a Cleveland-gold Democrat) into the candidate of progressive Democrats in 1912. Bryan played a major role in securing the nomination for Woodrow Wilson, wrote the 1912 platform that charted the path of reform for the "New Freedom" years, and coached the candidate through the campaign. And it was Bryan who inspired the congressional Democrats to push the president on antitrust, labor, banking, currency, farm credit, and Philippine independence and who encouraged them to restrain Wilson's momentum toward preparedness and war.[43]

Writing of Bryan's lifelong devotion to political reform, Claude Bowers observed in the early 1950s, "Almost everything we've got today in the way of reforms originated with Bryan."[44] Later scholars and pundits associated him more with the event that immediately preceded his death: the Scopes evolution trial. However, even that involvement, which reflected the aged reformer's commitments to evangelical Protestantism and strong local religious communities, had more to do with the political reform impulse than has been generally recognized. Bryan strongly objected to arguments that drew on the social implications of Darwinism to justify the exploitation of workers and consumers and to discourage reform movements. Against those tenets he wrote in 1921, "Pure food laws have become necessary to keep manufacturers from poisoning their customers; child-labor laws have become necessary to keep employers from dwarfing the bodies, minds and souls of children; anti-trust laws have become necessary to keep over-grown corporations from strangling smaller corporations, and we are still in a death grapple with profiteers and gamblers in farm products."[45] The Antimonopoly-Greenback-Populist creed that Bryan embodied was naturally antithetical to Darwinism, whose founder, in *The Descent of Man,* had argued against reforms that checked the salutary process of weeding out the weak and less fit. In addition, Bryan abhorred Nietzsche's Darwinist defense of war as both necessary and desirable for human progress. Such ideas, he believed, were important factors in the development of German militarism leading to World War I.[46]

Agrarianism as a Regional Program

Despite the common description of the progressive reform leaders as representatives of the urban business and professional classes, the farmers were the most numerous constituents for expanded public power in the southern and midwestern states where the reform movements were strongest. In the South, where the social origins of Populist and progressive leaders have been sharply contrasted, the new middle-class reformers embraced and elaborated on the older agrarian agenda. "Under the growing pressure of monopoly," wrote C. Vann Woodward, "the small businessmen and urban middle class overcame their fear of reform and joined hands with the discontented farmers. They envisaged as a common enemy the plutocracy of the northeast, together with its agents, banks, insurance companies, public utilities, oil companies, pipelines and railroads."[47]

This metamorphosis could also be observed in the Midwest, where a relatively young, dissident, middle-class cohort emerged within the dominant

Republican Party. These men, many of whom had been anti-Populists in the 1890s, now embraced much of the agrarian program as if they had invented it themselves.[48] To what could the farmers attribute this fortuitous conversion of their old urban antagonists? A major factor was undoubtedly the disappearance of the Populist Party. The return of the Populists to the major parties and the inauguration of primary elections contributed to the new sensitivities in the political leadership class. But principally, the urbanites had come to realize that not only the farmers but also the periphery (and, to a lesser extent, the diverse) regions generally occupied dependent and disadvantaged positions within the national political economy. Their rudimentary industry and commerce suffered the stifling competition of "trusts" grown even larger and more powerful in the unprecedented merger wave of 1897–1903; likewise, they still bore regionally discriminatory freight rates and an increasing tariff tax on the manufactured goods they imported, and the problems of low bank deposits, insufficient credit, and high interest rates had scarcely eased. . . .[49] In regions dependent on agriculture, the plight of the farmer reverberated strongly in the small towns and cities. In the cotton belt, the rate of tenancy—which served as a barometer of that region's continued economic distress—continued its inexorable rise. About 38 and 80 percent of white and black farmers, respectively, aged thirty-five to forty-four were tenants in 1910; the numbers would grow to 50 and 81 percent by 1930.[50]

The share of the nation's wealth in the periphery states of the south Atlantic, west-north-central, and mountain regions declined or showed no significant increase between 1890 and 1912;[51] and this measure of "wealth" is a figure that overestimates landed wealth and understates wealth derived from stocks and bonds or embodied in personal property. Further, the mining, manufacturing, and transportation assets counted as "wealth" in these regions were frequently owned by residents of other (mainly core) regions. The South had an estimated per capita wealth of $509 in 1900, compared with a national average of $1,165; in 1919, per capita income in the South remained 40 percent below the national level.[52] Thus the problems to which farmers were peculiarly sensitive were also regional disadvantages perceived as thwarting social and economic advancement.

In view of these regional tendencies, it seems appropriate to recognize the major reform legislation of the Progressive Era—the tariff, banking, income tax, railroad, shipping, and commodity exchange regulation and the antitrust, farm credit, highway, and education measures—as an "agrarian" agenda, albeit one now broadly endorsed in the periphery. The progressive reforms of 1909–17 had their roots in programs advocated by a long succession of Grangers, Antimonopolists, Greenbackers, Farmers' Alliance members, Populists, and Farmers' Unionists. Whatever the social origins of Progressive Era reform leaders (up to and including President Wilson), the periphery regions that provided the necessary votes for these bills had economies dependent on agriculture, forestry, and other natural-resource-based activity, and farmers constituted the largest and best-organized voting blocks there.

However, formal local-interest organization was less important to the shaping of public policy in this formative period than the fact that the Democratic Party, having deposed most of its northern conservative wing in 1896, was an *agrarian* party, itself the foremost political organization of the periphery farmers. In the Republican Party, the bulk of midwestern and western progressive reformers who would break with the eastern capital wing to support the new surge of legislation either represented periphery states and districts or—in the case of some Wisconsin, Illinois, and Iowa legislators—were dependent on farmers for essential electoral support.

Regions, Parties, and Progressive Reform

In sheer numbers of congressional seats, the nonindustrial periphery appeared to possess a decisive political advantage in the Progressive Era. The agriculture, timber, and mining regions held the largest block of members in all four Congresses from 1910 to 1917, with 47 percent of House seats and 57–58 percent of the Senate. Indeed, it is surprising, from this perspective, that the significant political victories finally won in the insurgent Republican and Wilson eras were so long in coming. However, . . . the interests of the periphery were by no means homogeneous. Despite the fact that this vast region was overwhelmingly rural[53] and depended for its livelihood on products extracted from the soil, the nature of the markets enjoyed by those products propelled some sections of the periphery into political alliance with northeastern capital. The sheep, cattle, timber, and sugar-beet regions of the West produced almost entirely for a domestic market, and their products could be purchased at a significantly lower price from other countries (particularly from Latin American countries, Australia, and New Zealand but also from Canada in some cases). The South, on the other hand, was the world's prime cotton-growing area and the low-cost cotton producer through the 1930s.[54] Sixty percent of the cotton crop was exported in 1910, at prices set internationally. Selling in the world market, the South preferred to buy there as well, so that its customers might accumulate dollars and its necessities might be purchased at the lowest price.

Thus it was that on the tariff issue—which was a fundamental line of political cleavage for much of American history—the South and the West had different interests. The wheat-growing areas, which enjoyed only a modest export trade, and the domestically oriented corn-hog-grain belt in the Midwest were usually reluctant to coalesce with the South. Recognizing the conflicting interests of regions within the periphery, representatives of eastern manufacturing firms years before had crafted a political program that could penetrate the agrarian sections. A high tariff on finished woolen goods produced in the Northeast could be balanced with protective duties for raw wool and sheep. Similarly, the tariff coalition sponsored by the East could embrace a wide variety of other periphery products threatened by imports (for example, sugar, fruits and nuts, hides, lumber, and some metals). Like a balance with a fulcrum somewhere in Iowa, the Republican Party deftly brought eastern and western producer interests into a rough parity and thus dominated national politics, to the broad advantage of eastern capital. Given the unpopularity in the West of the Democratic stand on the tariff issue, it was not surprising that the Populists ignored the issue and Bryan talked mainly of bimetallism in 1896. Currency inflation was an issue on which periphery farmers, ranchers, and miners could agree.

The failure of the Populist-Democratic coalition did not diminish the willingness of the southern periphery to pursue an alliance with northern labor. Just as eastern capital had penetrated the western periphery, southern agriculture sought to penetrate the industrial core.[55] The cities of the manufacturing belt were growing rapidly in the early twentieth century, and the interests of the expanding labor force were generally ignored by the party of capital. The draconian labor policies of the era's capitalists made their arguments for common benefit through the tariff seem increasingly flimsy to the working class (who did notice the rising costs of consumer goods). Since the interests of northern labor could be accommodated at little or no cost to the nonindustrial South, a political alliance against their mutual enemy (northern capital) recommended itself. This alliance formed the basis for a revitalized Democratic Party in the Progressive Era.

In the early twentieth century, then, the most sharply antagonistic interests existed between northern industrial capital and southern agriculture. The two major political parties had formed around these two poles of regional interest. By 1909, the Democratic Party was almost entirely confined to the periphery (see table 1). Its strongholds were in the cotton and tobacco states, with a sprinkling of representatives from midwestern and western farm and mining regions. Core industrial areas, on the other hand, elected Republicans by a 3-to-1 margin, despite Bryan's labor strategy in the 1908 election. The tendency of more recently settled immigrant groups in some core cities to vote Democratic for state and local offices produced only a weak echo in national politics. Residents of manufacturing-belt truck-garden* and dairy sections were overwhelmingly Republican; the same was true of the corn, hog, cattle, and grain sections of the Midwest (the Chicago and Cincinnati trade areas). The western strategy of the Republican Party was splendidly affirmed by an overwhelmingly GOP vote in the San Francisco, Seattle, Portland, Helena, Spokane, and Salt Lake City trade areas.

However, by 1910, partisan patterns were clearly shifting in the industrial and diverse farm-industry regions. Holding their solid southern base, the Democrats won a majority of the House in 1910 and added sixty-three more seats in 1912. Although population growth in the southwestern periphery accounted for a portion of the Democratic gains, the bulk of the new Democratic seats were won in the manufacturing belt and the midwestern corn belt. In the 61st Congress, 72 percent of Democratic House seats were held by periphery representatives; in the 63rd, the periphery composed just under 55 percent of the Democratic Party. An indecisive Republican president and an intransigent congressional Republican leadership had failed to accommodate rising demands for public control of corporate power and for a more reasonable tariff. In three- and four-way elections contested by Progressives and Socialists, the Republicans temporarily lost their control of the core. As a result, a new reform coalition — consisting of a solid phalanx of southern and other periphery Democrats, joined by a new cadre of northern urban Democrats and a smaller number of progressive Republicans — was now in a position to challenge the Republican regime and construct a new national state.

Who Were the "Progressives"?

Attempts to uncover a single ideology at the root of Progressive Era reform have seemed destined either to fail empirical substantiation or to be so vague ("optimism," "activism," "status anxiety," "social justice") as to defy any effort at empirical demonstration.[56] One way of avoiding the quagmire of ideological labels is to focus on what people *did* during this period, as opposed to what they (presumably) were *thinking*. If the irrefutable identifying trait of a "reform" period is the large quantity of new programmatic legislation, then analysis should start there — with the new statutes — and work backward to the supporting coalitions that enacted them. Dealing only with federal statutes and formal public behavior (roll-call votes), supplemented by public debates and pronouncements, one may put aside some of the intriguing but frustrating questions about the origin and shape of progressive *ideas* and search for patterns in actual *events*. In this

*A truck-garden is a small to mid-sized garden in which vegetables are raised for market.

Table 1. Regions and Parties in the Progressive Era House of Representatives

Trade Area	Party Balance 61st Congress 1909–1911		Party Balance 62nd Congress 1911–1913		Party Balance 63rd Congress 1913–1915		Party Balance 64th Congress 1915–1917	
	D[a]	R[a]	D	R	D	R-Other[b]	D	R-Other[b]
Core Industrial								
Boston	4	24	7	21	17	14	6	25
Buffalo	1	4	2	3	3	3	2	4
Cleveland	6	8	11	3	14	1	7	9
Detroit	0	5	1	4	2	4	2	4
New York	13	27	28	12	38	9	21	26
Philadelphia	5	21	8	18	14	16	5	25
Pittsburgh	0	11	2	9	2	9	2	9
Seattle	0	2	0	2	0	4	0	3
Total	29	102	59	72	90	60	45	105
Diverse (industry, agriculture, timber, mining)								
Chicago	14	42	21	34	32	26	20	38
Cincinnati	4	8	8	4	8	4	5	6
Portland	0	2	0	2	0	3	0	3
San Francisco	1	6	1	6	2	7	2	7
Total	19	58	30	46	42	40	27	54
Periphery (cotton, wheat, grazing, mining)								
Atlanta	12	0	12	0	13	0	13	0
Baltimore	3	5	7	1	7	1	6	2

City								
Birmingham	8	0	8	0	9	0	9	0
Dallas^c	13	0	14	1	17	0	16	1
Denver	3	0	3	0	4	0	3	1
Helena	0	1	0	1	2	0	2	0
Houston	5	0	5	0	5	0	5	0
Jacksonville	3	0	3	0	4	0	4	0
Kansas City, Ks	2	9	3	8	8	3	9	2
Little Rock	5	0	5	0	5	0	5	0
Los Angeles^d	0	2	1	2	2	2	2	2
Louisville	7	0	7	0	7	0	7	0
Memphis	8	0	8	0	8	0	8	0
Minneapolis	1	15	1	16	1	18	2	17
Nashville	5	2	5	2	5	2	5	2
New Orleans	9	0	9	0	9	0	8	1
Omaha	3	4	3	4	3	4	3	4
Oklahoma City	2	3	3	2	6	2	7	1
Richmond	23	6	27	2	26	4	26	4
St. Louis	13	8	16	5	19	2	19	2
Salt Lake City	0	2	0	2	0	4	1	3
Spokane	0	1	0	1	0	1	1	1
Total	125	58	140	47	160	43	161	43

[a]Party designations are taken from the congressional directories for the first session, filling vacancies. In the 63rd Congress, for example, it includes 9 Progressives, 7 progressive Republicans, and 1 Independent. There was 1 Socialist in the Chicago trade area in the 62nd and 1 in the New York trade area in the 64th Congress.

[b]The "other" category mainly designates Progressives.

[c]Includes Texas portion of the El Paso trade area, where the majority of the population resided in the Dallas trade-area districts. The remainder of the El Paso trade area went to Los Angeles. Two New Mexico districts are added here in the 62nd Congress.

[d]The Los Angeles trade area includes newly admitted Arizona in the 62nd Congress.

method, it is not "where did the idea come from?" that is most important but "who had the incentive and provided the muscle to put this idea into national law?"

Biographies of "progressives" tend to overemphasize the role of their principles in securing legislation. The favored biographical subjects, of course, have been the Hamlet-like insurgent Republicans. Repelled by the corruption and conservatism of their party's leadership, but equally repulsed by the party of the cotton South, the insurgent Republicans stood apart from the old two-party axis of contention and freely criticized both poles. They collected and developed ideas for solving social problems and helped to mobilize public support for new legislation. Because these insurgents were well-educated, articulate, independent, and accessible, the middle-class "uplift" magazines (*Collier's, Success, McClure's,* and the *New Republic,* for example) found them very good copy. Such publications consciously served as mouthpieces and propagandists for their policy initiatives and indirectly helped the "partyless" insurgents build supporting organizations, both at home and within a larger national arena.[57] Once these Republicans became respected celebrities, nongovernment activists (such as Louis Brandeis) sought them out as sponsors for reform proposals.

At the turn of the century, widespread corruption permeated the political power structures of the states. In Iowa, for example, two great railroads had built an imposing network of control by distributing free passes to local notables and sponsoring political campaigns for state offices. As a result, the railroads were able to keep their taxes low and avoid rate and service regulation. What the railroads did in the Midwest and California, powerful mining trusts (like the Rockefeller-Guggenheim Mineral Coal and Iron Company) did in western states, along with even more shameless exploitation of their workers. The Republican Party in these essentially one-party states sanctioned and furthered corporate policy goals. The party became, in Thomas J. Bray's words, a "bulwark of plunder and special interests."[58] Because the South had already adopted the direct primary, southern progressives could work more easily within a loosely organized one-party system. In the Midwest, however, it was necessary to reorganize the dominant Republican Party in order to attack "the interests." Electoral reform, particularly the direct primary and the popular election of senators, became the opening wedge in that reorganization. Civil-service laws provided methods for undermining the patronage that supported reactionary incumbents.

Most of those destined to rebel against the Republican Party in the 61st Congress shared two traits, one personal and the other regional: they were ambitious politicians who found their careers thwarted by the Old Guard

Republican leadership; and they represented areas of the Midwest where the policy direction imposed by the core GOP was increasingly unpopular. Most began their political careers as straight-arrow Republicans, strongly supportive of the protective tariff and contemptuous of Bryan and his party.[59] They lived in small towns or cities in the Midwest and West, almost all located in the corn, sugar-beet, and wheat regions. William Borah of Idaho was something of an exception, representing a predominantly mining and sheep-raising state in the West (such tariff-dependent regions typically produced Republican loyalists).[60] Comfortable, conservative lawyers, the insurgent Republicans were preeminently good politicians. When the people of their states and districts began to show dissatisfaction with national Republican policies and local Republican corruption, they seized on that discontent and turned failed or failing political careers into near invincibility.[61]

Less articulate and often less well educated, the rustic spokesmen for the South and border states have attracted far less (and less favorable) attention from Progressive Era historians, and the Democratic Party, in the years before it acquired a large urban wing, has generally been seen as traditional and ineffectual. Champ Clark, who led the resurgent Democratic Party in the House, was ridiculed in the eastern press and treated condescendingly by historians. Southern members of Congress were less prolific memorialists, which may explain some of the omission, as David Sarasohn has suggested.[62] But more important, the most senior southern congressional leaders, men like John Sharp Williams of Mississippi and Texas Sens. Joseph Bailey and Charles Culberson, had not been associated with the Populist or Democratic reform factions in their home states. Although from the standpoint of regional economic imperatives it was quite possible for politicians representing middle- and upper-class interests in intrastate politics to become ardent progressives in the national arena, historians have been understandably reluctant to include these regional champions among the ranks of those progressives for whom national reform efforts were logical extensions of state careers as reform leaders.[63] It was particularly difficult to do so in the 1960s and early 1970s, when much of Progressive Era history was being written and when the oppressive southern segregation system was finally under concerted attack.

The southern congressmen often performed less brilliantly in debate than the insurgent Republicans. Few of them had attended universities or law schools of the first rank,[64] and one suspects that small-town life in the cotton belt failed to impart a sophisticated understanding of the industrial economy they were struggling to control. Nevertheless, southern committee leaders could swiftly graft appealing ideas onto their own legislative proposals, and the great majority of their rank-and-file colleagues joined the supporting side on almost all issues commonly designated "progressive" in this era. They did so not because they were farsighted idealists but because such positions went over very well with their constituents. The insurgent Republicans were progressive for the same reason.

By 1910 the progressive movement in the states—particularly the states of the Midwest, South, and West—had secured electoral reforms, regulatory restraints on railroads and insurance companies, taxes on powerful corporations, and mitigation of some of the most reprehensible employment practices. However, the effectiveness of state laws was limited. Corporations harassed by state regulators could threaten to move their operations elsewhere, and federal court decisions made it impossible for states to have much influence on corporations heavily engaged in interstate commerce. If a state like New Jersey opened its arms to trusts and holding companies, redress for their abuses of farmers, businesspeople, and consumers in other states was beyond the reach of those victims. When the U.S. Department of Justice refused to act, or pursued the transgressors halfheartedly, the immunity of the offending corporations was almost complete. Where national legislation existed, as in the Interstate Commerce and Sherman Acts, federal court interpretation often rendered it useless or applied it perversely to protect corporations from their workers or would-be competitors. Reformers were compelled to turn their attention to national politics.[65]

While Theodore Roosevelt was president, it appeared that the reform movement could be accommodated within the national Republican Party, in the same way that the movement was transforming state parties in the Midwest. Roosevelt's actions in the *Northern Securities* and other cases gave new vitality to the Sherman Act. His antitrust efforts, his arbitration of the 1902 coal strike, and his support for railroad, conservation, reclamation, and meat inspection laws convinced reform-minded Republicans that their party had stepped into the vanguard of a popular movement to cure the ills of industrial society.[66] However, with William Howard Taft in the White House, this hope faded. The "standpatters"—senators like Rhode Island's Nelson Aldrich, New York's Elihu Root, Pennsylvania's Boies Penrose, Connecticut's Orville Platt, Massachusetts's Henry Cabot Lodge, New Hampshire's Jacob Gallinger, Utah's Reed Smoot, and Wisconsin's John Spooner and Speaker Joseph Cannon and his circle in the House—balked at serious reform, and the president declined to push them. Under standpat leadership, the Republicans lifted protection to prohibitive levels, provoking cries that high tariffs milked the consumer and nurtured monopolies. When midwestern farmers complained about the tariff, party leaders offered to cut duties on *their* products. When reformers pressed for an income tax, Republican leaders came forward with a corporation tax, easily passed on to consumers. When farmers and small businesspeople complained about railroads, Taft offered them a "Commerce Court" and schemes to facilitate railroad "cooperation." Revolt within the party was inevitable, and it was inevitably most pronounced in regions where the debilities of Republican policy (particularly policy on the tariff, railroads, and trusts) outweighed the benefits.

In the House of Representatives, the first clearly identifiable group of "progressives" among Republicans were those who, in 1909 and 1910, successfully moved (with Democratic cooperation) to strip the autocratic Speaker of his most important powers and to change the rules by which bills were brought to the floor and debated. Some of the insurgents were motivated only by annoyance at what they perceived as Cannon's unfair handling of their committee assignments or legislative proposals, but most insurgents either were or soon would be "progressives" in support of reform legislation previously blocked by the Republican leadership.

Within the Republican Party, it was mainly farm-state representatives who were restless, but agricultural economies alone were not the determining factor. Farm areas within the manufacturing belt remained steadfast under the Republican standard, and western wool and sugar-beet areas, dependent on the protective system, dared not desert the Republican coalition. Among the thirty-three insurgent Republicans in the 61st Congress,[67] only six represented districts in the industrial heartland, and the evidence strongly suggests that the "insurgency" of the latter resulted from personal pique at Cannon's tactics rather than from policy incongruity with the majority (see table 2). They were faithful to a man on the tariff and cast only a few sporadic votes with the opposition on other divisive issues. The policy-oriented insurgents came overwhelmingly from the corn and wheat sections of the Midwest. In the West, only Miles Poindexter, from wheat-growing eastern Washington (Spokane), and San Francisco representative Everis Hayes, whose dissent was mostly confined to labor issues, joined the insurgent ranks. The wheat sections of the periphery were more favorable to the southern Democratic position on the tariff than were the corn-belt districts in the Chicago trade area. The latter were both closer to manufacturing centers and less involved in international trade.

Sympathy with labor's legislative goals was expressed by many Republican insurgents, particularly representatives from the Milwaukee and Minneapolis areas, where there were significant numbers of industrial workers. However, as the second labor vote in table 2 indicates, this was a "soft" issue for the dissident Republicans. The third vote in table 2 provides a measure of support for strong railroad regulation. The most popular issue for the agrarian insurgents (but clearly a zero for the core contingent) was

Table 2. House Republican Insurgents and Issue Positions

Reps.	District		Region	Defeat Payne Tariff[a]	Labor Exemption[b]		Defeat Commerce Court[c]	Corporate Suits in State Courts[d]	Put Murdock on Rules Committee[e]
					I	II			
Ames	MA	5	C						
Cary	WI	4	D	X	X	X	X	X	X
Cooper	WI	1	D		X				X
Davidson	WI	8	D						
Davis	MN	4	P	X	X	X	X	X	X
Fish	NY	21	C		X	X			
Foelker	NY	3	C						
Fowler	NJ	5	C				X		X
Gardner	MA	6	C						
Good	IA	5	D		X		X	X	
Gronna	ND	AL	P	X	X		X		
Haugen	IA	4	D	X	X		X		
Hayes	CA	5	D		X	X			
Hinshaw	NE	4	P		X			X	
Hubbard	IA	11	D	X	X	X	X	X	X
Kendall	IA	6	D	X	X	X		X	
Kinkaid	NE	6	P		X			X	
Kopp	WI	3	D		X			X	
Lenroot	WI	11	P	X	X	X	X	X	X

Name	State	Dist.	Party	a	b	b	c	d	e
Lindbergh	MN	6	P	X	X			X	X
Madison	KS	7	P		X			X	X
Martin	SD	AL	P						
Miller	MN	8	P	X	X				
Morse	WI	10	D		X			X	X
Murdock	KS	AL	P	X	X	X	X	X	
Nelson	WI	2	D	X	X	X	X	X	X
Norris	NE	5	P		X			X	X
Pickett	IA	3	D	X					
Poindexter	WA	3	P	X	X	X	X	X	
Steenerson	MN	9	P	X	X				
Taylor	OH	12	C						
Volstead	MN	7	P	X	X		X	X	
Woods	IA	10	D	X	X	X	X	X	X
Total by Issue				15	20	12	12	18	12

Regional Totals	
Core	6
Diverse	13
Periphery	14

aPayne-Aldrich Tariff Conference Report, CR, 61-1, July 21, 1909, 4755.

bAmendment to prohibit the use of federal monies to prosecute labor violations of the antitrust laws, two votes, CR, 61-2, June 21, 1910, and June 23, 1910, 8656, 8852–53.

cMotion to recommit Mann-Elkins bill and strike the provision for a commerce court, CR, 61-2, May 10, 1910, 6032 (a yea vote favors strong railroad regulations).

dHubbard (West Virginia) amendment to weaken Garrett (Tennessee) amendment facilitating suits against out-of-state corporations, CR, 61-3, January 18, 1911, 1070.

eMotion by Rep. Norris to appoint insurgent Rep. Murdock of Kansas to Rules Committee in place of the regular Republican nominated by the leadership, CR, 62-2, January 11, 1912, 864–65.

control of corporate malfeasance and protection of small competitors. There are few House roll calls that tap this sentiment in 1909–10, but the fourth roll call reported in the table is indicative. Eighteen of the twenty-seven periphery- and diverse-area insurgents voted with the southern Democrats to keep in state courts all suits against distant corporations — the goal being greater convenience for the local plaintiff and considerably greater chance of conviction.

In the Senate, there was no rules fight to galvanize the intraparty rebellion, but a small group of midwestern senators began to conspicuously oppose the Old Guard during the 61st Congress. The early leaders of the "insurgent" group were Robert La Follette of Wisconsin, Albert Cummins of Iowa, Cummins's colleague Jonathan Dolliver (recently transformed from standpatter to progressive), Joseph Bristow of Kansas, and Albert Beveridge of Indiana. Death and defeat removed Dolliver and Beveridge in 1910, but insurgent ranks expanded with election reforms in the western and midwestern states and the promotion of House insurgents to the Senate. By 1912 the group of rebellious Senate Republicans had gained George Norris of Nebraska, William Borah and James Brady of Idaho, Miles Poindexter of Washington, Moses Clapp of Minnesota, William Kenyon of Iowa, Ash Gronna of North Dakota, and Coe Crawford of South Dakota.[68] The issues that most clearly distinguished the insurgents from the Senate leaders were the tariff, the Mann-Elkins railroad bill, and to a lesser extent, labor issues. As in the House, however, Senate insurgents were not "progressive" on all issues. They were much more consistent on railroad and subsequent corporate regulatory legislation than on labor. It must be remembered that on each of the roll calls reported in table 2, there were about four Democrats for every Republican on the "progressive" side. Republican insurgency seldom involved more than 15 percent of the party (20–30 members) in the House, and it lost considerable momentum in the 62nd Congress even as the Democrats were achieving remarkable cohesion within their own ranks. It was periphery Democrats and their less numerous northern labor allies who provided the foot soldiers for the progressive program.[69]

In table 3, a summary of regional and party patterns for 1909–11 has been constructed from data provided in an unpublished Ph.D. dissertation by Jerome M. Clubb. Three-quarters of the "reformers" on these issues (which encompassed tariff, taxation, railroad, banking, conservation, and political reform proposals) were Democrats. The largest bloc came from the South, where reformers constituted almost 80 percent of representatives. The next-largest group was midwestern, mainly Democrats but with a substantial cohort of Republicans from the (periphery) states of the west-north-central region. Reform-oriented representatives were scarcer in the

Table 3. House Supporters of "Progressive" Reform, by Census Region, 61st Congress

	Reformers/All Representatives from Region (%)	Democrats/All Reformers (%)
Northeast (New England & Mid-Atlantic)	$\frac{33}{112}$ (29.5)	$\frac{20}{33}$ (60.6)
Midwest (East-North-Central & West-North-Central)	$\frac{73}{137}$ (53.3)	$\frac{38}{73}$ (52.1)
South (South Atlantic, East-South-Central & West-South-Central)	$\frac{103}{131}$ (78.6)	$\frac{98}{103}$ (95.1)
West (Mountain & Pacific)	$\frac{7}{22}$ (31.8)	$\frac{4}{7}$ (57.1)

Source: Jerome M. Clubb, "Congressional Opponents of Reform, 1901–1913" (Ph.D. diss., University of Washington, 1963), table 26, 190–91.

northeastern (core) states and were usually Democrats following an agenda set by the majority agrarian wing of the party. In the South, over 80 percent of the reformers represented districts that contained no large cities; but even among the small urban contingent, supporters outnumbered opponents of reform by almost six to one.[70] In the Midwest, rural representatives also dominated the group of reformers, but in the northeastern and Pacific states, rural districts were more conservative than big-city districts.[71] Thus early progressivism in Congress was not a program of farmers in general but of farmers in the less-industrial regions of the South and Midwest.

Notes

1. E. E. Schattsneider, *The Semi-Sovereign People* (New York: Holt, Rinehart and Winston, 1960), 78–86; Walter Dean Burnham, "The System of 1896: An Analysis," in *The Evolution of American Electoral Systems,* by Paul Kleppner et al. (Westport, Conn.: Greenwood Press, 1981), 147–202.

2. J. Morgan Kousser, *The Shaping of Southern Politics* (New Haven, Conn.: Yale University Press, 1974), 139–223; V. O. Key, *Southern Politics* (New York: Random House, 1949), 533–50; C. Vann Woodward, *Origins of the New South* (Baton Rouge: Louisiana State University Press, 1951), 321–49.

3. Key, *Southern Politics,* 232–33, 263–71, 304–5.

4. Works attributing the progressive reform movements in the states to the new urban business and professional classes include Sheldon Hackney, *Populism to Progressivism in Alabama* (Princeton: Princeton University Press, 1969); Kousser,

Shaping of Southern Politics; Dewey W. Grantham, *Southern Progressivism* (Knoxville: University of Tennessee Press, 1983); George E. Mowry, *The Era of Theodore Roosevelt* (New York: Harper & Row, 1958); Woodward, *Origins of the New South;* and William A. Link, *The Paradox of Southern Progressivism, 1880–1930* (Chapel Hill: University of North Carolina Press, 1992).

5. The most notable works in this genre are Gabriel Kolko, *The Triumph of Conservatism* (Chicago: Quadrangle Books, 1963); James Weinstein, *The Corporate Ideal in the Liberal State* (Boston: Beacon Press, 1968); and Martin J. Sklar, *The Corporate Reconstruction of American Capitalism, 1890–1916* (New York: Cambridge University Press, 1988).

6. Carl C. Taylor, *The Farmers' Movement, 1670–1920* (Westport, Conn.: Greenwood Press, 1953), 332–33; Solon J. Buck, *The Granger Movement* (Cambridge: Harvard University Press, 1913), 306.

7. Lowell K. Dyson, *Farmers' Organizations* (New York: Greenwood Press, 1986), 369.

8. Marilyn P. Watkins, *Rural Democracy: Community, Gender, and Politics in Western Washington, 1890–1925* (Ithaca, N.Y.: Cornell University Press, 1995), chap. 5.

9. Robert Lee Hunt, *A History of Farmers' Movements in the Southwest, 1873–1925* (College Station: Texas A&M University Press, 1935), 41–49.

10. Taylor, *Farmers' Movement,* 336–43; Hunt, *History of Farmers' Movements in the Southwest,* 52–53. The following were the first five (of thirteen) goals listed: "To establish justice. To secure equity. To apply the Golden Rule. To discourage the credit and mortgage system. To assist our members in buying and selling." Charles S. Barrett, *The Mission, History, and Times of the Farmers Union* (Lincoln: University of Nebraska Press, 1960), 107.

11. Woodward, *Origins of the New South,* 413; *Minutes of the National Farmers' Educational and Cooperative Union of America,* 1908 (Fort Worth, Texas), 14.

12. Taylor, *Farmers' Movement,* 349–50. According to Charles P. Loomis, of North Carolina locals that reported the gender of their members, 37 percent were female. "The Rise and Decline of the North Carolina Farmers' Union," *North Carolina Historical Review* 7 (July 1930): 314. As convention minutes (major speeches, committee service, etc.) make clear, women played an active role in the national organization. At the 1908 convention, for example, of the eight people delivering addresses to the assembled members (including President Barrett and Samuel Gompers), five were women. However, with the exception of the Committee on Education, which they dominated, women were not listed on the executive board or on committees concerned with cooperation and legislation. *Minutes,* 1908.

13. Taylor, *Farmers' Movement,* 346–48; Gilbert C. Fite, *Cotton Fields No More* (Lexington: University Press of Kentucky, 1984), 64. The Midwest also spawned other farm organizations in this period. For a description, see Dyson, *Farmers' Organizations,* entries under American Society of Equity, Nonpartisan League, and Farmers' National Congress. On the radical agrarian Nonpartisan League, founded in North Dakota in 1915, see Grant McConnell, *The Decline of Agrarian Democracy* (Berkeley: University of California Press, 1953), 41; and Richard M. Valelly, *Radicalism in the States* (Chicago: University of Chicago Press, 1989), 17–21.

14. The Texas and Oklahoma organizations, however, did conduct some collaborative activities across racial lines. On the race issue in the FU, see Theodore Saloutos, *Farmer Movements in the South, 1865–1933* (Lincoln: University of Nebraska Press, 1960), 192–94, 203. Some breach in the racial exclusiveness of

membership was permitted for "Indians of industrious habits." Barrett, *Mission, History, and Times of the Farmers Union,* 107.

15. Fite, *Cotton Fields No More,* 63; Hunt, *History of Farmers' Movements in the Southwest,* 62 (quotation).

16. Taylor, *Farmers' Movement,* 350–55 (quotation at 355). See also Woodward, *Origins of the New South,* 414; Fite, *Cotton Fields No More,* 64; Saloutos, *Farmer Movements in the South,* 200–204.

17. Woodward, *Origins of the New South,* 413–15.

18. The FU's legislative demands of 1912 ran the gamut of economic, social, and political reforms. See *Minutes,* 1912 (Chattanooga, Tennessee), 31–33. One of the constituent committees of the organization was the Committee on Child and Animal Protection, whose reports declaimed against the evils of child labor and mental or physical child abuse, as well as the poor treatment of domestic animals in both the United States and abroad (in terms that call to mind 1990s animal rights organizations). See, for example, *Minutes,* 1911 (Shawnee, Oklahoma), 86–91; *Minutes,* 1913 (Salina, Kansas), 68–71; and *Minutes,* 1914 (Fort Worth, Texas), 26, 38–40. The protection of both classes of "dependent" creatures was portrayed as a logical extension of the organization's humane moral philosophy. Child labor in mines and factories during the school year was condemned as a "curse to civilization" calling for national legislation (*Minutes,* 1913, 68). The 1911 *Minutes* proclaimed: "The proper protection of children and animals by law constitutes the highest state of civilization. No country nor state can claim to be civilized at this date that has not provided reasonable protection, not only for the child, but for . . . the lesser animals. A wilful injury to one of these dependent, helpless creatures not only injures the child or animal, but it also injures the one who does it and the community that carelessly or willingly permits it" (86–87).

19. Barrett, *Mission, History, and Times of the Farmers Union,* 31–32, 45–48. In the old producerist language, Barrett argued that when "the farmers and the laborers convince[d] the world that they know their strength and their rights, and are determined to use the one to secure the other," the political system would not dare to refuse their demands (415).

20. Taylor, *Farmers' Movement,* 358–59; *Minutes,* 1911, 65–67; *Minutes,* 1912, 31–33. See also Hunt, *History of Farmers' Movements in the Southwest,* 70, 76–80, 82–83, 131–32, and William C. Tucker, "Populism Up-to-Date: The Story of the Farmers' Union," *Agricultural History* 21 (October 1947): 200–202.

21. McConnell, *Decline of Agrarian Democracy,* 39; Samuel Gompers, *Seventy Years of Life and Labor,* 2 vols. (New York: E. P. Dutton, 1925), 2:271; Tucker, "Populism Up-to-Date," 200–201. In 1908, for example, the first (and only) "outsider" to address the FU convention was Samuel Gompers. *Minutes,* 1911, 1. The 1915 FU convention directed its national offices "to cooperate with the Federation of Labor in national legislation for the benefit of labor" and expressed appreciation to the AFL for "the help it has extended this organization in this past." *Minutes,* 1915 (Lincoln, Nebraska), 53. Cooperation between labor and farm groups within the southern states was apparently stronger in Texas, Oklahoma, and North Carolina than elsewhere. Grantham, *Southern Progressivism,* 295–97.

22. Hunt, *History of Farmers' Movements in the Southwest,* 70, 76, 80. The condemnation of convict labor was not without loopholes. The Texas FU endorsed convict labor for road repair and for activities providing competition with monopolies — such as in the prison manufacture of cotton bagging and the development of iron

resources. Ibid., 82, 91, 98; Jack Temple Kirby, *Darkness at the Dawning* (Philadelphia: J. B. Lippincott, 1972), 152–54.

23. James Aubrey Tinsley, "The Progressive Movement in Texas" (Ph.D. diss., University of Wisconsin, 1953), 67, 135–37.

24. Worth R. Miller, "Building a Progressive Coalition in Texas: The Populist-Reform Democrat Rapprochement, 1900–1907," *Journal of Southern History* 52 (May 1986): 176–77, 181–82.

25. Taylor, *Farmers' Movement*, 359. See also Grantham, *Southern Progressivism*, 330–31, and Saloutos, *Farmer Movements in the South*, 191–92. FU President Barrett was appointed to a variety of advisory groups by Presidents Roosevelt, Taft, and Wilson (Saloutos, *Farmer Movements in the South*).

26. On the tenant farmers' organization, see James Green, *Grass Roots Socialism* (Baton Rouge: Louisiana State University Press, 1978), 108–15, 224–25, 323–27, and Tinsley, "Progressive Movement in Texas," 170–72. In 1906–8, Kentucky, Tennessee, and Virginia tobacco growers, ranging from sharecroppers to planters, battled the "tobacco trust" (American Tobacco) in the "Black Patch War." Participants blew up factories, burned warehouses, and destroyed plant beds in a wave of violence that had to be curbed by military force. Cotton growers in Texas, Arkansas, Mississippi, and Georgia imitated their tactics in efforts to enforce a collective reduction of surplus cotton production after admonitions from the FU leadership failed to reduce planting. Woodward, *Origins of the New South*, 386–87; Fite, *Cotton Fields No More*, 66; Saloutos, *Farmer Movements in the South*, 198–99; George L. Robson Jr., "The Farmers' Union in Mississippi," *Journal of Mississippi History* 27 (November 1965): 381–83.

27. Woodward, *Origins of the New South*, 372–73; Paul Lewinson, *Race, Class, and Party* (New York: Russell and Russell, 1963), 111–20, 153–56; Kousser, *Shaping of Southern Politics*, 72–80. By 1903 a majority of southern states, and by 1913 all but North Carolina (which waited until 1915), had primaries. The absence of primary elections may account for some of the failures of the reform movement in the latter state (see Joseph F. Steelman, "The Progressive Era in North Carolina" [Ph.D. diss., University of North Carolina, 1955]). In Alabama, Arkansas, Florida, Mississippi, and Texas, the institution of primary elections paved the way for progressive reforms. Woodward, *Origins of the New South*, 373.

28. Key, *Southern Politics*, 298–310; Lewinson, *Race, Class, and Party*, 190–91; Kousser, *Shaping of Southern Politics*, 80.

29. Albert D. Kirwan, *Revolt of the Rednecks* (New York: Harper Torchbooks, 1951), 314. Nevertheless, one might argue that reforms aimed at improving the position of periphery farmers in the national political economy had even more significance for black than white southerners. Blocked from most urban careers, blacks were even more bound to the land than whites and landownership was a potential escape route from poverty. On campaigns for black land purchase and their surprising successes, see Kirby, *Darkness at the Dawning*, 159–76.

30. Kirwan, *Revolt of the Rednecks*, 144, 163–77.

31. Kousser, *Shaping of Southern Politics*, 234.

32. Kirwan, *Revolt of the Rednecks*, 259–67.

33. Louis W. Koenig, *Bryan* (New York: Capricorn Books, 1971), 354–68.

34. Ibid., 333.

35. Paolo Coletta, *William Jennings Bryan*, 3 vols. (Lincoln: University of Nebraska Press, 1964–69), 1:252.

36. Koenig, *Bryan,* 305, 329–44; Coletta, *Bryan* 1:252–85. However, McKinley's plurality increased by only about 100,000 votes.

37. Coletta, *Bryan* 1:306–52; Koenig, *Bryan,* 368–98. The conservative faction, with critical support from New York City financiers, was led by David Bennett Hill, Grover Cleveland, Abram S. Hewitt, and Alton B. Parker of New York, John G. Carlisle of Kentucky, and Sen. Arthur Pue Gorman of Maryland.

38. Coletta, *Bryan* 1:353–73; Koenig, *Bryan,* 400–405; and see also David Sara-sohn, *The Party of Reform* (Jackson: University of Mississippi Press, 1989), ix–xv, 22–23, 35–58.

39. Willard H. Smith, *The Social and Religious Thought of William Jennings Bryan* (Lawrence, Kans.: Coronado Press, 1975), 41–65. For some more positive evidence, see Koenig, *Bryan,* 334–35, 357–58, 449–50, and Kirby, *Darkness at the Dawning,* 125.

40. Koenig, *Bryan,* 358, 417; Smith, *Social and Religious Thought of William Jennings Bryan,* 13.

41. "Oklahoma's Radical Constitution," *Outlook* 87 (1907): 229–31. See also Charles A. Beard's more favorable description in "The Constitution of Oklahoma," *Political Science Quarterly* 24 (1909): 95–114.

42. Koenig, *Bryan,* 436–37.

43. On the Wilson–Bryan relationship and the 1912 platform, see Arthur S. Link, *Wilson,* vol. 1, *The Road to the White House* (Princeton: Princeton University Press, 1947), 316–27, 341, 452–65; Koenig, *Bryan,* 473–96; Coletta, *Bryan* 2:27–32, 54–78; and Sarasohn, *Party of Reform,* 119–44. For Bryan's influence on New Freedom legislation and the antiwar effort in Congress, see Coletta, *Bryan* 2:121–46, and Lawrence W. Levine, *Defender of the Faith, William Jennings Bryan: The Last Decade, 1915–1925* (New York: Oxford University Press, 1965), 39–90.

44. Quoted in David Burner, *The Politics of Provincialism* (New York: W. W. Norton, 1975), 13. Robert M. La Follette described Bryan as "a great moral teacher" who exerted "a powerful influence for good upon the political thought and standards of his time." *La Follette's Autobiography* (Madison: University of Wisconsin Press, 1960), 148–49.

45. Quoted in Smith, *Social and Religious Thought of William Jennings Bryan,* 191.

46. Ibid., 189–92. See also Levine, *Defender of the Faith,* 261–66, and Koenig, *Bryan,* 606–45.

47. Woodward, *Origins of the New South,* 371.

48. See, for example, Robert S. La Forte, *Leaders of Reform: Progressive Republicans in Kansas, 1900–1916* (Lawrence: University Press of Kansas, 1974), 6–7.

49. For a discussion of the South's colonial status in the early twentieth century, see Woodward, *Origins of the New South,* 291–320, 371–72. On income trends in agriculture, see Willford I. King, *The National Income and Its Purchasing Power* (New York: National Bureau of Economic Research, 1930), 152, 297, 304–14. King wrote that in nine of the seventeen years between 1909 and 1927, "the return on the farmer's investment was less than nothing" (314).

50. Rupert B. Vance, *All These People* (New York: Russell and Russell, 1945), 217, 224.

51. U.S. Department of Commerce, Bureau of the Census, *Statistical Abstract of the United States, 1933* (Washington, D.C.: GPO, 1933), 259 (table). Nonperiphery Delaware and the District of Columbia were subtracted from the South Atlantic totals; Delaware was added to the mid-Atlantic census region. Nevada (a diverse

state due to its location in the San Francisco trade area) was subtracted from the mountain region for these comparisons.

52. Woodward, *Origins of the New South*, 318–19.

53. The 1910 census found 46.3 percent of all Americans living in towns or cities of 2,500 or more population. In the core industrial states, the range was from 47.5 percent in Vermont to over 92 percent in Rhode Island and Massachusetts. In the periphery, the southern state average was 19.8; the midwestern and plains states, 32.6; and the mountain states, 32.6. U.S. Department of Commerce, Bureau of the Census, *Statistical Abstract of the United States, 1913* (Washington, D.C.: GPO, 1914), 41.

54. Harold Hull McCarty, *The Geographic Basis of American Economic Life* (Port Washington, N.Y.: Kennikat Press, 1940), vol. 2, 331.

55. On the formation of these biregional alliances, see Richard F. Bensel, *Sectionalism and American Political Development* (Madison: University of Wisconsin Press, 1984), chap. 7.

56. The complexity is captured in Daniel T. Rodgers's summary description of the period as "an era of shifting, ideologically fluid, issue-focused coalitions, all competing for the reshaping of American society." Daniel T. Rodgers, "In Search of Progressivism," in *The Promise of American History: Progress and Prospects,* ed. Stanley I. Kutler and Stanley N. Katz (Baltimore: Johns Hopkins University Press, 1982), 114.

57. A. Bower Sagaser, *Joseph L. Bristow: Kansas Progressive* (Lawrence: University of Kansas Press, 1968), 99–100; David P. Thelen, *Robert M. La Follette and the Insurgent Spirit* (Boston: Little, Brown, 1976), 41–44; George E. Mowry, *Theodore Roosevelt and the Progressive Movement* (New York: Hill and Wang, 1946), 173; Sarasohn, *Party of Reform*, 85–86.

58. Thomas J. Bray, *Rebirth of Freedom* (Indianola, Iowa: Record and Tribune Press, 1957), 15–16. See also Mowry, *Theodore Roosevelt and the Progressive Movement,* 15–16, and Kenneth Hechler, *Insurgency* (New York: Columbia University Press, 1940), 18–19.

59. Richard Lowitt, *George Norris,* vol. 1, *The Making of a Progressive* (Syracuse, N.Y.: Syracuse University Press, 1963), 27–62; Howard W. Allen, *Poindexter of Washington* (Carbondale: Southern Illinois University Press, 1981), 10–31; Patrick F. Palermo, "Republicans in Revolt: The Sources of Insurgency" (Ph.D. diss., State University of New York, 1973), 119–83; Harlan Hahn, *Urban-Rural Conflict: The Politics of Change* (Beverly Hills, Calif.: Sage, 1971), 53–55; Claudius O. Johnson, *Borah of Idaho* (Seattle: Washington University Press, 1967), 31–97; Thelen, *Robert M. La Follette and the Insurgent Spirit,* 1–31; James Holt, *Congressional Insurgents and the Party System* (Cambridge: Harvard University Press, 1967), 4–5.

60. Borah was not "progressive" on the tariff or on most labor issues, and on roll-call votes he lagged behind the midwesterners in support for "reform" issues. He did, however, support antitrust laws, the income tax, financial decentralization, and railroad regulation.

61. Lowitt, *The Making of a Progressive,* 16–96; Palermo, "Republicans in Revolt," 148–90; Hahn, *Urban-Rural Conflict,* 53–56. Among the leading progressive Republicans, only Beveridge failed reelection in 1910, defeated by a progressive Democrat.

62. Sarasohn, *Party of Reform,* 30, 61–86, 240–42.

63. So reluctant was one historian to label southerners "progressive" that he adopted a dual standard. Republican senators who voted the "progressive" position at least 50 percent of the time were labeled progressive, whereas Democrats had to achieve at least a 90 percent score to win the label. Howard W. Allen, "Geography and Politics: Voting on Reform Issues in the U.S. Senate, 1911–1916," *Journal of Southern History* 27 (May 1961): 218–19. Allen goes on to derive a second, broader list of progressive-issue roll calls but unaccountably subtracts from the list all votes that were highly partisan. This procedure sharply reduces the "progressive" scores of southern Democrats. Another often-cited study employed selective and misleading roll-call descriptions to argue that southern congressional members were actually opponents, rather than leaders (or even followers), of reform. Richard Abrams, "Woodrow Wilson and the Southern Congressmen," *Journal of Southern History* 22 (November 1956): 417–37. The latter contains numerous errors in the descriptions and omissions of essential context of roll calls. . . . The typical study of Republican insurgents seldom mentions the southern Democrats who provided the great bulk of supporting votes on most issues championed by the insurgents, or it takes note of their voting patterns only when they deviate from the norm.

64. John Wells Davidson, "The Response of the South to Woodrow Wilson's New Freedom, 1912–1914" (Ph.D. diss., Yale University, 1954), 95–96.

65. Historians who focus on the state political arena are prone to see agrarian radicalism as more symbol than substance (in Arsenault's view, as a "culturally confused" program serving mainly as a kind of psychological affirmation by increasingly marginalized farmers). The fact that local elites got off lightly as farmers directed their wrath at a national economic system is used as evidence of the farmers' confusion and their addiction to symbolic politics. But a national focus makes sense from a political-economy perspective. Local redistribution could not greatly improve the periphery farmers' position; a rearrangement of the national production, marketing, and monetary system could. Whether, as Arsenault argues, agrarians "wanted respect" above all else is impossible to prove. See Raymond Arsenault, *The Wild Ass of the Ozarks: Jeff Davis and the Social Bases of Southern Politics* (Knoxville: University of Tennessee Press, 1988), 14–15. But the national program of the periphery agrarians was about economics and was quite pragmatic.

66. Mowry, *Era of Theodore Roosevelt*, 198–223; John Braeman, *Albert F. Beveridge* (Chicago: University of Chicago Press, 1971), 98–121.

67. This count is based on the March 19, 1910, vote, specifically the Dalzell motion to table Norris's appeal from the Speaker's ruling (that it was not in order) — the first vote of the Norris rules change series. *Congressional Record (CR)*, 61st Cong., 2d sess. . . ., 3426–27. The first vote is probably a better gauge of "insurgency," since it avoids much of the "bandwagon" effect of later votes. As leaders of the House Republican insurgency, Hechler lists Norris (NE), Madison (KS), Nelson (WI), Murdock (KS), Poindexter (WA), and Lindbergh (MN). Gardner (MA), Fish (NY), and Fowler (NJ) opposed Cannon, mainly for personal reasons. Hechler, *Insurgency*, 34–42.

68. On identification of Senate "insurgents," see Holt, *Congressional Insurgents and the Party System*, 3–9; Edgar G. Robinson, *The Evolution of American Political Parties* (New York: Harcourt, Brace and World, 1924), 313; Hechler, *Insurgency*, 83–91; Mowry, *Era of Theodore Roosevelt*, 244; and Allen, *Poindexter of Washington*, 60–61. Perkins and Works of California, Dixon of Montana, Nelson of Minnesota, and

Brown and Burkett of Nebraska are sometimes identified as Senate "progressives" or "insurgents" but clearly were not among the group's major activists. In Allen's study, the five senators voting most in opposition to their party on progressive issues were La Follette, Clapp, Gronna, Kenyon, and Poindexter. Of the fourteen senators listed in the text, eight represented periphery, five diverse, and one (Poindexter of Washington) core states.

69. On the rules fight, Hechler reports that Democratic leaders were miffed that the insurgent Republicans "monopolized the limelight." Clayton of Alabama branded it "a case of the tail wagging the dog" (quoted in Hechler, *Insurgency*, 74). However, as Sarasohn argues, it was good politics to let the insurgents lead the charge in the years when the Republicans held the majority (*Party of Reform*, 65), and the Democrats seemed much more gracious about sharing the limelight than did the insurgents, who "tended to treat the Democrats as political untouchables who happened to be voting the same way" (ibid., 63). The progressive Republicans were particularly ungracious and increasingly uncooperative when the tables were turned and Democrats led the Congress and the executive branch. As Sarasohn summarizes, the insurgents "played an important role in the politics of the Progressive Era. But they were rarely as radical and never as numerous as the Democrats whom they denounced, despised, and depended upon" (ibid., 86; see also 76, 80–81).

70. Computed from Jerome M. Clubb, "Congressional Opponents of Reform, 1901–1913" (Ph.D. diss., University of Washington, 1963), table 28, 209–10.

71. Ibid. Six of the ten rural "opponents of reform" were from the Pacific states. All were Republican.

2. How much influence did middle-class businessmen have on the Progressive agenda?

Robert H. Wiebe

Progressivism Arrives

Robert H. Wiebe, one of the foremost historians of Progressivism, led a long and distinguished career at Northwestern University. The selection that follows, "Progressivism Arrives," is excerpted from his classic 1967 history, *The Search for Order*. Wiebe argues that Progressivism occurred in both urban and small-town settings. He finds reform divided among voluntary associations, cities, states, and the federal government and exercised by members of a new middle class eager to bring order to their rapidly expanding world. Moreover, this is the only article you will read that discusses Progressivism on the level of state government. Wiebe makes sense of this pattern of reform by arguing that all the reformers shared a passion for organization and efficiency. Thus he is a founder of the "organizational" school of Progressive Era historiography.

Wiebe opens *The Search for Order* with an eloquent portrait of rural life in the nineteenth century, before industrialization and urbanization. He aptly describes most people as living in "island communities," places where people were tied to each other by geography, trading, and kinship—places where they knew each other. The breakdown of these island communities because of migration, industrialization, and urbanization caused the unrest and chaos that prompted people to reform their new world.

In many ways, Wiebe was responding to Hofstadter's argument that the Progressives came from an old professional group who found themselves pushed off center stage with urbanization and industrialization. Although Wiebe's Progressives resemble Hofstadter's in many ways, they are not the old-stock middle class who held moral authority in less complicated times. Rather, they are a new middle class—men whose fathers might have been craftsmen or farmers. The sons are now trying to make a go of careers in town. Moreover, Wiebe's Progressive leaders are not only from New England, but from other regions as well.

Questions for a Closer Reading

1. Find three quotes from Wiebe describing the Progressives and contrast them with three quotes from Hofstadter. How do they differ and what do they have in common?

2. What role does expertise play in Wiebe's argument? How did businesses and professionals reorganize themselves to meet the challenges they faced at the turn of the twentieth century?

3. What sorts of reform could state governments enact? What were their limitations?

4. How did reform impulses penetrate the federal government? How important was the federal government's role in reform compared to the local reform efforts that Wiebe also discusses? Compare Wiebe's analysis of federal reform to Sanders's version of how national Progressive policy was made.

5. Wiebe gives little credit to the Populists for inspiring Progressivism. In fact, it is as if the Populists remained back on the farm in their "island communities," while their smarter sons went to town, joined associations, and became Progressives. Sketch points of argument between Sanders and Wiebe. How do their sources differ? Is there any way to reconcile their positions?

Progressivism Arrives

Attributing omnipotence to abstractions—the Trust and Wall Street, the Political Machine and the System of Influence—had become a national habit by the end of the nineteenth century. This was the American way of expressing the contrast between a familiar environment and the strange world beyond. In the town, or even in restricted areas of the city, power was personal. Almost any interested citizen could separate the leader from the follower and the partisan from the apathetic. If he cared, he could also discover the men who combined to make the important decisions; and among these, who controlled wealth or votes, who held the strategic posts, and who simply had a reputation for offering wise counsel. With a little more effort, he could probably uncover the men who financed campaigns and something of the privileges they reaped. Never simple, often fluctuating, it was still a manageable pattern, an eminently human network of relations.

As long as Americans were content to operate within that familiar setting, the outside world posed no serious problems. They translated its events into the language of local power, then dismissed them. When they moved into a broader arena, however, they soon found that they could neither see, know, nor even know about the people upon whom they had to depend. The legal framework changed; new groups, some abiding by quite different values, complicated the pattern; and relationships often followed an alien logic. The system was so impersonal, so vast, seemingly without beginning or end.

Some sallied forth and returned, licking their wounds, to stay. But the urge to fight again and again infected ever increasing numbers, particularly those from the new middle class. They demanded the right to pursue their ambitions outward rather than simply to be left alone at home, and that in turn required far-reaching social changes. To improve public health, for example, doctors might insist upon the renovation of an entire

Robert H. Wiebe, "Progressivism Arrives," from *The Search for Order: 1877–1920* (New York: Hill and Wang, 1967), 164–95.

city. Some social workers quite literally called for a new American society. Expansionists in business, labor, agriculture, and the professions, in other words, formulated their interests in terms of continuous policies that necessitated regularity and predictability from unseen thousands.

These men and women stood in the forefront of the reforms that had spread across the land by the beginning of the twentieth century. In contrast to the grim defenses of the community only a decade before, these movements were founded in stability. If frustration also drove the new reformers, it was a frustration born of confidence, an impatience with the inertia that slowed their irresistible march to victory. Most of them lived and worked in the midst of modern society and accepting its major thrust drew both their inspiration and their programs from its peculiar traits. Where their predecessors would have destroyed many of urban-industrial America's outstanding characteristics, the new reformers wanted to adapt an existing order to their own ends. They prized their organizations not merely as reflections of an ideal but as sources of everyday strength, and generally they also accepted the organizations that were multiplying about them. Theirs was an unusually open, expansive scheme of reform which took them farther and farther into modern society's hitherto unexamined corners. The challengers of the late nineteenth century had, in almost all instances, sought a single objective—the autonomous community—through sweeping, redundant programs. Their successors sought a great variety of objectives through a technique of reform which they came to believe could resolve each of these problems, and tomorrow's as well. The heart of progressivism was the ambition of the new middle class to fulfill its destiny through bureaucratic means.

The two initial centers of progressive reform were the large cities of the East and Midwest and the predominantly agrarian states of the Midwest and portions of the South. By priority, complexity, and sophistication, the urban wing led the rural. It was in the major cities that a fair number of citizens first gained a sufficient grip upon their lives to look anew at the society around them. Making sense out of this impersonal world had been a slow, painful process that the depression of the nineties had seriously retarded. Those who did find their way emerged with a consuming sense of accomplishment, a conviction that now no challenge could overwhelm them. Later changes would largely appear as more of the same—additional electric trolleys and broader expanses of commuter housing, more modern factories and stronger trade unions, bigger skyscrapers and denser tenement districts. An elusive yet fundamental maturity appeared in the great cities around 1900, with an aggressive, optimistic, new middle class the prime beneficiary.

Urban progressivism originated in these calculated second thoughts. No divine logic designated this place and this time for full-scale reform. If anyone had cared to examine them, county governments were at least as corrupt and incompetent, but their half-hearted renovation awaited the twenties. Rural poverty and disease were just as obvious and as appalling in their setting as slum squalor was in its, but aside from some educational philanthropy and Dr. Charles Stiles' attack upon hookworm few paid them much attention. Moreover, as city officials gained some experience in dealing with metropolitan problems late in the nineteenth century, urban government had gradually grown more efficient and more responsive. At that same steady, unspectacular rate both the government and the privately owned utilities had been expanding, improving, and lowering the costs of their essential services. A change in the quality of perceptions, not in the quantity of unique evils, produced a broad reappraisal of the cities around 1900.

In the larger cities, the hectic period of growth—what Theodore Dreiser called "the furnace stage of [their] existence" when "everything was in the making"—had largely passed, and the heroes of yesterday had become the villains of a more settled era. Once city dwellers had noticed only the presence or absence of a basic service. Now they took its existence for granted and scrutinized the details, grumbling over inconveniences and omissions and shoddy work. Contracts excused or ignored in the panting demand for sewers and fresh water now seemed vicious, and franchise privileges granted out of a confused need for something at once were regarded as nothing less than theft. Some of the critics were the very ones who had promoted the city's helter-skelter growth only a few years before. Many more, however, were rising young men and women who had had no part in the decisions, who had never shared the moon-struck atmosphere surrounding them—and could not comprehend it. They arrived fresh, intolerant, and eager to take hold.

At the center of their discontent lay a fairly simple condition. A patchwork government could no longer manage the range of urban problems with the expertise and economy that articulate citizens now believed they must have. In one of the grand ironies of the era, the reformers described their opposition as a devilishly effective pact between bosses and businessmen which financed the machines and sold public favors on request. Partly in self-delusion and partly in self-defense, they declared that they would destroy that System and, by implication, substitute a natural, individualistic democracy. Of course the urban progressives were the systematizers and their opponents the slovenly, albeit sometimes democratic, governors. The typical business ally of the boss, moreover, was a rather marginal operator [and an] anathema to the chamber of commerce. The few important businessmen who did purchase franchises invariably complained of political larceny. Hidden behind the stereotypes, well-to-do merchants, manufacturers, and bankers who sought more dependable and rewarding relations with government were moving in the vanguard of urban reform.

Impatiently dismissing all half-measures, the reformers reached out for the power to reorder the government themselves, and though they fell short, they did accomplish a good deal. In a series of highly publicized struggles involving almost every major city, they extended the scope of utility regulation and sharply limited the privileges and duration of the franchises. Tax assessment, decades out of date and badly skewed in favor of large corporations, was modernized. Completing an older movement to introduce the secret ballot, urban progressives also shortened the ballot, and that, in conjunction with the expansion of government services, increased the number of appointive posts. Reformers were remarkably successful in reserving these positions for specialists, either by broadening the civil service or by private understandings with the city's leading officials. The experts in turn devised rudimentary government budgets, introduced central, audited purchasing, and partially rationalized the structure of offices. Bureaus of research provided endless data on all of these matters as well as the skill for drafting some of the more complex ordinances.

While some reformers were streamlining the government, others entered the slums. Settlement houses multiplied in the new century. Campaigns for public health, originating in the eighties as drives against filth and then broadening into attacks upon particular diseases, developed around 1900 into integrated, city-wide programs. Just as naturally, slum life involved the progressives in housing and factory conditions, and that in turn led to new regulations covering both areas. These reformers asked and to a surprising degree received one another's assistance. When a child labor committee brought its bill before the New York legislature in 1903, for instance, an extraordinary collection of settlement workers, union officials, young lawyers, public administrators, and other professionals eagerly gathered to lobby for the measure. With some exceptions, the humanitarian progressives came to form a loose confederation, increasingly aware of the ways their special interests fitted into a common cause.

If humanitarian progressivism had a central theme, it was the child. He united the campaigns for health, education, and a richer city environment, and he dominated much of the interest in labor legislation. Female wage earners—mothers in absentia—received far closer attention than male, movements for industrial safety and workmen's compensation invariably raised the specter of the unprotected young, and child labor laws drew the progressives' unanimous support. The most popular versions of legal and penal reform also emphasized the needs of youth. Something more than sympathy for the helpless, or even the powerful influence of women in this portion of progressivism, explained that intense preoccupation. The child was the carrier of tomorrow's hope whose innocence and freedom made him singularly receptive to education in rational, humane behavior. Protect him, nurture him, and in his manhood he would create that bright new world of the progressives' vision. Here was a dream utterly alien to the late nineteenth century. Instead of molding youth in a slightly improved pattern of their fathers, like cyclically reproducing like, the new reformers thought in terms of fluid progress, a process of growth that demanded constant vigilance.

Whatever the reformer's specialty, his program relied ultimately upon administration. "For two generations," Frederic Howe wrote in 1905, "we have wrought out the most admirable laws and then left the government to run itself. This has been our greatest fault." Now laws established an outline for management, a flexible authority to meet and follow the major issues of urban living. In fact, the fewer laws the better if those few properly empowered the experts, for administration was expected to replace the tedious, haphazard process of legislative compromise. In the regulation of factory conditions, for example, urban progressives spent far less time listing novel rules than perfecting inspection according to the basic ones. Of course discretionary phrasing had long been a common part of legislation. But where the leeway in the New York Housing Act of 1867 served as a sieve through which any agile landlord might escape, the latitude in the New York Health Law of 1913 enabled the state commissioner to manage such matters as quarantines by his personal standards of medical efficiency. Because the reformers viewed organization quite simply as anti-chaos, they conceived their administrative solutions in terms of broad executive mandates, with a mayor holding full general authority and subordinates enjoying virtual autonomy in their limited areas of expertise. The model government formed a simple pyramid free from the cross-checks and intersecting lines of divided responsibility.

Scientific government, the urban reformers believed, would bring opportunity, progress, order, and community. Once emancipated from fear and exploitation, all men would enjoy a fair chance for success. The coarseness, the jagged violence, of city life that so deeply disturbed them would dissolve into a new urban unity, the progressive version of the old community ideal. At first, the urban progressives had expected to transplant village intimacy into the city, either directly through the kind of neighborhood cohesion settlement workers were cultivating or through the "organic city" of brotherhood and compassion, their mystic compromise between the town's face-to-face society and the metropolitan crowds.

Early in the twentieth century this goal rapidly lost ground to a very different one predicated upon the assumption that every man, properly educated, would desire a functional, efficient society. The new bureaucratic vision accepted the impersonal flux of the city and anticipated its perfect systematization. When a band of urban progressives went in search of utopia in 1916, they travelled not to a country retreat but to an industrial subdivision of Cincinnati where they tried to build a model for the professionally serviced city. If memories of the friendly village still lingered about the corners of their thoughts, most of them were now dreaming of an urban world that they would control for the benefit of all, a paradise of new-middle-class rationality.

Although many topics of late-nineteenth-century reform reappeared after 1900, most of the old issues had changed beyond recognition. Civil service, for instance, had once been a negative, absolute goal, self-contained and self-fulfilling. Now the panacea of the patrician had given way to the administrative tool of the expert, with efficiency rather than moral purity its objective. The long-standing ambition of urban home rule underwent a comparable metamorphosis. Earlier it had anticipated no more than the removal of outside influence, a simple dream of the uncontaminated community reclaimed. Now it was a precondition for reform. It prepared the laboratory for uninterrupted experimentation. Similarly, the enemies of child labor changed an uncomplicated demand for abolition into a complex social movement. What would become of the emancipated children? The urban progressives advocated nurseries and kindergartens, better schools and tighter attendance laws, recreational facilities and social clubs. Was the child any safer outside the factory? They spread the gospel of personal hygiene and public sanitation, proper diet and prompt inoculation. And what of the child's home environment? Many of them supported adult labor laws and adult education, trade unions and family courts. Perhaps only half-aware of what they were doing, they transformed the sin of child labor into the sin of the unprotected child.

As these changes occurred early in the twentieth century, the industrial centers of the East which had set the pace in almost every area of reform now retraced their steps and modernized their pioneer accomplishments. Massachusetts, for example, which in 1900 had seemed so far advanced in the regulation of industry, was undertaking a general renovation of its reform laws only five years later under Governor Curtis Guild, Jr. Moreover, many of the experiments in the nineties, such as the first purified milk stations and the first campaigns against diphtheria and tuberculosis, had been financed by private funds, a natural extension of nineteenth-century charity reform and obviously unsuitable to the progressive goal of systematic, city-wide coverage. For that the government had to assume responsibility, which it began to do around the turn of the century. The change in orientation among settlement workers illustrated the same process. Dedicated in the nineties to personal service among the poor, they had operated from a most traditional attitude about the private nature of man's improvement. Only as they grew convinced that their ambitions involved a whole society and required a modern government of experts did they become an important part of the new urban progressivism.

Of course the older brands of reform did not suddenly disappear. Just as progressivism was emerging, in fact, a rash of old-fashioned graft prosecutions spread among many of the nation's major cities: Joseph W. Folk, for instance, attacked bosses and bribers in St. Louis, righteous citizens battled an alliance between criminals and city hall in Minneapolis, and Francis J. Heney prosecuted a corrupt triangle of politicians, labor leaders, and businessmen in San Francisco. In a widely read series for *McClure's,* the muckraker Lincoln Steffens described the uprisings as if they were startlingly new phenomena, and to many then and later these moral crusades seemed the finest flower of a new reform. Actually the labors of such men as Folk and Heney lay outside the mainstream of progressivism. With no purpose beyond disclosure and conviction and very little organized support behind them, they captured the headlines, then disappeared.

Divergent types of protest often marched side by side within the same city, especially where someone loosely identified with "reform" gained power. In 1901 a diffuse discontent over greedy traction executives and complacent city councilmen threw out the old crowd in Cleveland. The new mayor, Tom L. Johnson, had gained a fortune manipulating franchises before his conversion to Henry George's single tax, and he was able to fight the traction companies* on their own terms for eight exciting years. Reformers of the old school, sweeping and moralistic, collected in and around city hall throughout his tenure. If a group of zealous and well-trained young men had not counselled Johnson, his administration would have accomplished little more than Hazen Pingree's sterile war against the utility "octopus" in Detroit a decade before. Such men as Frederic Howe, Newton D. Baker, and Edward Bemis brought a wealth of new ideas on tax assessment, the treatment of criminals, and rational executive procedures; they even contributed expert knowledge about the regulation of utilities that fell beyond the mayor's experience. Willing to listen and eager to succeed, the unpretentious Johnson allowed his lieutenants to fashion their own programs. Early in the century these amalgams of old and new were

---

*Traction companies were power-generating companies that also ran electric railways. Thus, they often had a monopoly in a single town on electrical power and public transportation.

the standard content of any reform administration, whose simple, popular slogans—"a three-cent fare for Cleveland"—usually concealed the more substantial changes within.

Actually, reformers never fully controlled the government of a metropolis. The larger the city and the more heterogeneous its life, the looser its power structure. A multiplicity of functions created many independent centers; ethnic differences spawned more. No one group could possibly manage more than a fraction of its political services, and that complexity encouraged ambitious citizens to try their luck in the scramble. A New York or Chicago, impersonal and diffuse, invited competition. At the same time, the problems of consolidation were immense. The very intricacies that produced so many cracks kept the way open to one's enemies as well. In a very rough sense, the power to decide came increasingly to be parcelled along lines of functional specialization. Businessmen who restricted themselves to particular taxes and economic regulations, administrative experts who concentrated upon the government's procedure, doctors who limited themselves to public health, tended to have more and more success, while the men who attempted to combine all of these programs into general policy seldom left a mark on the big city.

In order to compete effectively, members of the new middle class organized to ensure a continuity of influence. Where respectable citizens in the eighties typically had called a conference and passed resolutions, the new breed around 1900 formed associations with long-range policies and delegated one or two officers to act for the entire body. As late as 1894 only Chicago boasted an urban reform league with a paid executive; ten years later comparable associations in every major city employed full-time directors. Although the new professional, business, and labor organizations had some grumbling members and even an occasional palace coup, these scarcely affected the trend. For instance, when the so-called socialist opposition won office in the United Mine Workers and the International Association of Machinists, its leaders, too, shelved their plans for democratic unionism in favor of a centralized command.

As reformers sought to expand their influence, they found two important avenues open before them. Newly self-conscious businessmen offered one. They alone among the prominent progressive groups had the inherent resources—the critical positions in the local economy, the money, and the prestige—to command some sort of response from the government. Weaker reformers, therefore, tried to attach their causes to these men's ambitions, relying upon their need for expert advice and their general sympathy for systematization and order. The boss provided the second avenue. "Professionally [the boss] desires to play his role [as benefactor] in the fullest sense," wrote the settlement worker Robert A. Woods, "and if public improvement or general welfare be part of the tradition he is among the first to catch and hold it." Capable of recognizing when he was beyond his depth, the boss also depended upon the special skills of the new reformers.

It was the expert who benefited most directly from the new framework of politics. The more intricate such fields as the law and the sciences became, the greater the need for men with highly developed skills. The more complex the competition for power, the more organizational leaders relied on experts to decipher and to prescribe. Above all, the more elaborate men's aspirations grew, the greater their dependence upon specialists who could transcribe principles into policy. A chamber of commerce, mobilized and formidable, desired a cleaner, safer, more beautiful, and more economically operated city. Only the professional administrator, the doctor, the social worker, the architect, the economist, could show the way. Knowing that, the chamber's president had to accept at least some of their technical schemes or abandon his goals. By placing a specialist, Lawrence Veiller, in charge of New York City's movement for better housing in 1898, its backers transformed an expensive avocation into an efficient campaign. Meanwhile, professors like Frank Goodnow, Leo Rowe, and Edmund James were telling the National Municipal League what urban reforms it really wanted. For the same reason, legislators faced with such involved problems as utility franchises and factory inspection also came to depend upon the new professionals who as a result proved to be remarkably effective lobbyists. As the definer of general impulses, the expert who timed his entry properly and presented his plans cleverly could become the indispensable man.

Supplementing these primary routes to power, some progressives also used moral suasion to excellent effect. In particular, women of good families such as Jane Addams and Florence Kelley were learning how to shame their contemporaries with surprising results. Rant though they might, men in authority simply could not seal themselves from these voices as they had a generation before from a Terence Powderly or a Henry George. Politicians who would otherwise have turned their backs gave at least token response, and the rich subsidized many a venture that on its own merits would never have appealed to them.

Such a heavy reliance upon other people's good graces meant that many urban progressives functioned under constant pressure. At any moment the very rich might close their checkbooks. The boss would never willingly relinquish any control he deemed essential to his organization's power. The reform-minded businessman, moreover, usually pictured the ideal city as an extension of his commercial values. Desiring continuous services that were also inexpensive, he resented taxes that would take away with one hand the benefits he was just then extracting with the other. His modern city was a business community; a clean, attractive appearance, an atmosphere of growth and progress, raised the general level of the economy. This excluded a great deal that other progressives were urgently seeking, and as dependents they had somehow to show their sponsors that better schools and parks in the slums would produce a more peaceful, industrious citizenry, that higher costs for welfare services would save the taxpayer "in the long run." Tortuous logic brought limited results. By 1905 urban progressives were already separating along two paths. While one group used the language of the budget, boosterism, and social control, the other talked of economic justice, human opportunities, and rehabilitated democracy. Efficiency-as-economy diverged further and further from efficiency-as-social-service.

State progressivism in the industrial East simply rephrased urban problems in the artificial terms of a larger jurisdiction. During the late nineteenth century, the rising metropolitan centers had already come to dominate these states' politics, which often comprised so many responses to the dynamics of their major cities. Progressivism deepened that tradition. In New York, for example, the great victory of the progressive Governor, Charles Evans Hughes, was the creation of a state commission to regulate urban public utilities, particularly those in New York City; and in Ohio the triumph of reform merely relieved the cities of excessive interference from the state legislature.

State governments in the East were certainly not the cordial allies of urban progressivism. By a combination of custom, majority rule, and the gerrymander, they served as rural strongholds where the enemies of the city generally held sway. Assistance came grudgingly and sparingly. When the New York legislature passed measures to regulate urban housing and public utilities, it did so primarily out of upstate Republican antagonism to Tammany Hall. The laws pried the city open to state politicians. Urban home rule succeeded in Ohio largely because a number of country legislators hoped to tip a very close electoral balance in favor of their party. More often, these state governments rejected urban reforms almost as a matter of policy.

In most of the Midwest, South, and Far West, however, state progressivism enjoyed an independent existence. Once again, a new social maturity lay immediately behind the reform movements. Out of the disruptions of the late nineteenth century, a number of men on the farms and in the towns and smaller cities had gradually built stable careers around the new modes of distribution and finance. Slowed by the uncertainties of the late eighties and nineties, they had suddenly found themselves in highly advantageous positions around 1900. They were prospering, and tomorrow's promise now seemed exceptionally bright. These merchants and commercial farmers, bankers and lawyers, promoters and editors—men whose success was rooted in their own areas even as it drew them far into a national society—constituted an indigenous socioeconomic power that their regions had not known in any strength since the full-scale arrival of the railroads. Like the urban progressives, they were taking a calculated second look at the world around them.

Generally younger men with a passion for the future, they manifested much of that same zest and self-confident drive which characterized the urban progressives. Yet by contrast they were quite narrow. Lacking a strong contingent of new professionals, they concentrated upon a relatively few matters of economic policy and political power. The nature of reform in the smaller cities of the Midwest and South provided one excellent illustration of that difference. In these centers of limited function—a commercial way-station, a home for one or two simple industries—a handful controlling its primary business usually monopolized power. Progressivism generally emanated from an influential group of citizens who were just then appreciating the advantages of modernization as an aid to their expanding interests. Implemented with little of the pulling and hauling that attended urban progressivism, their reforms moved far more smoothly to a logical conclusion. In many instances, that meant substituting either a city manager or a set of specialized commissions for the mayor and introducing city-wide, nonpartisan elections to break down all little enclaves of political power. By the First World War about six hundred of these smaller cities had adopted such a system, an utter impossibility in the metropolis, and quite often the local chamber of commerce or its equivalent openly selected the important officials.

Even in a city the size of Memphis, which passed one hundred thousand early in the century, reform followed a similar pattern. A commercial center specializing in the cotton trade, Memphis contained relatively few elements of a complex urban-industrial society. When leading citizens suddenly became dissatisfied with an alliance between city hall and the underworld, they brought in a new mayor, Edward H. Crump, who modernized taxes and rationalized government in a businesslike fashion. If Crump later asserted his independence and outlasted his sponsors, that told much more about his political acumen than it did about the lost opportunities of progressive reform. In Memphis the sources for social-welfare reform scarcely existed.

That narrowness, which characterized the towns and farms as well as the smaller cities, also stood in marked contrast to late-nineteenth-century reform. Very few of these progressives had looked kindly upon Populism or its near relations. Struggling to secure a place for themselves during the eighties and nineties, they had either avoided such movements or opposed them as a direct threat to their ambitions. Now they replaced the older programs with far more concrete yet subtle proposals which envisaged an administered progress rather than immediate wholesale changes. It was men of this stripe, no less determined and much better organized than their predecessors, who collected about Governors Robert La Follette in Wisconsin, Albert Cummins in Iowa, John Johnson in Minnesota, Walter Stubbs in Kansas, Braxton Bragg Comer in Alabama, Robert Glenn in North Carolina, and Hoke Smith in Georgia, and somewhat later Hiram Johnson in California, as well as the lesser figures in several other western and southern states.

They gathered, but they did not necessarily control. Without the focus of a big city, politics in these states tended toward a diffuse factionalism. Local leaders endlessly jostled each other for petty advantage, and only the skillful manager of loose coalitions held any chance of success. Except for Alabama's Comer, a Birmingham businessman turned politician, each of the important progressive Governors launched his state career as just such a factional chieftain, concentrating initially upon intraparty power rather than upon a specific program. Consequently, even after he had allied himself to certain new-middle-class groups, his campaigns continued to reflect a much broader segment of the state's population. In Wisconsin, for example, La Follette's early margins of victory came from newly assertive Americans a generation removed from Scandinavia who had relatively little at stake in the Governor's progressivism. Cummins of Iowa constructed his first coalition out of Republican antiprohibition sentiment, an issue that bore only tangentially on progressive reform. And Hoke Smith's dependence upon the followers of Tom Watson, now a pathological racist, meant that as Governor of Georgia he would have to mix a large measure of Jim Crow into any plans for reform.

Leadership played an exceptionally important role in the state progressivism of the West and South. The Governors not only had to maintain their coalitions, but they had to do so while directing legislative and administrative programs of unprecedented complexity. The best of them compensated in two ways. They marshalled the reformers to browbeat legislators; and they veiled much of their program with those traditional appeals to localism which still attracted a large if disorganized rural audience. The kings of state progressivism—La Follette, Cummins, and Johnson of California—mastered these managerial and rhetorical techniques with startling results. As Governors they set standards for the nation; and when they moved on in time to the Senate, they still commanded the kind of veneration at home that almost assured re-election. A fumbling leader, on the other hand, such as Stubbs of Kansas or Folk of Missouri only scattered the reformers and stunted his own career.

Not all of the localist rhetoric was a sham. Most members of the new middle class in these agricultural states also felt something of that vague threat which had obsessed the community reformers of the late nineteenth century, and a desire to break the grip of oppressive national forces continued to influence their progressivism. Particularly in the South, where the economic dominance of outsiders was too pervasive for any ambitious man to ignore, the urge for local independence remained a very powerful sentiment indeed. After 1900 the familiar cries to emulate a successful northern capitalism included a new and stronger emphasis upon southern control. A younger group of promoters still called for a modern South but one in which they would hold the power. Similar themes, though somewhat more subdued, appeared in the western movements as well.

Partly from expediency and partly from conviction, therefore, the progressive platforms in the West and South included a good deal of old-fashioned reform. Leaders demanded stern antitrust laws, discriminated in favor of state enterprise in such areas as insurance, and insisted upon rigid rules to restrain the political activities of the large corporations. In several states, moreover, they introduced direct primaries and some version of the initiative, referendum, and recall with all the fanfare of a Populist camp meeting. At the same time, however, they expanded the discretionary power of the executive, copied many of the new techniques for efficient government, stressed the law's continuous implementation, rationalized tax structures, and in many of these matters drew upon the new professional's advice.

In this mingling of old and new, of suspicion and optimism, the new clearly predominated. Railroad regulation, the major issue in state progressivism, illustrated that supremacy. Earlier champions of the community had demanded an arithmetic equality in rates and a flat prohibition against anything hinting at special privilege. They had looked to the legislature for relief. The right laws, often designating exact rates, would ensure right principles. In this conception the regulatory commission had served exclusively as an arm of the legislature, to enforce its laws and to gather its data. In the twentieth century the commission became the master instead of the servant. Once empowered, it operated apart from the legislature, administering rather than enforcing. It was expected to oversee adjustments not only in rates but also in such highly technical matters as storage, transfer, and the general handling of cargo. Business-minded progressives, in other words, expected the commission to act as their agent in an endless series of maneuvers with the railroads. No precise legal wording could possibly have captured their purpose; that required an independent body responding to the flow of circumstances. In the end these commissions accomplished relatively little. Irrelevant to the natural flow of people and goods, the states simply could not manage the major problems of a national economy. Nevertheless, railroad regulation suggested how deeply a new orientation, derived from urban-industrial society and championed by a new middle class, had penetrated the minds of reformers throughout the nation.

Progressivism was the central force in a revolution that fundamentally altered the structure of politics and government early in the twentieth century. In no sense, however, did it monopolize the field. In fact the major corporations tended to move somewhat ahead of the reformers in attempts to extend the range and continuity of their power through bureaucratic means. Most large corporations had spread their nets far more rapidly during the eighties and nineties than their officers could comprehend, let alone manage. Beginning with the railroads, a few companies made an uneven start toward assimilating these gains toward the end of the century. Then around 1900 the rush to reorganize commenced, with one giant firm after another adopting some variant of administrative centralization. An age that assumed an automatic connection between accurate data and rational action naturally emphasized a few leaders linked by simple lines to the staff below. Information would flow upward through the corporate structure, decisions downward. A scheme guaranteed to produce ulcerous executives and evasive underlings, it still represented an important advance in marshalling the corporation's resources for long-range, nationwide policy.

As their interests grew more refined and their need for technical services increased, big businessmen also leaned more and more upon expert assistants. The first to profit from this trend had been a few specialists in corporate and financial law. Then around 1900 they were joined by a great variety of experts. When John D. Rockefeller wanted to do good with his millions, he turned to Frederick T. Gates, a pioneer specialist in spending other people's money, and when he wanted to rehabilitate his reputation, he hired a second pioneer, Ivy Lee, professional in public relations. The magnate no longer relied upon the family friend and the cooperative newspaper editor. In 1901 J. P. Morgan brought a partner into his firm who simply did not care much about stocks, bonds, and mortgages. George W. Perkins—organizer, mediator, publicist, and politician—added a new dimension to one of the nation's major centers of power. As one commentator remarked, Perkins served as "Secretary of State" for a company that had become involved in an increasingly complex set of public and private negotiations.

The political implications of the desire for continuity turned big businessmen into political innovators, and campaigning was one of the first areas affected. Particularly after 1896, such magnates as John McCall of New York Life Insurance, Henry H. Rogers of Standard Oil, and Edward Harriman began both to contribute more consistently and to grant funds for a party rather than a man. They were attempting to buy a good reputation, to incline all important party members in their favor instead of stringing a few as company puppets. The more extensive the magnate's political concern, the more important it was to condition countless, unknown officials in all parts of government to respond appropriately whenever his interests came under consideration. The managers of the Republican party, which was almost the exclusive beneficiary, were naturally delighted. Businessmen's detached representatives had only weakened party discipline. Discretionary funds now brought prestige and control back into the hands of such men as Mark Hanna, George Cortelyou, and Nelson Aldrich, and regular donations allowed them to plan campaigns rather than approach each election hat in hand.

The centralized associations from the new middle class had exactly the opposite effect on party discipline. When an office-seeker accepted their support, he was expected in return to abide by their platforms and their ideals. Unlike such precursors as the Grand Army of the Republic or the American Iron and Steel Association, which had become adjuncts to the Republican party, the new-middle-class groups showed far less regard for the party as such. A man became known as the candidate of the chamber of commerce or the social workers, whatever his party label, and in time a slate might appear as the candidates of Toledo's Independents or Chicago's Municipal Voters' League. Moreover, the directors of these organizations, often zestful political amateurs, usually held a tight rein on all funds. Such groups compiled impressive local gains early in the century; the most effective among them approximated small, autonomous political units with all the paraphernalia for nominating, electing, and controlling a handful of officials. Little wonder, then, that party professionals, especially Republicans, preferred corporate executives to earnest, middle-class reformers.

Lobbying underwent comparable changes around 1900. A time-honored and universally condemned device, it had never been the simple, static technique its enemies claimed. Again, the major corporations were the earliest experimenters. As long as they had viewed political problems as isolated challenges, they had awaited a crisis before throwing together a lobby. The railroad wanted a land grant or the utility a franchise, the insurance firm opposed a tax bill or the oil company a restriction on monopoly. Then, as their critics described the process, corporate agents—wealthy, smiling, and persuasive—would "descend upon the legislature." As formidable as it seemed to an onlooker, lobbying of that sort was casual, almost sloppy, predicated on the assumption that legislatures usually did not matter. Precisely that assumption had to be abandoned by the nineties, and along with it went the cavalier approach to lobbying. Perpetual ferment in dozens of states demanded the corporate leader's constant attention, so he assigned full-time agents to the important posts. He needed a continuous flow of political information, so he paid strategically placed men to supply it. He required coordination, so he often hired a manager to supervise these many local activities. Andrew Hamilton, whose expenses in the decade after 1895 exceeded a million dollars, directed a nationwide network of lobbies for New York Life Insurance with as much skill in his line as the company's president demonstrated in his. Other organizations adopted the same systematic approach on a smaller scale, employing a professional agent of their own or pooling resources in order to share one. The American Medical Association expected its county and state directors to train themselves in politics. Strictly local leagues simply designated men—or women—to follow the city council throughout its sessions.

Scores of alert, critical eyes, representing thousands of crucial dollars and votes, radically altered the operation of a legislature, and political managers discovered that they could no more dispense with the lobbyists than could the organizations who had hired them. Now it was the politician who required information. In former years, when agents had come from a corporation or a church league with their bill, lobbyists had been self-evident propositions. Everyone had known what they wanted and had either bowed or resisted. After 1900, that simple precision vanished. Varieties of competing organizations, often with diversified programs, left the legislative leader without the basis for decisions. Nor could he depend upon partisan loyalties to mellow their spirits. Only if the lobbyists translated the wishes of their clients, negotiated with other agents, and offered reasonable assurance of how their constituents would react to particular measures could the political broker calculate the risks and fashion the compromises. The reliable lobbyist had become an indispensable intermediary in representative government.

Relatively, however, legislatures were declining in importance. People who wanted a definite, self-contained political favor—a tariff or a tax exemption—had almost always sought it in the form of a law. Services of an indefinite duration covering somewhat nebulous fields—railroad regulation, for example—just as naturally led them to the administrators. Although many corporate executives had long added state and local officials to the payroll as a matter of course, no precedents really existed for the imaginative uses of administration as a means to widespread, long-range control. After 1900 the dynamics of American politics increasingly concentrated in administration, where businessmen sought freedom from antimonopoly rules, farmers the basis for modern marketing, urban reformers the techniques for economy or systematic law enforcement, professionals the right to police their fields, and countless conflicting interests the mechanisms for adjustment and compromise. To a striking degree, the major legislative battles now involved which administrative agencies would receive what mandates under whose supervision.

By far the most important part of that political revolution transformed the national government. Because most progressives chose to concentrate initially upon a government close at hand and because few of them had easy access to national power, the pressure for change mounted more slowly in Washington than it did in the city halls and state capitols. Nevertheless, a rudimentary national progressivism was already taking shape around 1900. Some reformers were turning to Washington because they needed truly national solutions to their problems. Even more looked there because the scope of their operations, though far less than nationwide, had still entangled them in too many conflicting jurisdictions. Others simply sought national weapons to use in their local wars.

One issue of rising concern was the conservation and rational management of natural resources. The most complicated political story of its time, the movement for conservation grew out of the confusion created over many decades of feverish exploitation. Railroad promoters and lumber kings, land speculators and mine owners, stockmen and farmers—a few rich men growing richer and many poor ones forever scrambling—had ripped through forests, abused precious water supplies, squandered minerals, and stripped grazing lands in a rape of Gargantuan proportions. By the end of the nineteenth century, enough bitter conflicts and blasted dreams had combined with a vague sense of diminishing bounty to generate a strong demand for order. Yet despite an assumption that somehow Washington should be tackling the big issues, neither the tradition nor the means for effective action existed. In what passed for public policy, innumerable centers of power, located mostly in the states that held the natural resources, had made the important decisions. The few Federal laws passed in the name of conservation had scarcely changed even the rules of procedure. Early in the twentieth century these feelings were beginning to acquire direction and consistent purpose.

A second issue was railroad regulation. The process of consolidating the railroads had gained such momentum during the nineties that within a few more years seven large groups dominated the nation's system. At each step the reorganizations followed Morgan's original formula: a heavy burden of common stock and, of course, generous bonuses for the financiers. Apparently no group of Americans had greater confidence in their nation's future, for only an unprecedented prosperity could have relieved that mountainous debt. As it was, the good times early in the century were not good enough. The roads still required investments they could no longer attract. Consequently they raised rates. Their customers protested; Wall Street's agents replied that they had no choice. Meanwhile, the carriers' equipment deteriorated and their services remained undependable. By 1900 a small but growing number of militants, largely new-middle-class businessmen who shipped to and from the major cities of the Midwest, had already lost faith in the value of piecemeal controls through state government and were demanding an expansion of the Interstate Commerce Commission's powers.

At the same time, certain magnates were themselves developing a new interest in the national government. The passion for stability in business had grown even more urgent during the depression of the nineties, and America's tiny elite of finance capitalists eagerly awaited an opportunity to apply its techniques of reorganization to other portions of the economy. In 1899 Standard Oil publicized the latest device for these experiments when it changed into a holding company, a more flexible, enduring form than the trust, less susceptible to prosecution, and uniquely suited to the liberal issuance of common stock. In a trend that included many smaller enterprises as well, companies of all sorts hastened to the states with the laxest incorporation laws—New Jersey, the early favorite, issued about two thousand charters each year from 1899 to 1901—and overnight the face of American business seemed transformed. Most prominent were the giant new holding companies, climaxed in 1901 by the nation's first billion-dollar concern, United States Steel. Behind these lurked the master organizers: Morgan; Kuhn, Loeb; the National City Bank of New York; Lee, Higginson of Boston; and a number of powerful financial satellites, most of which revolved about Morgan's firm.

The view was far more impressive at a distance. Each year more enterprising men competed with the original finance capitalists for access to America's investment surplus. Though Morgan's towering prestige enabled him to eliminate some of the least scrupulous independents during the panic of 1907, others always materialized, disrupting the work of the mighty. The magnates also struggled with the consequences of their own greed, as untimely and hollow promotions periodically glutted the stock exchanges. Their paper dragons, moreover, faced the challenges of an increasingly diversified urban market which was confusing executives throughout the business system. Little wonder that huge enterprises like Standard Oil and U.S. Steel not only lost ground to their competitors but often did not even contest the trend. It was enough to consolidate what they had, try to keep abreast of technological changes and new sources of raw materials, and seek some way of moderating the flux about them.

The old problems of establishing and maintaining order, then, continued without pause. If conditions never approached the chaos of the late nineteenth century, in the twentieth they produced a more conscious sense of individual helplessness. The best minds in business, it appeared, were not equal to the task. In part, the disappointments stemmed from higher expectations. Once stability had meant no more than the grossest forms of economic discipline; now it increasingly suggested elaborate patterns that might cover everything in a field of business from wages to a division of the market. Perhaps, as a few thoughtful corporate leaders were wondering, the national government could somehow be used to achieve that order which persistently eluded them when they acted alone.

At the same time, a rising group of financiers from the major cities of the Midwest were demanding a revision of the nation's archaic banking and currency laws in an effort to free themselves from the dominance of New York. In place of the ethical economics of the gold standard, they argued a technical case, insisting upon a currency geared to commercial and industrial credits so that it would automatically expand and contract in response to changing business conditions. In a similar spirit, an assortment of moderately prosperous businessmen seeking cheap raw materials or increased foreign trade called for reforms that would adjust the nation's import duties year by year without necessitating a complete overhaul of the tariff laws.

These basic issues and many lesser ones combined to force major changes in congressional procedure. In 1890, largely out of a desire for tighter party discipline, Speaker Thomas B. Reed had applied a sweeping set of new rules which enabled him to reward and punish through a variety of controls, especially his regulation of day-to-day proceedings in the House. But if Reed's coup had originated in partisan ambition, the rules remained only because of a bipartisan need to dispatch more business. Equally as impressive, the demands for greater efficiency in the Senate had placed almost dictatorial power in the hands of a few legislative directors, particularly Rhode Island's Senator Nelson Aldrich. The fundamental changes, however, came after 1900 with the flood of broad, new issues requiring national action. The premium on speed, efficiency, and technical competence mounted sharply. Powerful, impatient groups would no longer wait for a decade's deliberation. Far heavier responsibilities passed to the committees; the committees in turn relied increasingly upon experts. Congressmen learned that success meant specialization, and competition for that one choice committee assignment grew vicious. When rebels in the House broke Speaker Joseph Cannon's arbitrary rule in 1910, they made certain that no member could receive a place on more than one major committee and that each member who had won his vital post would retain it. During these same years the arrival of congressmen infected by the spirit of the new middle class and relatively indifferent to partisan obligations was compounding the problems of the party managers.

Though not so readily evident at the time, leadership in Congress had fallen beyond the capacity of congressmen, and the executive was rapidly acquiring that responsibility. Neither house was constituted to evaluate an array of complicated demands, place them in order of preference, pass on them swiftly, and then follow the process of administration. The executive, on the other hand, was uniquely situated to guide these functions. The conditions demanding much more joined with a man wanting much more when Theodore Roosevelt, scion of one of New York's great patrician families, became president on the assassination of William McKinley in September 1901.

A man of unlovely traits who relished killing human beings, nursed harsh personal prejudices, and juggled facts to enhance his fame, Roosevelt was at the same time an extraordinarily vital person whose effervescence and extrovertive political style appeared to catch the spirit of the nation—at least of that nation to which a great many citizens wanted to belong. For millions of Americans this politician, soldier, author, hunter, cowboy, and forceful preacher of the balanced banalities provided a delightful, warming show. Countless reformers, mistaking vigor for directness, adored him. Upon hearing of his death in 1919, the progressive Donald Richberg recalled, "I could only press my face into the pillow and cry like a child. There were many others who wept that day." Behind the flashing teeth and flailing arms lay a keen-edged intelligence and an insatiable ambition for power within the framework of popular acclaim. No one of his time better understood the operations of American politics, and no one more shrewdly turned his knowledge to the service of personal glory.

Roosevelt inherited an office of rising prominence. Those fears of the nineties which ultimately focused upon the horror Bryan would perpetrate if elected had already invested the presidency with a new importance. Significantly, the contributions that had poured in upon Hanna in 1896 returned again in 1900, establishing a pattern for Republican presidential campaigns. Once a man won the nomination he stepped apart from the rest of the candidates. A largely impersonal fund—an investment in the office—carried him the rest of the way. Of course if a presumed radical such as Robert La Follette had ever led the party, the tradition would have snapped. Yet only safe Republicans were nominated, and an ample fund always materialized. In that tacit fashion, a new definition for the presidency had already received financial form before Roosevelt's arrival, a definition with great potential and sharp limitations.

Soon after assuming office, Roosevelt set three interrelated goals: to establish himself as the pre-eminent figure in the Republican party, to elevate the executive as the dominant force in national government, and to make that government the most important single influence in national affairs. At almost every step he encountered the peculiar power of a few corporate and financial magnates, and he quickly marked these men as his primary opponents. More often than not, it was at this point that Roosevelt's urge to power and the several national progressive movements intersected. To the degree that he found personal relevance in their proposals, he joined the cause. An imperious master as well as an invaluable ally, he then tailored each project to fit his special style, leaving a private stamp on the whole of the early national movement.

In his drive for power Roosevelt relied heavily upon the ambitions and talents of his subordinates. An avid aggrandizer, the president understood and encouraged those aggrandizing executive officials who sought to construct small empires out of the growing demand for public management. He enjoyed a particularly close relationship with the well-born and hard-driving chief of the Division of Forestry, Gifford Pinchot, whose small corps of scientific experts was spreading the gospel of rational land use throughout the country. While Roosevelt more than doubled the acreage of the public reserve, Pinchot and his colleagues were rapidly extending a system of contracts for its regulated, private development. In a remarkably short span, the president and these specialists had built a permanent base within the executive for the supervision of natural resources. In 1903 Roosevelt also fought successfully to include a Bureau of Corporations in the new Department of Commerce and Labor, then urged its staff to expand their investigation and informal regulation of large business enterprises. Meanwhile, with far less assistance from the president, the ambitious Dr. Harvey Wiley, chief chemist in the Department of Agriculture, was coordinating a movement for pure food and drugs from an assortment of women, doctors, scientists, and those manufacturers and distributors who hoped a mild regulation would destroy their marginal competitors. With the Pure Food and Drug Act of 1906, the executive was headquarters for still another experiment in bureaucratic reform.

Drawing upon the slack resources of his office, Roosevelt employed an exceptional range of devices to spotlight his favorite issues and force congressional action. Special conferences, dramatic investigations, public condemnations, and private encouragement all found a place in the master's repertory. He negotiated with the legislative chieftains through a mixture of implied threats, quiet bargains, and clever flattery. Roosevelt's extraordinary ability to leave men believing that they, and they alone, enjoyed his most intimate confidence pacified innumerable opponents and won the services of many a deluded lieutenant. Increasingly the important bills, including those to outlaw rebating by the railroads, regulate the food and drug industries, and revise the Sherman Antitrust Act, were either drafted in an executive department or cleared there before they were introduced. This kind of leadership meant, of course, that those reforms the president rejected rarely survived in Congress. Roosevelt's unwillingness to support major changes in the tariff or in the financial system guaranteed that for a time Congress would meet neither of these basic problems. Moreover, his commitment to a strong, stable Republican party—the indispensable means to his influence—led him to protect both its congressional leaders and its far-flung network of professionals.

Throughout his tenure Roosevelt derived maximum benefit from each of the government's major achievements—"my policies," as he called them. After business shippers had struggled for years to strengthen the Interstate Commerce Commission, he entered late in the battle, helped to pass the Hepburn Act of 1906—perhaps the most significant law of his presidency—and received much of the credit for establishing the commission as a substantial regulatory agency. In the same fashion, he identified himself with the Pure Food and Drug Act by a last-minute assault against the meat-packing industry which mobilized support behind the bill. One shrewd, successful prosecution of a giant railroad combination gave him the reputation of "trust-buster," although he had little use for the Sherman Act's sledge-hammer approach.

Roosevelt, in other words, transformed important contributions into dramatic, personal victories. Both his overwhelming election in 1904 and the widespread demands in 1907 and 1908 that he seek another term testified to the magician's skill. Self-advertisement was part of the process by which he elevated the president as party leader in an entirely new sense. As interest increasingly riveted upon what Congress did instead of what congressmen said, it was the president who fixed the gauge for judgment. How did congressional behavior measure against his program—against "my policies"? What support had the Republicans, or any individual Republican provided? Because the president had a party label, every four years the party had a national record.

What a profound change from the days of Benjamin Harrison! Then the only bills composed in executive offices had been minor enough to pass the most jealous and imperious congressional scrutiny, often so inconsequential the president had not even known of them. Neither of the presidents succeeding Grover Cleveland had built upon that man's isolated initiatives in legislative policy, any more than Cleveland himself had done. No president from Hayes through Cleveland had been more than a factional leader, nor had a congressman's party standing suffered—even if his patronage sometimes did—simply because he voted with an antipresidential bloc. If McKinley surrounded himself with the aura of a general party leader, he had still led the Republicans with slogans, not programs. Like his predecessors, he had used his office to harmonize partisan differences and to ensure his re-election, not to guide Congress through the steps of legislation.

Now the subdivisions of the executive had assumed the task of studying and resolving the big problems. The president was expected to give priorities, then focus congressional attention on an issue at a time; in other words, provide and direct a rather precise legislative program. The president initiated, and Congress, if it wished, could veto. William Howard Taft would run in 1908 on Roosevelt's record, an innovation of tremendous consequence in national elections.

At the center of this revolution lay the same flexible, adaptive approach that characterized the reforms in city and state government. Each new administrative power, from the expansion of Pinchot's conservation program to the birth of an effective Interstate Commerce Commission, was predicated upon the continuous, expert management of indeterminate processes. Officials inclined in certain directions rather than committing themselves to specific goals. "The American mind . . . loves to see clear and definite solutions. . . ," wrote the president's friend Albert Shaw. "But the Roosevelt policy . . . makes [them] largely a matter of experiment from time to time to discover the just degree and method of public control."

Nothing better illustrated the new spirit than the gradual emergence of a policy toward giant corporations. Initially Roosevelt adopted the tactics of the skirmisher. Through selective antitrust prosecutions, investigations by the Bureau of Corporations, and such unpredictable intrusions as his interference in the anthracite strike of 1902, he would teach the nation's magnates at whose sufferance they operated. In a game of wills, of feints and thrusts, he hoped to maneuver them into the proper attitude of deference. Though Roosevelt overestimated the effect of these lessons, he had nonetheless found a raw nerve. Just when corporate leaders were disturbed by an inability to consolidate their empires, they confronted an unpredictable government whose chief executive seemed capable at any time of doing his worst.

Some magnates tried rather clumsily to protect themselves through straightforward deals with the executive, the sort of self-contained, man-to-man bargains traditional to nineteenth-century politics. Others waited grimly until the storm passed. Two men in Morgan's entourage—Elbert H. Gary, the unctuous chairman of U.S. Steel, and George Perkins, Morgan's aggressive young political partner—had the imagination to experiment. In an effort to immunize U.S. Steel and International Harvester (and by implication all of Morgan's major interests), they arranged a general understanding with Roosevelt by which, as the magnates interpreted it, they would cooperate in any investigation by the Bureau of Corporations in return for a guarantee of their companies' legality through private negotiations with the executive. A gentlemen's agreement between reasonable people: it was the natural extension of Wall Street's stock in trade.

Too clever to bind himself, Roosevelt still found this kind of arrangement very congenial. Of course he must always reserve the power to determine which corporations were the good ones and which the bad. Nevertheless, the agreement with Morgan's men seemed to combine a promise of stability with an essential subordination to executive direction. That appeared to be as far as anyone could go. Other big businessmen who talked favorably of a benign national regulation retreated at the first signs of trouble—the sudden, noisy demands in 1905 for meat inspection, or New York State's investigations that same year of chicanery between insurance executives and Wall Street bankers.

Roosevelt did not remain in office long enough to institutionalize his policy. Yet the parties to the gentlemen's agreement had roughed out a pattern that would eventually cover a large portion of progressive reform. The management of indeterminate processes invited exactly this kind of loose understanding. In order to achieve the adaptable order that both public officials and private interests sought, some sense of mutual purpose, some accommodation that still allowed each side ample room to maneuver, was considered indispensable. The bureaucratic answer, in other words, made reform a function of continuing, close negotiations.

Richard L. McCormick

The Discovery That Business Corrupts Politics: A Reappraisal of the Origins of Progressivism

Richard L. McCormick, a distinguished historian, is president of the University of Washington in Seattle. Until 1979, when he wrote this article, historians, following Wiebe's lead, saw the Progressive Era as a triumph for business and as the climax of a drive to organize society. If Progressivism amounted simply to a more efficient way of doing things that preserved the status quo, many historians in the 1970s and 1980s began to doubt that real reform had ever taken place. Perhaps business interests orchestrated Progressive Era changes to prevent anyone from challenging their power and to institutionalize their position in a rapidly changing society. In other words, perhaps Progressivism was simply a form of middle-class social control.

McCormick reminds us that causes cannot be discerned from results. Perhaps Progressivism restructured chaotic commerce, but shoring up business was not its aim, he argues. In the mid-1890s, people discovered with horror the extent of business corruption and rapacity. They worried that government as a whole was not strong enough to stand up to business. Through exposure of these problems on a municipal and state level, people began to demand full disclosure of business–government deals and to strengthen municipalities' and states' regulatory powers.

While citizens experienced business corruption at the local level, they also realized that the federal government must be expanded, primarily through the presidency and a new administrative regulatory structure. The federal government must monitor commerce and stand up to the interests of capital when they clashed with the public good. Certainly the regulatory task remained unfinished at the end of the Progressive Era. But the basic bargain—that business and governmental relationships should be open to public scrutiny and based on fair practices—forged the standard that the American people came to expect.

Questions for a Closer Reading

1. McCormick states, "Shortly after 1900, American politics and government experienced a . . . rather rapid transformation that affected both the patterns of popular political involvement and the nature and functions of government itself." Name two of the changes to which he refers and determine how those changes affected the role of government.

2. Compare McCormick's argument with Wiebe's. What kind of evidence does each use to make his argument? Find two contrasting quotes on business from each article and explain their differences.

3. Imagine that you live in a mid-sized urban area in 1905. What indications might you see around you of business involvement in municipal government and public services? How might corruption in the relationship between business and government on a local level affect your daily life?

4. What forces came together to expose the ways in which business had corrupted politics, and what methods did those forces use to expose them? Compare these approaches with how business is regulated and reformed today. Think of an industry that has recently come under fire. Who is criticizing it? What methods are they using? What is the role of government in this process?

5. What safeguards did Progressives enact to correct the problem of politics being corrupted by business? Many people today recommend privatization of what has been government's responsibility, for example, private companies running prisons. Based on the Progressive experience, what sort of regulation would you propose to ensure that privately run companies operating public services would continue to serve the public fairly and not corrupt government?

The Discovery That Business Corrupts Politics: A Reappraisal of the Origins of Progressivism

Almost any history textbook that covers the Progressive era and was written at least twenty years ago tells how early-twentieth-century Americans discovered how big business interests were corrupting politics in quest of special privileges and how an outraged people acted to reform the perceived evils. Commonly, the narrative offers ample anecdotal evidence to support this tale of scandal and reform. The autobiographies of leading progressives—including Theodore Roosevelt, Robert M. La Follette, William Allen White, Frederic C. Howe, and Lincoln Steffens, among others—are frequently cited, because all of them recounted the purported awakening of their authors to the corrupt politico-business alliance.[1] Muckraking journalism, not only by Steffens but also by David Graham Phillips, Charles E. Russell, Ray Stannard Baker, and numerous others, is often drawn upon too, along with evidence that the magazines for which they wrote achieved unprecedented circulation. Political speeches, party platforms, and newspaper editorials by the hundreds are also offered to buttress the contention that Americans of the early 1900s discovered the prevalence of illicit business influence in politics and demanded its removal. But all of this evidence would probably fail to persuade historians today that the old textbook scenario for progressivism is correct.

And for good reason. Every prominent interpretation of the Progressive movement now encourages us not to take the outcry against politico-business corruption too seriously. Some historians have seen progressivism as dichotomous: alongside the individualist, antibusiness strain of reform stood an equally vocal, and ultimately more successful, school that accepted industrial growth and sought even closer cooperation between

Richard L. McCormick, "The Discovery That Business Corrupts Politics: A Reappraisal of the Origins of Progressivism," *American Historical Review*, 86, no. 2 (April 1981), 247–74.

business and government.[2] Other recent interpreters have described progressivism as a pluralistic movement of diverse groups, including businessmen, who came together when their interests coincided and worked separately when they did not.[3] Still other historians have seen businessmen themselves as the key progressives, whose methods and techniques were copied by other reformers.[4] Whichever view of the movement they have favored, historians have increasingly recognized the Progressive Era as the age when Americans accommodated, rather than tried to escape, large-scale business organizations and their methods.[5] More often than not, the achievement of what used to be called reform now appears to have benefited big business interests. If our aim is to grasp the results and meaning of progressivism, the evidence in the typical textbook seems to lead in the wrong direction.

The currently dominant "organizational" interpretation of the Progressive movement has particularly little room for such evidence. Led by Samuel P. Hays and Robert H. Wiebe, a number of scholars have located the progressive impulse in the drive of newly formed business and professional groups to achieve their goals through organization and expertise. In a related study, Louis Galambos has described the progressive outcry against the trusts as merely a phase in the nation's growing acceptance of large corporations, and, with Hays and Wiebe, he has suggested that the rhetorical attack on business came to very little. The distinctive achievement of this interpretation lies in its account of how in the early twentieth century the United States became an organized, bureaucratic society whose model institution was the large corporation. Where reformers of the 1880s and 1890s had sought to resist the forces of industrialism, or at least to prevent their penetration of the local community, the progressives of the early 1900s accepted an industrial society and concentrated their efforts on controlling, ordering, and improving it. No interpretation of the era based on ideological evidence of a battle between the "people" and the "interests" can capture the enormous complexity of the adjustments to industrialism worked out by different social groups. Hays and Wiebe have succeeded better than any previous historians in describing and characterizing those adjustments and placing them in the context of large social and economic changes. In this light the progressives' claims to have discovered and opposed the corruption of politics by business seem to become a curiosity of the era, not a clue to its meaning, a diversion to the serious historian exploring the organizational achievements that constituted true progressivism, a suitable subject for old textbooks.[6]

Despite its great strengths, however, the organizational model neglects too much.[7] Missing is the progressives' moral intensity. Missing, too, are their surprise and animation upon discovering political and social evils.

Also absent are their own explanations of what they felt and what they were doing. And absent, above all, is a description, much less an analysis, of the particular political circumstances from which progressivism emerged in the first years of the twentieth century. In place of these vivid actualities, the organizational historians offer a vague account of what motivated the reformers who advocated bureaucratic solutions and an exaggerated estimation of their capacity to predict and control events. Actually, progressive reform was not characterized by remarkable rationality or foresight; nor were the "organizers" always at the forefront of the movement. Often the results the progressives achieved were unexpected and ironical; and, along the way, crucial roles were sometimes played by men and ideas that, in the end, met defeat.

The perception that privileged businesses corrupted politics was one such ultimately unsuccessful idea of particular short-run instrumentality. Especially in the cities and states, around the middle of the first decade of the twentieth century, the discovery of such corruption precipitated crises that led to the most significant political changes of the time. When the crises had passed, the results for political participation and public policy were roughly those that the organizational interpretation predicts, but the way these changes came about is far from adequately described by that thesis. The pages that follow here sketch an account of political change in the early twentieth century and show how the discovery of politico-business corruption played this central, transforming role—though not with quite the same results that the old textbooks describe.

Admittedly, to interpret progressivism on the basis of its political and governmental side is a more risky endeavor than it once was. Indeed, a major thrust of contemporary scholarship has been to subordinate the Progressive Era's political achievements to the larger social and economic changes associated with what Wiebe has called "the process of America's modernization."[8] From such a perspective, "developments in politics" become, as John C. Burnham has observed, "mere epiphenomena of more basic forces and changes."[9] But what if political behavior fails to fit trends that the rest of society seems to be experiencing? What conclusions are to be drawn, for instance, from the observation that American political rhetoric was preoccupied with attacking corporations at precisely the moment in the early twentieth century when such businesses were becoming ascendant in economic and social life? One approach simply ignores the anomalous behavior or, at most, considers it spurious or deceptive. Another answer lies in the notions that American politics is fundamentally discontinuous with the rest of national life and that, as several political scientists have suggested, it has always retained a "premodern" character.[10] A better solution, however, rests upon a close study of the ways in which apparently anachronistic political events and the ideas they inspired became essential catalysts for "modernizing" developments. Studied in this manner, politics has more to tell us about progressivism than contemporary wisdom generally admits.

Shortly after 1900, American politics and government experienced a decisive and rather rapid transformation that affected both the patterns of popular political involvement and the nature and functions of government itself. To be sure, the changes were not revolutionary, but, considering how relatively undevelopmental the political system of the United States has been, they are of considerable historical importance. The basic features of this political transformation can be easily described, but its causes and significance are somewhat more difficult to grasp.

One important category of change involved the manner and methods of popular participation in politics. For most of the nineteenth century, high rates of partisan voting—based on complex sectional, cultural, and communal influences—formed the American people's main means of political expression and involvement. Only in exceptional circumstances did most individuals or groups rely on nonelectoral methods of influencing the government. Indeed, almost no such means existed within the normal bounds of politics. After 1900, this structure of political participation changed. Voter turnout fell, and, even among those electors who remained active, pure and simple partisanship became less pervasive. At approximately the same time, interest-group organizations of all sorts successfully forged permanent, nonelectoral means of influencing the government and its agencies. Only recently have historians begun to explore with care what caused these changes in the patterns of political participation and to delineate the redistribution of power that they entailed.[11]

American governance, too, went through a fundamental transition in the early 1900s. Wiebe has accurately described it as the emergence of "a government broadly and continuously involved in society's operations."[12] Both the institutions of government and the content of policy reflected the change. Where the legislature had been the dominant branch of government at every level, lawmakers now saw their power curtailed by an enlarged executive and, even more, by the creation of an essentially new branch of government composed of administrative boards and agencies. Where nineteenth-century policy had generally focused on distinct groups and locales (most characteristically through the distribution of resources and privileges to enterprising individuals and corporations), the government now began to take explicit account of clashing interests and to assume the responsibility for mitigating their conflicts through regulation, administration, and planning. In 1900, government did very little in the way of recognizing and adjusting group differences. Fifteen years later, innumerable policies committed officials to that formal purpose and provided the bureaucratic structures for achieving it.[13]

Most political historians consider these changes to be the products of long-term social and economic developments. Accordingly, they have devoted much of their attention to tracing the interconnecting paths leading from industrialization, urbanization, and immigration to the political and governmental responses. Some of the general trends have been firmly documented in scholarship: the organization of functional groups whose needs the established political parties could not meet; the creation of new demands for government policies to make life bearable in crowded cities, where huge industries were located; and the determination of certain cultural and economic groups to curtail the political power of people they considered threatening. All of these developments, along with others, occurred over a period of decades — now speeded, now slowed by depression, migration, prosperity, fortune, and the talents of individual men and women.

Yet, given the long-term forces involved, it is notable how suddenly the main elements of the new political order went into place. The first fifteen years of the twentieth century witnessed most of the changes; more precisely, the brief period from 1904 to 1908 saw a remarkably compressed political transformation. During these years the regulatory revolution peaked; new and powerful agencies of government came into being everywhere.[14] At the same time, voter turnout declined, ticket-splitting increased, and organized social, economic, and reform-minded groups began to exercise power more systematically than ever before.[15] An understanding of how the new polity crystallized so rapidly can be obtained by exploring, first, the latent threat to the old system represented by fears of "corruption"; then, the pressures for political change that had built up by about 1904; and, finally, the way in which the old fears abruptly took on new meaning and inspired a resolution of the crisis.

Long before 1900 — indeed, since before the Revolution — Americans had been aware that governmental promotion of private interests, which became the dominant form of nineteenth-century economic policy, carried with it risks of corruption. From the English opposition of Walpole's day, colonists in America had absorbed the theory that commercial development threatened republican government in two ways: (1) by spreading greed, extravagance, and luxury among the people; and (2) by encouraging a designing ministry to conspire with monied interests for the purpose of overwhelming the independence of the legislature. Neither theme ever entirely disappeared from American politics, although each was significantly revised as time passed. For Jeffersonians in the 1790s, as Lance Banning has demonstrated, both understandings remained substantially intact. In their belief, Alexander Hamilton's program of public aid to commercial enterprises would inevitably make an agrarian people less virtuous and would also create a phalanx of privileged interests—including bank directors, speculators, and stock-jobbers—pledged to support the administration faction that had nurtured them. Even after classical republican thought waned and the structure of government-business relations changed, these eighteenth-century fears that corruption inevitably flowed from government-assisted commercial development continued to echo in American politics.[16]

For much of the nineteenth century, as Fred Somkin has shown, thoughtful citizens remained ambivalent about economic abundance, because they feared its potential to corrupt them and their government. "Over and over again," Somkin stated, "Americans called attention to the danger which prosperity posed for the safety of free institutions and for the maintenance of republicanism."[17] In the 1830s the Democratic Party's official ideology began to give voice to these fears. Using language similar to that of Walpole's and Hamilton's critics, Andrew Jackson decried "special privileges" from government as dangerous to liberty and demanded their abolition. Much of his wrath was directed against the Second Bank of the United States. That "monster," he said, was "a vast electioneering engine"; it has "already attempted to subject the government to its will." The Bank clearly raised the question of "whether the people of the United States are to govern . . . or whether the power and money of a great corporation are to be secretly exerted to influence their judgment and control their decisions." In a different context Jackson made the point with simple clarity: "Money," he said, "is power." Yet Jackson's anti-Bank rhetoric also carried a new understanding of politico-business corruption, different from that of the eighteenth century. For the danger that Jackson apprehended came not from a corrupt ministry, whose tool the monied interests were, but from privileged monsters, acting independently from public authorities and presenting a danger not only to the government but also to the welfare of other social and economic groups ("the farmers, mechanics, and laborers") whose interests conflicted with theirs. Jackson's remedy was to scale down governmental undertakings, on the grounds that public privileges led to both corruption and inequality.[18]

Despite the prestige that Jackson lent to the attack on privilege, it was not a predominant fear for Americans in the nineteenth century. So many forms of thought and avarice disguised the dangers Jackson saw. First of

all, Americans were far from agreed that governmental assistance for some
groups hurt the rest, as he proclaimed. Both the "commonwealth" notion
of a harmonious community and its successor, the Whig-Republican concept of interlocking producer interests, suggested that economic benefits
from government would be shared throughout society. Even when differences emerged over who should get what, an abundance of land and
resources disguised the conflicts, while the inherent divisibility of public
benefits encouraged their widespread distribution. Especially at the state
and local levels, Democrats, as well as Whigs and Republicans, freely suc-
cumbed to the nearly universal desire for government aid. Not to have
done so would have been as remarkable as to have withheld patronage
from deserving partisans.[19] Nor, in the second place, was it evident to most
nineteenth-century Americans that private interests represented a threat
to the commonweal. While their eighteenth-century republican heritage
warned them of the danger to free government from a designing ministry
that manipulated monied interests, classical economics denied that there
was a comparable danger to the public from private enterprises that were
independent of the government. Indeed, the public–private distinction
tended to be blurred for nineteenth-century Americans, and not until it
came into focus did new threats of politico-business corruption seem as
real as the old ones had in the 1700s.[20]

As time passed, Jackson's Democratic Party proved to be a weak vehicle
for the insight that privileged businesses corrupted politics and government. The party's platforms, which in the 1840s had declared a national
bank "dangerous to our republican institutions," afterwards dropped such
rhetoric. The party of Stephen A. Douglas, Samuel J. Tilden, and Grover
Cleveland all but abandoned serious criticism of politico-business corruption. Cleveland's annual message of 1887, which he devoted wholly to
the tariff issue, stands as the Gilded Age's equivalent to Jackson's Bank
veto. But, unlike Jackson, Cleveland made his case entirely on economic
grounds and did not suggest that the protected interests corrupted government. Nor did William Jennings Bryan pay much attention to the
theme in 1896. Unlike his Populist supporters who charged that public
officials had "basely surrendered . . . to corporate monopolies," the Democrat Bryan made only fleeting mention of the political influence of big corporations or the danger to liberty from privileged businesses.[21]

From outside the political mainstream, the danger was more visible.
Workingmen's parties, Mugwumps, Greenbackers, Prohibitionists, and
Populists all voiced their own versions of the accusation that business corrupted politics and government. The Greenbackers charged that the
major parties were tools of the monopolies; the Prohibitionists believed
that the liquor corporations endangered free institutions; and the Populists

powerfully indicted both the Democrats and Republicans for truckling to the interests "to secure corruption funds from the millionaires." In *Progress and Poverty* (1879), Henry George asked, "Is there not growing up among us a class who have all the power . . . ? We have simple citizens who control thousands of miles of railroad, millions of acres of land, the means of livelihood of great numbers of men; who name the governors of sovereign states as they name their clerks, choose senators as they choose attorneys, and whose will is as supreme with legislatures as that of a French king sitting in a bed of justice."[22] But these were the voices of dissenters and frail minorities. Their accusations of corruption posed a latent challenge to an economic policy based on distributing privileges to private interests, but for most of the nineteenth century their warnings were not widely accepted or even listened to by the political majority.

The late 1860s and early and mid-1870s, however, offer an apparent exception. These were the years when the Crédit Mobilier* and other scandals—local and national—aroused a furor against politico-business corruption. "Perhaps the offense most discredited by the exposures," according to C. Vann Woodward, "was the corrupting of politicians to secure government subsidies and grants to big corporations—particularly railroads." For several years, in consequence, there was a widespread revulsion against a policy of bestowing public privileges and benefits on private companies. Editorializing in 1873 on the Crédit Mobilier scandal, E. L. Godkin of the *Nation* declared, "The remedy is simple. The Government must get out of the 'protective' business and the 'subsidy' business and the 'improvement' and the 'development' business. It must let trade, and commerce, and manufactures, and steamboats, and railroads, and telegraphs alone. It cannot touch them without breeding corruption." Yet even in the mid-1870s, by Woodward's own account, it was possible for railroad and other promoters, especially in the South and Midwest, to organize local meetings that rekindled the fervor for subsidies in town after town. The fear of corruption that Godkin voiced simply was not compelling enough to override the demand for policies of unchecked promotion.[23]

Even the nineteenth century's most brilliant and sustained analysis of business and politics—that provided by the Adams brothers, Charles Francis, Jr. and Henry, in their *Chapters of Erie* (1871)—failed to portray the danger convincingly. Recounting the classic Gilded Age roguery of Jay Gould and Jim Fisk, including their corruption of courts and legislatures and their influence on the president himself, the Adamses warned that, as

---

*In 1873 Americans discovered that the Crédit Mobilier of America, the construction company set up to build the Union Pacific Railroad, had bribed congressmen by selling them stock at discount rates in return for legislation that gave the company public land and rights of way.

Henry put it, "the day is at hand when corporations . . . —having created a system of quiet but irresistible corruption—will ultimately succeed in directing government itself." But the Adams brothers presented Gould and Fisk as so fantastic that readers could not believe that ordinary businessmen could accomplish such feats. Rather than describing a process of politico-business corruption, the Adamses gave only the dramatic particulars of it. Words like "astounding," "unique," and "extraordinary" marked their account. Writing of the effort by Gould and Fisk to corner the market on gold in 1869, Henry said, "Even the most dramatic of modern authors, even Balzac himself, . . . or Alexandre Dumas, with all his extravagance of imagination, never have reached a conception bolder or more melodramatic than this, nor have they ever ventured to conceive a plot so enormous, or a catastrophe so original." Far from supporting the Adamses' thesis, such descriptions must have undermined it by raising doubts that what Gould and Fisk did could be widely or systematically repeated.[24]

Expressed by third parties and by elite spokesmen like Godkin and the Adamses, the fear that business corrupted politics exerted only minor influence in the late nineteenth century. When they recognized corruption, ordinary people seem to have blamed "bad" politicians, like James G. Blaine, and to have considered the businessmen guiltless. Even when Americans saw that corruption involved the use of money, they showed more interest in how the money was spent—for example, to bribe voters—than in where it came from. Wanting governmental assistance for their enterprises, but only sporadically scrutinizing its political implications, most people probably failed to perceive what the Adamses saw.[25] Nor did they, until social and industrial developments created deep dissatisfaction with the existing policy process. Then, the discovery that privileged businesses corrupted politics played a vital, if short-lived, role in facilitating the momentous transition from the nineteenth-century polity to the one Americans fashioned at the beginning of the twentieth century.

By the 1890s, large-scale industrialization was creating the felt need for new government policies in two distinct but related ways. The first process, which Hays and Wiebe have described so well, was the increasing organization of diverse producer groups, conscious of their own identities and special needs. Each demanded specific public protections for its own endeavors and questioned the allocation of benefits to others. The second development was less tangible: the unorganized public's dawning sense of vulnerability, unease, and anger in the face of economic changes wrought by big corporations. Sometimes, the people's inchoate feelings focused on the ill-understood "trusts"; at other times, their negative emotions found more specific, local targets in street-railway or electric-power companies.

Older interpretations of progressivism gave too much weight to the second of these developments; recently, only a few historians have sufficiently recognized it.[26]

Together, these processes created a political crisis by making people conscious of uncomfortable truths that earlier nineteenth-century conditions had obscured: that society's diverse producer groups did not exist in harmony or share equally in government benefits, and that private interests posed a danger to the public's interests. The crisis brought on by the recognition of these two problems extended approximately from the onset of depression in 1893 until 1908 and passed through three distinct phases: (1) the years of realignment, 1893–96; (2) the years of experimentation and uncertainty, 1897–1904; and (3) the years of discovery and resolution, 1905–08. When the crisis was over, the American political system was different in important respects from what it had been before.

During the first phase, the depression and the alleged radicalism of the Populists preoccupied politics and led to a decisive change in the national balance of party power. Willingly or unwillingly, many former voters now ceased to participate in politics, while others from almost every social group in the North and Midwest shifted their allegiance to the Republicans. As a result, that party established a national majority that endured until the 1930s. Yet, given how decisive the realignment of the 1890s was, it is striking how quickly the particular issues of 1896—tariff protection and free silver—faded and how little of long-standing importance the realignment resolved.[27] To be sure, the defeat of Bryan and the destruction of Populism established who would not have control of the process of accommodating the nation to industrial realities, but the election of 1896 did much less in determining who would be in charge or what the solutions would be.

In the aftermath of realignment, a subtler form of crisis took hold—although several happy circumstances partially hid it, both from people then and from historians since. The war with Spain boosted national pride and self-confidence; economic prosperity returned after the depression; and the Republican Party with its new majority gave the appearance of having doctrines that were relevant to industrial problems. Soon, President Theodore Roosevelt's activism and appeal helped foster an impression of political command over the economy. However disguised, the crisis nonetheless was real, and, in the years after 1896, many voices quietly questioned whether traditional politics and government could resolve interest-group conflicts or allay the sense of vulnerability that ordinary people felt.

Central to the issue were the dual problems of how powerful government should be and whether it ought to acknowledge and adjust group differences. Industrialism and its consequences seemed to demand strong public policies based on a recognition of social conflict. At the very least, privileged corporations had to be restrained, weaker elements in the community protected, and regular means established for newer interest groups to participate in government. But the will, the energy, and the imagination to bring about these changes seemed missing. Deeply felt ideological beliefs help explain this paralysis. The historic American commitment, on the one hand, to weak government, local autonomy, and the preservation of individual liberties—reflected in the doctrines of the Democratic Party—presented a strong barrier to any significant expansion of governmental authority. The ingrained resistance, on the other hand, to having the government acknowledge that the country's producing interests were not harmonious—voiced in the doctrines of the Republican Party—presented an equally strong obstacle to the recognition and adjustment of group differences.[28]

Weighted down by their doctrines as well as by an unwillingness to alienate elements of their heterogeneous coalitions, both parties floundered in attempting to deal with these problems. The Democrats were merely more conspicuous in failing than were the Republicans. Blatantly divided into two wings, neither of which succeeded in coming to grips with the new issues, the Democrats blazoned their perplexity by nominating Bryan for president for a second time in 1900, abandoning him for the conservative Alton B. Parker in 1904, and then returning to the Great Commoner (who was having trouble deciding whether to stand for nationalizing the railroads) in 1908. The Republicans, for their part, were only a little less contradictory in moving from McKinley to Roosevelt to Taft. Roosevelt, moreover, for all of the excitement he brought to the presidency in 1901, veered wildly in his approach to the problems of big business during his first term—from "publicity" to trust-busting to jawboning to conspiring with the House of Morgan.[29]

While the national leaders wavered and confidence in the parties waned, a good deal of experimenting went on in the cities and states—much of it haphazard and unsuccessful. Every large city found it difficult to obtain cheap and efficient utilities, equitable taxes, and the variety of public services required by an expanding, heterogeneous population. A few, notably Detroit and later Cleveland and New York, made adjustments during the last years of the nineteenth and the first years of the twentieth centuries that other cities later copied: the adoption of restrictions on utility and transportation franchises, the imposition of new taxes on intangible personalty, and the inauguration of innovative municipal services. But most cities were less successful in aligning governance with industrialism. Utility regulation was a particularly difficult problem. Franchise "grabs" agreed to by city councilmen came under increasing attack, but the chaotic competition between divergent theories of regulation (home rule versus state supervision versus municipal ownership) caused the continuance of poor public policy.[30] In the states, too, the late 1890s and early 1900s were years of experimentation with various methods of regulation and administration. What Gerald D. Nash has found for California seems to have been true elsewhere as well: the state's railroad commission "floundered" in the late nineteenth century due to ignorance, inexperience, and a lack of both manpower and money. These were, Nash says, times of "trial and error." Antitrust policy also illuminates the uncertainty that was characteristic of the period before about 1905. By the turn of the century, two-thirds of the states had already passed antitrust laws, but in the great majority the provisions for enforcement were negligible. Some states simply preferred encouraging business to restraining it; others felt that the laxity of neighboring states and of the federal government made antitrust action futile; still others saw their enforcement policies frustrated by court decisions and administrative weaknesses. The result was unsuccessful policy—and a consequent failure to relieve the crisis that large-scale industrialization presented to nineteenth-century politics and government.[31]

In September 1899, that failure was searchingly probed at a conference on trusts held under the auspices of the Chicago Civic Federation. Attended by a broad spectrum of the country's political figures and economic thinkers, the meeting's four days of debates and speeches amply expressed the agitation, the uncertainty, and the discouragement engendered by the nation's search for solutions to the problems caused by large business combinations. In exploring whether and to what extent the government should regulate corporations and how to adjust social-group differences, the speakers addressed basic questions about the nineteenth-century American polity.[32] Following the conference, the search for answers continued unabated, for there was little consensus and considerable resistance to change. In the years immediately following, pressure to do *something* mounted. And roughly by the middle of the next decade, many of the elements were in place for a blaze of political innovation. The spark that finally served to ignite them was a series of disclosures reawakening and refashioning the old fear that privileged business corrupted politics and government.

The evidence concerning these disclosures is familiar to students of progressivism, but its meaning has not been fully explored. The period 1904–08 comprised the muckraking years, not only in national magazines but also in local newspapers and legislative halls across the country. During 1905 and 1906 in particular, a remarkable number of cities and states experienced wrenching moments of discovery that led directly to signifi-

cant political changes. Usually, a scandal, an investigation, an intraparty battle, or a particularly divisive election campaign exposed an illicit alliance of politics and business and made corruption apparent to the community, affecting party rhetoric, popular expectations, electoral behavior, and government policies.[33]

Just before it exploded in city and state affairs, business corruption of politics had already emerged as a leading theme of the new magazine journalism created by the muckrakers. Their primary contribution was to give a national audience the first systematic accounts of how modern American society operated. In so doing, journalists like Steffens, Baker, Russell, and Phillips created insights and pioneered ways of describing social and political relationships that crucially affected how people saw things in their home towns and states. Since so many of the muckrakers' articles identified the widespread tendency for privilege-seeking businessmen to bribe legislators, conspire with party leaders, and control nominations, an awareness of such corruption soon entered local politics. Indeed, many of the muckraking articles concerned particular locales—including Steffens's early series on the cities (1902–03); his subsequent exposures of Missouri, Illinois, Wisconsin, Rhode Island, New Jersey, and Ohio (1904–05); Rudolph Blankenburg's articles on Pennsylvania (1905); and C. P. Connolly's treatment of Montana (1906). All of these accounts featured descriptions of politico-business corruption, as did many of the contemporaneous exposures of individual industries, such as oil, railroads, and meat-packing. Almost immediately after this literature began to flourish, citizens across the country discovered local examples of the same corrupt behavior that Steffens and the others had described elsewhere.[34]

In New York, the occasion was the 1905 legislative investigation of the life insurance industry. One by one, insurance executives and Republican politicians took the witness stand and were compelled to bare the details of their corrupt relations. The companies received legislative protection, and the Republicans got bribes and campaign funds. In California, the graft trials of San Francisco city officials, beginning in 1906, threw light on the illicit cooperation between businessmen and public officials. Boss Abraham Ruef had delivered special privileges to public utility corporations in return for fees, of which he kept some and used the rest to bribe members of the city's Board of Supervisors. San Francisco's awakening revitalized reform elsewhere in California, and the next year insurgent Republicans formally organized to combat their party's alliance with the Southern Pacific Railroad. In Vermont, the railroad commissioners charged the 1906 legislature with yielding "supinely to the unfortunate influence of railroad representatives." Then the legislature investigated and found that the commissioners themselves were corrupt![35]

evolution

Other states, in all parts of the country, experienced their own versions of these events during 1905 and 1906. In South Dakota, as in a number of midwestern states, hostility to railroad influence in politics—by means of free passes and a statewide network of paid henchmen—was the issue around which insurgent Republicans coalesced against the regular machine. Some of those who joined the opposition did so purely from expediency; but their charges of corruption excited the popular imagination, and they captured the state in 1906 with pledges of electoral reform and business regulation. Farther west Denver's major utilities, including the Denver Tramway Company and the Denver Gas and Electric Company, applied for new franchises in 1906, and these applications went before the voters at the spring elections. When the franchises all narrowly carried, opponents of the companies produced evidence that the Democratic and Republican Parties had obtained fraudulent votes for the utilities. The case made its way through the courts during the next several months, and, although they ultimately lost, Colorado's nascent progressives derived an immense boost from the well-publicized judicial battle. As a result, the focus of reform shifted to the state. Dissidents in the Republican Party organized to demand direct primary nominations and a judiciary untainted by corporate influence. These questions dominated Colorado's three-way gubernatorial election that fall.[36]

To the south, in Alabama, Georgia, and Mississippi, similar accusations of politico-business corruption were heard that same year, only in a different regional accent. In Alabama, Braxton Bragg Comer rode the issue from his position on the state's railroad commission to the governorship. His "main theme," according to Sheldon Hackney, "was that the railroads had for years deprived the people of Alabama of their right to rule their own state and that the time had come to free the people from alien and arbitrary rule." Mississippi voters heard similar rhetoric from Governor James K. Vardaman in his unsuccessful campaign against John Sharp Williams for a seat in the U.S. Senate. Georgia's Tom Watson conjured up some inane but effective imagery to illustrate how Vardaman's opponent would serve the business interests: "If the Hon. John Sharp Williams should win out in the fight with Governor Vardaman, the corporations would have just one more doodle-bug in the United States Senate. Every time that a Railroad lobbyist stopped over the hole and called 'Doodle, Doodle, Doodle'—soft and slow—the sand at the little end of the funnel would be seen to stir, and then the little head of J. Sharp would pop up." In Watson's own state, Hoke Smith trumpeted the issue, too, in 1905 and 1906.[37]

New Hampshire, Rhode Island, New Jersey, Pennsylvania, Ohio, Indiana, North Dakota, Nebraska, Texas, and Montana, among other states, also had their muckraking moments during these same years. Although the details varied from place to place, there were three basic routes by which the issue of politico-business corruption entered state politics. In some states, including New York, Colorado, and California, a legislative investigation or judicial proceeding captured attention by uncovering a fresh scandal or by unexpectedly focusing public attention on a recognized political sore. Elsewhere, as in New Hampshire, South Dakota, and Kansas, a factional battle in the dominant Republican Party inspired dissidents to drag their opponents' misdeeds into public view; in several Southern states, the Democrats divided in similar fashion, and each side told tales of the other's corruption by business interests. Finally, city politics often became a vehicle for spreading the issue of a politico-business alliance to the state. Philadelphia, Jersey City, Cincinnati, Denver, and San Francisco all played the role of inspiring state reform movements based on this issue. Some states took more than one of these three routes; and the politicians and reformers in a few states simply echoed what their counterparts elsewhere were saying without having any outstanding local stimulus for doing so. This pattern is, of course, not perfect. In Wisconsin and Oregon, the discovery of politico-business corruption came earlier than 1905–06; in Virginia its arrival engendered almost no popular excitement, while it scarcely got to Massachusetts at all.[38]

An anonymous Kansan, whose state became aware of business domination of its politics and government in 1905 and 1906, later gave a description of the discovery that also illuminates what happened elsewhere. When he first entered politics in the 1890s, the Kansan recalled, "three great railroad systems governed" the state. "This was a matter of common knowledge, but nobody objected or was in any way outraged by it." Then "an awakening began" during Roosevelt's first term as president, due to his "hammering on the square deal" and to a growing resentment of discriminatory railroad rates. Finally, after the railroads succeeded in using their political influence to block rate reform, "it began to dawn upon me," the Kansan reported, "that the railway contributions to campaign funds were part of the general game. . . . I saw they were in politics so that they could run things as they pleased." He and his fellow citizens had "really been converted," he declared. "We have got our eyes open now. . . . We have seen that the old sort of politics was used to promote all sorts of private ends, and we have got the idea now that the new politics can be used to promote the general welfare."[39]

State party platforms provide further evidence of the awakening to politico-business corruption. In Iowa, to take a midwestern state, charges of corporation influence in politics were almost entirely confined to the minor parties during the years from 1900 to 1904. Prohibitionists believed that the liquor industry brought political corruption, while socialists felt that the powers of government belonged to the capitalists. For their part, the Democrats and Republicans saw little of this—until 1906, when both major parties gushed in opposition to what the Republicans now called "the domination of corporate influences in public affairs." The Democrats agreed: "We favor the complete elimination of railway and other public service corporations from the politics of the state." In Missouri, a different but parallel pattern emerges from the platforms. There, what had been a subordinate theme of the Democratic Party (and minor parties) in 1900 and 1902 became of central importance to both parties in 1904 and 1906. The Democrats now called "the eradication of bribery" the "paramount issue" in the state and declared opposition to campaign contributions "by great corporations and by those interested in special industries enjoying special privileges under the law." In New Hampshire, where nothing had been said of politico-business corruption in 1900 and 1904, both major parties wrote platforms in 1906 that attacked the issuance of free transportation passes and the prevalence of corrupt legislative lobbies. Party platforms in other states also suggest how suddenly major-party politicians discovered that business corrupted politics.[40]

The annual messages of the state governors from 1902 to 1908 point to the same pattern. In the first three years, the chief executives almost never mentioned the influence of business in politics. Albert Cummins of Iowa was exceptional; as early as 1902 he declared, "Corporations have, and ought to have, many privileges, but among them is not the privilege to sit in political conventions or occupy seats in legislative chambers." Then in 1905, governors across the Midwest suddenly let loose denunciations of corporate bribery, lobbying, campaign contributions, and free passes. Nebraska's John H. Mickey was typical in attacking "the onslaught of private and corporation lobbyists who seek to accomplish pernicious ends by the exercise of undue influence." Missouri's Joseph W. Folk advised that "all franchises, rights and privileges secured by bribery should be declared null and void." By 1906, 1907, and 1908, such observations and recommendations were common to the governors of every region. In 1907 alone, no less than nineteen state executives called for the regulation of lobbying, while a similar number advised the abolition of free passes.[41]

What is the meaning of this awakening to something that Americans had, in a sense, known about all along? Should we accept the originality of the "discovery" that monied interests endangered free government or lay stress instead on the familiar elements the charge contained? It had, after all, been a part of American political thought since the eighteenth century and had been powerfully repeated, in one form or another, by major and minor figures throughout the nineteenth century. According to Richard

Hofstadter, "there was nothing new in the awareness of these things."[42] In fact, however, there was much that was new. First, many of the details of politico-business corruption had never been publicly revealed before. No one had ever probed the subject as thoroughly as journalists and legislative investigators were now doing, and, moreover, some of the practices they uncovered had only recently come into being. Large-scale corporation campaign contributions, for instance, were a product of the 1880s and 1890s. Highly organized legislative lobbying operations by competing interest groups represented an even more recent development. In his systematic study of American legislative practices, published in 1907, Paul S. Reinsch devoted a lengthy chapter to describing how business interests had developed a new and "far more efficient system of dealing with legislatures than [the old methods of] haphazard corruption."[43]

Even more startling than the new practices themselves was the fresh meaning they acquired from the nationwide character of the patterns that were now disclosed. The point is not simply that more people than ever before became aware of politico-business corruption but that the perception of such a national pattern itself created new political understandings. Lincoln Steffens's autobiography is brilliant on this point. As Steffens acknowledged, much of the corruption he observed in his series on the "shame" of the cities had already come to light locally before he reported it to a national audience. What he did was take the facts in city after city, apply imagination to their transcription, and form a new truth by showing the same process at work everywhere. Here was a solution to the problem the Adams brothers had encountered in writing *Chapters of Erie:* how to report shocking corruption without making it seem too astounding to be representative. The solution was breadth of coverage. Instead of looking at only two businessmen, study dozens; explore city after city and state after state and report the facts to a people who were vaguely aware of corruption in their own home towns but had never before seen that a single process was at work across the country.[44] This concept of a "process" of corruption was central to the new understanding. Uncovered through systematic journalistic research and probing legislative investigations, corruption was now seen to be the result of concrete historical developments. It could not just be dismissed as the product of misbehavior by "bad" men (although that kind of rhetoric continued too) but had to be regarded as an outcome of identifiable economic and political forces. In particular, corruption resulted from an outmoded policy of indiscriminate distribution, which could not safely withstand an onslaught of demands from private corporations that were larger than the government itself.[45]

Thus in its systematic character, as well as in its particular details, the corruption that Americans discovered in 1905 and 1906 was different from the kind their eighteenth- and nineteenth-century forebears had known.

Compared to the eighteenth-century republican understanding, the progressive concept of corruption regarded the monied interests not as tools of a designing administration but as independent agents. If any branch of government was in alliance with them, it was probably the legislature. In a curious way, however, the old republican view that commerce inherently threatened the people's virtue still persisted, now informed by a new understanding of the actual process at work. Compared to Andrew Jackson, the progressives saw big corporations not as monsters but as products of social and industrial development. And their activist remedies differed entirely from his negativistic ones. But, like Jackson, those who now discovered corruption grasped that private interests could conflict with the public interest and that government benefits for some groups often hurt others. The recognition of these two things—both painfully at odds with the nineteenth century's conventional wisdom—had been at the root of the floundering over principles of political economy in the 1890s and early 1900s. Now, rather suddenly, the discovery that business corrupts politics suggested concrete answers to a people who were ready for new policies but had been uncertain how to get them or what exactly they should be.

Enacted in a burst of legislative activity immediately following the awakening of 1905 and 1906, the new policies brought to an end the paralysis that had gripped the polity and constituted a decisive break with nineteenth-century patterns of governance. Many states passed laws explicitly designed to curtail illicit business influence in politics. These included measures regulating legislative lobbying, prohibiting corporate campaign contributions, and outlawing the acceptance of free transportation passes by public officials. In 1903 and 1904, there had been almost no legislation on these three subjects; during 1905 and 1906, several states acted on each question; and, by 1907 and 1908, ten states passed lobbying laws, nineteen took steps to prevent corporate contributions, and fourteen acted on the question of passes (see table 1). If these laws failed to wipe out corporation influence in politics, they at least curtailed important means through which businesses had exercised political power in the late nineteenth and early twentieth centuries. To be sure, other means were soon found, but the flood of state lawmaking on these subjects, together with the corresponding attention they received from the federal government in these same years, shows how prevalent was the determination to abolish existing forms of politico-business corruption.[46]

Closely associated with these three measures were two more important categories of legislation, often considered to represent the essence of progressivism in the states: mandatory direct primary laws and measures establishing or strengthening the regulation of utility and transportation

Table 1. Selected Categories of State Legislation, 1903–08

Type of Legislation	1903–04	1905–06	1907–08	1903–08
Regulation of Lobbying	0	2	10	12
Prohibition of Corporate Campaign Contributions	0	3	19	22
Regulation or Prohibition of Free Railroad Passes for Public Officials	4	6	14	24
Mandatory Direct Primary	4	9	18	31
Regulation of Railroad Corporations by Commission	5	8	28	41
Totals	13	28	89	130

Note: Figures represent the number of states that passed legislation in the given category during the specified years.
Source: New York State Library, *Index of Legislation* (Albany, N.Y., 1904–09).

corporations by commission. These types of legislation, too, reached a peak in the years just after 1905–06, when so many states had experienced a crisis disclosing the extent of politico-business corruption. Like the laws concerning lobbying, contributions, and passes, primary and regulatory measures were brought forth amidst intense public concern with business influence in politics and were presented by their advocates as remedies for that problem. Both types of laws had been talked about for years, but the disclosures of 1905–06 provided the catalyst for their enactment.

Even before 1905, the direct primary had already been adopted in some states. In Wisconsin, where it was approved in 1904, Robert M. La Follette had campaigned for direct nominations since the late 1890s on the grounds that they would "emancipate the legislature from all subserviency to the corporations." In his well-known speech, "The Menace of the Machine" (1897), La Follette explicitly offered the direct primary as "the remedy" for corporate control of politics. Now, after the awakening of 1905–06, that same argument inspired many states that had failed to act before to adopt mandatory direct primary laws (see table 1). In New York, Charles Evans Hughes, who was elected governor in 1906 because of his role as chief counsel in the previous year's life insurance investigation, argued that the direct primary would curtail the power of the special interests. "Those interests," he declared, "are ever at work stealthily and persistently endeavoring to pervert the government to the service of their own ends. All that is worst in our public life finds its readiest means of access to power through the control of the nominating machinery of parties."

In other states, too, in the years after 1905–06, the direct primary was urged and approved for the same reasons that La Follette and Hughes advanced it.[47]

The creation of effective regulatory boards—progressivism's most distinctive governmental achievement—also followed upon the discovery of politico-business corruption. From 1905 to 1907 alone, fifteen new state railroad commissions were established, and at least as many existing boards were strengthened. Most of the new commissions were "strong" ones, having rate-setting powers and a wide range of administrative authority to supervise service, safety, and finance. In the years to come, many of them extended their jurisdiction to other public utilities, including gas, electricity, telephones, and telegraphs. Direct legislative supervision of business corporations was also significantly expanded in these years. Life insurance companies—whose corruption of the New York State government Hughes had dramatically disclosed—provide one example. "In 1907," as a result of Hughes's investigation and several others conducted in imitation of it, Morton Keller has reported, "forty-two state legislatures met; thirty considered life insurance legislation; twenty-nine passed laws. . . . By 1908 . . . [the basic] lines of twentieth century life insurance supervision were set, and thereafter only minor adjustments occurred." The federal regulatory machinery, too, was greatly strengthened at this time, most notably by the railroad, meat inspection, and food and drug acts of 1906.[48]

The adoption of these measures marked the moment of transition from a structure of economic policy based largely on the allocation of resources and benefits to one in which regulation and administration played permanent and significant roles. Not confined for long to the transportation, utility, and insurance companies that formed its most immediate objects, regulatory policies soon were extended to other industries as well. Sometimes the legislative branch took responsibility for the ongoing tasks of supervision and administration, but more commonly they became the duty of independent boards and commissions, staffed by experts and entrusted with significant powers of oversight and enforcement. Certainly, regulation was not previously unknown, nor did promoting commerce and industry now cease to be a governmental purpose. But the middle years of the first decade of the twentieth century unmistakably mark a turning point—that point when the direction shifted, when the weight of opinion changed, when the forces of localism and opposition to governmental authority that had sustained the distribution of privileges but opposed regulation and administration now lost the upper hand to the forces of centralization, bureaucratization, and government actions to recognize and adjust group differences. Besides economic regulation, other governmental policy areas, including health, education, taxation, correction, and the control of natural resources, increasingly came under the jurisdiction of independent boards and commissions. The establishment of these agencies and the expansion of their duties meant that American governance in the twentieth century was significantly different from what it had been in the nineteenth.[49]

The developments of 1905–08 also changed the nature of political participation in the United States. Parties emerged from the years of turmoil altered and, on balance, less important vehicles of popular expression than they had been. The disclosures of politico-business wrongdoing disgraced the regular party organizations, and many voters showed their loss of faith by staying at home on election day or by casting split tickets. These trends had been in progress before 1905–06—encouraged by new election laws as well as by the crisis of confidence in traditional politics and government—but in several ways the discovery of corruption strengthened them. Some reigning party organizations were toppled by the disclosures, and the insurgents who came to power lacked the old bosses' experience and inclination when it came to rallying the electorate. And the legal prohibition of corporate campaign contributions now meant, moreover, that less money was available for pre-election entertainment, transportation to the polls, and bribes.[50]

While the party organizations were thus weakened, they were also more firmly embedded in the legal machinery of elections than ever before. In many states the direct primary completed a series of new election laws (beginning with the Australian ballot in the late 1880s and early 1890s) that gave the parties official status as nominating bodies, regulated their practices, and converted them into durable, official bureaucracies. Less popular now but also more respectable, the party organizations surrendered to state regulation and relinquished much of their ability to express community opinion in return for legal guarantees that they alone would be permanently certified to place nominees on the official ballot.[51]

Interest organizations took over much of the parties' old job of articulating popular demands and pressing them upon the government. More exclusive and single-minded than parties, the new organizations became regular elements of the polity. Their right to represent their members before the government's new boards and agencies received implicit recognition, and, indeed, the commissions in some cases became captives of the groups they were supposed to regulate. The result was a fairly drastic transformation of the rules of political participation: who could compete, the kinds of resources required, and the rewards of participation all changed. These developments were not brand new in the first years of the twentieth century, but, like the contemporaneous changes in government policy, they derived impressive, decisive confirmation from the political upheaval that occurred between 1905 and 1908.

Political and governmental changes thus followed upon the discovery that business corrupts politics. And Americans of the day explicitly linked the two developments: the reforms adopted in 1907–08 were to remedy the ills uncovered in 1905–06. But these chronological and rhetorical connections between discovery and reform do not fully explain the relationship between them. Why, having paid relatively little heed to similar charges before, did people now take such strong actions in response to the disclosures? Why, moreover, did the perception of wrongdoing precipitate the particular pattern of responses that it did—namely, the triumph of bureaucracy and organization? Of most importance, what distinctive effects did the discovery of corruption have upon the final outcome of the crisis?

By 1905 a political explosion of some sort was likely, due to the accumulated frustrations people felt about the government's failure to deal with the problems of industrialization. So combustible were the elements present that another spark besides the discovery of politico-business corruption might well have ignited them. But the recognition of such corruption was an especially effective torch. Upon close analysis, its ignition of the volatile political mass is unsurprising. The accusations made in 1905–06 were serious, widespread, and full of damaging information; they explained the actual corrupt process behind a danger that Americans had historically worried about, if not always responded to with vigor; they linked in dark scandal the two main villains—party bosses and big businessmen—already on the American scene; they inherently discredited the existing structure of economic policy based on the distribution of privileges; and they dramatically suggested the necessity for new kinds of politics and government. That businessmen systematically corrupted politics was incendiary knowledge; given the circumstances of 1905, it could hardly have failed to set off an explosion.

The organizational results that followed, however, seem less inevitable. There were, after all, several other known ways of curtailing corruption besides expert regulation and administration. For one, there was the continued reliance on direct legislative action against the corruption of politics by businessmen. The lobbying, anti-free pass, and campaign-contribution measures of 1907–08 exemplified this approach. So did the extension of legislative controls over the offending corporations. Such measures were familiar, but obviously they were considered inadequate to the crisis at hand. A second approach, favored by Edward Alsworth Ross and later by Woodrow Wilson, was to hold business leaders personally responsible for their "sins" and to punish them accordingly. There were a few attempts to bring individuals to justice, but, because of the inadequacy of the criminal statutes, the skill of high-priced lawyers, and the public's lack of appetite for personal vendettas, few sinners were jailed. Finally, there were proposals for large structural solutions changing the political and economic environment so that the old corrupt practices became impossible. Some men, like Frederic C. Howe, still advocated the single tax and the abolition of all privileges granted by government.[52] Many more believed in the municipal ownership of public utilities. Hundreds of thousands (to judge from election returns) favored socialist solutions, but most Americans did not. In their response to politico-business corruption, they went beyond existing legislative remedies and avoided the temptation to personalize all the blame, but they fell short of wanting socialism, short even of accepting the single tax.

Regulation and administration represented a fourth available approach. Well before the discoveries of 1905–06, groups who stood to benefit from governmental control of utility and transportation corporations had placed strong regulatory proposals on the political agendas of the states and the nation. In other policy areas, the proponents of an administrative approach had not advanced that far prior to 1905–06, but theirs was a large and growing movement, supported—as recent historians have shown—by many different groups for varied, often contradictory, reasons.[53] The popular awakening to corruption increased the opportunity of these groups to obtain enactment of their measures. Where their proposals met the particular political needs of 1905–08, they succeeded most quickly. Regulation by commissions seemed to be an effective way to halt corruption by transferring the responsibility for business-government relations from party bosses and legislators to impartial experts. That approach also possessed the additional political advantages of appearing sane and moderate, of meeting consumer demands for government protection, and, above all, of being sufficiently malleable that a diversity of groups could be induced to anticipate favorable results from the new policies.[54]

In consequence, the passions of 1905–06 added support to an existing movement toward regulation and administration, enormously speeded it up, shaped the timing and form of its victory, and probably made the organizational revolution more complete—certainly more sudden—than it otherwise would have been. These accomplishments alone must make the discovery of corruption pivotal in any adequate interpretation of progressivism. But the awakening did more than hurry along a movement that already possessed formidable political strength and would probably have triumphed eventually even without the events of 1905–06. By pushing the political process toward so quick a resolution of the long-standing crisis over industrialism, the passions of those years caused the outcome to be more conservative than it otherwise might have been. This is the ultimate irony of the discovery that business corrupts politics.

Muckraking accounts of politico-business evils suggest one reason for the discovery's conservative impact. Full of facts and revelations, these writings were also dangerously devoid of effective solutions. Charles E. Russell's *Lawless Wealth* (1908) — the title itself epitomizes the perceptions of 1905–06 — illustrates the flaw. Published originally in *Everybody's Magazine* under the accusatory title, "Where Did You Get It, Gentlemen?," the book recounts numerous instances of riches obtained through the corruption of politics but, in its closing pages, merely suggests that citizens recognize the evils and be determined to stop them. This reliance on trying to change how people felt (to "shame" them, in Steffens's phrase) was characteristic of muckraking and of the exposures of 1905–06. One can admire the muckrakers' reporting, can even accept David P. Thelen's judgment that their writing "contained at least as deep a moral revulsion toward capitalism and profit as did more orthodox forms of Marxism," yet can still feel that their proposed remedy was superficial. Because the perception of politico-business corruption carried no far-reaching solutions of its own or genuine economic grievances, but only a desire to clean up politics and government, the passions of 1905–06 were easily diverted to the support of other people's remedies, especially administrative answers. Had the muckrakers and their local imitators penetrated more deeply into the way that business operated and its real relationship to government, popular emotions might not have been so readily mobilized in support of regulatory and administrative agencies that business interests could often dominate. At the very least, there might have been a more determined effort to prevent the supervised corporations themselves from shaping the details of regulatory legislation. Thus, for all of their radical implications, the passions of 1905–06 dulled the capacity of ordinary people to get reforms in their own interest.[55]

The circumstances in which the discovery of corruption became a political force also assist in explaining its conservatism. The passions of 1905–06 were primarily expressed in state, rather than local or national, politics. Indeed, those passions often served to shift the focus of reform from the cities to the state capitals. There — in Albany, or Madison, or Sacramento — the remedies were worked out in relative isolation from the local, insurgent forces that had in many cases originally called attention to the evils. Usually the policy consequences were more favorable to large business interests than local solutions would have been. State utility boards, for example, which had always been considered more conservative in their policies than comparable local commissions, now took the regulatory power away from cities and foreclosed experimentation with such alternatives as municipal ownership or popularly chosen regulatory boards. In gaining a statewide hearing for reform, the accusations of politico-business corruption actually increased the likelihood that conservative solutions would be adopted.[56]

Considering the intensity of the feelings aroused in 1905 and 1906 ("the wrath of thousands of private citizens . . . is at white heat over the disclosures," declared a Rochester newspaper) and the catalytic political role they played, the awakened opposition to corruption was surprisingly short-lived. As early as 1907 and 1908, the years of the most significant state legislative responses to the discovery, the messages of the governors began to exhibit a more stylized, less passionate way of describing politico-business wrongdoing. Now the governors emphasized remedies rather than abuses, and most seemed confident that the remedies would work. Criticism of business influence in government continued to be a staple of political rhetoric throughout the Progressive era, but it ceased to have the intensity it did in 1905–06. In place of the burning attack on corruption, politicans offered advanced progressive programs, including further regulation and election-law reforms.[57] The deep concern with business corruption of politics and government thus waned. It had stirred people to consciousness of wrongdoing, crystalized their discontent with existing policies, and pointed toward concrete solutions for the ills of industrialism. But it had not sustained the more radical, antibusiness possibilities suggested by the discoveries of 1905–06.

Indeed, the passions of those years probably weakened the insurgent, democratic qualities of the ensuing political transformation and strengthened its bureaucratic aspects. This result was ironical, but its causes were not conspiratorial. They lay instead in the tendency—shared by the muckrakers and their audience—to accept remedies unequal to the problems at hand and in political circumstances that isolated insurgents from decision making. Once the changes in policy were under way after 1906, those organized groups whose interests were most directly affected entered the fray, jockeyed for position, and heavily shaped the outcomes. We do not yet know enough about how this happened, but studies such as Stanley P. Caine's examination of railroad regulation in Wisconsin suggest how difficult it was to translate popular concern on an "issue" into the details of a law.[58] It is hardly surprising that, as regulation and administration became accepted public functions, the affected interests exerted much more influence on policy than did those who cared most passionately about restoring clean government.

But the failure to pursue antibusiness policies does not mean the outcry against corruption was either insincere or irrelevant. Quite the contrary. It was sufficiently genuine and widespread to dominate the nation's public life in 1905 and 1906 and to play a decisive part in bringing about the transformation of American politics and government. Political changes do not, of course, embrace everything that is meant by progressivism. Nor was the discovery that business corrupts politics the only catalytic agent at work; certainly the rise of consumer discontent with utility and transportation corporations and the vigorous impetus toward new policies given by Theodore Roosevelt during his second term as president played complementary roles. But the awakening to corruption—as it was newly understood—provided an essential dynamic, pushing the states and the nation toward what many of its leading men and women considered progressive reform.

The organizational thesis sheds much light on the values and methods of those who succeeded in dominating the new types of politics and government but very little on the political circumstances in which they came forward. Robert H. Wiebe, in particular, has downplayed key aspects of the political context, including the outcry against corruption. Local uprisings against the alliance of bosses and businessmen, Wiebe has stated, "lay outside the mainstream of progressivism"; measures instituting the direct primary and curtailing the political influence of business were "old-fashioned reform."[59] Yet those local crusades, by spreading the dynamic perception that business corrupts politics, created a popular demand for the regulatory and administrative measures that Wiebe has claimed are characteristic of true progressivism; and those "old-fashioned" laws were enacted amidst the same political furor that produced the stunningly rapid bureaucratic triumph whose significance for twentieth-century America Wiebe has explained so convincingly. What the organizational thesis mainly lacks is the sense that political action is open-ended and unpredictable. Consequences are often unexpected, outcomes surprising when matched against origins. While it is misleading, as Samuel P. Hays has said, to interpret progressivism solely on the basis of its antibusiness ideology, it is equally misleading to fail to appreciate that reform gained decisive initial strength from ideas and feelings that were not able to sustain the movement in the end.[60] The farsighted organizers from business and the professions thus gained the opportunity to complete a political transformation that had been begun by people who were momentarily shocked into action but who stopped far short of pursuing the full implications of their discovery.

Notes

1. Although it is a common autobiographical convention to recount one's growth from ignorance to knowledge, it is nonetheless striking that so many progressive autobiographies should identify the same point of ignorance and trace a

similar path to knowledge. See Roosevelt, *An Autobiography* (New York, 1913), 85–86, 186, 297–300, 306, 321–23; La Follette, *La Follette's Autobiography: A Personal Narrative of Political Experiences* (Madison, Wisc., 1960), 3–97; White, *The Autobiography of William Allen White* (New York, 1946), 149–50, 160–61, 177–79, 192–93, 215–16, 232–34, 325–26, 345, 351, 364, 428–29, 439–40, 465; Howe, *The Confessions of a Reformer* (New York, 1925), 70–72, 100–12; and Steffens, *The Autobiography of Lincoln Steffens* (New York, 1931), 357–627.

2. Richard Hofstadter, *The Age of Reform: From Bryan to F.D.R.* (New York, 1955), 133; George E. Mowry, *The Era of Theodore Roosevelt, 1900–1912* (New York, 1958), 55–58; John Braeman, "Seven Progressives," *Business History Review*, 35 (1961): 581–92; and Sheldon Hackney, *Populism to Progressivism in Alabama* (Princeton, 1969), xii–xiii, 329–30.

3. John D. Buenker, "The Progressive Era: A Search for a Synthesis," *Mid-America*, 51 (1969): 175–93; David P. Thelen, "Social Tensions and the Origins of Progressivism," *Journal of American History* [hereafter, *JAH*], 56 (1969): 323–41; and Peter G. Filene, "An Obituary for 'The Progressive Movement,'" *American Quarterly*, 22 (1970): 20–34.

4. Robert H. Wiebe, *Businessmen and Reform: A Study of the Progressive Movement* (Cambridge, Mass., 1962); Gabriel Kolko, *The Triumph of Conservatism: A Reinterpretation of American History, 1900–1916* (New York, 1963); and Samuel P. Hays, "The Politics of Reform in Municipal Government in the Progressive Era," *Pacific Northwest Quarterly*, 55 (1964): 157–69.

5. Samuel P. Hays, *The Response to Industrialism, 1885–1914* (Chicago, 1957); Robert H. Wiebe, *The Search for Order, 1877–1920* (New York, 1967); Louis Galambos, *The Public Image of Big Business in America, 1880–1940: A Quantitative Study in Social Change* (Baltimore, 1975); William L. O'Neill, *The Progressive Years: America Comes of Age* (New York, 1975); and David P. Thelen, *Robert M. La Follette and the Insurgent Spirit* (Boston, 1976).

6. Louis Galambos provided a sympathetic introduction to the work of the "organizational" school; see his "The Emerging Organizational Synthesis in Modern American History," *Business History Review*, 44 (1970): 279–90. For another effort to place the work of these historians in perspective, see Robert H. Wiebe, "The Progressive Years, 1900–1917," in William H. Cartwright and Richard L. Watson, Jr., eds., *The Reinterpretation of American History and Culture* (Washington, 1973), 425–42. In addition to the works by Wiebe, Hays, and Galambos, already cited, several other studies by Hays also rank among the most important products of the organizational school: Samuel P. Hays, *Conservation and the Gospel of Efficiency: The Progressive Conservation Movement, 1890–1920* (Cambridge, Mass., 1959), "Political Parties and the Community-Society Continuum," in William Nisbet Chambers and Walter Dean Burnham, eds., *The American Party Systems: Stages of Political Development* (New York, 1967), 152–81, and "The New Organizational Society," in Jerry Israel, ed., *Building the Organizational Society: Essays on Associational Activities in Modern America* (New York, 1972), 1–15. Although Wiebe and Hays share the same broad interpretation of the period, their works make quite distinctive contributions, and there are certain matters on which they have disagreed. Some of Wiebe's most important insights concern the complex relationships between business and reform, while Hays has demonstrated particular originality on the subjects of urban politics and political parties. Concerning the middle classes, they have differing views: Wiebe has included the middle classes among the "organizers," while

Hays has emphasized their persistent individualism. Compare Wiebe, *The Search for Order, 1877–1920,* chap. 5, and Hays, *The Response to Industrialism, 1885–1914,* chap. 4.

7. For related comments on the organizational model's shortcomings, see William G. Anderson, "Progressivism: An Historiographical Essay," *History Teacher,* 6 (1973): 427–52; David M. Kennedy, "Overview: The Progressive Era," *Historian,* 37 (1975): 453–68; O'Neill, *The Progressive Years,* x, 45; and Morton Keller, *Affairs of State: Public Life in Late-Nineteenth-Century America* (Cambridge, Mass., 1977), 285–87.

8. Wiebe, "The Progressive Years, 1900–1917," 429.

9. John D. Buenker, John C. Burnham, and Robert M. Crunden, *Progressivism* (Cambridge, Mass., 1977), 4. For some disagreements among these three authors about how central politics was to progressivism, see *ibid.,* 107–29.

10. Samuel P. Huntington, *Political Order in Changing Societies* (New Haven, 1968), 93–139; Walter Dean Burnham, *Critical Elections and the Mainsprings of American Politics* (New York, 1970), 175–93; and J. G. A. Pocock, *The Machiavellian Moment: Florentine Political Thought and the Atlantic Republican Tradition* (Princeton, 1975), 549.

11. I have elsewhere cited many of the sources on which these generalizations are based; see my "The Party Period and Public Policy: An Exploratory Hypothesis," *JAH,* 66 (1979): 279–98. On the decline in turnout and the increase in ticket-splitting, see Walter Dean Burnham, "The Changing Shape of the American Political Universe," *American Political Science Review* [hereafter, *APSR*], 59 (1965): 7–28. On the rise of interest-group organizations, see Hays, "Political Parties and the Community-Society Continuum." For two studies that make significant contributions to an understanding of how the political changes of the early twentieth century altered the power relationships among groups, see J. Morgan Kousser, *The Shaping of Southern Politics: Suffrage Restriction and the Establishment of the One-Party South, 1880–1910* (New Haven, 1974); and Carl V. Harris, *Political Power in Birmingham, 1871–1921* (Knoxville, 1977).

12. Wiebe, *The Search for Order, 1877–1920,* 160.

13. McCormick, "The Party Period and Public Policy"; Robert A. Lively, "The American System: A Review Article," *Business History Review,* 29 (1955): 81–96; James Willard Hurst, *Law and the Conditions of Freedom in the Nineteenth-Century United States* (Madison, Wisc., 1956); Theodore J. Lowi, "American Business, Public Policy, Case-Studies, and Political Theory," *World Politics,* 16 (1964): 677–715; and Wiebe, *The Search for Order, 1877–1920,* 159–95.

14. James Willard Hurst, *Law and Social Order in the United States* (Ithaca, 1977), 33, 36, and *Law and the Conditions of Freedom,* 71–108; and Grover G. Huebner, "Five Years of Railroad Regulation by the States," *Annals of the American Academy of Political and Social Science,* 32 (1908): 138–56. . . .

15. Burnham, "The Changing Shape of the American Political Universe," and *Critical Elections and the Mainsprings of American Politics,* 71–90, 115; and Jerrold G. Rusk, "The Effect of the Australian Ballot Reform on Split-Ticket Voting, 1876–1908," *APSR,* 64 (1970): 1220–38. For a contemporary effort to estimate and assess split-ticket voting, see Philip Loring Allen, "Ballot Laws and Their Workings," *Political Science Quarterly,* 21 (1906): 38–58.

16. Banning, *The Jeffersonian Persuasion: Evolution of a Party Ideology* (Ithaca, 1978); J. G. A. Pocock, "Virtue and Commerce in the Eighteenth Century," *Journal of Interdisciplinary History,* 3 (1972): 119–34, and *The Machiavellian Moment,* 506–52;

Gordon S. Sood, *The Creation of the American Republic, 1776–1787* (Chapel Hill, 1969), 32–33, 52, 64–65, 107–14, 400–03, 416–21; Morton Keller, "Corruption in America: Continuity and Change," in Abraham S. Eisenstadt *et al.,* eds., *Before Watergate: Problems of Corruption in American Society* (New York, 1979), 7–19; and Edwin G. Burrows, "Albert Gallatin and the Problem of Corruption in the Federalist Era," *ibid.,* 51–67.

17. Somkin, *Unquiet Eagle: Memory and Desire in the Idea of American Freedom, 1815–1860* (Ithaca, 1967), 24.

18. [Jackson] *Annual Messages, Veto Messages, Protests, &c. of Andrew Jackson, President of the United States* (Baltimore, 1835), 162, 165, 179, 197, 244. Numerous studies document the Democratic Party's use of the accusation that privileged business was corrupting politics: Lee Benson, *The Concept of Jacksonian Democracy: New York as a Test Case* (Princeton, 1961), 52–56, 96–97, 236; William G. Shade, *Banks or No Banks: The Money Issue in Western Politics, 1832–1865* (Detroit, 1972), 56–59; Marvin Meyers, *The Jacksonian Persuasion: Politics and Belief* (Stanford, 1957), 23–24, 30, 157–58, 196, 198; and Edward K. Spann, *Ideals and Politics: New York Intellectuals and Liberal Democracy, 1820–1880* (Albany, N.Y., 1972), 60, 68–78, 105–06. President Martin Van Buren's special message to Congress proposing the subtreasury system in 1837 contained accusations against the Bank similar to those Jackson had made, except that Van Buren expressed them more in "pure," eighteenth-century republican language; James D. Richardson, ed., *A Compilation of the Messages and Papers of the Presidents, 1789–1897,* 10 vols. (Washington, 1896–99), 3: 324–46.

19. McCormick, "The Party Period and Public Policy," 286–88. On the "commonwealth" ideal, see Oscar Handlin and Mary Flug Handlin, *Commonwealth—A Study of the Role of Government in the American Economy: Massachusetts, 1774–1861* (New York, 1947); and Louis Hartz, *Economic Policy and Democratic Thought: Pennsylvania, 1776–1860* (Cambridge, Mass., 1948). For a classic expression of the Whig concept of interlocking producer interests, see Calvin Colton, ed., *The Works of Henry Clay, Comprising His Life, Correspondence, and Speeches,* 5 (New York, 1897): 437–86; and, for a later Republican expression of the same point of view, see Benjamin Harrison, *Speeches of Benjamin Harrison, Twenty-Third President of the United States* (New York, 1892), 62, 72, 157, 167, 181, 197. For a discussion of the Republican ideology and economic policy, see Eric Foner, *Free Soil, Free Labor, Free Men: The Ideology of the Republican Party before the Civil War* (New York, 1970), 18–23.

20. Lively, "The American System," 94; Carter Goodrich, "The Revulsion against Internal Improvements," *Journal of Economic History,* 10 (1950): 169; and Hays, *The Response to Industrialism, 1885–1914,* 39–40. On the reluctance of state legislatures to prohibit their members from mixing public and private business, see Ari Hoogenboom, "Did Gilded Age Scandals Bring Reform?" in Eisenstadt *et al., Before Watergate,* 127–31.

21. Compare the Democratic platforms of 1840–52 with those for the rest of the century; see Donald Bruce Johnson and Kirk H. Porter, eds., *National Party Platforms, 1840–1972* (Urbana, 1973); for the People's Party platform of 1896, see *ibid.,* 104. For Cleveland's message of 1887, see Richardson, *Messages and Papers of the Presidents, 1789–1897,* 8: 580–91; and, for a compilation of Bryan's speeches of 1896, see his *The First Battle: A Story of the Campaign of 1896* (Chicago, 1896).

22. Johnson and Porter, *National Party Platforms, 1840–1972,* 90; and George, *Progress and Poverty—An Inquiry into the Cause of Industrial Depressions and of Increase of Want with Increase of Wealth: The Remedy* (New York, 1880), 481. For examples of

other late-nineteenth-century dissenters who recognized the corruption of politics and government by business interests, see H. R. Chamberlain, *The Farmers' Alliance: What It Aims to Accomplish* (New York, 1891), 12, 37–38; and Henry Demarest Lloyd, *Wealth against Commonwealth* (New York, 1894), 369–404.

23. Woodward, *Reunion and Reaction: The Compromise of 1877 and the End of Reconstruction* (Boston, 1951), 65; and Godkin, "The Moral of the Crédit Mobilier Scandal," *Nation*, 16 (1873): 68. Also see Allan Nevins, *The Emergence of Modern America, 1865–1878* (New York, 1927), 178–202; and John G. Sproat, *"The Best Men": Liberal Reformers in the Gilded Age* (New York, 1968), 72–73. For the ebb and flow of public aid to private enterprise in this era, see Keller, *Affairs of State*, 162–96. For other expressions of Godkin's opinion, see the *Nation*, 16 (1873): 328–29, and 24 (1877): 82–83.

24. Adams and Adams, *Chapters of Erie* (reprint ed., Ithaca, 1956), 136, 107. Originally published as articles during the late 1860s and early 1870s, these essays were first issued in book form in 1871 under the title *Chapters of Erie and Other Essays* (Boston).

25. For the vivid expression of a similar point, see Wiebe, *The Search for Order, 1877–1920*, 28.

26. Hays, *the Response to Industrialism, 1885–1914*; and Wiebe, *The Search for Order, 1877–1920*. On the fear and anger of the unorganized, see Hofstadter, *The Age of Reform*, 213–69; Irwin Unger and Debi Unger, *The Vulnerable Years: The United States, 1896–1917* (Hinsdale, Ill., 1977), 102–08; and David P. Thelen, *The New Citizenship: Origins of Progressivism in Wisconsin, 1885–1900* (Columbia, Mo., 1972).

27. The three most important studies of the electoral realignment of the 1890s are Paul Kleppner, *The Cross of Culture: A Social Analysis of Midwestern Politics, 1850–1900* (New York, 1970); Richard Jensen, *The Winning of the Midwest: Social and Political Conflict, 1888–1896* (Chicago, 1971); and Samuel T. McSeveney, *The Politics of Depression: Political Behavior in the Northeast, 1893–1896* (New York, 1972). A number of studies associate the realignment with subsequent changes in government policy: Walter Dean Burnham *et al.*, "Partisan Realignment: A Systemic Perspective," in Joel H. Silbey *et al.*, eds., *The History of American Electoral Behavior* (Princeton, 1978), 45–77; and David W. Brady, "Critical Elections, Congressional Parties, and Clusters of Policy Changes," *British Journal of Political Science*, 8 (1978): 79–99.

28. For a discussion of the major parties' ideological beliefs, see Robert Kelley, "Ideology and Political Culture from Jefferson to Nixon," *AHR*, 82 (1977): 531–62. And, for a brilliant account of the resistance to change, see Keller, *Affairs of State*.

29. On the Democratic Party's doctrinal floundering in these years, see J. Rogers Hollingsworth, *The Whirligig of Politics: The Democracy of Cleveland and Bryan* (New York, 1963). For the Republican side of the story, see Nathaniel W. Stephenson, *Nelson W. Aldrich: A Leader in American Politics* (New York, 1930); and John M. Blum, *The Republican Roosevelt* (Cambridge, Mass., 1954). Roosevelt's doctrinal uncertainties can be traced in his annual messages as president; see Hermann Hagedorn, ed., *The Works of Theodore Roosevelt*, memorial edition, 17 (New York, 1925): 93–641. For a recent treatment of these matters, see Lewis L. Gould, *Reform and Regulation: American Politics, 1900–1916* (New York, 1978).

30. Melvin G. Holli, *Reform in Detroit: Hazen S. Pingree and Urban Politics* (New York, 1969); Martin J. Schiesl, *The Politics of Efficiency: Municipal Administration and Reform in America, 1880–1920* (Berkeley and Los Angeles, 1977); Mowry, *The Era of Theodore Roosevelt, 1900–1912*, 59–67; Thelen, *The New Citizenship*, 130–201; and David Nord, "The Experts versus the Experts: Conflicting Philosophies of Munici-

pal Utility Regulation in the Progressive Era," *Wisconsin Magazine of History,* 58 (1975): 219–36.

31. Nash, "The California Railroad Commission, 1876–1911," *Southern California Quarterly,* 44 (1962): 293, 303; Harry L. Purdy *et al., Corporate Concentration and Public Policy* (2d ed., New York, 1950), 317–22; Hans B. Thorelli, *The Federal Antitrust Policy: Origination of an American Tradition* (Baltimore, 1955), 155–56, 265, 352–55, 607; and William Letwin, *Law and Economic Policy in America: The Evolution of the Sherman Antitrust Act* (New York, 1965), 182–247.

32. Civic Federation of Chicago, *Chicago Conference on Trusts* (Chicago, 1900).

33. For other analyses that indicate the importance of the year 1906 in state politics around the country, see Richard M. Abrams, *Conservatism in a Progressive Era: Massachusetts Politics, 1900–1912* (Cambridge, Mass., 1964), 131; and Dewey W. Grantham, Jr., "The Progressive Era and the Reform Tradition," *Mid-America,* 46 (1964): 233–35.

34. The fullest treatment of the muckrakers is still Louis Filler's *The Muckrakers,* a new and enlarged edition of his *Crusaders for American Liberalism* (University Park, Pa., 1976). Filler's chronology provides a convenient list of the major muckraking articles; *ibid.,* 417–24. Steffen's initial series on the cities was published as *The Shame of the Cities* (New York, 1904). His subsequent articles on the states appeared in *McClure's Magazine* between April 1904 and July 1905; these essays were later published as *The Struggle for Self-Government* (New York, 1906). Blankenburg's articles on Pennsylvania appeared in *The Arena* between January and June 1905; Connolly's "The Story of Montana" was published in *McClure's Magazine* between August and December 1906. Other major magazine articles probing politico-business corruption include "The Confessions of a Commercial Senator," *World's Work,* April–May 1905; Charles Edward Russell, "The Greatest Trust in the World" [the meat-packing industry], *Everybody's Magazine,* 1905; and David Graham Phillips, "The Treason of the Senate," *Cosmopolitan Magazine,* 1906.

35. Robert F. Wesser, *Charles Evans Hughes: Politics and Reform in New York, 1905–1910* (Ithaca, 1967), 18–69; Richard L. McCormick, *From Realignment to Reform: Political Change in New York State, 1893–1910* (Ithaca, 1981), chap. 7; George E. Mowry, *The California Progressives* (Berkeley and Los Angeles, 1951), 23–85; Spencer C. Olin, Jr., *California's Prodigal Sons: Hiram Johnson and the Progressives, 1911–1917* (Berkeley and Los Angeles, 1968), 1–19; Winston Allen Flint, *The Progressive Movement in Vermont* (Washington, 1941), 42–51; and the *Tenth Biennial Report of the Board of Railroad Commissioners of the State of Vermont* (Bradford, Vt., 1906), 25.

36. Herbert S. Schell, *History of South Dakota* (Lincoln, Neb., 1961), 258–61; Fred Greenbaum, "The Colorado Progressives in 1906," *Arizona and the West,* 7 (1965): 21–32; and Carl Abbott, *Colorado: A History of the Centennial State* (Boulder, 1976), 203–06.

37. Hackney, *Populism to Progressivism in Alabama,* 257; Watson's *Weekly Jeffersonian,* July 25, 1907, as quoted in William F. Holmes, *The White Chief: James Kimble Vardaman* (Baton Rouge, 1970), 184; Dewey W. Grantham, Jr., *Hoke Smith and the Politics of the New South* (Baton Rouge, 1958), 131–46; and C. Vann Woodward, *Origins of the New South, 1877–1913* (Baton Rouge, 1951), 369–95.

38. Geoffrey Blodgett, "Winston Churchill: The Novelist as Reformer," *New England Quarterly,* 47 (1974): 495–517; Thomas Agan, "The New Hampshire Progressives: Who and What Were They?" *Historical New Hampshire,* 34 (1979): 32–53; Charles Carroll, *Rhode Island: Three Centuries of Democracy,* 2 (New York, 1932): 676–78; Erwin L. Levine, *Theodore Francis Green: The Rhode Island Years, 1906–36*

(Providence, 1963), 1–19; Arthur S. Link, *Wilson: The Road to the White House* (Princeton, 1947), 133–40; Ransom E. Noble, Jr., *New Jersey Progressivism before Wilson* (Princeton, 1946), 24–81; Eugene M. Tobin, "The Progressive as Politician: Jersey City, 1896–1907," *New Jersey History*, 91 (1973): 5–23; Lloyd M. Abernethy, "Insurgency in Philadelphia, 1905," *Pennsylvania Magazine of History and Biography*, 87 (1963): 3–20; Hoyt Landon Warner, *Progressivism in Ohio, 1897–1917* (Columbus, 1964), 143–210; Clifton J. Phillips, *Indiana in Transition: The Emergence of an Industrial Commonwealth, 1880–1920* (Indianapolis, 1968), 93–100; Charles N. Glaab, "The Failure of North Dakota Progressivism," *Mid-America*, 39 (1957): 195–209; James C. Olson, *History of Nebraska* (Lincoln, Neb., 1955), 250–53; Alwyn Barr, *Reconstruction to Reform: Texas Politics, 1876–1906* (Austin, 1971), 229–42; Michael P. Malone and Richard B. Roeder, *Montana: A History of Two Centuries* (Seattle, 1976), 196–99; Robert S. Maxwell, *La Follette and the Rise of the Progressives in Wisconsin* (Madison, Wisc., 1956); Herbert F. Margulies, *The Decline of the Progressive Movement in Wisconsin, 1890–1920* (Madison, Wisc., 1968); Raymond H. Pully, *Old Virginia Restored: An Interpretation of the Progressive Impulse, 1870–1930* (Charlottesville, 1968); and Abrams, *Conservatism in a Progressive Era.*

39. "How I Was Converted—Politically: By a Kansas Progressive Republican," *Outlook*, 96 (1910): 857–59. Also see Robert Sherman La Forte, *Leaders of Reform: Progressive Republicans in Kansas, 1900–1916* (Lawrence, Kans., 1974), 13–88.

40. *The Iowa Official Register for the Years 1907–1908* (Des Moines, 1907), 389, 393; *Official Manual of the State of Missouri for the Years 1905–1906* (Jefferson City, Mo., 1905), 254; and *Official Manual of the State of Missouri for the Years 1907–1908* (Jefferson City, Mo., 1907), 365. Also see State of New Hampshire, *Manual for the General Court, 1907* (Concord, N.H., 1907), 61–63. State party platforms for the early 1900s are surprisingly hard to locate. For some states, particularly in the Northeast and Midwest, the platforms were printed in the annual legislative manuals and blue books, but otherwise they must be found in newspapers. Of the ten states—Iowa, Missouri, New Hampshire, New York, New Jersey, Indiana, Pennsylvania, Illinois, Wisconsin, and South Dakota—for which I was able to survey the party platforms of 1900–10 fairly completely (using the manuals, supplemented when necessary by newspapers), only two fail to support the generalization given here: Wisconsin, where an awareness of politico-business corruption was demonstrated in the platforms of 1900 and 1902 as well as those of later years; and New Jersey, where the Democrats used the issue sparingly in 1901 and 1904, while the Republicans almost completely ignored it throughout the decade.

41. New York State Library, *Digest of Governors' Messages* (Albany, N.Y., 1903–09). This annual document, published for the years 1902–08, classifies the contents of the governors' messages by subject and permits easy comparison among them. For Mickey's and Folk's denunciations, see New York State Library, *Digest of Governors' Messages, 1905*, classifications 99 (legislative lobbying), 96 (legislative bribery).

42. Hofstadter, *The Age of Reform*, 185.

43. Reinsch, *American Legislatures and Legislative Methods* (New York, 1907), 231. On the history of party campaign funds, see James K. Pollock, Jr., *Party Campaign Funds* (New York, 1926); Earl R. Sikes, *State and Federal Corrupt-Practices Legislation* (Durham, N.C., 1928); and Louise Overacker, *Money in Elections* (New York, 1932).

44. Steffens later commented insightfully on his own (and, by implication, the country's) process of "discovery" during these years; see his *Autobiography*, 357–627. Also see his *Shame of the Cities*, 3–26; and Filler, *The Muckrakers*, 257–59.

45. Around 1905 a social-science literature emerged that attempted to explain the process of corruption and to suggest suitable remedies. In addition to Reinsch's *American Legislatures and Legislative Methods,* see Frederic C. Howe, *The City: The Hope of Democracy* (New York, 1905), and *Privilege and Democracy in America* (New York, 1910); and Robert C. Brooks, *Corruption in American Politics and Life* (New York, 1910). Several less scholarly works also analyze the cause of politico-business corruption; see, for example, George W. Berge, *The Free Pass Bribery System* (Lincoln, Neb., 1905); Philip Loring Allen, *America's Awakening: The Triumph of Righteousness in High Places* (New York, 1906); and William Allen White, *The Old Order Changeth: A View of American Democracy* (New York, 1910).

46. The figures in this paragraph (and in the accompanying table) are based on an analysis of the yearly summaries of state legislation reported in New York State Library, *Index of Legislation* (Albany, N.Y., 1904–09). The laws included here are drawn from among those classified in categories 99 (lobbying), 154 (corporate campaign contributions), 1237 (free passes), 160 (direct nominations), and 1267, 1286 (transportation regulation). The legislative years are paired because so many state legislatures met only biennially, usually in the odd-numbered years; no state is counted more than once in any one category in any pair of years. The *Index of Legislation* should be used in conjunction with the accompanying annual *Review of Legislation* (Albany, N.Y., 1904–09).

47. Ellen Torelle, comp., *The Political Philosophy of Robert M. La Follette* (Madison, Wisc., 1920), 28; and Hughes, *Public Papers of Charles E. Hughes, Governor, 1909* (Albany, 1910), 37. Also see Maxwell, *La Follette and the Rise of the Progressives,* 13, 27–35, 48–50, 53–54, 74; Allen Fraser Lovejoy, *La Follette and the Establishment of the Direct Primary in Wisconsin, 1890–1094* (New Haven, 1941); Wesser, *Charles Evans Hughes,* 250–301; Direct Primaries Association of the State of New York, *Direct Primary Nominations: Why Voters Demand Them. Why Bosses Oppose Them* (New York, 1909); Ralph Simpson Boots, *The Direct Primary in New Jersey* (New York, 1917), 59–70; Grantham, *Hoke Smith and the Politics of the New South,* 158, 162, 172–73, 178, 193; Schell, *History of South Dakota,* 260; Olin, *California's Prodigal Sons,* 13; and Charles Edward Merriam and Louise Overacker, *Primary Elections* (Chicago, 1928), 4–7, 60–66.

48. Huebner, "Five Years of Railroad Regulation by the States"; Robert Emmett Ireton, "The Legislatures and the Railroads," *Review of Reviews,* 36 (1907): 217–20; and Keller, *The Life Insurance Enterprise, 1885–1910: A Study in the Limits of Corporate Power* (Cambridge, Mass., 1963), 257, 259. The manner in which the states copied each other's legislation in this period is a subject deserving of study; for a suggestive approach, see Jack L. Walker, "The Diffusion of Innovations among the American States," *APSR,* 63 (1969): 880–99.

49. Among the best accounts of this transformation in policy are Herbert Croly, *Marcus Alonzo Hanna: His Life and Work* (New York, 1912), 465–79; Hurst, *Law and the Conditions of Freedom,* 71–108; and Wiebe, *The Search for Order, 1877–1920,* 164–95.

50. The causes of the decline in party voting have been the subject of considerable debate and disagreement among political scientists and historians in recent years. Walter Dean Burnham began the controversy when he first described the early-twentieth-century changes in voting behavior and explained them by suggesting that an antipartisan industrial elite had captured the political system after the realignment of the 1890s; "Changing Shape of the American Political

Universe." Jerrold G. Rusk and Philip E. Converse responded by contending that legal-institutional factors could better account for the behavioral changes that Burnham had observed; Rusk, "The Effect of the Australian Ballot Reform on Split Ticket Voting"; and Converse, "Change in the American Electorate," in Angus Campbell and Philip E. Converse, eds., *The Human Meaning of Social Change* (New York, 1972), 263–337. All three political scientists carried the debate forward— and all withdrew a bit from their original positions—in the September 1974 issue of the *American Political Science Review*. At present, the weight of developing evidence seems to indicate that, while new election laws alone cannot explain the voters' changed behavior, Burnham's notion of an elite takeover after 1896 is also inadequate to account for what happened; McCormick, *From Realignment to Reform*, chap. 9. What I am suggesting here is that the shock given to party politics by the awakening of 1905–06 played an important part in solidifying the new tendencies toward lower rates of voter participation and higher levels of ticket splitting. On the relative scarcity of campaign funds in the election of 1908, see Pollock, *Party Campaign Funds*, 37, 66–67; Overacker, *Money in Elections*, 234–38; and Brooks, *Corruption in American Politics and Life*, 234–35.

51. Peter H. Argersinger, " 'A Place on the Ballot': Fusion Politics and Antifusion Laws," *AHR*, 85 (1980): 287–306; Merriam and Overacker, *Primary Elections;* and William Mills Ivins, *On the Electoral System of the State of New York* (Albany, 1906).

52. Ross, *Sin and Society: An Analysis of Latter-Day Iniquity* (Boston, 1907); John M. Blum, *Woodrow Wilson and the Politics of Morality* (Boston, 1956); John B. Roberts, "The Real Cause of Municipal Corruption," in Clinton Rogers Woodruff, ed., *Proceedings of the New York Conference for Good City Government*, National Municipal League publication (Philadelphia, 1905), 148–53; and Howe, *Privilege and Democracy in America.*

53. For an astute analysis of which groups favored and which groups opposed federal railroad legislation, see Richard H. K. Vietor, "Businessmen and the Political Economy: The Railroad Rate Controversy of 1905," *JAH*, 64 (1977): 47–66; and, for an excellent survey of the literature on regulation, see Thomas K. McCraw, "Regulation in America: A Review Article," *Business History Review*, 49 (1975): 159–83. The best account of the emergence of administrative ideas is, of course, Wiebe, *The Search for Order, 1877–1920*, 133–95.

54. On the adaptability of administrative government, see Otis L. Graham, Jr., *The Great Campaigns: Reform and War in America, 1900–1928* (Englewood Cliffs, N.J., 1971), 50–51; and Wiebe, *The Search for Order, 1877–1920*, 222–23, 302.

55. Russell, *Lawless Wealth: The Origin of Some Great American Fortunes* (New York, 1908), 30–35, 52–55, 274–79; and Thelen, "Lincoln Steffens and the Muckrakers: A Review Essay," *Wisconsin Magazine of History*, 58 (1975): 316.

56. Nord, "The Experts versus the Experts"; and Thelen, *Robert M. La Follette and the Insurgent Spirit*, 50–51.

57. Rochester *Democrat and Chronicle*, October 18, 1905; and New York State Library, *Digest of Governors' Messages, 1907, 1908*. In a number of states where politico-business corruption had been an issue in the party platforms around 1906, the platforms were silent on the subject by 1910.

58. Caine, *The Myth of a Progressive Reform: Railroad Regulation in Wisconsin, 1903–1910* (Madison, Wisc., 1970), 70. Also see Mansel G. Blackford, *The Politics of Business in California, 1890–1920* (Columbus, Ohio, 1977); Bruce W. Dearstyne, "Regulation in the Progressive Era: The New York Public Service Commission,"

New York History, 58 (1977): 331–47; and McCraw, "Regulation in America." These and other studies cast considerable doubt on the applicability at the state level of Gabriel Kolko's interpretation of regulatory legislation; for that position, see his *The Triumph of Conservatism*. Commonly, the affected interests opposed state regulation until its passage became inevitable, at which point they entered the contest in order to influence the details of the law. Businessmen often had considerable, but not complete, success in helping shape such legislation, and they frequently found it beneficial in practice.

59. Wiebe, *The Search for Order, 1877–1920*, 172, 180.

60. Hays, "The Politics of Reform in Municipal Government."

3. How do class and ethnicity complicate our conception of the Progressives?

Shelton Stromquist

The Crucible of Class: Cleveland Politics and the Origins of Municipal Reform in the Progressive Era

Shelton Stromquist is the author of several books on labor movements and social change. He is Professor of History at the University of Iowa. In this article, he strikes a powerful blow against the selections we have read so far that put the middle class at the helm of Progressive leadership. At the same time, he gives us a view of immigrants as workers and citizens in an urban area. Rather than seeing immigrants as a Progressive Era problem, he argues that they are part of Progressive Era solutions.

To Stromquist, change is a dynamic process that comes about in an interlocking struggle between demands and concessions. Here, he looks at that process in Cleveland, Ohio, where the working class protested several issues with direct action. How the middle class responded and how those accommodations came to be incorporated in politics illustrate, Stromquist believes, the agency of the working class in Progressivism.

As you read Stromquist's article, ask yourself how his setting and the range of his argument differ from those of Hofstadter, Sanders, Wiebe, and McCormick. This is the first of several articles you will read that move from a national stage to a single urban setting. The nature of a historian's evidence changes with that move, offering much richer detail. But this detail comes at a cost. It is more difficult to argue that what happened in one city might have happened in another; thus it is more difficult to argue for the significance of someone's findings.

Questions for a Closer Reading

1. What did Cleveland workers organize to change? How did they define the problems around them? What were their goals? What tactics did they use to win those goals? Compare this grassroots movement to another social movement with which you are familiar—for example, Populism or the Civil Rights movement.

2. Stromquist argues that you don't have to be involved directly in Progressive lawmaking to have an influence on the laws that are made. Write a treatment of that argument, being sure to give two examples of ways workers influenced Progressive politics, municipal regulation, and legislation.

3. Think about the national range of Sanders's or Wiebe's articles and reflect on what is lost by limiting research to one city. Why might it be easier to talk about working-class activism in a municipal setting than in a national setting? In what ways is Stromquist careful not to overstate his argument as it is based on the evidence of one city? What general claims does he make for it that extend beyond the Cleveland experience?

4. Are there any similarities between Stromquist's workers and Sanders's rural-based Democrats? What does Sanders say about the Democrats' urban support?

5. What does Stromquist think that Wiebe left out of his portrayal of the Progressives as middle-class organizers? If you accept Stromquist's argument that workers influenced Progressivism, how does that acceptance change your evaluation of the ultimate goals of Progressivism?

The Crucible of Class: Cleveland Politics and the Origins of Municipal Reform in the Progressive Era

Progressivism has proved to be a resilient, if somewhat opaque, concept for historians. Yet we seem unable to do without it. Despite "obituaries" for the progressive movement, reports of its demise as a useful historical concept are greatly exaggerated. Like the proverbial cat, progressivism comes back from the latest historiographical fray mangled and scarred, almost beyond recognition, but very much alive.[1]

If new, more promising openings for understanding the nature and meaning of progressive reform have appeared in recent years, it is in large measure because urban historians have made the city a primary venue for the study of class relations, social movements, and the impact of structural reforms in governance and political participation on urban politics. As a result of richly detailed local studies, we see more clearly the intersections of class conflict, political reform, and the social recomposition of cities during the industrial era.[2] And it is on this foundation that we can begin to reconceive progressivism.

Two problems have hindered the reconception of progressivism. The first has been an inability by historians to look beyond the agency* of a "middle class," however defined. The "organizational" historians have replaced an anxious "old middle class" with a new breed of middle-class professionals confident in their mastery of technique. But the revisionism of the organizational school has largely blocked further interpretive advances for nearly a generation.[3] It is now thirty-two years since Joseph Huthmacher took issue with the emphasis on the middle-class origins of progressive reform. Arguing that "the urban lower class provided an active, numerically strong, and politically necessary force for reform," he insisted

---

*Agency means the ability of a group to act on its own behalf.

Shelton Stromquist, "The Crucible of Class: Cleveland Politics and the Origins of Municipal Reform in the Progressive Era," *Journal of Urban History*, 23 (January 1997), 192–220.

that it was *their* "experience" that gave "urban liberalism" its programmatic direction.[4] Promising though his argument was, it failed to recast in any fundamental way the historiography of progressivism.

The second problem that has inhibited a rethinking of progressivism is the failure of historians to provide a credible account of the contentious politics of reform. What both the organizational interpretation and Huthmacher's "urban liberal" alternative lacked was a convincing account of the politics by which its middle-class or lower-class agents fulfilled their "destiny" politically. A group of historians, loosely described as "neo-progressives," has reasserted the centrality of politics to the study of progressivism.[5] While offering no unified interpretation or fully detailed rendering, they have managed to shift attention from categorical analysis of the psychological and sociological attributes of the progressives themselves to the political processes that generated reform. They have identified the historically contingent character of the movement, its diverse composition, and its explosive character. In Richard McCormick's words, an accurate portrait of progressivism must now account for the fact "that political action is open-ended and unpredictable. Consequences are often unexpected, outcomes surprising when matched against origins."[6]

To examine the politics of progressive reform, especially at state and local levels, is to reintroduce the question of agency. Following the organizational historians, Kenneth Finegold has argued that "the incorporation of expertise into city government made possible political coalitions" that were broader than those of "traditional reformers." But Finegold also provides a politics missing from Wiebe's account. In his view, the mediation of experts and the "strategic calculations" of politicians were responsible for assembling successful reform coalitions that could enlist the support of "municipal populists" and their immigrant working-class voters.[7] If Thelen and McCormick did not adequately specify the politics of reform coalition building at the municipal level, Finegold overestimates the agency of middle-class experts and fails to account for the dynamic restructuring of local politics that emanated from episodes of class conflict and that reshaped partisan loyalties and reform agendas.

It is my argument that progressive reform at the municipal level congealed in a crucible of class polarization and conflict. Workers were agents in the construction of a new urban politics of reform, not simply its constituents or for that matter its beneficiaries. Municipal politics in a number of cities around the turn of the century was restructured by the pulse of class warfare that realigned the field of social polarities and party identities.[8] This article seeks to unravel, in one setting, that social context and the contentious political process it spawned.

The argument must not be overdrawn. Class conflict and mass protest created conditions that invited reform but did not wholly dictate the outcomes. Episodes of conflict, frequently centered around streetcar strikes, had an impact on local political alignments and the programmatic direction of reform. They gave a temporary spin and direction to municipal progressivism by calling forth responses from other organized interests. They stimulated intraparty factionalism, resuscitated communities of labor populist reformers, and prompted the formation of cross-class alliances that sought to articulate and manage reform sentiment. But workers' actions were also limited by several factors: the nativist and racist cultural currents within the old immigrant, skilled working class, a persistent ambivalence toward politics within the trade unions, and the political alienation of large segments of the new immigrant working class who were effectively disfranchised by the new politics of reform.[9] As David Thelen, Richard McCormick, and Samuel P. Hays have shown, political and social reformers, whether in the name of a "new citizenship" or arrayed against seemingly pervasive business or political "corruption," sought a political equilibrium that would mitigate the politics of class.[10]

A reexamination of the origins of progressivism is appropriate not only because of the renewed appeal of a narrative history of politics that stresses contingent outcomes but because new work on the social crisis of the late nineteenth century refocuses attention on the agency and distinctive vision of popular movements and their impact on the political process.[11] Mass strikes, political insurgency, and the "social crisis" of American capitalism in the 1890s created a unique set of conditions that served as a breeding ground for corporate consolidation and social and political reform.[12] What we have lacked is a more precise understanding of how the social turmoil of these decades intersected with a decaying party system to produce changes in American politics, particularly at the municipal level, that created openings for reform.

New research in a number of other areas supports such a reassessment of politics in the progressive era. Recent work on labor politics demonstrates that the voluntarist political ideology of the American Federation of Labor (AFL) had a more tenuous hold on the political ideas and practice of trade unionists than was previously thought. Trade unions, particularly at the level of the city central, were deeply engaged in politics, even when the federation officially foreswore partisan alignment.[13] New studies of municipal politics in the progressive era reveal the dynamic role that workers played, through the agency of their trade unions and central labor unions, in the process of municipal reform.[14] These studies, and others for the nineteenth century, suggest that working-class struggles centered on

Sheeton

the workplace cannot be isolated from the political arena.[15] Nowhere is this more apparent than in the epidemic of streetcar strikes that swept through American cities between 1895 and 1919.[16] Finally, studies of municipal politics across the industrializing world of the early twentieth century reveal patterns of working-class political behavior and influence, that make the experience of American workers appear less exceptional. Class politics, in Europe as well as the United States, was governed by an underlying pragmatism that was responsive to the specific conditions of party structure and competition workers confronted.[17]

The party system in the United States offered a limited range of options for the articulation of a working-class political agenda. Those options varied from one locality to another. But in most circumstances the dominance of well-entrenched parties with deeply embedded patronage networks, restrictive rules governing voter participation, and a growing "party of nonvoters," whose numbers swelled annually with new immigrant arrivals, forced working-class activists normally to operate within the interstices of the two-party system as they sought to mobilize and focus what political power they could muster on behalf of their reform agenda. Circumstances could change and moments of great political portent appear suddenly, often on the heels of industrial conflict or with surging intraparty factionalism. These shifting circumstances created openings in which a politically pragmatic working class guided by a distinctive social vision exercised some influence over the direction of reform.

The pattern varied from one city to another. What was common across many cases was the new political energy for reform that class conflict generated. In San Francisco, for instance, a new era of reform politics dominated by the Union Labor Party (ULP) was ignited by a bitter general strike under the leadership of the City Front Federation in 1901.[18] In St. Louis, a streetcar strike and consumer boycott in May 1900 precipitated the formation of a Public Ownership Party whose candidate, state labor commissioner Lee Meriwether, Republicans and Democrats feared just might become a "pyrotechnically proletarian mayor" of the city. Defeated in a questionable tally of the votes, this political insurgency nonetheless disrupted established party loyalties within the city's electorate.[19] An 1896 streetcar strike in Milwaukee brought Democrat David Rose to power with the promise to "get" the streetcar company. Although he disappointed his more radical supporters, the heightened expectations voters had for his administration helped fuel support over the next decade for the Social Democrats and the fight for public ownership.[20] Between 1890 and 1914, industrial conflict played a significant role in constituting a new politics of reform in a host of other cities.[21]

This article examines the politics of class and the origins of municipal reform in one specific setting—Cleveland at the turn of the century. Cleveland is a case worthy of examination. Its economy, built on transportation and heavy manufacturing, had attracted by the end of the nineteenth century a large and ethnically diverse working class. The city had witnessed its share of class conflict in the era of "Great Upheaval," but unlike Chicago, Detroit, or Pittsburgh, it was not a primary storm center of late nineteenth-century labor conflict. Its party system, like those of so many other cities, had grown more competitive in the waning years of the century, but even at the height of populist agitation it offered little promise of third party triumph. Yet, within a few years, Cleveland found itself with a dynamic reform administration under businessman and Democrat Tom Johnson, whom Lincoln Steffens in 1905 would proclaim "the best mayor of the best-governed city in the United States," and whom Mark Hanna a few years before had called a "socialist-anarchist-nihilist."[22] While Cleveland may not be representative of a large class of American municipalities, it is a case that reveals with particular clarity the interplay of class forces in constituting a new politics of reform. Other cities would reveal different "scenes set" and different "dramas enacted."[23]

Cleveland, like other major cities, was beset with periodic industrial conflict in the 1890s. Streetcar strikes in 1892 and 1899, an ore handlers strike in 1891, riots of unemployed workers in 1894, molders strikes in 1890 and 1891, and a violent lockout at Brown Hoisting Company in 1896 shattered the city's industrial peace. Between 1893 and 1898, some eighty-three strikes were reported in the city.[24]

The Cleveland Central Labor Union (CLU) brought unity to a divided labor movement in the early 1890s. Led by militant printers Robert Bandlow and Max Hayes, the CLU established its own newspaper, the *Cleveland Citizen,* and through its columns codified a political program of local, state, and federal demands. Throughout the 1890s, it remained the primary voice of the Cleveland labor movement, articulating a political vision that was increasingly at odds with the national leadership of the American Federation of Labor after 1896.[25]

Ideologically, the embrace of the CLU was broad, from the single tax to Bellamyite nationalism* and on occasion even support for DeLeon's Socialist Labor Party.[26] In an 1892 editorial, the *Cleveland Citizen* suggested the breadth of its vision in the remedies advocated for the problem of

---

*Edward Bellamy wrote *Looking Backward* in 1888, a utopian novel that advocated a nationally planned society that produced economic equality among its citizens through socialism.

unemployment: "The workingmen of this nation can put an end to involuntary idleness and poverty if they will persistently vote to place all taxes upon land values, vote to have all money issued upon the resources of the government, and vote for government control of railroads, telephone and telegraph lines." And during the Homestead strike it expanded those demands to include "the governmental absorption and ownership of such great corporations as that of the soulless Carnegie."[27]

Closely allied with the working-class movement in Cleveland was a collection of radical reformers (single taxers, populists, greenbackers, nationalists) who persistently sought to build a third-party presence in the city but on occasion threw their support to reform-minded Democrats, like former cooper Martin Foran. The central figure in this reform coalition was Dr. L. B. Tuckerman, a physician, who had come to Cleveland in the early 1880s. He published a newspaper, *The Workman,* from 1885 to 1888, advocated a third party, and drafted a "labor platform" that called for "better hospital facilities, more adequate health services, labor representation on the police board, public ownership of utilities and an improved school system."[28]

After 1893, radical reform centered around the Franklin Club, whose founding inspiration was Dr. Tuckerman. The club's regular meetings on Sunday afternoons and network of affiliated reform clubs throughout the city provided what one newspaper called "a chain of soapboxes for leading progressives and labor leaders." The club brought together middle-class reformers of a radical variety and working-class activists from a number of skilled trades—cabinetmakers, blacksmiths, iron molders, printers, and cigar makers. Max Hayes recalled that often workers who received "their first baptism as polemicists at the Central Labor Union," took a "postgraduate course" at the Franklin Club.[29]

This broad-based labor reform coalition, anchored in the CLU and the Franklin Club, spearheaded the Populist Party in the city. In the spring 1893 mayoral campaign, the Peoples' Party held the balance of power with 16 percent of the popular vote, and in some working-class wards it polled as much as 25 percent. Although the Populists never achieved greater electoral success in the city, they continued to have a strategic effect on local electoral outcomes as late as the 1897 mayoral campaign, when their votes denied victory to the Democratic candidate, John Farley.[30]

As the end of the century approached, Cleveland's working-class movement was firmly organized and growing. Unions experienced the energizing effects of returning prosperity and a tighter labor market. By 1900, the city had sixty-two unions affiliated with the AFL, twenty-four unaffiliated, and fourteen local assemblies of the nationally moribund Knights of Labor. Ideologically the movement's leadership was unequivocally commit-

ted to a radical program whose roots lay in the working-class republicanism of the 1880s and whose branches were closely intertwined with the
developing socialist movement.[31] But as an independent presence in the
political process, the working class had enjoyed only modest success.
Labor candidates under Greenback, ULP, and Populist banners had
attracted limited support, and on only a few occasions had a "labor vote"
effectively influenced the selection of Democratic party candidates and
their platforms.

The Structure of Local Politics

Cleveland city politics in the late nineteenth century was essentially a story
of Republican party domination, with occasional interludes of Democratic
success. Both parties were beset by intensifying factionalism in the 1890s
that inhibited the formation of an effective or dominant local machine in
the ranks of either.

Among the Democrats, John Farley, who served as mayor from 1883–85
and as director of public works in the Democratic administration of
Robert Blee from 1893–95, occupied a central role, supported by a coalition of ward leaders led by Charles P. Salen. But Farley and the regular
organization faced perpetual challenges from labor reform and populist
interests that threatened to withhold their support. The Republicans were
divided after 1895 into a faction that coalesced around upstart mayoral
candidate Robert E. McKisson and the regular organization associated
with Mark Hanna. McKisson, elected in 1895 after challenging Hanna's
candidate in the primary, was reelected in 1897. Although he never managed to root out Hanna's influence and construct a durable machine of
his own, McKisson's brand of independent republicanism left the ranks of
the Grand Old Party unsettled.[32]

The critical developments that transformed Cleveland politics began
with the mayoral campaign in the spring of 1899 and lasted through the
subsequent mayoral contest two years later. The Democratic organization
again put forward as its candidate, John Farley, whom Mayor McKisson
had defeated in 1897. McKisson won the Republican primary in spite of
the active opposition of Hanna.

The 1899 campaign revealed the bewildering disarray of Cleveland politics. Hanna, more or less openly, threw his support to the Democrat Farley,
as did the mugwumpish Municipal Association, a local "good government"
coalition of middle- and upper-class reformers that was aggrieved with
McKisson's machine-building efforts. On the other hand, key "municipal
populists" lined up their working-class supporters behind Republican
McKisson, who pledged his support for municipal ownership of utilities

and attacked the Municipal Association as "tax dodgers and corpora-
tionists."[33] The Farley organization had been associated with the anti-
Bryan wing of the Democratic party and was therefore further out of favor
with the populist-leaning Democrats. Farley's victory only intensified the
divisions in both parties. According to the *Cleveland Citizen,* the spring
campaign left party regulars "panic stricken and floundering out of the
frying pan into the fire. . . . The old crowds almost completely obliterated
party lines."[34]

While populist reformers had demonstrated some capacity to mobilize
working-class voters on behalf of their agenda and the local labor movement was solidly committed to a political program that went beyond that
of the reformers, class was not the dominant substructure of local politics.
Indeed, factional and party loyalties were a tangled web in early 1899.

Two events untangled the political web in Cleveland and defined a
structure of partisan alignment that had a strong class character. The
streetcar strike of the summer of 1899 and the nonpartisan gubernatorial
campaign of Samuel "Golden Rule" Jones, mayor of Toledo, in the fall,
realigned the local political universe around class poles.

Streetcar Strike of 1899

In early June 1899, motormen and conductors for the Big Consolidated
streetcar company struck over work rules they found objectionable and
demanded recognition of their union, organized just a few months
before.[35] The strike occurred in the context of growing public hostility
toward the company over the speed with which cars traveled through
densely populated working-class neighborhoods. Accidents that took the
lives of several children within the space of a few weeks brought angry
crowds into the streets in early June.[36] Between the beginning of the strike
on June 11 and June 22, when a tentative settlement was reached, streetcar
service was badly disrupted as crowds attacked cars operating with scab*
labor. For the next several weeks, disgruntled strikers claimed that the
company was not abiding by its agreement to rehire 80 percent of the
strikers and to segregate the scabs on separate runs. Attacks on nonunion
crews continued sporadically until July 18 when the union, out of frustration, reimposed the strike.[37] For the remainder of July and well into
August, Cleveland was the scene of nightly warfare. Huge roving crowds,
numbering in the thousands, attacked the cars and their nonunion operators, while the city's police force, augmented by 1,200 members of the

Scab is unionists' term for a strikebreaker.

state militia, arrested strike sympathizers and attempted to keep the street-cars operating.[38]

Sporadic rioting continued into September. Hundreds of persons were arrested for offenses that ranged from dynamiting cars to calling nonunion motormen "scabs." The strike was accompanied by a thoroughly organized boycott of the streetcars. Women acted as spotters and followed those who rode the cars into shops where proprietors were told not to serve them on penalty of being boycotted themselves.[39] Wagons, jitneys, and omnibuses were enlisted to provide alternative transportation in the working-class neighborhoods. Although the strike and boycott were not officially declared off until October, they enjoyed diminishing effectiveness by the end of August.

Several features of the conflict are particularly noteworthy for our purposes. First, the streetcar men enjoyed widespread support among Cleveland's working classes. Cars traveling through the factory district near the center of the city were perpetually attacked by workers throwing missiles from workshop windows or gathering at noon to attack the nonunion crews.[40] A wide range of organized trades declared their official support for the strike and boycott and contributed handsomely to the strike fund. They included granite cutters, steamfitters, lithographers, plumbers, cigar makers, structural iron workers, waiters, machinists, retail clerks, lathers, and railroad yardmen.[41] As Labor Day approached, the preparations for a massive show of solidarity suggested that the strike had invigorated the local labor movement. A reporter noted that "local labor agitators claim that there has been a big revival in trade unionism as a result of the street car strike."[42] Organizers were not disappointed. The streetcar men led the parade of between eight and ten thousand workers, the biggest turnout in years. As they passed city hall and the mayor's reviewing stand, each union masked its colors and marched by in silence. All twelve bands in the procession, with one exception, ceased playing. Max Hayes, secretary of the CLU, confirmed that the action was intended as a "rebuke to the mayor for his official conduct during the street car strike."[43]

A second important dimension of the strike is revealed in the support that it generated across the diverse ethnic working-class communities of the city. Hostility toward the streetcar companies was classwide. The legions of labor reached deep into the ethnic communities of the city. At the height of the crowd activity, the local police refused protection to Big Con cars operating in the Polish district in the vicinity of Broadway. Captain Hutchinson said that "it would be suicide to attempt to operate cars through the Polish district at any time, much less on Sunday, when all the men in the district are idle." The presence of militia in the neighborhoods of "Bohemians and other foreigners," who were traditionally hostile to all forms of militarism, was like "waving a red flag in front of a bull," according to a reporter who witnessed the crowd attacking a car guarded by two militia men on a Sunday afternoon. "In less time than it takes to tell, the crowd had increased to nearly 2000 people and commenced charging the cars."[44] In other incidents, a Polish woman weighing nearly 280 pounds (the newspaper called her an "Amazon") incited a crowd of men and boys to riot, pelting streetcars with stones. She refused to desist when ordered to do so by the police. As part of the boycott activity, anonymous persons placed stakes in the yards of those who rode nonunion cars. The inscription read "scabs live here," but the newspaper reported that "the spelling is worthy of note and indicates that the printer is on unfamiliar terms with the English language."[45]

Organizations in the immigrant communities were visible and active on behalf of the strikers. Prominent leaders of the Bohemian community organized meetings at the Turn Hall and urged the hundreds in attendance to support the boycott. The Massini Italian Republican Club, some three hundred strong, pledged their support to the strikers. In the east side neighborhoods around Broadway, Orange, Scoville, Central, Union, and Quincy, largely populated by Polish, Italian, Russian Jewish, Hungarian, and Bohemian immigrants, few passengers were found on streetcars because, according to the *Plain Dealer*, "the majority of people residing in that section are working people and to a great extent are members of a labor union or reform organization."[46] Polish community leader, M. P. Knicka, wrote to a friend that "cars are running, but nobody wants to take them, and to go to the city people take carriages." The community newspaper, *Polonia w Ameryce* reported regularly on the effectiveness of the boycott.[47]

Although incidents of crowd and boycott activity were widely reported throughout the city, the most concentrated action, almost daily for a period of several weeks in July and August, occurred in two quite different areas. On the east side, a cluster of "new" immigrant neighborhoods radiating outward from the center of the city along Broadway, Orange, and Scoville streets as far as Willson Avenue was one center of activity. A second, more concentrated area lay just west of the Cuyahoga River in neighborhoods stretching south along Pearl Street as far as the village of Brooklyn. This area was populated largely by persons of older immigrant stock, both first and second generation Germans and Irish. It was also an area with a larger concentration of skilled workers. In each of these districts, crowds of several thousand gathered night after night to attack streetcars and their nonunion crews and for a period of time thoroughly disrupted traffic.[48]

What does this mean?

The Politics of Class

The labor turmoil in the streets of Cleveland during the summer months of 1899 had direct and unmistakable political repercussions. The political effects were in part an accident of timing — the streetcar strike coincided with a nonpartisan gubernatorial campaign by Samuel "Golden Rule" Jones, reform mayor of Toledo and a man closely identified with the aspirations of working people. They were in part a product of a fluid political situation in which both major parties were deeply factionalized and neither party had a very powerful hold on its constituents. But finally they were also the product of a reform political tradition that had kept a working-class reform agenda before the public throughout the 1890s.

The strike created the conditions necessary for a reform administration to capture and hold city government for the next fifteen years. Workers realigned the universe of local politics through their collective actions in the streets. In doing so, they exerted some influence in defining the reform agenda and, in the polarized atmosphere of the months following the strike, recast the Democratic party into an instrument of reform. The politics of those months between the summer of 1899 and the spring election of 1901 reveal a good deal about the origins and dynamics of "progressive" reform in the municipal arena, as well as the limits that class politics faced.[49]

What made the working class agents in constituting the politics of urban reform in a variety of cities was not their organized strength or effective mobilization as a voting bloc, though occasionally they did exercise such direct influence. Rather, it was the intermittent pulse of labor conflict that realigned local politics. These episodes, often brief but intense and frequently centered around streetcar strikes, had an impact on local party alignments and the programmatic direction of reform. But lacking, as they most often did, permanent political organization, workers could not in the end dictate outcomes. They called forth responses by other organized interests. The intraparty factions in Cleveland are particularly interesting to observe in this regard. Those segments of the working class that were inside the contracting universe of local politics — native-born and old immigrant skilled workers for the most part — did form an important segment of the constituency for reform. But political initiative most often lay in the hands of others.[50]

The Cleveland case illustrates these more general patterns. Workers may have created the conditions for reform — even dictated certain aspects of the reform program — but they could not control the political process. Without effective political organization and without overcoming the internal divisions that inhibited a wider working-class solidarity, they could do little more than periodically shatter the class harmony that progressives and standpatters both sought to create. Such actions got the attention of party leaders and local elites; they even extracted some accommodation to working-class demands. In that sense, they gave shape and direction to progressivism. But as the force of such impulses ebbed, so did working-class influence over the direction of municipal reform.[51]

Late in the spring of 1899, after winning a second term as mayor of Toledo, largely on the strength of the support he enjoyed in working-class wards, Samuel P. Jones began to explore the possibility of a run for the governorship of Ohio.[52] Seeking a wider field for his reform views and frustrated by the lack of municipal home rule, he found the appeals from workingmen and central labor unions around the state persuasive.[53] His decision was not officially announced until August, but his correspondence and the tenor of his speeches throughout the summer made clear his intentions. Although he defined his mission in nonpartisan terms—"principle before party"—he called himself on occasion a socialist, while refusing outright affiliation with a socialist party. "I am," he wrote, "just as willing to be called a collectivist, a mutualist, or Brotherhood of man." When he spoke at a Cleveland streetcar strikers' picnic in early August, he insisted, to enthusiastic applause, that the "social disorder" in the city was not the fault of the strikers. "It is the inevitable result of allowing our cities to be used for the profit of private corporations."[54]

With Jones's announcement that he would run a nonpartisan campaign, Democratic politicians immediately saw the dangers ahead. Some, like Allen W. Thurman of Columbus, argued that the party must itself nominate a reformer if it hoped "to hold Democratic workingmen in line with their party." The great danger was "that Jones would poll such a tremendous vote that it would not only demoralize our party . . . but so encourage these people all over the country who think that no good can ever come out of either of the old parties."[55]

In Cleveland, the Jones campaign gathered momentum in September. A Jones organization called the "People's Club" was formed at a meeting hall on Broadway in the strike-torn south side. A business agent of the Electrical Workers' Union predicted that a majority of workers in the building trades in Cleveland would support him. "We have become tired of being knocked about by both the old parties, and have decided to take a stand for Jones."[56] As Jones's support grew, squabbling in the ranks of the Democratic party over control of the organization deepened. Operatives for both parties noted Jones's strength among the "foreign element." A Republican agent reported from Cleveland in late September that dozens of Jones's men "are spending their time in the foreign settlements organizing Jones clubs and it is also said that shortly some of the foreign newspapers may come into line for the Toledoan. The movement is also strong among the union laboring men. The recent labor troubles are believed to be responsible for a good share of the defections."[57]

As the campaign reached its final stages, Jones was particularly active in Cleveland. Huge, wildly enthusiastic meetings were held in the working-class neighborhoods at Germania Hall, Bohemia Hall, Hungaria Hall, and Gray's Armory during the last days of the campaign. One speaker predicted that whether or not he was elected, the Jones vote "will greatly influence the action of the other parties in the future and will hasten the time of the adoption of the system represented by Jones." When the vote was tallied, Jones had won a stunning victory in Cleveland, while losing the statewide contest. In the three-cornered race, 56 percent of Cleveland's voters supported Jones, while the Republican Nash won 30 percent, and the Democrat McLean a mere 11 percent. In the key east side working-class wards, Jones had won 74 and 76 percent, and 72 percent in the heart of the south side immigrant working-class neighborhood.[58]

The fall campaign was "a clearing of the atmosphere" in Cleveland politics, according to the *Plain Dealer.* "The great mass of people who voted for Jones are now aware of their power and will cause further trouble to leading political parties. The *Cleveland Citizen,* which by 1899 was outspokenly socialist in its affiliation, had initially belittled the Jonesites as being reformers who simply "weep the downfall of humpty-dumpty capitalism." By November, the *Citizen* was noting that the "Jones craze" was "sidetracking a good many well-meaning voters who were headed for the Socialist movement."[59] Charles Salen, Democratic boss of the city, was resigned to the outcome, claiming to have "expected and predicted" it all along. He noted that the "portion of the labor vote which is not subject to corporate influence united solidly for [Jones], and as this vote is really the bulwark of the Democratic party in Cleveland, the party was the sufferer. The streetcar strike helped to combine it." Finally, Jones himself argued that the Democratic party must take seriously the lessons of the campaign. Its own reform wing must be "born again," if it hoped to compete for the votes of working people who had traditionally identified with it. "There may be some kind of upheaval yet that may make it a party of good morals."[60]

The events of 1899 had done more than unsettle Cleveland politics. They threatened permanently to restructure party loyalties and competition on the basis of class. While both Democrats and Republicans had been losers in the process, and party managers in each camp struggled to devise a strategy for recovery, the Democrats faced a more critical juncture. Their very existence as a second party seemed threatened.

Agents of this political restructuring were, in one sense, the working men and women whose collective action during the summer had revealed the bankruptcy of the Democratic Farley administration. A different kind of agency is also evident in the activities of a cadre of skilled workingmen who had become politically active in the reform campaigns of the 1890s. No individual played a more central role than Peter Witt. Witt, born in 1869, had quit school at age fifteen. After short stints working in a basket factory and as a printer's devil, he found a job in an iron foundry and in 1886 began learning the trade of molder. In the same year, he joined the Knights of Labor. He also came to be deeply influenced by Dr. Tuckerman and the single-tax ideas that were enjoying wide exposure in working-class circles. He participated in several strikes in the early 1890s, lost his job on more than one occasion, and in 1891 joined the Peoples' Party. His attacks on "special privilege" won him the nickname of "foul-mouthed Pete." Witt was president of Molders' Union No. 218 from 1891–93 and again in 1896. He represented the molders at the Ohio Trades and Labor Assembly and was a delegate to the national convention in Chicago in 1895. During these same years, he was a regular participant in the Franklin Club and its associated reform activities. In 1896, Witt, the devoted single taxer and tireless "street corner agitator," campaigned enthusiastically for William Jennings Bryan.[61]

When Samuel Jones brought his nonpartisan campaign to Cleveland in the late summer of 1899, he found in Peter Witt a ready and enthusiastic recruit to his cause. Witt was already deeply involved in mobilizing support for the streetcar strikers, speaking at nightly rallies in various parts of the city, advocating municipal ownership, and bitterly attacking the Farley administration.[62] Witt and other working-class leaders in the local reform movement spoke with Samuel Jones at the strikers' picnic on August 9. Then in September, he joined Edmund Vail and Thomas Fitzsimmons (old allies from the Franklin Club) in forming the executive committee of the Jones campaign. A nonpartisan legislative ticket was constructed, at least a majority of whose candidates were skilled working men. In early October, as secretary of the organization, he officially opened the campaign headquarters on the public square and was thereafter highly visible in the "Jones craze."

Peter Witt was a crucial bridge between Cleveland's organized working class of old immigrant stock and its community of radical reformers. He also was a direct conduit for these constituencies and their program into the Democratic administration of Tom L. Johnson, elected in 1901. Witt became a key figure in Johnson's campaign and in his subsequent administration. He ran Johnson's so-called "tax school," responsible for uncovering inequities in tax assessments, and served as his city clerk.[63]

Witt articulated a class ideology that he absorbed as a young labor activist and Knights of Labor member. The outlines of that ideology are evident in the text of a popular illustrated lecture he gave many times in Cleveland during the last years of the 1890s. Published as *Cleveland Before St. Peter, A Handful of Hotstuff,* the text reflects Witt's painstaking research in city and county tax ledgers, his unfailing eye for inequality, and his utter contempt for the elite classes. Describing in sarcastic detail the bacchanalian feasts of the "city's representatives of wealth and refinement" at the Union Club and the "overfed and underworked society women" giving exclusive doll shows, he contrasted the city's poor.

> Hundreds of human beings . . . trying to sleep in dry goods boxes and coal sheds; babies nursing at empty breasts, and mothers standing at washtubs for eighteen hours a day in hovels in which the rich would not even think of sheltering their dogs, is certainly presenting with a vengeance the damnableness of our present rotten, corrupt and contemptible social system.

Even his future political ally and fellow single taxer, Tom Johnson, did not emerge unscathed from this attack fueled with class hatred.[64]

Cleveland Politics and the Origins of Municipal Reform

Between the fall of 1899 and the spring mayoral election of 1901, Cleveland's political universe was reconstructed. That project had several dimensions. First, the major parties, but most notably the Democrats, overcame their internal fragmentation and reemerged under new leadership. The threat of nonpartisanism, in an organized form, was dissipated. Second, the Democratic party moved decisively to recapture its lost constituency, the working-class voters who had been deeply infected with the Jones virus. Third, that project of "recapture" was more complex than it might seem or than it has been portrayed. The price for the return of working-class voters was a high one—a mayoral candidate with solid reform credentials and a platform that, at least in part, embodied working-class reform aspirations. What these voters wanted was no mystery. It had been clearly articulated by Jones and was, in fact, a program, elements of which had been around in one reform context or another for a considerable time. Fourth, the "urban populism" that Tom Johnson came to embody was in the end something less than the mobilized working classes of 1899 had demanded. In the "expert" administrators that Johnson surrounded himself with, he revealed a cross-class strategy that in the long run lessened his dependence on the votes of workingmen and, to the degree that it succeeded, left less incentive for him to expand his political base among newly arriving and not yet naturalized immigrant workers.

Over the course of his administration, the class character of his appeal ebbed and flowed, as political circumstances changed.[65]

The reconstruction of Cleveland politics in this critical period centered around the person of Tom L. Johnson. Johnson brought a peculiar blend of business acumen—enormous success as a streetcar magnate—and single-tax principles to his administration. He was converted—by his own account—to Henry George's single tax in the mid-1880s, played an important role in financing and advising George's 1886 United Labor Party campaign for mayor of New York, and abandoned his own business career to serve as a Democratic congressman from Cleveland, succeeding Martin A. Foran.[66] Whereas Foran had enjoyed strong labor support, Johnson in his congressional campaigns did not. Despite his single-tax ideas, he had no record of support for labor, and his background in street railways made workers "suspicious if not openly hostile," according to historian James Whipple.[67] After three terms in Congress, Johnson reportedly told Frederic Howe that "there is not much to be done there. The place to begin is in the city."[68] In the meantime, he returned to his streetcar interests in Detroit and New York.

Johnson reappeared fleetingly during the streetcar strike of 1899, when rumors circulated that he was contributing funds toward the purchase of omnibuses that would serve as alternative transportation to the boycotted streetcars. Peter Witt, as late as August 1899, made light of his fellow single taxer, "smiling Tom," who pledged to abandon his business interests so as to devote himself to the cause of the single tax, and "then came to Cleveland and voted for Mark Hanna's mayoralty candidate [John Farley]."[69]

In late September, with the drift of the fall campaign toward support for Samuel Jones clearly established, Johnson again returned to Cleveland. He paid courtesy calls on Farley and Democratic party leader Charles Salen. He declined to talk politics, although an article in a local newspaper published just prior to his arrival quoted him as recently saying, "I have always been a Democrat and am one still, and I believe in organization, but whether or not I shall work within party lines I am not yet prepared to say. Still, I have my own ideas, although it is rather my custom to act than to talk in advance." Rumors around town had it that he would return with his family in May 1900 to take up permanent residence in the city. In the meantime, he returned by train to his adopted home of New York, with Charles Salen as his traveling companion.[70]

After Cleveland Democrats' ignominious defeat at the hands of Jones's nonpartisan legions, shifts within the party were occurring that prepared the way for a reform movement capable of recapturing working-class votes. The spring 1900 campaign for school director again saw a deeply factionalized Democratic party in a three-cornered race. But the nonpartisan candidate, closely associated with the mugwumpish Municipal Association, was the candidate of only one faction of Jones's supporters from the fall campaign and generated little enthusiasm in working-class districts. The various Democratic factions and Jones partisans jockeyed for control of the congressional nominating convention and the selection of delegates to the national convention.[71]

Once Bryan's nomination was assured, the presidential contest overshadowed local party factionalism. Reformers like Peter Witt reentered the ranks of the party on behalf of Bryan but with no clear commitments beyond that. Johnson's return to Cleveland, as promised, helped bridge the divisions within the party, and Samuel Jones aligned his nonpartisan forces with the Democrats in the presidential contest and campaigned actively for "the great commoner."[72]

Not until the fall election had passed did public attention within the city turn again to municipal politics and the impending spring election for mayor. In early January, the press alluded to efforts by Salenites to recruit a "reluctant" Tom Johnson as their mayoral candidate. Johnson, who had been highly visible in the effort to orchestrate Democratic unity for the fall campaign, busied himself speaking to reform groups on the single tax, and on one notable occasion praised Peter Witt's service on the decennial board of appraisers, for raising Johnson's own taxes![73]

By late January, a Johnson "boom" was under way, with petitions circulating throughout the city calling for his candidacy. Finally, on February 6, a large committee, carrying petitions with the signatures of 15,000 citizens, called at Johnson's palatial home in a carefully orchestrated direct appeal. Johnson was well prepared for the visit, accepted the draft, and announced his candidacy. He read a neatly typed statement of acceptance and outlined his platform. He called for equal rights for all and special privileges to none, made clear that he would conduct public affairs on a corruption-free "business" basis, advocated home rule, lower streetcar fares, opposed quick franchise renewal, and made clear that personally he advocated "municipal ownership of street railroads and some other public utilities, in their nature monopolies, and . . . the philosophy of Henry George." Taxes, he asserted, should be "made a charge on monopoly and privilege." Among the committee of fifty were key figures in the labor reform community, Thomas Fitzsimmons and Edmund Vail.[74]

By the time of the Democratic primary on February 19, all formal opposition within the party had dissolved. Mayor Farley remained hostile to Johnson's candidacy but did not enter the race himself, declaring instead his intention to support the Republican candidate. Renewal of the streetcar franchises, which Farley intended to push ahead with, emerged as a central issue in the campaign, and mass meetings protesting renewal were held across the city, even as the Democratic primary ratified the inevitable Johnson candidacy.

As Johnson's campaign unfolded, the deep support that he enjoyed among the city's workingmen became evident. His direct style of campaigning with open-air rallies in working-class wards, and his increasingly focused attacks on the streetcar companies and their demands for franchise renewal, set in motion what the *Plain Dealer* called "a tidal wave" of enthusiasm for Johnson. At the same time, he appealed for support from all classes by emphasizing his intention to run city government on a "progressive" business basis.[75]

Tom Johnson won the mayoral contest by a comfortable plurality of 6,033 votes in an election that the *Plain Dealer* portrayed as "the people arrayed against McKissonism, the corporations in the shape of the street railway companies, the gas companies and the steam railroad companies and the contractors' ring." The vote followed closely the traditional lines of partisanship reflected in the 1900 presidential contest. Johnson's support was particularly strong among second generation, immigrant-stock voters, whereas his Republican opponent drew most heavily on native-born voters living in outlying areas. Johnson's vote correlated weakly with both Democratic and nonpartisan (Jones) votes in the disordered 1899 gubernatorial campaign, where Jones had shattered the Democratic base; Akers' vote followed closely the Republican vote in that campaign, suggesting the extent to which the Republican base had remained intact.[76] In those immigrant, working-class wards that lay at the heart of the 1899 streetcar strike, where the Democrat Farley had won 54–60 percent of the vote during his last run for office in the spring of 1899, and where Samuel Jones that fall had buried both Democrats and Republicans with majorities in excess of 70 percent, Tom Johnson and the Democrats again won solid majorities ranging from 54–66 percent.

The results, then, confirmed a reconstitution of the Democratic party along traditional lines of partisanship in the municipal arena. The losses of 1899 were recovered. The fissures in the party's ranks were healed, and, under Johnson's leadership, the city administration was set on a new course.

The question remains: how do we explain the appearance and programmatic direction of municipal reform in progressive-era Cleveland? One line of interpretation has suggested the important role of a new, professionalizing middle class, eager to apply its techniques to the realms of public policy. That view was classically stated by Robert Wiebe: "The heart of progressivism was the ambition of the new middle class to fulfill its destiny through bureaucratic means."[77] This interpretation has been reinforced in Kenneth Finegold's comparative study of municipal reform in Cleveland, New York, and Chicago. Finegold believes that it was the incorporation of experts into Johnson's administration that produced reform. "Fundamental change in politics and policy did take place *after* Johnson's election" (my emphasis). Despite their support for Johnson's candidacy in 1901, organizational politicians and businessmen had limited influence on public policy. Instead, policy was initiated and implemented by experts and quasi-experts who were directly incorporated into Johnson's administration.[78] This view stresses partisan continuity between 1899 and 1901 and the instrumental role of Johnson and his experts in constructing a new brand of progressivism. But the "organizational" interpretation of progressivism has paid scant attention to the immediate context of class polarization in many progressive-era cities and the political process that gave birth to reform.

This article has shown that political behavior and patterns of partisanship did undergo significant change during the critical years of 1899 to 1901. The streetcar strike and the Jones campaign of 1899, together with long-standing commitments among leaders of the skilled, old-stock immigrant working class and their radical allies to a reform agenda, redefined the terms of municipal politics. Class polarities undermined the local Democratic party, making the recruitment of a "radical" candidate for mayor and the creation of a new municipal platform imperative. Johnson's candidacy and his program are difficult to imagine in the absence of these polarities. For the Democratic party to recover its old working-class base, it had to be transformed into an instrument of reform. On the surface, traditional partisan alignments were reestablished. But the polarizing events of 1899 had injected class issues into the political process, dislodged large numbers of working-class Democratic voters from their traditional partisan moorings, and defined new conditions for their return to the ranks of the party faithful. Those conditions were clearly understood by Democratic party managers, and they were met. The party of Tom Johnson was not the party of old. The working-class segment of his constituency, deeply affected by the upheavals of 1899, reshaped municipal politics to reflect its reform aspirations. The limits of that influence were evident as the Johnson administration and that of his anointed successor, Newton Baker, unfolded over the next fifteen years.

Urban progressivism, at least in this context, was animated by a working-class reform tradition, given new salience by class conflict. It was not the creation of "experts and quasi-experts," although they became its functionaries, and they in time recast its program and its constituency.

Notes

1. The most widely cited "obituary" is Peter G. Filene, "An Obituary for 'The Progressive Movement,'" *American Quarterly*, 22 (1970), 20–34; See also John D.

Buenker, "The Progressive Era: A Search for Synthesis," *Mid-America*, 51 (1969), 175–93. For a useful review of the 1970s crisis in progressive era historiography, see Daniel Rodgers, "In Search of Progressivism," *Reviews in American History* (December 1982), 113–31.

2. Path-breaking work includes Samuel P. Hays, "The Politics of Reform in Municipal Government in the Progressive Era," *Pacific Northwest Quarterly*, LV (1964); Melvin G. Holli, *Reform in Detroit: Hazen S. Pingree and Urban Politics* (New York, 1968); and Zane Miller, *Boss Cox's Cincinnati: Urban Politics in the Progressive Era* (New York, 1968). Newer studies introduce workers as agents in municipal politics: see, especially, Leon Fink, *Workingmen's Democracy: The Knights of Labor and American Politics* (Urbana, 1983); Michael Kazin, *Barons of Labor: The San Francisco Building Trades and Union Power in the Progressive Era* (Urbana, 1987); Daniel Cornford, *Workers and Dissent in the Redwood Empire* (Philadelphia, 1987). New studies of the relationship between immigrant and African American urban residents and the social reform movement are complicating traditional views; see Rivka Lissak, *Pluralism and the Progressives: Hull House and the New Immigrants* (Chicago, 1989); Ruth Crocker, *Social Work and Social Order: The Settlement Movement in Industrial Cities, 1889–1930* (Urbana, 1992); and Elisabeth Lasch-Quinn, *Black Neighbors: Race and the Limits of Reform in the American Settlement House Movement, 1890–1945* (Chapel Hill, 1993).

3. Robert Wiebe, *The Search for Order, 1877–1920* (New York, 1967), 166. See also Samuel P. Hays, *The Response to Industrialism, 1885–1914* (Chicago, 1957).

4. J. Joseph Hutmacher, "Urban Liberalism and the Age of Reform," *Mississippi Valley Historical Review*, XLIX (September 1962), 234–5. See also John Buenker, *Urban Liberalism and Progressive Reform* (New York, 1973).

5. The term "neo-progressive" is used by David M. Kennedy, "Overview: The Progressive Era," *The Historian*, 37 (1975), 453–68.

6. Richard L. McCormick, "The Discovery That Business Corrupts Politics: A Reappraisal of the Origins of Progressivism," in McCormick, *The Party Period and Public Policy: American Politics from the Age of Jackson to the Progressive Era* (New York, 1986), 311–56, especially 355. See also McCormick, *From Realignment to Reform: Political Change in New York State, 1893–1910* (Ithaca, 1981), which stresses the political process by which state reform emerged. Also, David Thelen, "Social Tensions and the Origins of Progressivism," *Journal of American History,* 56 (1969), 341. And Thelen, *The New Citizenship: The Origins of Progressivism in Wisconsin, 1885–1900* (Columbia, 1972).

7. Kenneth H. Finegold, "Progressivism, Electoral Change, and Public Policy: Reform Outcomes in New York, Cleveland, and Chicago" (Ph.D. dissertation, Harvard University, 1985), 1–51, especially 5–6, 30–1, 35–49. See also Kenneth Finegold, *Experts and Politicians: Reform Challenges to Machine Politics in New York, Cleveland, and Chicago* (Princeton, N.J., 1995). Finegold links political behavior to policy outcomes but fails to recognize working-class agency in the political mobilization for reform. Useful on more general patterns of working-class political mobilization are Michael Rogin and John Shover, *Political Change in California, Critical Elections and Social Movements, 1890–1966* (Westport, 1970); Melvyn Dubofsky, *When Workers Organize: New York City in the Progressive Era* (Amherst, 1968); and Gary M. Fink, *Labor's Search for Political Order: The Political Behavior of the Missouri Labor Movement, 1890–1940* (Columbia, 1974).

8. The "field of force" metaphor was introduced into discussions of class formation by Edward P. Thompson, "Eighteenth-Century English Society: Class Struggle

Without Class?" *Social History*, 3 (May 1978), 151–2, and taken up in the American context by Alan Dawley, "Workers, Capital and the State in the Twentieth Century," and David Brody, "On Creating a New Synthesis of American Labor History: A Comment," in Carroll Moody and Alice Kessler-Harris, eds., *Perspectives on American Labor History, the Problems of Synthesis* (DeKalb, 1989), 154, 213–4.

9. For explorations of the nativist and racist currents within labor and reform communities, see Gwendolyn Mink, *Old Labor and New Immigrants in American Political Development, Union, Party and State, 1875–1920* (Ithaca, 1986), 22, 152–4, and Rivka Lissak, *Pluralism and Progressives*.

10. David Thelen, "Social Tensions and the Origins of Progressivism"; Richard L. McCormick, "The Discovery That Business Corrupts Politics"; Samuel P. Hays, "The Politics of Municipal Reform in the Progressive Era," *Pacific Northwest Quarterly*, LV (1964). What Dorothy Ross called "the liberal revision of American exceptionalism" was the intellectual project that underlay the new pluralist politics that marginalized class interests; see Ross, *The Origins of American Social Science* (New York, 1991), 143–54. See also Shelton Stromquist, *The Progressive Movement and the Reinvention of a Classless People* (forthcoming).

11. Synthetic works that integrate the crises of the late nineteenth century and the reform impulses of the twentieth with an emphasis on popular agency are Nell Irvin Painter, *Standing at Armageddon: The United States 1877–1919* (New York, 1987), and Alan Dawley, *Struggles for Justice: Social Responsibility and the Liberal State* (Cambridge, Mass., 1991).

12. James Livingston, "The Social Analysis of Economic History and Theory: Conjectures on Late Nineteenth-Century American Development," *American Historical Review*, 92 (February 1987), 69–95; Shelton Stromquist, "The United States, 1870–1914," in Marcel van der Linden, ed., *The Formation of Labour Movements: An International Perspective* II (Leiden, 1990), 543–78.

13. See Gary M. Fink, "The Rejection of Voluntarism," *Industrial and Labor Relations Review*, xxvi (1973), 805–19; Julia Greene, " 'The Strike at the Ballot Box': The American Federation of Labor's Entrance into Electoral Politics, 1906–1909," *Labor History*, 32 (Spring 1991), 165–92. Gwendolyn Mink, *Old Labor and New Immigrants in American Political Development*. Also, Melvyn Dubofsky, *When Workers Organize*, and Gary M. Fink, *Labor's Search for Political Order*.

14. Michael Kazin, *Barons of Labor*; Gregory Zieren, "The Propertied Worker: Working Class Formation in Toledo, Ohio, 1870–1900" (unpublished dissertation, University of Delaware, 1981); Daniel A. Cornford, *Workers and Dissent in the Redwood Empire*; Richard William Judd, *Socialist Cities: Municipal Politics and the Grassroots of American Socialism* (Albany, 1989); and Donald T. Critchlow, ed., *Socialism in the Heartland: The Midwestern Experience 1900–1925* (South Bend, 1986).

15. David Scoby, "Boycotting the Politics Factory: Land Radicalism and the New York City Mayoral Election of 1884 [sic]," *Radical History Review*, xxviii–xxx (1984); Leon Fink, *Workingmen's Democracy*, suggests the practical, workplace concerns that drove the Knights to enter politics; Ira Katznelson, *City Trenches, Urban Politics and the Patterning of Class in the United States* (New York, 1981), and Richard Oestreicher, "Urban Working-Class Political Behavior and Theories of American Electoral Politics, 1870–1940," *Journal of American History*, 74 (March 1988), 1257–86, have asserted that a gulf separated workplace and community spheres of working-class life and insulated local politics from class concerns. I see, rather, the connections between workplace and community as a defining characteristic of working-class political activity in this period.

16. See *The Motorman and Conductor,* the journal of the Amalgamated Association of Street Railway Employees, for descriptions of numerous street railway strikes throughout the period; Emerson P. Schmidt, *Industrial Relations in Urban Transportation* (Minneapolis, 1937) provides brief accounts of some of the period's bitterly contested streetcar strikes.

17. See, for instance, Joan Scott, "Social History and the History of Socialism: French Socialist Municipalities in the 1890s," *Le Mouvement Social,* 111 (April–June 1980); Mary Nolan, *Social Democracy and Society, Working Class Radicalism in Düsseldorf, 1890–1920* (Cambridge, 1981); Michael Savage, *The Dynamics of Working-Class Politics, The Labour Movement in Preston, 1880–1940* (Cambridge, 1987); J. Reynolds and K. Laybourn, "The Emergence of the Independent Labour Party in Bradford," *International Review of Social History,* xx (1975), 313–46; and Marcel van der Linden and Jürgen Rojahn, eds., *The Formation of Labour Movements, 1870–1914: An International Perspective* (Leiden, 1990).

18. Michael Kazin, *Barons of Labor,* 35–59, 113–20, 136–9, 181–202, and Jules E. Tygiel, "Workingmen in San Francisco, 1880–1901" (unpublished Ph.D. dissertation, University of California, Los Angeles, 1977).

19. David Thelen, *Paths of Resistance: Tradition and Dignity in Industrializing Missouri* (New York, 1986), 222–4. Also, Steven L. Piott, *The Anti-Monopoly Persuasion: Popular Resistance to the Rise of Big Business in the Midwest* (Westport, 1985), 55–71. Thelen and Piott emphasize the cross-class, consumer orientation of the St. Louis revolt against the streetcar company.

20. Forrest McDonald, "Street Cars and Politics in Milwaukee, 1896–1901," *Wisconsin Magazine of History,* 39 (1955), 166–212, 253–7, 271–3.

21. Although these connections await further research for a number of cities, other cases would almost certainly include Detroit, Toledo, Chicago, New York, and a large number of smaller industrial towns, from Pawtucket, Rhode Island, to Hibbing, Minnesota, to Fresno, California.

22. Lincoln Steffens, "Ohio: A Tale of Two Cities," *McClure's,* 25 (July 1905), 301–2.

23. E. P. Thompson, "Eighteenth-Century English Society: Class Struggle Without Class?" 151–2, masterfully captures the contingent character of class formation and its political outcomes.

24. Leslie Seldon Hough, "The Turbulent Spirit: Violence and Coaction among Cleveland Workers, 1877–1899" (Ph.D. dissertation, University of Virginia, 1977), 157–83; Louis F. Post, "Notes for a Biography of Peter Witt," Peter Witt Papers, Western Reserve Historical Society (hereafter WRHS); Clyde Weasner, "A History of the Labor Movement in Cleveland from 1890 to 1896" (M.A. thesis, Ohio State University, 1933), 48–54, 62–6.

25. James B. Whipple, "Cleveland in Conflict: A Study in Urban Adolescence, 1876–1900" (Ph.D. dissertation, Western Reserve University, 1951), 208.

26. See the Declaration of Principles, Central Labor Union of Cleveland, *Trades and Labor Directory of Cleveland and Vicinity, 1893* (Cleveland, 1893), 9.

27. *Cleveland Citizen,* June 11, August 27, 1892. On the evolving ideology of the Central Labor Union of Cleveland, see T. L. Sudlo, "Socialism and Trade-Unionism, A Study of Their Relation in Cleveland," *Western Reserve University Bulletin,* 12 (1909), 127–8.

28. Whipple, 134–45; Louis F. Post, "Notes."

29. Whipple, 198–202; "Minutes of the Franklin Club, 1893–1896," Franklin Club Papers, WRHS; see frequent reports in *Cleveland Citizen,* e.g., January 12, 19,

16, February 2, 9, March 23, 30, 1895. Parallel discussion/reform clubs appeared in many cities. Perhaps the most widely known was "The Hull House Social Science Club" whose activities were recounted in "A Decade of Economic Discussion," Chapter 9 in Jane Addams, *Twenty Years at Hull House* (New York, 1910), 133–47.

30. *Cleveland Citizen*, August 27, 1892.

31. Whipple, 196. On the linkages between republicanism and socialism in the late nineteenth century, see Dorothy Ross, "Socialism and American Liberalism: Academic Social Thought in the 1880s," *Perspectives in American History*, XI (1977–1978), 5–80.

32. James B. Whipple, "Municipal Government in an Average City: Cleveland, 1876–1900," *Ohio State Archaeological and Historical Quarterly*, 62 (January 1963), 18–20; Kenneth Howard Finegold, "Progressivism, Electoral Change, and Public Policy: Reform Outcomes in New York, Cleveland and Chicago" (Ph.D. dissertation, Harvard University, 1985), 140–8. The McKisson era in Cleveland municipal politics is most thoroughly examined in Thomas Francis Campbell, "Background for Progressivism: Machine Politics in the Administration of Robert E. McKisson, Mayor 1895–1899" (M.A. Thesis, Western Reserve University, June, 1960), and also his article, "Mounting Crisis and Reform: Cleveland's Political Development," in Thomas F. Campbell and Edward M. Miggins, eds., *The Birth of Modern Cleveland, 1865–1930* (Cleveland, 1988).

33. *Cincinnati Enquirer*, April 2, 1899; see also Finegold on divisions among "municipal populists" (the term is his), 148–9, and Frederic C. Howe, *Confessions of a Reformer* (New York, 1925), on the shock that a young "good government" reformer felt at seeing Hanna support with impunity the Democrat Farley. Also Whipple, "Cleveland in Conflict," 363–5.

34. *Cleveland Citizen*, March 4, 18, April 1, 1899.

35. On the organization of streetcar men, see Amalgamated Association of Street Railway Employees periodical, *The Motorman and Conductor*, April, 1899, 2; *Cleveland Plain Dealer*, June 3, 1899.

36. *Cleveland Plain Dealer*, June 6, 8, 9, 1899, has extensive reporting on the crowds of angry citizens protesting streetcar speeds and the loss of life that resulted.

37. *Cleveland Plain Dealer*, July 2, 5, 12, 18, 1899.

38. Nightly rioting and crowd action was reported between July 18 and 28. Naval reservists were called up on July 22 to help police suppress the crowds that were disrupting streetcar service. Their numbers were increased with regular state militia to a total of 1,200 on July 26. See daily reports in *Cleveland Plain Dealer* and *Cleveland Press*.

39. The boycott was extensively reported for a couple of weeks and then minimized by a daily press that seemed particularly eager to discourage it. The thoroughness of the boycott was reflected in the following report. "A well known resident of Newburg said [after riding a nonunion streetcar] . . . that being thirsty Thursday noon he walked into a saloon and requested a glass of beer. He was surprised when it was refused and demanded an explanation. He was told that because he had ridden on a car he could not be accommodated. The gentleman then walked to a saloon a few doors away and met with the same treatment. This incensed him and he determined to order a case of beer. Accordingly, he walked into a nearby drug store for the purpose of telephoning an order. The use of the telephone was, however, refused him. He then entered a barber shop. The proprietor was in a back room and called out to him to wait a moment. The boycotted

man then took off his hat and coat and sat himself in the barber chair. The proprietor appeared in a few moments, but as soon as he saw him informed him with many apologies that he could not be shaved in that shop. All because he had ridden on a nonunion car." *Cleveland Plain Dealer,* July 29, 1899, 2.

40. *Cleveland Plain Dealer* reported numerous incidents of attacks by factory workers in sympathy with the streetcar men, June 15, July 5, 18, 20, 1899. When the police entered Hirschheimer's cloak factory looking for those who had hurled missiles at the cars from shop windows, one worker reported, "Wherever they went they were given the laugh."

41. *Cleveland Plain Dealer,* August 1, 2, 9, 10, 11, 1899. The Butchers' Union led a huge sympathy parade on August 18, at the end of which Big Con cars were attacked.

42. Ibid., September 4, 1899.

43. Ibid., September 5, 1899.

44. Ibid., July 24, 27, 1899.

45. Ibid., July 22, 27, 1899.

46. Ibid., July 28, 31, August 4, 1899.

47. M. P. Knicka to Kwiatkowski, Kniola Travel Bureau Records, Series 1, Cont. 1, Fold. 4, 544, WRHS; and *Polonia w Ameryce,* July 20, 27, August 3, 10, 1899, quoted in Adam Walaszek, "Poles and the Other Ethnic Groups in Cleveland: Cooperation Until the Beginning of the 20th Century" (unpublished paper presented at the Annual Meeting of the Social Science History Association, November, 1989).

48. All strike and boycott incidents reported in the press have been plotted on maps of the city to determine the areas of most concentrated strike support. The west side neighborhoods included large portions of wards 1, 2, 15, 16, 17, and 24. On the east side, activity was concentrated in wards 37, 38, and 39.

49. None of the standard histories of Cleveland politics in this period give adequate attention to either the streetcar labor conflict or the Jones campaign. See for example, Whipple, Campbell, Finegold, or Hoyt L. Warner, *Progressivism in Ohio, 1897–1917* (Columbus, 1964).

50. Huthmacher and Buenker focus their attention primarily on old immigrant, working-class voters who supported progressive reform. What they neglect is the vast number of newer immigrants who were underrepresented in the political process but who were a significant factor in the mass strikes of the period, as the Cleveland evidence illustrates. The "revolt of the laborers" between 1907 and 1913, which the IWW among others tapped, is another manifestation of this phenomenon. The political consequences of these mass strikes have yet to be adequately explored. See David Montgomery, *The Fall of the House of Labor* (New York, 1987), 178–9, 288–9, 310–29, for a discussion of such strikes.

51. For a preliminary discussion of the evolving character of progressive reform in Cleveland during the Tom Johnson and Newton Baker administrations, see Shelton Stromquist, "The Politics of Class: Urban Reform and Working-Class Mobilization in Cleveland and Milwaukee, 1890–1910" (paper presented at the Annual Convention of the Organization of American Historians, Reno, Nevada, March 26, 1988).

52. On the support for Jones among Toledo's working classes, see Gregory R. Zieren, "The Propertied Worker: Working Class Formation in Toledo, Ohio, 1870–1900" (Ph.D. dissertation, University of Delaware, 1981).

53. Samuel Milton Jones, Papers, Incoming correspondence, H. L. Shyrock to Samuel M. Jones, May 22, 1899, also S. M. Jones to N. O. Nelson, May 9, 1899.

54. S. M. Jones to Fred Warren, May 13, 1899, Jones Papers; *Cleveland Citizen,* August 26, 1899.

55. *Cleveland Plain Dealer,* August 24, 1899.

56. Ibid., September 17, 22, 1899.

57. Ibid., September 28, 1899.

58. Ibid., October 13, 16, 20, November 5, 1899.

59. *Cleveland Citizen,* March 4, 18, November 11, 1899.

60. *Cleveland Plain Dealer,* November 8, 1899, and S. M. Jones to N. H. Motsinger, June 16, 1899, Jones Papers.

61. The essential sources on Peter Witt's early life are: Louis F. Post, "Notes for a Biography of Peter Witt," Peter Witt Papers, WRHS, "From Molder to Mayor: High Spots in Peter Witt's Labor Record," 1915, Witt Papers, WRHS, and Carl Wittke, "Peter Witt, Tribune of the People," *Ohio Archaeological and Historical Quarterly,* 58 (October 1949), 361–77.

62. *Cleveland Plain Dealer,* August 3, 4, 5, 6, 9, 1899. Witt's inflammatory attacks on the Farley administration prompted the latter to call Witt and other leaders "Jawsmiths . . . professional working men."

63. On Peter Witt's role in the Johnson administration, see Carl Lorenz, *Tom L. Johnson, Mayor of Cleveland* (New York, 1911), and Tom L. Johnson, *My Story* (New York, 1911). See Hoyt L. Warner, *Progressivism in Ohio,* 56, n. 6, on Witt and Fitzsimmons's "nonpartisan campaigns for Johnson." "They made a nonpartisan fight for him in the immigrant-labor wards as they had for Jones," according to Warner, based on a personal interview with Witt in 1948.

64. Peter Witt, *Cleveland Before St. Peter, A Handful of Hotstuff* (Cleveland, 1899), 6–8, 34–6, 46–8.

65. Kenneth Finegold, "Progressivism, Electoral Change, and Public Policy." For my specific differences with this interpretation that stresses the role of outside experts in shaping Johnson's "urban populism," see below. A preliminary analysis of the ebb and flow of Johnson's working-class support is offered in Shelton Stromquist, "The Politics of Class: Urban Reform and Working Class Mobilization in Cleveland and Milwaukee, 1890–1910."

66. Tom L. Johnson, *My Story* (New York, 1911).

67. James B. Whipple, "Cleveland in Conflict," 130–45.

68. Frederic Howe, *Confessions of a Reformer* (New York, 1925), 97. See also Eugene Converse Burdock, "The Life of Tom L. Johnson" (Ph.D. dissertation, Columbia University, 1951), 52.

69. *Cleveland Plain Dealer,* July 29, 1899; Peter Witt, "Cleveland Before St. Peter," 46.

70. *Cleveland Plain Dealer,* September 24, 26, 1899.

71. Factional squabbling in the Democratic party is closely reported in the *Plain Dealer.* See especially, January 24, February 11, March 3, 6, 28, 29, April 3, 1900.

72. *Cleveland Plain Dealer,* September 15, 18, 30, October 15, 24, 1900.

73. *Cleveland Plain Dealer,* January 10, 15, 1901.

74. Ibid., February 1, 7, 1901.

75. See daily reports in the *Plain Dealer,* but especially, March 7, 14, 17, 23, 28, 29, 30, 1901.

76. See Kenneth Finegold, "Progressivism, Electoral Change, and Public Policy," 161–6, for an analysis that stresses the reconstitution of traditional lines of partisanship in the 1901 mayoral election: correlations (Pearson's r) are from my own analysis of the ward-level voting data: Johnson with 1899 Dem. —.42, Johnson with Jones 1899 vote —.37, Akers with 1899 Rep. —.66.

77. Robert Wiebe, *The Search for Order* (New York, 1967), 166.

78. Finegold, 164.

James J. Connolly

From *The Dimensions of Progressivism*

James J. Connolly is an assistant professor of history at Ball State University. This reading selection is from one of his chapters in *The Triumph of Ethnic Progressivism: Urban Political Culture in Boston, 1900–1925.*

Connolly depicts the rise of ethnic politics in Boston from 1900 to 1925. His selection is one of the most recent of the readings in this book, and it opens a window on a new way of thinking about Progressivism. Connolly looks closely at how Progressivism played out on the ground, not at how national leaders and writers hoped reform might work. He finds that Progressivism gave ethnic groups, many of them made up of recent immigrants, a way to gain access to municipal power in the name of the "people."

In *The Triumph of Ethnic Progressivism,* Connolly argues that Progressivism provided a way to talk about changing government outside traditional political parties, a way to talk about the public as if it was not divided by class interests, and a way to make popular reforms that involved both men and women. As you read about the diverse ethnic groups that used Progressive rhetoric to their advantage, think about Connolly's argument that Progressivism operated in a "multiplicity of contexts" and took on "many meanings."

Questions for a Closer Reading

1. Who are the people Connolly calls Progressives? How do they differ from Hofstadter's, Wiebe's, and Sanders's Progressives? Stromquist and Connolly are both writing about ethnic people in urban areas who became Progressives. What difference did ethnic diversity make to workers in Cleveland? What difference did it make to those Connolly is writing about in Boston?

2. What factors worked against Boston's Italians gaining a voice in municipal government? How did their leaders use Progressivism to even the odds? How did Jewish and Irish Bostonians use Progressivism to challenge political machines in their neighborhoods and in the city at large?

3. Connolly uses phrases such as "the language of reform" and "the Progressive fiction of a morally aroused citizenry." Taking into account all your readings, what do you think he means when he speaks of Progressivism as a language or a fiction?

4. Thinking back to Wiebe and McCormick, find examples of how the ethnic Progressives in this selection use the language of efficiency and the discovery that business corrupts politics to back their campaigns for change.

5. Now refer back to Cleveland. The ethnic unity among workers that Stromquist stresses contrasts with the ethnic conflict Connolly portrays. Did workers in Cleveland overcome ethnic conflict or might they have been more divided than Stromquist emphasizes? Based on Connolly's sources and style of analysis, write a paragraph outlining how and where you would begin to look at interethnic relations in Cleveland.

The Dimensions of Progressivism

The language of reform had a specific resonance in Boston's immigrant communities. It provided an explanation for why they were excluded from public office and positions of power and influence, and why social conditions in their districts were deteriorating. Most importantly, it offered them, too, a way to construct a political identity outside of party politics. Progressivism helped leaders and would-be leaders of the city's Italians, Jews, and especially its Irish majority to establish the civic credentials of their communities. By devoting themselves to the public good, Boston's immigrants would demonstrate their willingness to transcend partisan loyalties and act as unselfish citizens. But while spokesmen for several cultural groups developed versions of reform with enough similarities to share the label "ethnic Progressivism," each was designed to suit its group's particular circumstances.

Purveyors of ethnic Progressivisms used them in a fashion similar to that of the city's business and suburban leaders and middle-class women. They legitimized their claims to be the representatives of their neighborhood or ethnic group. The Progressive fiction of a unified, morally aroused citizenry allowed small bodies of men and women to speak on behalf of particular communities. How convincingly they did so varied from case to case.

Historians have described some but not all of the dimensions of these ethnic Progressivisms. They argue that while immigrants favored social welfare reform as well as many democratizing measures, including the popular nomination of U.S. senators, direct primaries, and woman suffrage, these same immigrants opposed most attempts to remake city governments. Historians agree that the attempts of upper- and middle-class reformers to launch investigations of corruption at city hall, establish city-wide elections, and remove partisanship from city politics were efforts to strip political power from working-class ethnic neighborhoods; as such,

From James J. Connolly, "The Dimensions of Progressivism," from *The Triumph of Ethnic Progressivism: Urban Political Culture in Boston, 1900–1925* (Cambridge: Harvard University Press, 1998), 55–76.

municipal reform supposedly met with strong resistance from the inhabitants of these districts. But these assumptions are based on little careful examination of ground-level, urban public life. A closer look reveals that many ethnic leaders found in Progressivism and its assault on city politics a formula with which to pursue their own ends.[1]

Though just a few miles away from Jamaica Plain, Boston's immigrant-filled North End enclosed a different social and cultural world. The home first of Irish then of Jewish immigrants, by the early twentieth century the North End had become a predominantly Italian neighborhood. Children of Italian parents constituted 60 percent of the district's population in 1905. The 1910 census classified 76 percent of the working members of that population as semi- or unskilled laborers; the remaining 24 percent had managed to climb to the higher rungs of the socioeconomic ladder. Fourteen percent were white-collar workers. Members of this better-off group spearheaded the attempt to create an Italian-American political identity in Boston.[2]

Numerical supremacy did not translate into political dominance for the North End's Italians. The principal reason for this failure was a low rate of electoral participation. "Italians without a doubt take the least interest in politics of any nationality," declared one social worker. In 1896 just 13 percent of Italian males with five years of residence in Boston registered to vote; by 1900 only 36 percent of the same group had become citizens. Nor were Italians a cohesive group. Rather, they were divided by provincial loyalties, which remained strong in the North End. Barriers of language and custom prevented them from becoming an organized political force, a difficulty many never tried to overcome because they planned to return to Italy.[3]

Nevertheless, a basic infrastructure of public leadership had developed among leading Italians by the early 1900s. Its essential building blocks were unions and cooperative societies. Forty-four mutual aid societies operated in the North End in 1908. Two years later the number had grown to one hundred. Out of this activity emerged a tier of local *prominenti*. Dominic D'Alessandro, who came from a small village near Rome to Boston in 1898, rose to prominence as an organizer of the Italian Laborers' Union. In connection with the union he established the Benevolent Aid Society, a federation of smaller mutual aid associations. He also helped found a bank and a branch of the Dante Alighieri Society, an Italian cultural organization. He was aided by George Scigliano, a second-generation lawyer with ties to the North End Democratic Party leaders and a reputation for supporting working-class causes while in the state legislature.

James Donnaruma, editor and publisher of the *Gazzetta del Massachusetts,* the North End–based Italian weekly, also played a central role in neighborhood public life. Rounding out this collection of local elite were political lawyers Jerome Petitti and Frank Leveroni, and a handful of other business and professional men.[4]

By virtue of his position at the helm of the *Gazzetta,* Donnaruma became the dominant public voice in Boston's Italian community. Arriving in the United States at the age of nine, he was educated in the Boston public schools. After purchasing the Italian-language *Gazzetta* in 1897, he launched an aggressive campaign to expand his Italian audience. In 1904 he helped D'Alessandro form the Italian Laborers' Union, and relentlessly publicized its activities in exchange for the guaranteed subscriptions of its members. Aggressively marketing his paper, Donnaruma played a central role in constructing a public identity for the Italian-American community in Boston.[5]

Donnaruma and his fellow North End *prominenti* had little opportunity to translate their civic status into political power. The local Democratic organization, still in the hands of the district's Irish remnant, blocked their path to public office. John F. "Honey Fitz" Fitzgerald, who was elected mayor of Boston in 1909, was a former resident; and although its namesake had long since departed for wealthier suburbs, the Fitzgerald organization still dominated North End politics. The failure of most Italian immigrants to vote made that task much easier. The North End's Irish politicians had learned by 1900 to placate the few Italians who voted by placing one Italian candidate on the ballot each year.[6]

For the North End's emerging Italian elite, power depended on its ability to represent the community convincingly, a difficult task in a community split along provincial lines. The Fitzgerald organization's continued success made this difficult. So they turned to the Progressive formula to establish themselves as civic spokesmen. Progressivism offered a vocabulary that allowed them to speak for North End Italians and at the same time provided a rhetoric for criticizing Fitzgerald and his supporters.

The choice of Fitzgerald as villain was revealing. He had not lived in the North End for nearly a decade when he was elected mayor in 1905, but his notoriety made him an ideal scapegoat for a Progressive crusade. His political exploits first received widespread public notice in settlement worker Robert A. Woods's *Americans in Process,* a study of life in Boston's North and West Ends published in 1902. Woods depicted Fitzgerald, "the Young Napoleon of the North End," and the West End's Martin Lomasney as corrupt, all-powerful bosses preventing social progress in the city's immigrant districts. Fitzgerald and several other politicians threatened to sue Woods for libel after the book appeared. Fitzgerald's image as an unscrupulous politician grew after he was elected mayor, when a series of scandals uncovered by the GGA* and the Boston Finance Commission, a state-sponsored investigative body, rocked his administration.[7]

The attack on Fitzgerald began in earnest when several Italian leaders openly opposed his 1905 mayoral bid. Casting Fitzgerald as a political predator, a group led by Dominic D'Alessandro called on Italians to unite to help defeat him and break his organization's hold on the North End. Fitzgerald was a "dictator," they charged, whose "oppression" was responsible for the deteriorating condition of the North End. The failure of local Italians to "cooperate for the benefit of their district" in the past allowed boss rule to continue. Only when they worked together would they achieve their "political emancipation."[8]

Another prominent North End Italian, State Representative George Scigliano, joined the anti-Fitzgerald insurgency. Although he owed his seat in the state legislature to the Fitzgerald organization, Scigliano broke with it in 1905 as part of the larger factional dispute with the Democratic Party. Opposing Fitzgerald's mayoral aspirations in the name of the "Italian people," he attacked the candidate as a boss who was working "against the interests of the Italians of the North End." The momentum from Scigliano's bolt carried over into the municipal elections that followed. With Fitzgerald battling the Democratic leaders in Boston over the mayoralty, North End Italians formed a "Partito Italiano Independente" and ran two local lawyers, Jerome Petitti and Frank Leveroni, for Common Council.[9]

Although the efforts to create a distinct political identity for North End Italians originated largely from factional disputes within the Democratic Party, they received their greatest support from the *Gazzetta del Massachusetts*. The revelations of the Boston Finance Commission and the attacks of the GGA during Fitzgerald's first term received front-page coverage. The paper presented a long analysis of municipal expenditures and services under Fitzgerald taken from the Finance Commission's highly publicized findings. With the commissioners, Donnaruma concluded that "graft" was the source of the city's growing expenditures and declining local services. During Fitzgerald's term Donnaruma was quick to point out every deficiency in the North End and to blame it on the mayor. "For the people of Boston, Fitzgerald is a new Attila, a divine scourge," the *Gazzetta* concluded, though it claimed in proper reform fashion that the campaign was "not against an individual, but a system."[10]

The sound and fury generated by the anti-Fitzgerald campaign signified little in the way of votes. Fitzgerald carried the district in 1905, and his fol-

*Good Government Association.

lowers controlled most local offices. But he remained a useful foil for efforts to create an effective Italian-American political identity in Boston. Appeals to the "Italian independent vote" became staples of Donnaruma's editorials, with the terms "Italian" and "independent" becoming virtually interchangeable. The Partito Italiano Independente persisted, with opposition to boss Fitzgerald remaining the primary plank of its platform. The *Gazzetta*'s attacks on the mayor borrowed heavily from the revelations of the GGA, the Finance Commission, and the daily press. And the paper continued to present local public life as a battle between the "Italian people" and the corrupt Fitzgerald machine. When Thomas Grady, a candidate opposed to the Fitzgerald organization, won a state representative seat from the North End in 1908, the *Gazzetta* declared that he had "broken the chain" that had bound the people of the North End, and credited the upset to the ubiquitous "Italian independent vote." Grady's victory marked "the triumph of the Italians," who had represented reform in the context of the *Gazzetta*'s portrayal of North End politics.[11]

That the North End Italians' "triumph" took the form of the election of an Irishman was a good measure of their limited political clout. Despite the efforts of Donnaruma and his allies to fashion a reform-based political identity for North End Italians, the Fitzgerald forces remained in control. Grady's victory was the only defeat for the Fitzgerald organization in the North End between 1900 and 1915. The high-water mark of 1908, when Grady won and Republican (and "Italian independent") Jerome Petitti fell just ten votes short of securing the second state representative spot, soon receded. In the city elections that followed, the independent Italian candidates were defeated, and both Grady and Petitti lost in the following year. The size of the nonvoting segment of the Italian population and the willingness of the Democratic organization to nominate a few popular Italians severely restricted the ability of other immigrant leaders to develop a political base outside party politics.[12]

Nor did gender prove a useful basis for sparking political action among Italian women. Efforts to establish a public role for them were limited to a few settlement workers and had little impact. Italian-American demographics were the greatest obstacle to such efforts. The Italian migration to Boston and the rest of the United States was predominantly male. Those women who did migrate either remained at home in traditional domestic roles or performed unskilled labor. Few of them participated in the women's reform campaigns becoming so prevalent in Boston during the first years of the twentieth century.

However limited its impact in the short run, the language and imagery of Progressive reform proved flexible enough to serve the interests of North End *prominenti*. The investigations of settlement house workers, the revelations of local muckrakers, and the exposés of the daily press provided rhetorical tools for Italian spokesmen, just as they did for the businessmen of the GGA, the women of the WML,* or middle-class suburbanites. Italian leaders in the North End used Progressivism to create a distinctive local Italian-American political identity and to establish themselves as the legitimate representatives of the Italian-American community in Boston. Though an ineffective fiction at first, the formula would prove more potent over the long term, when changes in the workings of politics gave nonpartisan action a more important place in urban public life.

Boston's Jewish voices crafted their own Progressivism designed to suit their particular experiences and circumstances. As in the case of Italian spokesmen, Jews' access to political power was limited. Although the roots of the Jewish community in Boston reached back further than those of Italians, they were fragile. Most of the five thousand Jews in Boston in 1880 were German immigrants who had arrived in the middle of the nineteenth century. Between 1880 and 1914, seventy thousand eastern European Jews poured into the city, carrying with them a language and customs that made assimilation into American life difficult. Their arrival also sparked tensions within the ranks of Boston Jewry, as the well-adapted Germans eyed their recently arrived coreligionists with suspicion. The effort by Jewish leaders to bridge this gap involved the creation of a clear Jewish political identity. Progressivism would be a crucial tool in the attempt to create that consciousness.[13]

Prior to the influx of new immigrants, the city's German-Jewish population experienced a fair degree of social and political success. Many prospered in local businesses and lived in Boston's growing suburban sections. They won a share of local public offices as well. Several rabbis, including reform leader Solomon Schindler, served on the School Committee, and a number of Jewish businessmen earned seats on the Common Council and in the state legislature. The most successful of them, Leopold Morse, served a term as a U.S. congressman in the 1880s.[14]

But Boston's Jews had no distinctive political identity. Jewish candidates were just as likely to appear on a Republican as a Democratic ballot. Indeed, the absence of a clear partisan loyalty or ethnic politics was perceived positively, as evidence of their successful assimilation. The city's German Jews created few specifically Jewish institutions, striving instead to blend fully into American life, in politics as well as in social activities. "We have no special Jewish interests to defend," insisted Boston's *Jewish Chron-*

*Women's Municipal League.

icle in 1892, "and we would not antagonize our Christian neighbors by continually forcing our religion to the surface."[15]

The note of defensiveness in the *Chronicle*'s comment reflected the changing circumstances of Jewish Boston. The flood of new immigrants shattered any hope that Jews could slip unnoticed into the mainstream of political and social life. The distinctive customs and language of the Russian, Polish, and other Jews who flooded Boston gave Boston Judaism a markedly ethnic character. Immigration also changed the social geography of Boston Jewry, establishing ward eight in the West End as the center of Jewish life by 1900.[16] By 1910, almost 70 percent of the district's 32,430 residents were Jewish, and they represented the majority of the city's total Jewish population. Crowded into the tenements of ward eight, these immigrants became the most visible Jewish presence in Boston, particularly after Robert Woods and his South End House settlement colleagues published *Americans in Process,* their well-publicized examination of slum life in Boston's North and West Ends.[17]

With so distinctive a public image now attached to Boston's Jews, the main challenge facing Jewish leaders became the forging of a respectable public identity. On the social front they began to develop charitable institutions that cut across the boundaries between German and Russian Jews. Politically, they turned to Progressivism as a way of establishing a distinctively Jewish presence in the city's public life. While Jewish men and women worked in separate spheres, they drew on a similar reform theme — the battle against the ward boss — to claim the mantle of reform for themselves and their community.[18]

The articulators of Jewish Progressivism in Boston belonged to various reform wings. They included labor leader Henry Abrahams, Harvard professor Horace Kallen, and settlement workers Philip Davis, Eva Hoffman, Meyer Bloomfield, and Henry Levenson, all of whom concentrated on social reform. Lawyer-reformer Louis Brandeis, Zionist editor Jacob de Haas, and David Ellis, a lawyer from Brandeis's firm involved in School Committee affairs, were other key figures of Jewish Progressivism. They devoted themselves not only to social reform but also to politics and political reform, using the Progressive motif in an attempt to create a Jewish political movement.[19]

With the hope of sharpening Jewish political consciousness, political reform advocates trained their sights on Martin Lomasney of ward eight. Lomasney was not only the acknowledged political power in the West End, where the largest and most visible portion of Boston's Jews lived, but also the quintessential urban boss. Woods's *Americans in Process* had chronicled Lomasney's exploits as the "czar of ward eight" alongside its portrait of

Fitzgerald's North End activities, winning Lomasney wide and unflattering public notice. His grip on the votes of West Enders became legendary. Between 1888 and 1909 Lomasney's candidates never lost a local race. He even delivered his Democratic ward to a Republican candidate in one instance. His control over a predominantly Jewish district—largely by virtue of the low voting rates of recent immigrants—made him anathema to those seeking a respectable Jewish political identity.[20]

The Jewish reform offensive began with school politics. Robert Silverman, a young Jewish lawyer and settlement worker at the West End Educational Union, accused Walter Harrington, headmaster of a nearby grammar school, of "misappropriation of funds." Harrington, who had political ties to Lomasney and whose sister Julia Duff served on the school board, escaped punishment when the Boston School Committee dismissed the charges in a narrow vote. Boston's Jewish leaders cried foul, claiming that the Committee had suppressed evidence in response to political pressure from Harrington's allies. Harrington filed suit against Silverman for libel, further fueling public interest in the controversy.[21]

Boston's Jewish Progressives mobilized in support of Silverman. David Ellis, a Democrat and member of the School Committee, deserted the party as a result of the controversy. He ran instead as an independent battling against political corruption, with the endorsement of the Public School Association (PSA), Boston's educational reform organization. Brandeis's law firm represented Silverman in hearings before the school board. Leading the way was Jacob de Haas, editor and publisher of the *Jewish Advocate,* Boston's Jewish newspaper. As the case played out over the fall of 1905, the *Advocate* repeatedly described the issue as one pitting "the people" against a political machine. Silverman's actions, it declared, constituted an "offer of assistance from the people"; the rejection of his claim, an act of "gross partisanship."[22]

De Haas and the *Advocate* used the subsequent school board election to link Jewish interests with reform. He urged Jews to vote as a bloc for Ellis and the PSA candidates. Calling the Association a defender of Jewish "flesh and blood," he told his readers that the "decent members" of the School Committee "find their efforts continuously thwarted by the evil elements placed on board by a political machine." Support for the reform candidates in opposition to those who acted as "the tools of some corporation or political machine" was "a paramount duty on the part of Jewish voters."[23]

The Silverman case blossomed into an all-out campaign by Jewish leaders against ward bosses in general, and Lomasney in particular. "These bosses are enemies of the immigrant," declared the *Advocate.* "Remember what our people suffered through the influence of ward bosses," the newspaper warned another time; "the bosses want you today but forget your interests tomorrow." When a Lomasney foe won an election, de Haas's paper welcomed the "triumph for clean politics and against the Eighth ward boss." Louis Brandeis, who was already at the forefront of political reform activities in Boston, urged opposition to machine politics in a pre-election address entitled "What Loyalty Demands" before a Jewish audience in 1905. He linked Jewish ideals with principles of American citizenship and appealed to Boston's Jews to place themselves on the side of clean politics.[24]

Jewish reform activism intensified further when social worker Henry Levenson opposed Lomasney in the 1906 race for state representative from ward eight. Casting himself as the "people's independent candidate," Levenson relentlessly attacked Lomasney and attempted to mobilize Jews against him. "This is a campaign of the people against the boss," he declared, and he left no doubt who "the people" were in this instance. The campaign aimed to secure "representation for the Jews," as one backer put it. Levenson trumpeted the endorsement of prominent local Jews, including Robert Silverman, Horace Kallen, and several synagogue leaders. Lomasney was the "czar" of the West End, they declared, a term with powerful significance in a neighborhood where 60 percent of the residents were Russian Jews. Levenson's backers blamed Lomasney for the poor sanitation of the West End and the prevalence of political corruption in the district. Although Lomasney won, the campaign drew wide attention and was seen as a spur to Jewish political activism in the district.[25]

In battling bossism, the city's leading Jews also sought to create a nonpartisan, specifically Jewish political movement. They held a meeting in November 1905 to discuss plans for nominating Jewish candidates for City Council and considered the possibility of sending a delegation to the GGA to lobby for the inclusion of a Jew on its slate. Although no immediate results came of the meeting, it set a precedent for further activity. It also reflected the emerging push for political unity among Jews in Boston.[26]

As popular clamor for reform increased in Boston after 1905, the drive to define Boston's Jewish community as politically independent and reform-minded accelerated. Spearheading this effort was de Haas's *Advocate*, which claimed to speak for "the solid Jewish vote of Boston." Often citing "the natural political morality of the Jews" in its editorials and reporting, the *Advocate* insisted that its readers strongly favored clean politics. "The Jewish vote is finally on the side of morality," the paper declared in 1907. Two years later, when municipal reform fever in Boston neared its apogee, de Haas observed: "There has grown up a quiet movement which shows distinctly enough that the tendency of the Jews, now as at all times, is to combine with the forces that make for righteousness in municipal affairs."[27]

Efforts at mobilizing Jewish women also drew on Progressive themes, including opposition to ward boss Lomasney. Encouraged to organize by settlement worker Eva Hoffman and other social reformers after a series of riots over high food prices early in the twentieth century, Jewish women in Boston's West End slums finally united in 1912 to battle the "beef trust." This effort evolved into a permanent body, the West End Mothers' Club, which lobbied the state legislature for price regulation, organized boycotts, and staged protest marches. They also singled out Lomasney for sharp criticism, blaming him for the difficult living conditions in the West End. Like their Protestant and Catholic counterparts, Jewish women turned their roles as wives and mothers into a springboard to political power. But they did so separately, never joining with the WML or any of the other citywide reform bodies dominated by middle-class Protestant women.[28]

As both Jewish women and men sought distinctive political identities in Boston, Lomasney remained the biggest obstacle. He continued to dominate the political life of the West End, a symbol of the failure of efforts to wean Jewish voters away from him. While part of Lomasney's success came from his willingness to accommodate some local Jews, the primary reason for his ability to remain in power was the limited interest in voting shown by the eastern European Jews who crowded into his district. Between 1900 and 1910, voter registration in ward eight averaged just 38 percent of the district's total adult male population. A considerable number of the neighborhood's Jews either were not eligible or did not bother to register to vote. The *Advocate* estimated that only one-third of qualified Jews registered in 1905, a view echoed by other observers. With so large a portion of Jewish residents electorally inert, Lomasney faced no real threat to his preeminence.[29]

But the true significance of the Jews' use of Progressivism in Boston did not rest in election results. Rather, Boston's Jewish leaders established a model for future political activity along Jewish lines. As internal social tensions diminished, as they migrated to other parts of the city, and as new national and international issues emerged that linked them together, Boston's Jews would begin to act more cohesively in public life. The groundwork for that activity lay in the appropriation of Progressive concepts and language by the city's Jewish leaders.

a means of uniting

For Boston's most famous immigrants, the language of Progressive reform had yet other meanings. The Irish, who made up a majority of the city's population, dominated its electoral politics. On the surface, they had little reason to embrace Progressivism. But civic authority did not automatically follow from electoral triumphs in Boston. Though the Irish governed, they struggled to win the respect of their Yankee contemporaries. It was in this context that some Irish men and women employed Progressivism as a vehicle to demonstrate their legitimacy as inheritors of the civic ideals of Brahmin Boston.

The unwillingness of the Yankee elite to accept Irish claims to social authority manifested itself outside electoral politics. Despite their numerical and political supremacy, the Boston Irish lacked entry to important corridors of social and economic power. State Street financial institutions, Back Bay clubs, and corporate law firms remained the exclusive preserves of the city's Anglo elite. Even in those areas where they gained a foothold, as in the legal profession, access to such Yankee strongholds as the Boston Bar Association was still limited.[30]

Nevertheless, they had gained considerable social and economic ground by the end of the nineteenth century. A significant number climbed to at least the middle rungs of the socioeconomic ladder. Fully a third held white-collar jobs, and more than half had graduated beyond unskilled or semiskilled labor by 1910. "Their institutions are at once the largest, strongest, and best managed that one comes upon," noted one observer of ethnic Boston. "It seems necessary to emphasize the obvious fact because so many people who should realize it have failed to do so," he added pointedly.[31]

South Boston was among the city's Irish strongholds. Located on a peninsula jutting out into Boston Harbor, it had been a prosperous Anglo-Saxon enclave in the mid–nineteenth century. Unskilled Irish laborers began arriving after the Civil War, settling primarily on the western, inland edge of the peninsula. They gradually edged the remaining native-born and a growing number of middle-class Irish toward the harbor, where the newly displaced built large houses on the wide streets of the City Point section. By 1900, South Boston was an Irish neighborhood. "The main current of South Boston life," a South End House investigator noted, "carries one into the story of the assimilation of the Irish people to the particular social, industrial and commercial conditions of Boston and New England during the past fifty years."[32]

Contrary to prevailing assumptions about Progressive Era Irish neighborhoods, the principal fact of South Boston public life was not machine politics. While the Irish influx made the district solidly Democratic, it did not yield a boss or a machine. Factionalism plagued neighborhood politics. "South Boston has not had a real leader of the 'Pat' Maguire or the Martin Lomasney or the 'Jim' Curley type," the *South Boston Gazette* noted in 1906. Each of the district's three wards had prominent party leaders, but none could unite either his own ward or the larger neighborhood into a single political machine. Factions and alliances rapidly came and went, and politicians often abruptly switched from one group to another between one election and the next. A smoothly run political organization never materialized out of South Boston's chaotic electoral life.[33]

This relentless feuding kindled dissatisfaction with local politics. Frustration over the inability of district politicians to cooperate in pursuit of common goals fed public criticism. Echoing broader calls for political reform, a local priest demanded "the sinking of all party lines and the rallying of all our citizens in support of local aims and objects for the benefit of all." Factionalism discouraged and embarrassed civic leaders. After John Fitzgerald was "hissed and disturbed" at a campaign rally in the neighborhood, the *South Boston Gazette* fretted over the damage done to the district's reputation. "It is unfortunate that such things occur to cause outsiders to talk about South Boston hoodlumism when other citizens are striving to have the district retain its good name." Ever conscious of the ongoing search for Irish legitimacy in Boston, many South Bostonians struggled to shape popular perceptions of the character of their district's public life.[34]

In their anxiety to obtain more-effective representation for their district and to refute stereotypes about Irish-American politics, some South Bostonians drew on Progressive rhetoric. The editor of a local paper and several leading legal and political figures in the district embraced reform as a way to overcome internal political feuding and to rehabilitate South Boston's political reputation. Their efforts yielded mixed results. Though reform-style candidates won a handful of elections, they did not unseat the district's dominant party politicians. Nor did they pry many local voters away from their staunch allegiance to the Democratic Party. But the activities of these candidates helped fuel an antimachine political style that would emerge more fully in later years.

A key figure in South Boston–Irish reform activism was John J. Toomey, editor and publisher of the *South Boston Gazette*. Along with his editorial duties, Toomey involved himself in local politics in the 1890s, running several times for state representative as an antiorganization candidate. He was successful in 1897 and again in 1899, when he ran as an Independent Citizens candidate after losing the Democratic nomination in a hotly contested race. While serving in the State House, he earned a reputation as a strong advocate of political reform, mainly for his outspoken backing of a measure to replace party caucuses with state-run primaries. He used the *Gazette* as a platform to rally support for political reform and clean politics in South Boston.[35]

Toomey had a number of partners among South Boston respectables in his proreform campaign, including two of the district's leading lawyers.

Judge Josiah Dean of the South Boston Municipal Court led the battle against Joseph Norton, ward fourteen's most successful party politician at that time. Dean's former law partner, Charles Slattery, also joined in the fight. Slattery was a Harvard College and Law School graduate who was first elected to the Board of Aldermen in 1901, where he won widespread praise and a reputation as a clean and honest politician. His political rectitude apparently irked Norton and other South Boston Democrats, who prevented him from receiving the customary renomination for a second term in 1902. The rejection sparked a contest that thrust reform issues directly into local public debate.[36]

Declaring himself an independent candidate, Slattery ran as a reformer against the local party leadership and attacked his opponent, veteran political figure and Norton ally John E. Baldwin, as a machine politician. "I have never been a gang fellow," Slattery proudly proclaimed, as he sought to distance himself from organizational politicians. He depicted Baldwin as a greedy, self-seeking candidate, whose sole political ambition was to obtain offices for self-enrichment. For their part, Slattery's opponents appeared content to let the race develop on these terms. They attacked Slattery as an ally of the PSA and other elite reformers and as a man who was out of touch with the needs of ordinary people.[37]

Despite his break with party leaders, Slattery won by a 354-vote margin with 6,244 ballots cast. He would win a third term as well, with the backing of the Good Government Association. He also had the support of Republicans, whose leaders endorsed him when no viable alternative arose from within the party. But his triumph also illustrated the growing appeal of reform politics, even in predominantly Irish districts. Slattery's success was merely the opening salvo in a broader attempt to formulate a Boston-Irish version of Progressive reform.[38]

As in other neighborhoods, the local press played a central role in cultivating proreform sentiment. John Toomey's *Gazette* constantly decried boss rule, the convention system, and self-seeking politicians. The boss has "unhesitatingly domineered over his followers," the *Gazette* declared, "and that has always been the first indication of the unfitness of the 'boss' to rule." Toomey's paper was "pleased" at the exposures of corruption by the Boston Finance Commission and complained about the incompetence of many city employees. Toomey and his staff also regularly attacked local machine politicians, especially John Baldwin and Joseph Norton. "It's been disgusting, to say the least, the way he has run things for many years," announced the *Gazette* after a Norton defeat, "and it was just about due for the people to rise up in their might and teach him a lesson."[39]

The *Gazette* repeatedly insisted that South Bostonians were undergoing a civic awakening of the sort promoted by Lincoln Steffens. It predicted imminent defeat for "the boss" in South Boston, claiming "the people have tired of 'boss' rule where the boss thinks himself bigger than all the people." Another observer argued that "a young man has more chance to win on merit than 'boss' influence than ever before." "The Critic," the *Gazette*'s political columnist, noted defensively that "there are some . . . who think that the voters of our district can be driven into line at the word of the so-called leaders or 'bosses.' The people, however, are mindful of their own responsibilities and duties, and they think and act for themselves."[40]

The *Gazette* contributed as well to the growing clamor for efficiency and nonpartisanship in city affairs. In language that might easily have come from the GGA, it called for a "citizen's candidate" for mayor in 1907: "A non-partisan administration would indeed be a novelty for Boston. An administration where the only qualification necessary for a position at City Hall would be fitness, not whether Democrat or Republican, where the city's money would be distributed with the special desire to do the most good, and not in order to please this or that alderman, or to satisfy the most influential sections." The *Gazette*'s proreform rhetoric did not prevent it from harboring suspicions about the Brahmin-tinged Good Government Association. But the flexibility of Progressive rhetoric allowed both the GGA and the *Gazette* to give it meanings that suited their particular social and political ends.

As Progressivism's themes became more popular in South Boston, politicians began to use them more aggressively. Candidates breathlessly endorsed "ADOPTION OF THE REFERENDUM AND THE INITIATIVE" to thwart boss rule. A South Boston grocer running for reelection to the Common Council in 1903 proudly recalled his vote "in favor of investigating charges of graft in the public building department," while another office seeker frantically "pointed to the charges and evidence of graft that are rampant throughout the country" in an effort to win popular support for his reform candidacy. Others began pointing to their business acumen instead of their political experience in the hopes of convincing voters that they would be responsible and efficient leaders.[41]

This growing reform sentiment was visible in the ground-level politics of other Irish neighborhoods as well. In Charlestown, the Irish-run *Charlestown Enterprise* encouraged reform in the same way the *South Boston Gazette* did, and politicians suddenly began to stress their independence. George Monahan, who had conducted several independent campaigns, prominently cited his fight "against machines and seasoned politicians" during his 1907 State Senate bid, while district attorney hopeful Joseph Dennison emphasized his defiance of local ward leaders in the 1902 congressional elections. Aldermanic candidate Arthur Dolan confidently declared that he would not suit "those who believe that the chief duty of an alderman is to obtain passes and patronage for their constituents." Even reputed ward boss Joseph Corbett caught reform fever, insisting that he "never cared to have anybody finance his campaigns. If he was to hold elective office he always preferred to hold it by the grace of the voters, not caring to be tied up in any way by financial assistance from friends or the public service corporations."[42]

Increased demand for good government prompted many candidates to present themselves as efficiency-minded businessmen, however convincing that claim might be. "The men who form the city government of Boston," Charlestown Alderman Edward Cauley declared, "are business directors of a stupendous corporation." During his reelection bid he naturally pronounced himself qualified for the job. "Alderman Cauley," one of his ads read, "represents that element of the community for which there is such an insistent and reasonable demand—the business man who is willing to enter public life." Another ad claimed that Cauley had succeeded in his field "by conducting his own business, by supervising every detail, and by making it a point to see that nothing is left undone which should be done for the comfort, benefit, and profit of patrons." He pledged to apply similar principles as an alderman. Of course his claims to business expertise may not have been what most people had in mind: he was a corner-store cigar dealer. Nonetheless, his aggressive presentation of himself as a business reformer reflected the growing popularity of the rhetoric of efficiency in local public life.[43]

A second Progressive theme was also present in the political culture of Boston's Irish neighborhoods. Local candidates pledged opposition to trusts and big business as often as they promised honest and efficient government. Charlestown's George Monahan warned that "corporations and trusts would find him a formidable opponent," while another candidate was outraged that "men who have spent their lives in helping great corporations defy the law have been advanced to high public places with large salaries." South Boston State Senator Frank Linehan alerted voters to their dire circumstances: "You men have no more control at the state house than a man way over in Russia," he told them; "The corporations have full control there and they completely run the state house."[44]

Perhaps the most aggressive use of antitrust rhetoric among Irish politicians was by a woman. Despite her connections to Martin Lomasney, Julia Duff found the anticorporation theme of Progressivism a useful political tool in her battles to win an at-large seat on the Boston City Council. Duff, who had long campaigned on the slogan "Boston schools for Boston girls," a not-so-subtle demand for greater employment of Catholic women as public schoolteachers, began to portray herself as a trustbuster as well. "Mrs. Duff," her supporters announced, "is backed by no machine, supported by no book trust, directed by no close corporation of politicians and financiers or educationalists. She has accomplished genuine reforms all along the line." Her campaign literature detailed her successful efforts as a member of the school board to rid the schools of out-of-date textbooks by "fearlessly" exposing the "machinations of the wealthy book trusts." Sinister forces backed Duff's opponents, her followers charged. She was "opposed solely by those influences which are everywhere shaking the foundations of our Republic—trusts and immense wealth."[45]

 The decision by Duff and her Irish male counterparts to use reform rhetoric does not prove that they sincerely desired to change the city's politics and government. But it is an indication of how powerful the language of Progressivism was becoming among their supporters. Irish voters did not automatically recoil from the idea of reform, even political reform, as so many scholars have suggested. Many of Boston's Irish shared the frustration of an angry letter writer from Charlestown who insisted that machine politics made public service "subservient to petty ward factions and political revenge." Much of the political rhetoric aiming to assuage these sentiments may have been hypocritical, but the sentiments themselves were not.[46]

Another strand of Progressivism that drew Irish participation was municipal housekeeping. But like their male counterparts, Irish women in Boston created a distinct version of reform that gave them their own place in local public life. Very few joined the Women's Municipal League. Instead they participated in the activities of the League of Catholic Women (LCW), a parish-based federation of women's clubs throughout the Boston Archdiocese. The LCW provided a vehicle for Catholic women to enter the public arena based on their ethnic and religious identities as well as on their gender.

A small group of Catholic laywomen launched the League in 1910, with the support of Archbishop William O'Connell. They modeled the new organization on the recently created English Catholic Women's League in Oxford, England. But the LCW was also quite clearly the Irish-Catholic response to the growth of predominantly Yankee women's groups such as the Women's Municipal League during the Progressive Era. O'Connell repeatedly insisted that Catholic women stay out of secular women's bodies. By working to "unite Catholic women for the promotion of religious, intellectual, and charitable work," the LCW provided them with a separate public platform free of Yankee Protestant influence and of the taint of the more controversial social reform programs sometimes favored by women's groups of the era.[47]

The LCW grew quickly. In 1915 its membership had surpassed 1,700 and was climbing steadily. By 1919 the League would blossom into a federation of more than forty local societies with over four thousand members. Virtually every parish had an affiliated women's guild or club, giving the LCW a far greater presence in many ethnic neighborhoods than the WML or any other reform or charitable group. Most members were middle-class Irish Catholics. Very few Catholic women from Boston's burgeoning Italian community joined. Nevertheless, the LCW succeeded in establishing itself as the voice of Boston's Catholic women.[48]

Progressive rhetoric lent credibility to the League's claims, while allowing it to remain distinctly Catholic and Irish. Like the WML, its secular counterpart, the Catholic League saw itself as a nonpartisan organization representing communal interests. But it conceived of the community differently. When a member described the LCW as "the material expression of an ever deepening movement among our women for unity," the "our" referred to Boston Catholics, not all Bostonians. LCW leaders used the same vocabulary of solidarity as Boston's other women reformers but gave those words different meanings.[49]

The League's work also paralleled the efforts of the WML and its other Protestant counterparts. The LCW's lecture series not only helped attract new members but encouraged Catholic women to participate in public affairs and presented reports on many social reform topics, including education, prison reform, and disease control. The LCW itself created a women's employment bureau, educated immigrants, engaged in social work, and helped the juvenile courts with their probation load. It became affiliated with several nonsectarian national groups, such as the North American Civic League for Immigrants. These endeavors not only gave the League credibility as a force for reform but also reinforced its claim to be the public embodiment of the views of Catholic women.[50]

Despite shared methods and goals, the LCW and the WML rarely cooperated. Archbishop (later Cardinal) O'Connell provided much of the funding for the LCW and was thus able to keep it on a short leash. He insisted that Catholic women not join Protestant or secular groups but instead operate separately. When some members attempted to combine efforts with a Protestant charity, O'Connell was forced to remind them that the LCW was organized "to assist in carrying on the work of Catholic charities" and should not become "a sort of subsidiary to the various organizations directing these non-Catholic activities."[51]

Much of the LCW's work had a sectarian slant as well. The efforts to educate and Americanize Italian immigrants, for instance, not only served a charitable purpose but also assured that the newcomers would not be lured away from their faith by Protestant social workers. The same impulse fueled the probation work the League performed with young Catholic girls. And in addition to its standard social welfare work, the LCW also dispatched members on home visits to "backslidden" Catholics in an effort to return them to the flock.[52]

In sum, the LCW constituted a distinctive variant of municipal house-keeping. It allowed Catholic women to use the same separate-spheres strategy as their Anglo-Protestant counterparts to establish a foothold in public affairs. Yet it also represented an assertion of a specifically Catholic Irish identity.

In the voice of Boston's Irish men and women, Progressive reform thus took on special significance. For male politicians, it was a way to debunk charges that the Irish were thoughtless followers of party bosses, incapable of acting as responsible, independent-minded citizens. For Irish women, it provided an avenue for gender-based civic activism within specific ethnic and religious boundaries. The openness of the Progressive formula allowed it to fit the needs and circumstances of Irish Boston, just as it did for Brahmin Boston and for the city's other social blocs.

 Social and political circumstance determined the possible variations of Progressivism. Ironically, its emphasis on a unified communal response to the corruption, self-interest, and inefficiency that seemed to plague American life in the early twentieth century was the source of its variety. In Boston, an urban setting buffeted by more than half a century of geographic expansion, spatial and social mobility, and immigration, the number of conceivable definitions of "community" was multiplying. As suburbs grew, as immigrant districts matured, as Boston's Irish became a majority, and as women became more active in public life, the openness of the political language of reform made it available to a variety of newly emerging local elites. Each set of leaders depicted themselves at the head of united political action by their own community, whether defined in neighborhood, religious, gender, or ethnic terms, or by various combinations of these elements.

None of the many versions of reform arose from a grassroots movement. Rather, each sought to create such a movement, or at least to create the impression of one. In every case, a handful of a community's most articulate leaders, usually in connection with a newspaper or publicity-minded organization, built a rhetorical facade of independent, reform-based action within their city, neighborhood, or social group. Initially, at least, none succeeded. But as the popular clamor for reform grew, and as party politicians increasingly found it useful, the new political language and the public endeavors that accompanied it became more widespread, and more powerful.

 In the short run, the growing popularity of the Progressive style made possible the construction of coalitions in support of municipal reform measures. The promise of more honest and efficient government, better and broader government services, and fairer politics appealed to a wide variety of interests.

But the shared words of reform masked different and sometimes contradictory expectations. The understanding of good government espoused by a Brahmin businessman differed from that favored by an immigrant editor. Gradually, city politics came to be a competition to make these divergent visions of urban public life real in practice. During the early twentieth century, the mechanics of city politics were changing, making Progressivism a more powerful electoral tool. As it became a more central part of public discourse, the differences embedded within reform rhetoric would begin to surface. Group identities—increasingly expressed in Progressive terms—eclipsed partisan loyalty as the principal category of political mobilization in Boston. Ironically, the language of Progressivism made possible the initial expression of those disparate identities in the name of unified public action.

Notes

1. J. Joseph Huthmacher, "Urban Liberalism and the Age of Reform," *Mississippi Valley Historical Review*, 44 (1962): 231–241. John D. Buenker's *Urban Liberalism and Progressive Reform* (New York: Charles Scribner and Sons, 1973) is the broadest statement of this perspective, and it focuses on the Progressive Era.

2. Robert A. Woods, ed., *Americans in Process: A Settlement Study by Residents and Associates of South End House* (Boston: Houghton Mifflin, 1902), p. 24. Massachusetts Bureau of Statistics and Labor, *Census of the Commonwealth of Massachusetts: 1905*, vol. 1; *Population and Social Statistics* (Boston: Wright and Potter, 1909), p. xcvii. Census data taken from Samuel H. Preston, "United States Census Data, 1910: Public Use Sample" (Ann Arbor: Inter-University Consortium for Political and Social Research, 1989). See Statistical Appendix for construction of data set. See also Edwin Fenton, *Immigrants and Unions, A Case Study: Italians and American Labor*, 2nd ed. (New York: Arno Press, 1975), p. 219; Anna Maria Martellone, *Una Little Italy: Nell'Atene d'America: La Comunità Italiana di Boston del 1880 al 1920* (Napoli: Guida Editori, 1973), p. 579; and William M. DeMarco, *Ethnics and Enclaves: Boston's Italian North End* (Ann Arbor: UMI Research Press, 1981), pp. 72–74.

3. Frederick A. Bushee, *Ethnic Factors in the Population of Boston* (Boston: South End House, 1903), p. 132. Gustave R. Serino, "Italians in the Political Life of Boston: A Study of the Role of an Immigrant and Ethnic Group in the Political Life of an Urban Community" (Ph.D. diss., Harvard University, 1950), p. 34. See also Woods, *Americans in Process*, pp. 64–65 and DeMarco, *Ethnics and Enclaves*.

4. Fenton, *Immigrants and Unions*, pp. 221–233. *Gazzetta del Massachusetts*, November 5, 1904; September 23, 1905.

5. Fenton, *Immigrants and Unions*, pp. 221–223. Donnaruma and D'Alessandro eventually split over D'Alessandro's cooperation with the Boston Central Labor Union, which insisted that such *prominenti* as Donnaruma and Scigliano sever their

connection with the Italian Laborers Union. D'Alessandro was eventually drawn into the Central Labor Union's orbit, and his role in purely local affairs diminished. See Fenton, *Immigrants and Unions*, p. 241.

6. Serino, "Italians in the Political Life of Boston," p. 39. *Il Moscone,* November 14, 1905, clipping, MLS, vol. 11. Ward 6 Democratic Party Flyer, MLS, vol. 15.

7. Woods, *Americans in Process*, pp. 163–170. Allen F. Davis, *Spearheads for Reform: The Social Settlements and the Progressive Movement, 1890–1914* (New York: Oxford University Press, 1967), p. 286, n. 4. Eleanor Woods, *Robert Woods, Champion of Democracy* (Boston: Houghton Mifflin, 1929), p. 169. *Boston Post,* November 2, 1902, clipping, MLS, vol. 8.

8. Ward 6 Regular Democratic Club Flyer, MLS, vol. 11.

9. *Gazzetta del Massachusetts,* November 11, December 9, 1905. *Boston Post,* November 9, 1905, clipping, MLS, vol. 12.

10. *Gazzetta del Massachusetts,* September 21, November 9, 16, 1907. See the *Gazzetta* generally between 1905 and 1914 for fierce anti-Fitzgerald rhetoric.

11. *Gazzetta del Massachusetts,* September 5, October 31, 1908.

12. Maurice Baskin, "Ward Boss Politics in Boston, 1896–1921" (senior honors thesis, Harvard University, 1975), p. 48. Boston Board of Election Commissioners, *Annual Report for the Year 1908* (Boston, 1909), p. 128. *Boston Herald,* December 16, 1908. *Gazzetta del Massachusetts,* November 6, 1909. *Boston Globe,* November 4, 1909.

13. Jacob Neusner, "The Rise of the Jewish Community, 1890–1914" (Ph.D. diss., Harvard University), pp. iii, 6–14. See also Jacob Neusner, "The Impact of Immigration and Philanthropy upon the Boston Jewish Community (1880–1914)," *Publication of the American Jewish Historical Society* 146 (1956): 71–85.

14. Neusner, "The Rise of the Jewish Community," p. 115. See *Boston Advocate,* September 1, 8, 15, 1905, for biographies of Jewish politicians. See also Albert Ehrenfield, *A Chronicle of Boston Jewry from the Colonial Settlement to 1900* (Boston: Irving Bernstein, 1963), and Ellen Smith, "Israelites in Boston, 1840–1880," in Jonathan D. Sarna and Ellen Smith, eds., *The Jews of Boston: Essays on the Occasion of the Centenary (1895–1995) of the Combined Jewish Philanthropies of Greater Boston* (Boston: Combined Jewish Philanthropies of Greater Boston, 1995), pp. 49–67.

15. Neusner, "The Rise of the Jewish Community," p. 67. *Jewish Chronicle,* September 9, 1892, quoted in Neusner, "The Rise of the Jewish Community," p. 117.

16. The West End neighborhood, lying north and west of the Boston Common, is no longer a residential district. Urban redevelopment turned it into a district of high-rise apartment and office buildings during the 1960s.

17. *Jewish Advocate,* August 26, 1910. Massachusetts Bureau of Statistics and Labor, *Census of Massachusetts: 1905,* vol. 1, *Population and Social Statistics,* p. xciii. The figures are for Russians, a proxy that probably underestimates the total number of Jews. Census data taken from Preston, "United States Census Data, 1910: Public Use Sample." See Statistical Appendix for data set construction. Gerald H. Gamm, "In Search of Suburbs: Boston's Jewish Districts, 1843–1994," in Sarna and Smith, eds., *The Jews of Boston,* p. 139, puts the Jewish population of the West End at 24,000.

18. On the development of Jewish charity institutions, see Neusner, "The Impact of Immigration and Philanthropy upon the Boston Jewish Community." On politics, see William A. Braverman, "The Emergence of a Unified Community, 1880–1917," in Sarna and Smith, eds., *The Jews of Boston,* pp. 85–86.

19. For biographical information, see James R. Green and Hugh Carter Donahue, *Boston Workers: A Labor History* (Boston: The Trustees of the Public Library of

the City of Boston, 1979), p. 75; Neusner, "The Rise of the Jewish Community," p. 78; Allon Gal, *Brandeis of Boston* (Cambridge: Harvard University Press, 1980); Neusner, "The Rise of the Jewish Community," pp. 94–95; Ehrenfield, *A Chronicle of Boston Jewry*, p. 639.

20. Woods, *Americans in Process*, pp. 183–189. Leslie G. Ainley, *Boston Mahatma* (Boston: Bruce Humphries, 1949), p. 45.

21. *Jewish Advocate*, September 29, 1905. *Proceedings of the Boston School Committee for 1905* (Boston: Municipal Printing Office, 1906), pp. 374–379, 401. *Jewish Advocate*, October 13, 1905. The Jewish leaders based their charges on the minority report, which singled out Lomasney for attempting to pressure the board. See also Braverman, "The Emergence of a Unified Community," p. 86.

22. See Gal, *Brandeis of Boston*, pp. 87–90, for a summary of the Silverman issue. *Proceedings of the School Committee for 1905*, p. 401. *Jewish Advocate*, December 5, October 6, 1905.

23. *Jewish Advocate*, October 27, December 8, 1905.

24. *Jewish Advocate*, February 22, 1906, quoted in Neusner, "The Rise of the Jewish Community," p. 118. *Jewish Advocate*, October 20, 1905. Gal, *Brandeis of Boston*, p. 93.

25. *Boston Post*, October 14, 1906, clipping, MLS, vol. 14. Levenson Campaign Flyer, MLS, vol. 14. *Boston Herald*, October 22, 1906, clipping, MLS, vol. 14.

26. *Jewish Advocate*, November 12, 1905.

27. *Jewish Advocate*, December 13, 1905. Neusner, "The Rise of the Jewish Community," p. 118. *Jewish Advocate*, December 1, 1909.

28. Marlene Rockmore, "The Kosher Meat Riots: A Study in the Process of Adaption Among Jewish Immigrant Housewives to Urban America, 1902–1917" (M.A. thesis, University of Massachusetts–Boston, 1980), pp. 35–57.

29. Boston Board of Election Commissioners, *Annual Reports for 1900–1910* (Boston, 1901–1911). *Jewish Advocate*, December 10, 1905.

30. Douglas L. Jones et al., *Discovering the Public Interest: A History of the Boston Bar Association* (Canoga Park, Calif.: CCA Press, 1993), p. 64.

31. Census data taken from Preston, "United States Census Data, 1910: Public Use Sample."

32. Thomas O'Connor, *South Boston, My Hometown: The History of an Ethnic Neighborhood* (Boston: Quinlan Press, 1988), pp. 7–33, 87. Robert A. Woods and Albert J. Kennedy, eds., *The Zone of Emergence: Observations of Lower, Middle, and Upper Working Class Communities in Boston, 1905–1914* (Cambridge: M.I.T. Press, 1962), pp. 174–176. David Ward, "Nineteenth-Century Boston: A Study in the Role of Antecedent and Adjacent Conditions in the Spatial Aspects of Urban Growth" (Ph.D. diss., University of Wisconsin, 1963), pp. 223–228. Massachusetts Bureau of Statistics and Labor, *Census of Massachusetts: 1905*, pp. xcix, c, 638–639, and Preston, "United States Census Data, 1910: Public Use Sample."

33. *South Boston Gazette*, October 6, 1906. O'Connor, *South Boston, My Hometown*, pp. 83–91.

34. John J. Toomey and Edward P. B. Rankin, *History of South Boston (Its Past and Present and Prospects for the Future with Sketches of Prominent Men)* (Boston: By the authors, 1901), p. 467. *South Boston Gazette*, October 13, 1916.

35. Toomey and Rankin, *History of South Boston*, p. 563. *South Boston Gazette*, September 4, 1909.

36. *Boston Post*, November 8, 1897. *Boston Herald*, November 25, 1941. Toomey and Rankin, *History of South Boston*, p. 558.

37. On Baldwin, see Toomey and Rankin, *History of South Boston*, p. 483; *Boston Post*, November 12, December 3, 6, 1902.

38. Boston Board of Election Commissioners, *Annual Report for 1902* (Boston, 1903), p. 71. Good Government Association Election Flyer, GGA, Files and History, file 2.

39. *South Boston Gazette*, October 13, 1906; August 31, 1907; November 16, 1907. See also September 14, 1907, for further proreform commentary. Toomey was not the only Irish editor in Boston who looked favorably on reform. John S. Flanagan, editor of the *Charlestown Enterprise*, encouraged many reforms and advocated non-partisan political action in his Irish neighborhood. In his editorials he supported Democratic candidates but looked askance on the factional maneuverings of many neighborhood politicians, often attacking their self-serving political motivation and lack of public spirit. See for example *Charlestown Enterprise*, October 30, 1915.

40. *South Boston Gazette*, October 13, 1906; November 16, 1907; September 26, 1908.

41. *South Boston Gazette*, September 20, 1913; September 21, 1907; September 8, 1906; November 3, 1906.

42. *Charlestown Enterprise*, October 12, November 2, 1907; August 27, 1910.

43. *South Boston Gazette*, September 28, 1907; November 3, 1906. *Charlestown Enterprise*, November 10, 1906; November 9, 1907.

44. *South Boston Gazette*, September 21, 1909. *Charlestown Enterprise*, September 3, 1910. *South Boston Gazette*, September 19, 1908.

45. Polly Kaufman, "Boston Women and School Committee Politics: Women on the School Committee, 1872–1905" (Ed.D. diss., Boston University, 1978), pp. 341–378. Burns, "The Irony of Progressive Reform," pp. 140–141. *Charlestown Enterprise*, November 30, 1907; December 2, 1907; December 8, 1906; December 9, 1905. *South Boston Gazette*, December 1, 1906.

46. *Charlestown Enterprise*, December 2, 1905.

47. "Constitution and By-Laws of the League of Catholic Women," Record Group VI.4, box 1, folder 1, League of Catholic Women's Papers.

48. Paula M. Kane, *Separatism and Subculture: Boston Catholicism, 1900–1920* (Chapel Hill: University of North Carolina Press, 1994), p. 213.

49. Unidentified typescript, October 1920, Chancery Correspondence, Archives, Archdiocese of Boston, Record Group III.E.10, folder 14.

50. Elizabeth Dwight to Archbishop O'Connell, November 11, 1914, Chancery Correspondence, Archives, Archdiocese of Boston, Record Group III.E.10, box 1, folder 2. "Second Report of the League of Catholic Women, 1912–1913," Chancery Correspondence, Archives, Archdiocese of Boston, Record Group III.E.10, box 1, folder 2. Kane, *Separatism and Subculture*, p. 217.

51. Kane, *Separatism and Subculture*, p. 214. R. J. Haberlin to Msgr. Splaine, November 18, 1916, Chancery Correspondence, Archives, Archdiocese of Boston, RG III.E.10, box 1, folder 3.

52. Kane, *Separatism and Subculture*, p. 216.

4. How did gender affect Progressivism, and which women became Progressives?

Maureen A. Flanagan

Gender and Urban Political Reform: The City Club and the Woman's City Club of Chicago in the Progressive Era

Maureen A. Flanagan is an associate professor of history at Michigan State University and serves as the editor of *The Journal of the Gilded Age and Progressive Era*. This article, "Gender and Urban Political Reform: The City Club and the Woman's City Club of Chicago in the Progressive Era," appeared in an issue of *The American Historical Review* that included articles on reform in several countries during the Progressive Era.

Until you read James J. Connolly's article, it may not have occurred to you that women were Progressives. The inclusion of women in his article, as well as in the selections by Flanagan and Gilmore, reflects scholarship of the past fifteen years that puts women at the center of Progressivism, playing roles as vigorously as men. This new gendered history of Progressivism has moved past asking whether women contributed to Progressivism and now asks how women's participation shaped Progressivism as a whole.

Flanagan's article exemplifies this inquiry as she examines the differences between how men and women defined problems and tackled them. Her setting is Chicago, a city that had fostered women's involvement in politics. It was the home of Jane Addams's Hull House and of a progressive university that trained women in social work. In Chicago, women voted in municipal elections before they won suffrage on the federal level in the Nineteenth Amendment. But Chicago is not an exception in its female activism. Most American cities had an active cadre of Progressive women, and the problems that they sought to solve had much in common with those of the women of the Woman's City Club of Chicago. In many cities across the nation, women could vote in elections for certain municipal offices, such as school boards. Moreover, women found ways to influence politics without themselves being fully enfranchised citizens.

Questions for a Closer Reading

1. What did the women in Flanagan's article mean when they used the term *municipal housekeeping*? How did they understand their relationship with city government?

2. In Flanagan's article, men and women of the same class had different ideas about the best way to reform municipal garbage disposal, to structure the public educational system, and to respond to strikes. Do you see any patterns in the way the men and women approach these three reforms? How do you account for the differences between the reforms men and women want and the way they go about implementing those reforms?

3. Think about Hofstadter's explanation of Progressivism as a reaction of elite men to their loss of status and influence in their communities. Does that analysis apply to either the men's or the women's club members about whom Flanagan writes? Using the case of the Woman's City Club of Chicago, formulate a thesis to challenge Hofstadter on who the Progressives were and why they wanted reform.

4. Many of the authors of selections that you have read in this book sought to discover who the Progressives were without thinking that they might include women. Choose one author who does not include them and confront that author's conclusions with the fact that women played an important role in Progressivism. How might that fact cause the author to revise his or her argument? How might the author justify the exclusion of women?

5. Flanagan argues that middle-class women leaders differed from men of their own class in their reaction to strikes.

Review her argument and think about what it might
mean to Stromquist's analysis. Study Flanagan's sources
and write a research agenda to discover the role women
might have played in working-class Cleveland politics.

Gender and Urban Political Reform: The City Club and the Woman's City Club of Chicago in the Progressive Era

*To bring together . . . as many as possible of those men . . . who
sincerely desire to meet the full measure of their responsibility as citizens,
who are genuinely interested in the improvement, by non-partisan and
disinterested methods, of the political, social, and economic conditions
of the community in which we live . . . [who] are united in the sincerity
of their desire to promote the public welfare.*
　　　　　　　　　　—City Club of Chicago Statement of Purpose[1]

*To bring together women interested in promoting the welfare of the city;
to coordinate and render more effective the scattered social and civic
activities in which they are engaged; to extend a knowledge of public
affairs; to aid in improving civic conditions and to assist in arousing
an increased sense of social responsibility for the safeguarding of the
home, the maintenance of good government, and the ennobling of that
larger home of all—the city.*
　　　　　　　　　—Woman's City Club of Chicago Statement of Purpose[2]

On one political reform issue after another, the men and
women of the Chicago City Clubs disagreed over the means and ends of
Progressive Era reform. In the second decade of the twentieth century,
the men of the City Club of Chicago, a civic reform organization, were
working with businessmen's clubs to implement a vocational education

Maureen A. Flanagan, "Gender and Urban Political Reform: The City Club and the Woman's
City Club of Chicago in the Progressive Era," *The American Historical Review*, 95, no. 4 (October 1990), 1032–50.

curriculum in the public schools designed to train workers for the benefit of industry. Simultaneously, the female counterpart of the City Club, the Woman's City Club of Chicago, was cooperating with the Chicago Federation of Labor, the Chicago Federation of Teachers, the Women's Trade Union League, the Woman's party, and the Socialist party of Illinois in sponsoring a talk in Chicago by Congressman David L. Lewis advocating government ownership of the telephones. The men of the City Club strongly opposed any attempt to implement government ownership of utilities as anticapitalist; they also would never have dreamed of cooperating with workers' organizations or the Socialist party on any issue.[3]

It is commonly accepted that male and female reformers in the first two decades of the twentieth century had different agendas for reform; that these differences stemmed primarily from gender concerns is also assumed.[4] Yet historians have rarely compared the political activities of men and women of the same class. Most works on Progressive Era politics and reform concentrate on men, ignoring women's roles, viewing them only as partners with their husbands or assigning them to the periphery of charity and church work.[5] The idea that women were actively concerned with politics is ignored in favor of seeing them as interested in social, not political, causes and reforms.[6] By ignoring women as political reformers, historians assume that women have little or no political history, at least until we can count their votes. As a result, the processes that led women to pursue political activity and political goals in the first place, and the reasons why their political goals differed from men of their own class, have not been examined.

The members of both the Woman's City Club and the City Club were deeply engaged in political action of the sort Eric Foner has characterized as concerned with "how power in civil society is ordered and exercised [and] the way in which power was wielded and conceptualized."[7] Feeling assaulted by numerous and vexatious municipal problems, they sought to solve them by changing the structure of government, reorganizing the urban environment, and reallocating power within it. Streets and sidewalks in Chicago were in constant disrepair; the public utilities provided abysmal service; the sewer and garbage collection and disposal systems could not handle the volume of waste produced every day in the city; the public school system was overcrowded, understaffed, and underfunded; the smoke, fumes, and waste from industrial plants polluted the air and ground; a large percentage of the populace lived in crowded, rickety, unsanitary tenement houses that flourished in the face of minimal building regulations; and the city's police force neither controlled crime nor kept the peace. Moreover, in the early twentieth century, municipal governments in the United States often lacked institutional authority for

attacking these and other urban problems. Chicago's municipal government was structurally weak, the locus of political power was diffuse and
decentralized, and no consensus existed on who should wield power and
to what purposes. Such issues as how to collect and dispose of municipal
garbage and waste, how to restructure and run the system of public education, and how, and to what ends, to regulate the use of police power within
the city were controversial, and no consensus existed among the citizenry
about the appropriate solutions. Because of their different relationships to
the urban power structure, to daily life within the city, and to other individuals, when the members of the Woman's City Club confronted these problems, they came to a vision of a good city and specific proposals of how
best to provide for the welfare of its residents that were very different from
those of their male counterparts in the City Club.

The contrasting approaches of the two City Clubs is particularly significant because in other respects the groups resembled each other. Both
were founded as municipal reform organizations, the men's club in 1903
and the women's club in 1910, on the principle that the citizens of a city
were responsible for the welfare of the community in which they lived.[8]
The two clubs drew their membership largely from the same class of
upper-middle-class white men and women within the city. The men were
generally businessmen or professionals; often, husbands in the City Club
had wives who belonged to the Woman's City Club. Of the 909 married
women who joined the Woman's City Club in its inaugural year of
1910–11, almost 10 percent were married to men who were members of
the City Club; five years later, the total percentage had risen to 16. A
smaller percentage of women who joined the Woman's City Club were the
sisters, mothers, and daughters of men in the City Club. During this same
period, 1910–15, more women joined the Woman's City Club whose husbands had previously been in the City Club and who had either died or
dropped membership for other reasons, a circumstance that adds to the
picture of a membership drawn from a similar pool of people within the
city. Among the leadership of the Woman's City Club, the correlation
between husbands and wives belonging to their respective clubs is higher:
55 percent of the married women serving as officers and directors of the
Woman's City Club in 1915–16, for example, were married to men in the
City Club; one other officer was the widow of a former City Club member.
Of the married women who chaired the club's standing and civic committees, 75 percent had husbands as members of the City Club; and 33 percent of the married women who headed the ward organization committees
were married to men in the City Club.[9]

Some of the founding members of the City Club were from the prominent, wealthy Chicago families who had built industrial Chicago: Medill

McCormick, John V. Farwell, Jr., Charles R. Crane, Murry Nelson, Jr., and Kellogg Fairbank, for example. But the majority of the membership came from the newer business and professional ranks, which furnished most of the city's middle-class reformers. Among them were real estate developer Arthur Aldis, manufacturer T. K. Webster, and stationer George Cole; lawyers Walter L. Fisher, Victor Elting, and Hoyt King; university professor Charles Merriam and newspaper editor Slason Thompson. At the Woman's City Club, first-year members included the wives of some of these men—Ruth McCormick, Mabel Fisher, Emma Webster, Mary Nelson, Julia Thompson, and Mary Aldis; the wives of other prominent Chicago business and professional men—Ellen Henrotin, Mary Emily Blatchford, Harriet McCormick, Edith Rockefeller McCormick, Anita McCormick Blaine, Paulette Palmer, and Julia Wolf; and settlement house workers—Jane Addams, Mary McDowell, Anna Nicholes, and Harriet Vittum.[10]

A goodly number of unmarried professional women, including some social workers, belonged to the Woman's City Club. It would be a mistake to assume, however, that the settlement house workers wielded a disproportionate influence over the policies pursued by the club. Of the 1,243 members of the Woman's City Club in 1910–11, twenty-three listed one of five settlement houses as their residence; two other women were married to male settlement house workers. Five years later, of 2,789 members, forty-three gave their residence as a settlement house with another three married to male settlement house workers. In no year between 1910 and 1916 did settlement house workers occupy more than five of the twenty-eight positions of officers and directors of the Woman's City Club, nor did they hold a higher percentage of chairs of standing, civic, and ward committees.[11] Solidly middle to upper-class women—either married or widowed—were considerably more numerous than settlement house workers. In 1915, for instance, 388 members listed a residence in the city's affluent twenty-first ward; eighty of these women had husbands or fathers in the City Club. Such prominent Chicago women as Ruth Hanna (Mrs. Medill) McCormick, Ellen (Mrs. Charles) Henrotin, Louise DeKoven (Mrs. Joseph) Bowen, and Elizabeth (Mrs. Charles E.) Merriam, for example, served as vice presidents, directors, and as chairs of standing, civic, and ward committees during the years covered by this study.[12] During the club's first six years, its presidency was held by three prominent Chicago women: Mary (Mrs. H. W.) Wilmarth, Louise DeKoven Bowen, and University of Chicago Professor Sophonisba Breckenridge; and two settlement house workers: Harriet Vittum and Mary McDowell.[13]

It is more difficult to determine how many male settlement house workers may have belonged to the City Club because its membership lists do not give addresses or professions. Raymond Robins and Graham Taylor, two of the city's most prominent settlement house workers, joined the club in early 1904.[14] One or the other of these two men were among the club's thirteen directors during its first four years; neither held a higher position, but both men were consistently active in club affairs and programs and in attempting to influence club policies.

Despite the similar constituencies and statements of purpose of the two City Clubs, they took opposing positions on several current municipal issues in a way that reveals profound differences in their conceptions of city government and its responsibility for the general welfare of its residents. For example, the two clubs took very different approaches to the noxious problem of municipal sanitation when the city's contract with the Chicago Reduction Company expired in 1913. Following standard municipal policy at the time, the city had contracted out to this private business most of the task of municipal garbage and waste disposal. The city itself only collected garbage from houses and small buildings, and it hired private contractors to collect from apartment buildings, hotels, hospitals, and other large establishments. It then paid the Chicago Reduction Company $47,500 per year to dispose of the garbage, and the company made profits from selling the by-products produced from the garbage. On the whole, the citizens of Chicago were unhappy with the system. They complained of infrequent garbage collection, of unsanitary and rickety wagons used for collection that leaked garbage and refuse onto the streets and alleys through which they traveled, of having to separate garbage from other types of waste, and of the reeking fumes emanating from the Reduction Company's plant on the city's near southwest side. When the contract expired, the city had several options to improve service. It could sign a new contract with the Chicago Reduction Company requiring the company to provide better services, it could seek a new company with which to contract, or it could assume direct municipal ownership and operation of all garbage and waste disposal.

The problem of how best to dispose of garbage was part of a larger dilemma faced by U.S. cities during the early twentieth century over the provision of vital municipal services. It was a dilemma not simply because it involved choosing the best possible means but because there was no agreement among urban residents about what criteria defined the best means. One group wished to replace the system of contracting out (franchising) with municipal ownership and operation of municipal services. Another wanted to retain the present system, albeit more tightly regulated. As everyone involved realized, there was a critical difference between these two positions: with municipal ownership and operation of municipal services, the city government would assume far more power than it currently possessed. It would also deprive private enterprise and the city's business-men of an arena for profit.

In 1913, both the City Club and the Woman's City Club considered the garbage issue in ways that suggest significant differences between the members of the two clubs. The City Club's approach typified its method of investigating municipal problems. The club constituted a committee and charged it to study the problem, consult with "experts" in the field, and make recommendations to the club as a whole. The club also scheduled meetings to which it invited various people concerned with the problem to present their ideas and recommendations to the general membership. It directed the committee to collect all possible information on garbage dumps, refuse loading stations, ward dump yards, and any and all real property used for the purpose of garbage disposal. The committee was also to visit and inspect the plant used by the Chicago Reduction Company. Most important, the City Club instructed the committee to gain all the information it could about the "financial details of the reduction business."[15]

On the basis of the committee's findings and reports, and a competing bid offered by the Illinois Rendering Company, the City Club firmly sup-ported the option of keeping the system in private hands for financial rea-sons. The only question in the club members' minds was how to secure the most favorable contract arrangement from one of the two reduction com-panies.[16] In all its deliberations, the City Club rejected outright the option of municipal ownership, contending that there were no "facts and figures" to show that municipal ownership and operation would be more finan-cially rewarding than private ownership.[17] Under the club's calculations, if the city retained its system of private contractors, it would continue to pay costs of collection and reduction, estimated at nearly $500,000 per year, but would avoid the costs of purchasing and operating a reduction plant. This approach, the City Club argued, would be more fiscally efficient.[18] The City Club also proposed that the one costly item for the city, its collec-tion from private residences, be reduced by making the garbage wagon drivers civil servants.[19]

The City Club carried forward its opposition to municipal ownership when it recommended that its membership oppose an ordinance before the City Council in 1914 to appropriate money for city purchase of the reduction plant, which would then be operated by the city's department of health. Even when the ordinance passed, the club refused to withdraw its opposition. In early 1915, it grudgingly supported a bond issue of $700,000 for the health department, saying that, since the money had already been spent (for the purchase and renovation of the plant), the bonds had to be approved.[20] The City Club, however, never ceased fighting municipal ownership of this and other public utilities.[21]

It was not just its cost-benefit analysis of municipal ownership that motivated the City Club. The debate over garbage disposal also concerned whether to continue with reduction—the disposal method used by both the companies bidding for the city contract—or to shift to the incineration method. When Willis Nance, an alderman and a member of the City Waste Commission, spoke to the City Club, he emphasized that reduction "has proven in certain cities to be of immense value from a commercial standpoint." In Chicago, for example, the profit realized from reduction (a process that rendered an oil product used in the manufacture of soaps) had reached as high as $150,000 per year. "It is a question worth considering if in burning all our waste [that is, incineration] we will not become a bit extravagant in our method."[22] Nance admitted that incineration plants were virtually odorless, that because the extreme heat destroyed almost everything this method was certainly sanitary, and that the heat generated by burning refuse could be used to create electricity for the city. Yet Nance, and the City Club, rejected these considerations in favor of reduction. In its refusal to consider creating a municipally owned and operated garbage system, and its support of reduction over incineration, the City Club remained solidly on the side of private profit and limited municipal power over city services. The club did not even investigate possible long-term savings to the city of buying and operating the disposal equipment. Implicit in its stance was the notion that the good of the city lay in maximizing private profits from the provision of municipal services and minimizing governmental involvement.

The Woman's City Club, on the other hand, favored both municipal control over and incineration of garbage on the grounds that they would maximize the healthiness of the urban environment. The Woman's City Club did not concentrate on fiscal details but directed Mary McDowell to explore the variety of sanitation methods used in the United States and in Europe. McDowell, a settlement house worker and chair of the club's Committee on City Waste, undertook an extensive tour of waste disposal operations on both continents in 1913. On her return, she addressed the men's club about her findings. Her tour had convinced her that incineration was a more efficient and sanitary way to dispose of garbage. All the incineration plants she had visited, she told her audience, were free of noxious fumes, the heat from incineration went to generate electricity, and the hardened ash left as a by-product was being used in Europe for street paving. She could see little to recommend in reduction and told the men of the City Club that it was wrong to think of garbage removal as a business rather than a question of health and sanitation. By thinking of it as a business, they failed to consider, for instance that, because a reduction plant could only handle pure garbage, citizens had to perform the unhealthy task of sorting pure garbage from unreducible refuse before it could be collected. Reduction, she bluntly told them, "fascinates the business man in America because you can extract money out of the garbage."[23]

Incineration was only one facet of the overall program for garbage collection and disposal reform favored by the members of the Woman's City Club. These women wanted to centralize power through the municipal ownership and operation of waste facilities, the same system specifically rejected by their male counterparts. After the city purchased the reduction plant in 1914, the men continued to decry the lack of facts and figures available to show whether municipal ownership could be profitable. The women responded by showing that it was indeed profitable. In contrast to the men of the City Club, who advocated maximizing private profits—as high as $150,000—while minimizing municipal expenditures, the women showed that the city had made a profit of almost $6,000 in the year after it purchased the reduction plant. According to their calculations, once the initial outlay had been made to purchase equipment, the possibilities of a small yearly profit for the city existed.[24] Moreover, while they never advocated waste or careless expenditure of municipal finances, they did not see profit as the primary issue. As debate continued during 1915, the Woman's City Club's Committee on City Waste stressed the primacy of health over economics. Where garbage disposal was concerned, announced the club, "the true measure of its efficiency in such work is not the financial returns to be received, but the character of the service given."[25]

In 1916, the Woman's City Club made municipal ownership and operation of all garbage and waste collection and disposal a provision of its Woman's Municipal Platform for Reform.[26] Later that year, the club proposed additionally that the city institutionalize garbage collection and disposal in a new municipal bureau, opposing a new bond issue of $2 million that neither provided for purchase and development of collection equipment nor established this municipal bureau.[27] Unlike the men of the City Club, these women believed that service and the good health and sanitation of the city should be the priority for settling this issue They rejected claims that municipal garbage disposal would not work, wondering aloud "why a municipality should not use the same sense in running their business that a packing plant does."[28]

On the issue of public education, the differences between the City Club and the Woman's City Club were, if anything, even more pronounced. For a number of years, the City Club had been seeking to increase the business efficiency of the school system by implementing a type of education "more in accordance with the demands of modern society and business conditions."[29] In 1908, in response to the statement of Superintendent of Schools Cooley that "instruction in the elementary grades of the city schools was hopelessly academic and unable to fit the mass of the children for the vocation upon which they were to enter,"[30] the City Club constituted a subcommittee to investigate the possibilities of instituting a curriculum stressing vocational education. The club followed its general operating premise that every issue should be scientifically investigated — a task made easier by its wealth — and hired an outside investigator, E. A. Wreidt of the University of Chicago, to pursue this issue for them.

The City Club was seeking a system of vocational education that would better train students for industrial jobs. This system, the club decided after some consideration, could best be established by businessmen and the board of education working together to design a program "directing school children toward proper occupations, and securing additional training for these children in the occupations themselves," while they were still in school.[31] To secure the requisite funding and administration, the City Club supported various measures in the state legislature. It especially liked a bill introduced by the Illinois Bankers' Association to give state support to schools providing vocational education within the general school curriculum.[32]

As was true of the City Club's attitude toward garbage and waste disposal, its proposals for vocational education, intended to create a dependable industrial work force, reflected members' preoccupation with financial reward for business. The subcommittee on vocational education declared industrial education "urgent if not imperative if we are to attain a place in the world's commerce commensurate with our possibilities and opportunities." Whether children or parents wanted this innovation did not concern the City Club. If anyone objected, he or she was accused of selfishness. The club's resolution in support of vocational education declared that "the nurture of intelligent skill in our hand workers is but increasing our effectiveness in industrial production. Certainly any measure looking to this end should have the hearty support of all classes of our citizens. What is good for the whole people can not possibly work harm to any section of our country."[33]

The Woman's City Club also supported vocational education but of a different type and for different means and ends. These women used no rhetoric about the productivity and advancement of industrial society. They were concerned instead with the fate of the individual child within the school and industrial work systems. The Woman's City Club did not establish a new subcommittee to study the problem, and they could not afford outside experts. Working jointly with more than two hundred women from thirty women's clubs across the city, the Woman's City Club approached the issue of vocational education with two goals in mind. The first was to find ways to keep children in school beyond age fourteen (the mandatory age limit for schooling) in order to educate and prepare them for better-paying jobs. These women believed it a social and personal tragedy that thousands of children left school every year to enter "low-grade industries, untrained, unguided and unguarded." They wanted children to understand "that the earning capacity of those who have had a technical or commercial training is much greater than those who have completed only the eighth grade." Their second goal was to provide advice and guidance to schoolchildren once they were ready to leave school and seek work. Children, the Woman's City Club believed, needed "help in choosing a job so as to prevent the wastage that comes to them and the employers from their own haphazard choice."[34]

To help carry out both these goals, in 1911 the Woman's City Club, along with the Chicago Woman's Club and the Association of Collegiate Alumnae, formed the Bureau for Vocational Supervision. The bureau took a personal interest in schoolchildren, working directly to place them in appropriate jobs when they left school and then to follow their subsequent progress. It also established a scholarship committee to raise funds to keep needy children between the ages of fourteen and sixteen in school "until they have acquired enough education, training and physical strength to guarantee them some chance of success in the industrial world." Scholarship money could be used for books, carfare, or as a stipend to replace the income a needy family could have earned from having a child leave school at fourteen; a book-loan fund was also established. The women's organizations, unlike their male counterparts, were always low on funds. The bureau raised the scholarship and book-loan monies through pledges of $1 a month from their memberships.[35]

The positions of the City Club and the Woman's City Club on two additional aspects of education reform also invite comparison. One is the question of whether to establish a system of vocational education separate from general education. Both groups opposed this proposition—which had been introduced into the state legislature with the avid support of the Commercial Club of Chicago—but for different reasons. The City Club thought a dual system would make it difficult to attract students into vocational education. Fearing that vocational education was viewed negatively by much of U.S. society, the club preferred that it be offered within the common schools as a separate curriculum.[36] The Woman's City Club, on the other hand, emphatically rejected a separate system of vocational education as discriminatory. Speaking before the club, Agnes Nestor, a glove worker who at the age of eighteen had led her fellow women workers in a successful strike, and who was both a labor organizer with the Women's Trade Union League and member of the Woman's City Club, urged her audience to reject a separate system of education. She reminded club members that while children might be trained for work in school, they deserved the privilege of cultural training as well as the practical. The women agreed. They passed a resolution stating, "All the children of the community, whether rich or poor are entitled . . . to the benefits of general education for citizenship . . . [and] the children who are to become efficient workmen must comprehend their work in relation to science, art, and to society in general."[37]

The second aspect of education reform over which the two clubs differed was that of maximum classroom size. After visiting public schools and talking to teachers, the Woman's City Club insisted that there be no more than thirty children to a classroom and urged the City Club to support this goal, or at the very least, some definite limit to classroom size. The women further declared that they would "insist that Chicago can afford and must have adequate facilities and a sufficient teaching force to insure a maximum of thirty in high school courses."[38] In other words, the principle of reduced class size demanded the municipality find and allocate the money to implement the changes. The City Club, for its part, refused to support any specific limits on class size, either the thirty initially proposed or the limits of forty-two and twenty-eight in elementary and secondary classrooms that the Woman's City Club later suggested as alternatives. In a letter to the women, the City Club sympathized with the idea of reducing the size of classrooms. It preferred, however, "to go into the question of the proper number of children under each teacher . . . with some care" and to make a future recommendation "based on the best evidence which can be obtained through the country after a rather careful search as to the maximum number of children that can be efficiently taught by a single teacher."[39]

The two organizations also clashed over the issue of police power in the city, especially police activities during labor strikes. Although the men of the City Club, unlike the members of the more ardent antilabor business clubs such as the Commercial Club, did not advocate or condone police violence against strikers, they were loath to condemn it when it happened. After a controversial strike in February 1914 by waitresses from the restaurant workers' union against the Henrici restaurant, the club confined itself to "investigating" both sides of the issue. During the strike, more than one hundred of the striking waitresses had been arrested on the picket line,[40] and the restaurant owners had secured a court injunction against picketing. On both issues—the injunction and the arrests—the chairman of the club's Committee on Labor Conditions, Frederick S. Deibler, presented a noncommittal report to the general membership. It acknowledged that the courts recognized the right to peaceful picketing and conceded that, in general, this was good for labor relations, but it also pointed out that courts could rule against picketing on the grounds that such activity "threatened irreparable injury to property." How to determine whether to issue an injunction was best left to the courts. If in this particular case a judge had found just cause in enjoining the Henrici strike, Deibler implied, that decision ought to be accepted by the club and all citizens.[41] He neither challenged the court's ruling nor questioned the prevailing idea that workers' rights to picket should be restricted to peaceful actions that caused no harm to property. The latter limitation was particularly important. Implicit in that notion was the protection of companies from the loss of any business or trade as a result of picketing.

Deibler did show more doubt about the propriety of the arrests of the striking waitresses and their treatment by the police. "When all the circumstances surrounding the dispute are concerned," he told the club members, "it is difficult to account for the necessity of 119 or more arrests." It looked, he reported, as if the police had been determined to halt the picketing, whatever the legal rights of the waitresses. He expressed doubts about the validity of the restaurant's claim that it had to employ private detectives, who were used against the strikers, in order to protect its property. However, he refused to condemn either the police or the owners for their actions.[42] Deibler's report merely suggested that police violence during strikes and the restaurant's use of private police during this particular strike did not help labor-business relations. The Henrici strike provoked no sentiment within the City Club to modify the exercise of police powers, at least as far as these affected labor activities.

By contrast, members of the Woman's City Club were actively involved in the strike itself: trying to resolve it and promoting reform of police powers. Several of these women, including Ruth Hanna McCormick (the wife of Medill McCormick, congressman, former publisher of the *Chicago Tribune,* and founding member of the City Club), had walked the picket lines with the striking waitresses.[43] Based on its experiences, the Woman's City Club accused the police and businessmen of brutality, demanded that policewomen be assigned to protect the picketers, and asked that all private guards be withdrawn.[44]

That police violence seemed endemic to labor situations in Chicago appalled the members of the Woman's City Club. At the mass meeting of the club called to consider the Woman's Municipal Platform in March 1916, they roundly condemned the 1,800 arrests made by police and private guards during the garment workers' strike of 1915. "It is time we challenged such things," Agnes Nestor told the assembly. "[The strikers] have come to this country because it holds out a promise to them. They come seeking freedom . . . and instead of that, they find they are exploited; and when they go on strike to protest against conditions, they are arrested. . . . They are arrested at the suggestion of the employer."[45] The women attending the meeting agreed with Nestor; they adopted a plank opposing the extraordinary use of police power against workers. "We condemn the practice of giving police power to private guards whose employment during industrial disputes we believe increases disorder," read the plank. "We protest against the illegal arrest of persons engaged in patrolling the district where a strike is in progress."[46] This last referred to the police practice of arresting private citizens who were walking the picket lines in order to protect the striking workers from police brutality.

Nestor was a working-class woman. The vast majority of women attending the meeting were not, and many were married to men who were employers. This did not keep them from sharing Nestor's sentiments, nor had it in the past. Six years earlier during a strike by the garment workers, Louise DeKoven Bowen, the wealthy Chicago reformer who chaired the meeting in 1916, had declared her sympathies to be on the side of the workers and their right to organize and protest.[47]

As part of their municipal platform, the Woman's City Club also demanded that the city create a municipal strike bureau. This bureau would require the office of chief of police to act as mediator in strikes, instead of acting on the behalf of employers, and would ban the use of private guards. The club declared that, while injustices or wrong-headedness might exist on the part of both employer and employee in labor disagreements, the workers' actions were quite often valid and justified. It advocated mediation, negotiation, and police protection of strikers rather than police power to arrest and abuse them. The men of the City Club, by contrast, were oriented to the needs and desires of businessmen on this issue as on most others. At a discussion meeting held to consider the proposed strike bureau, they listened to the attorney for the Illinois Manufacturers' Association speak against the measure as an infringement on the rights of business.[48] There is no evidence that the City Club held a different opinion or that it ever seriously considered supporting a municipal strike bureau.

It has been a prevailing idea of Progressive Era historiography that middle-class business and professional men, such as the members of the City Club, became municipal reformers because they had developed a citywide vision. This vision resulted from their realization that, as business affairs were conducted increasingly on a citywide basis, they needed to reform the entire urban structure in order to protect these affairs.[49] In Chicago, the men of the City Club viewed the city primarily as an arena in which to do business, and they advocated municipal reforms intended to protect and further the aims of business. If business and businessmen prospered, they argued, the city and the rest of its inhabitants would ultimately prosper. Thus, while they designed solutions for municipal problems that would, in practice, most directly profit one class, they argued that the benefits would spread through the remainder of the city. On one issue after another, they made fiscal efficiency and financial profitability the criteria for evaluating proposals for change.

I have argued elsewhere that, by the turn of the century, a broad range of urban residents, not just elite white males, had developed often-conflicting visions of the city as a whole.[50] The vision pursued by the members of the Woman's City Club has not been studied, in large part because of the tendency in Progressive Era political history to study men. That the women of the Woman's City Club had a citywide vision is apparent in their arguments and proposals for garbage disposal, public education, and the uses of police power. For them, municipal problems required solutions that guaranteed the well-being of everyone within the city, regardless of their immediate implications for business. The Woman's Municipal Platform of 1916 laid out the club's position on franchises, schools, housing, public health and sanitation, police and crime, among others. Underlying it was the belief that all municipal problems had to be solved before the city would be a good place in which to live.

One must, however, ask why the members of the Woman's City Club took strikingly different positions on municipal issues from the men of the City Club. As mentioned earlier, the different vision of the women of the Woman's City Club cannot be explained simply as one that the settlement house workers imposed on the rest of the membership. No one, we assume, forced Ruth McCormick to march the picket lines with the striking waitresses in 1914 in the company of Hull House resident Ellen Gates Starr. As president of the club, Louise DeKoven Bowen willingly took the lead in designing and promoting the Woman's Municipal Platform. Where the settlement house workers may well have made an impact on the Woman's City Club was in their skill in political organizing. Kathryn Kish Sklar's recent work on the activities of the women at Hull House suggests that the settlement house milieu gave women "a means of bypassing the control of male associations and institutions," one in which "women reformers were able to develop their capacity for political leadership free from many if not all of the constraints that otherwise might have been imposed on their power by the male-dominated parties or groups."[51] The activities of the Woman's City Club were the next step in the progression of building political leadership. Twenty-five years after the founding of Hull House, these Chicago women had gained more in the political arena than just the right to vote.[52]

In explaining why middle-class men and women had such different views of the city, and of political reform, it is also not sufficient to attribute the Woman's City Club positions to a received female culture both traditional and limited. Paula Baker has argued for the influence of a female culture, the basic tenets of which were shaped in the early nineteenth century. This female culture, emanating from a belief in the "special moral nature of women," compelled women to work to "ensure the moral and social order" of their surroundings, first through voluntary organizations and then government agencies. Women's efforts in the Progressive Era were thus, according to Baker, an extension of the pursuit of a morality-based social reform in which women passed "on to the state the work of social policy that they found increasingly unmanageable."[53] But the Woman's City Club did not speak about the higher morality of women. Mary McDowell described the club's work as "a constructive fight for better things, for higher standards, for a sense of collective responsibility for public safety and public morals. . . . Civic patriotism with a living daily sacrifice is the need of the hour."[54] Louise DeKoven Bowen, during her term as president of the Woman's City Club, proclaimed that the club "should act not only as a spotlight turned on our community . . . but it should also serve as an agency to correct the evils depicted and to guide women in their efforts to make of their citizenship a constructive force in the city's life."[55]

Further, even if Woman's City Club members may have learned from their mothers to concern themselves with the welfare of the poor, these received ideas do not explain the political strategies and the specific municipal proposals they developed in response to the problems of early twentieth-century Chicago. There is a crucial distinction between ideas received from previous generations and those that individuals create out of their own experiences. Received ideas had nothing to say about labor unions, for example, or municipal efficiency and municipal ownership. We know that businessmen, working out of their personal experiences of life and business in the city, changed their conception of politics and municipal government over the course of a generation.[56] Women went through the same process. But, as women's daily experiences were different from men's, they came to different conclusions about the direction political reform should take in Chicago.

The majority of men in the City Club were businessmen who drew on their professional experiences to design urban reform agendas. They were accustomed to thinking in terms of profitability and fiscal efficiency, of assessing a problem through the slow but steady accumulation of facts, and of seeking solutions that were best for themselves and their businesses. Their proposals for solving the problems of garbage disposal, public education, and police power make clear that they came easily to see as best for the city what was best for business and businessmen.[57]

The primary daily experience for most middle-class women, on the other hand, was the home. Women were used to organizing a home environment that ensured the well-being of everyone in the family. When they entered the political arena, they sought to achieve the same objective. "The struggle within the city is a fight for the welfare of all the children of all the people," declared Mary McDowell. The *Bulletin* decreed that women "must form a citywide organization. We must unite forces for the common good and act together."[58] "Suppose we had a system of municipal relief," asked DeKoven Bowen, "which is built upon the principle that the community is one great family and that each member of it is bound to help the other, the burden of support falling on all alike?"[59] Thus women applied their experience of how the home worked to what a city government should try to achieve.

The different gender experiences of the members of the City Club and Woman's City Club also shaped the recruitment and activities of the club. To begin with, members of the City Club established more rigorous membership requirements than did the Woman's City Club. Before joining the City Club, any proposed member had to have his name submitted along with "facts and references indicating his fitness for membership and facilitating corroborative inquiry among the members." One negative vote was enough to blackball a prospective member. The admission requirements were strict, not because the purpose of the club was to make business contacts (as was the case with the Commercial Club) but to ensure that men whose opinions might differ dramatically from the majority did not have access to the club. "The chief function of the club," read an early circular, "is to promote the acquaintance, the friendly intercourse, the accurate information and personal co-operation of those who are sincerely interested in practical methods of improving the public life and affairs of the community in which we live."[60] This sentiment was echoed by founding member Walter Fisher, who wrote that membership was "confined to those who are sincerely interested in practical methods of improving public conditions."[61] Careful admission requirements gave the City Club the leeway to define sincere interest and practical methods as it wished and to keep out those with whom its members might disagree. Entry into the Woman's City Club was easier. The club seems to have assumed that most women could contribute to its work, for all that was needed was nomination by one club member who believed that the nominee sympathized with the objectives of the organization.[62] Without records of who was proposed for membership, or who was turned down, no definitive statement can be made about the City Club's membership practices.[63] It is clear, however, that the City Club grew more slowly than did the Woman's City Club. From an initial membership of 335 in 1903–04, the City Club reached approximately 2,400 members in 1916; the members of the Woman's City Club numbered around 1,250 in its inaugural year of 1910–11 and stood at approximately 2,800 for 1915–16.[64]

Similarly reflective of their different experiences are the methods by which the two clubs investigated municipal problems. As businessmen, the members of the City Club were accustomed to experiencing firsthand only parts of the problem they were investigating. Employees often gathered facts and figures for the employer. Although social workers were members of the City Club, it is doubtful that the majority of the club members ever saw the places social workers lived and worked because the City Club carried on much of its work within its own quarters.[65] In contrast, the women focused on grass-roots activities out in the city itself. The Woman's City Club leaders directed members to organize according to their city ward (in its membership lists, the club provides the ward each woman lived in). They also instructed them to go out into the wards to investigate street, alley, and sidewalk conditions; housing, schools, and churches; infant mortality rates, numbers of children, and juvenile delinquency; parks, playgrounds, dance halls, saloons, hotels, jails, and courts.[66] A personal investigation of the garbage problem convinced the female reformers that only municipal ownership and operation of the means of garbage disposal would work well enough. Whether municipal ownership was the most financially profitable way to dispose of garbage was not their first concern; they asked whether it was the best way to promote the health and sanitation of the individuals whose neighborhoods they visited. When the answer seemed to be yes, they demanded municipal ownership.[67]

Gender experiences, finally, help explain why the Woman's City Club, and women involved in municipal reform movements throughout the country, used the term "municipal housekeeping" to describe their activities—a more complicated metaphor than has previously been acknowledged. The women of the Woman's City Club were not just attempting to keep the city clean, as they did their homes. They had tried that approach years earlier, for example, in 1894–95 when Jane Addams had organized women to go out and clean the streets themselves when the city was doing little about the problem. Rather, from their recognition of what it took to keep a home running, and running for the benefit of all is members, they developed ideas about how a good city should be run for the benefit of all its members. To characterize its work, the club talked in terms of "the Links that Bind the Home to the City Hall," with city hall in the middle, linked by chains to fourteen pairs of squares describing municipal activities and bureaus that affected life in the city.

The home and all life within the city, they argued, were inextricably "chained" to city hall. As one might expect, their illustration of these links includes the "traditional" female concerns about food inspection, factory safety, and clean air. But the two squares that depict the power of the city to license marriage and register birth showed that these women had become conscious of the power of the state to regulate and control their lives. "Whether she [the club member] likes it or not, the city government invades the privacy of her family life in the interests of the whole city," pointedly noted an essayist in the club's bulletin.[68] Marriage and birth may be viewed as primarily female concerns, but, without a political agenda to organize, investigate, and promote political municipal reforms in these and other areas, women had no say in that city government or over how it affected the home.

Using a term such as "municipal housekeeping" enabled women to become involved in every facet of urban affairs without arousing opposition from those who believed woman's only place was in the home.[69] Moreover, by depicting the city as the larger home, the women were asserting their right to involve themselves in every decision made by the Chicago city government, even to restructure that government. They supported the creation of a municipal strike bureau, for instance, in order to institutionalize within government protection for workers from businessmen.[70] When the club sought to institutionalize municipal ownership and operation of garbage disposal, it was advocating a radical change in Chicago's city government, for municipal ownership would dramatically change the political purposes and structures of city governments. In attempting to redefine what was economic in the political system, it came into direct conflict with established, male-dominated institutions.[71] In its positions on these issues, the Woman's City Club had thus moved beyond reliance on moral suasion to sophisticated participation in the political system.[72]

I do not to mean to suggest that gender was the only point of reference for these women or that they were political radicals. They wished to have the city control certain public services, but they did not vote for socialists; they belonged to the Women's Trade Union League but not the Industrial Workers of the World. They also tended to believe that theirs was the only appropriate municipal vision for women and that part of their task was to educate women of other classes to their point of view. Undoubtedly, there were people in the neighborhoods and institutions they visited who did not always welcome their presence. But, because of their gender experiences, the Woman's City Club members were more open to the possibilities of cross-class alliances than were most of their male counterparts.[73] These experiences also brought them to a different vision of good city government. Woman's City Club members seldom equated the good of the business community with the good of the citizenry as a whole. Instead, members of the Woman's City Club viewed the city as they had viewed their homes, a place where the health and welfare of all members should be sought.

Notes

1. City Club of Chicago, *Yearbook* (Chicago, 1904).
2. Woman's City Club of Chicago, *Bulletin*, 1 (July 1911).
3. For the City Club's position on vocational education, see "Yearly Report," Subcommittee on Vocational Education, March 1912, Box 13, folder 2, City Club of Chicago MS Collection, Chicago Historical Society, "Minutes of Subcommittee on Vocational Education," April 27, 1912, Box 14, folder 1, and letters of July 19, 1916, from City Club to the Chicago Association of Commerce, the Commercial Club, and the Hamilton Club, Box 18, folder 5. For positions on telephone ownership, see Woman's City Club of Chicago, *Bulletin*, 3 (March 1915); "Report of the Civic Committee on Lighting and Telephone," December 18, 1913, Box 15, folder 3, and May 28, 1915, Box 18, folder 2, City Club MS Collection; and City Club of Chicago, *Bulletin*, 8 (May 18, 1915), warning against allowing municipal ownership of utilities.
4. See Paula Baker, "The Domestication of Politics: Women and American Political Society, 1780–1920," *American Historical Review*, 89 (June 1984): 620–47; Karen Blair, *The Clubwoman as Feminist: True Womanhood Redefined, 1868–1914* (New York, 1980); Steven M. Buechler, *The Transformation of the Woman Suffrage Movement: The Case of Illinois, 1850–1920* (New Brunswick, N.J., 1986); Linda Cordon, *Woman's Body, Woman's Right: A Social History of Birth Control in America* (New York, 1977); and Adade Wheeler and Marlene Wortman, *The Roads They Made: Women in Illinois History* (Chicago, 1977). See Barbara Berg, *The Remembered Gate: Origins of American Feminism — The Woman and the City, 1800–1860* (New York, 1978), for an earlier period.
5. See John D. Buenker, "Sovereign Individuals and Organic Networks: Political Cultures in Conflict during the Progressive Era," *American Quarterly*, 40 (June 1988): 187–204; Michael Ebner and Eugene Tobin, eds., *The Age of Urban Reform: New Perspectives on the Progressive Era* (Port Washington, N.Y., 1977); Kenneth Fox, *Better City Government: Innovation in American Urban Politics, 1850–1937* (Philadelphia, 1972); David C. Hammack, *Power and Society: Greater New York at the Turn of the Century* (New York, 1982); Samuel Hays, "The Politics of Reform in Municipal Government in the Progressive Era," *Pacific Northwest Quarterly*, 55 (1964): 6–38; William Issel and Robert W. Cherney, *San Francisco, 1865–1932: Politics, Power, and Urban Development* (Berkeley, Calif., 1986); and Martin Schiesl, *The Politics of Efficiency: Municipal Administration and Reform in America, 1880–1920* (Berkeley, 1977). Works that compare men and women, such as Ruth Rosen, *The Lost Sisterhood: Prostitution in America, 1900–1918* (Baltimore, Md., 1982); and

Kathleen McCarthy, *Noblesse Oblige: Charity and Cultural Philanthropy in Chicago, 1849–1929* (Chicago, 1982), are concerned with social reform, not political reform movements.

6. Nancy F. Cott, "What's in a Name? The Limits of 'Social Feminism'; or, Expanding the Vocabulary of Women's History," *Journal of American History,* 76 (December 1989): 809–29, assesses the problems and limitations of seeing women in the Progressive Era as engaged primarily in "social feminism" and ignoring their political history.

7. Eric Foner, *Politics and Ideology in the Age of the Civil War* (New York, 1980), 9. The overwhelming tendency in women's history has been to analyze women's activities as socially directed, not as political. For a recent overview of the literature, see Linda Kerber, "Separate Spheres, Female Worlds, Woman's Place: The Rhetoric of Women's History," *Journal of American History,* 75 (June 1988): 9–39. For the Progressive Era, we historians need to rethink this analysis.

8. No other male and female organizations afford as good a comparison. For men, the socially elite Commercial, Merchants', and Union League clubs, for example, were primarily business organizations; for women, the elite Chicago Woman's Club was founded with more of a social than a reform agenda. All of these groups involved themselves in various reform issues, but none had as its primary purpose the pursuance of municipal reform.

9. The figures were compiled from the membership lists found in City Club of Chicago, *Yearbook* (1909–10; 1915–16), and the Woman's City Club, *Yearbook* (1910–11) and *Its Book* (1915); cross-checking of names was done from A. N. Marquis, ed., *The Book of Chicagoans: A Biographical Dictionary of Leading Living Men of the City of Chicago* (Chicago, 1911, 1917). The 1917 edition was retitled *Leading Living Men and Women. . . .*

10. The City Club was not as elite or as small as the older businessmen's clubs, the Commercial and the Union League. Most of the city's wealthiest capitalist industrialists belonged to the latter two but not to the City Club. On the other hand, the wives of Harold F. McCormick and Potter Palmer, Jr., and the wife and daughter of Cyrus H. McCormick did belong to the Woman's City Club. See Michael McCarthy, "Businessmen and Professionals in Municipal Reform: The Chicago Experience, 1887–1920" (Ph.D. dissertation, Northwestern University, 1970), for his explanation of the differences between the older industrialists and the newer businessmen and professionals.

11. Woman's City Club, *Yearbook* (1910–11); and *Its Book* (1915).

12. See Woman's City Club, *Its Book* (1915).

13. Mary (Mrs. H. W.) Wilmarth, 1910–11, 1911–12: Sophonisba Breckenridge, 1912–13; Harriet Vittum, 1913–14; Louise DeKoven (Mrs. Joseph) Bowen, 1914–15; Mary McDowell, 1915–16. After retiring as president, Mary Wilmarth served as honorary president during these years.

14. T. W. Allinson, Allen T. Burns, William Hard, George Hooker, James Mullenbach, and Charles Zueblin were associated with the settlement houses and members of the City Club.

15. "Minutes of Meetings," Committee on Garbage and Refuse Disposal, February 13, 1914, Box 14, folder 6, City Club MS Collection; "Yearly Report," Committee on Garbage and Refuse Disposal, April 7, 1914, *ibid.*

16. City Club of Chicago, "Chicago's Garbage Problem," *Bulletin,* 6 (December 20, 1913): 329–30.

17. "Minutes of Meetings," Committee on Garbage and Waste Disposal, July 30, 1914, Box 14, folder 6, City Club MS Collection.

18. The estimate supplied by Alderman Willis O. Nance to the City Club was $47,500 per year to the Reduction Company and $450,000 for collection. City Club, "Chicago's Garbage Problem," 330.

19. "Yearly Report," Committee on Garbage and Refuse Disposal, April 7, 1914, Box 14, folder 6, City Club MS Collection.

20. *Ibid.*, March 24, 1915, Box 16, folder 3.

21. See, for example, "Report of the Civic Committee on Lighting and Telephone Service," December 18, 1913, Box 15, folder 3, City Club MS Collection.

22. City Club, "Chicago's Garbage Problem," 331.

23. City Club, "Chicago's Garbage Problem," 336–37.

24. Their accounting can be found in the Woman's City Club, *Its Book*, 52–56. It had cost $650,000 to purchase and rehabilitate the plant; the $130,000 spent on operating the plant (with an additional $22,000 counted toward depreciation and interest) was offset by $114,000 profit on six months of selling the by-products and the savings of $47,500 that would have been paid under the old contract with the Chicago Reduction Company.

25. Woman's City Club, *Bulletin,* 4 (September 1915): 2.

26. "Report of Proceedings: Mass Meeting of Women to Protest against the Spoils System and Adopt a Woman's Municipal Platform," March 18, 1916, typescript, Box 1, folder 1, Woman's City Club of Chicago MS Collection, Chicago Historical Society. The provisions of the platform are also described in Louise DeKoven Bowen, *Speeches, Addresses and Letters,* 2 vols. (Ann Arbor, Mich., 1937), 1: 376–77.

27. Woman's City Club, *Bulletin,* 5 (November 1916).

28. Woman's City Club, *Bulletin,* 5 (December 1916): 11–12.

29. "Report of the Committee on Public Education," April 1, 1907, Box 9, folder 5, City Club MS Collection. For accounts of early twentieth-century municipal struggles on the issue of public education, see Maureen A. Flanagan, *Charter Reform in Chicago* (Carbondale, Ill., 1987); and David J. Hogan, *Class and Reform: School and Society in Chicago, 1880–1930* (Philadelphia, 1985).

30. Quoted in "Minutes of Meeting," Committee on Education, November 23, 1908, Box 10, folder 3, City Club MS Collection.

31. "Yearly Report," Subcommittee on Vocational Education, March 1912, Box 13, folder 2, City Club MS Collection. See also Box 14, folder 1, for report submitted to subcommittee by Mr. E. A. Wreidt recommending that the City Club "take steps to bring the business men of Chicago and the Board of Education together on this problem"; and copies of letters sent July 19, 1916, to the Chicago Association of Commerce and the Commercial and Hamilton clubs inviting them to confer over how to secure legislation for vocational education; Box 18, folder 5, City Club MS Collection.

32. "Minutes of Meetings," Subcommittee on Vocational Education, August 2, 1912, Box 14, folder 1, City Club MS Collection.

33. *Ibid.* For the progress of the vocational education proposals within the city and in the state legislature, and for the positions taken on this issue by various Chicagoans, see Hogan, *Class and Reform.*

34. Woman's City Club, *Its Book,* 86–87.

35. Woman's City Club, *Its Book,* 87–89.

36. Hogan, *Class and Reform,* 176. See also City Club, *Bulletin,* 5 (December 4, 1912): 373–77.

37. Woman's City Club, *Bulletin,* 3 (December 1914). Nestor was working class, but her opinions could not have prevailed without the agreement of the middle-class women who dominated the organization.

38. Woman's City Club, *Bulletin,* 5 (November 1916).

39. Woman's City Club, *Bulletin,* 5 (December 1916); letter from the City Club to the Woman's City Club, January 15, 1917, Box 18, folder 5, City Club MS Collection.

40. The exact number of arrests was disputed. The chair of the City Club sub-committee for investigating the strike said "119 or more"; Elizabeth Maloney, secretary of the Waitresses' Union, claimed "something like 139 arrests"; City Club, "The Henrici Strike," *Bulletin,* 7 (June 13, 1914): 198, 203.

41. *Ibid.,* 196–97. The club's general lack of engagement with this issue can be seen in the fact that the committee had decided that the investigation and preparation of the report could be feasibly undertaken by Deibler in consultation with the other members. There is no indication that the other committee members, or the membership as a whole, objected to Deibler's conclusions and recommendations.

42. City Club, "Henrici Strike," 198–99.

43. Agnes Nestor, *Woman's Labor Leader: The Autobiography of Her Life* (Rockford, Ill., 1954), 158–59.

44. *Chicago Tribune,* February 21, 23, 24, and 26, 1914. Policewomen were supplied, but they immediately arrested several women pickets; neither gender solidarity nor class solidarity was a given. Prominent Chicago women were not just opposed to labor violence against women strikers. In 1894, many of them had helped organize a relief committee for the male workers striking against the Pullman Company and in the process had incurred the wrath of the men who were their social equals. See Stanley Buder, *Pullman: An Experiment in Industrial Order and Community Planning, 1880–1930* (New York, 1967), 171–72. In 1910, they supported the predominantly male garment workers on strike that year (see note 47). By 1914–15, these women had moved beyond organizing relief committees to walking the picket lines.

45. "Report of the Proceedings: Mass Meeting of Women to Protest against the Spoils System and Adopt a Woman's Municipal Platform," Woman's City Club MS, Box 1, folder 1.

46. *Ibid.*

47. Newspaper clipping, November 1, 1910, Louise DeKoven Bowen Scrapbooks, Chicago Historical Society.

48. "Report of the Proceedings . . . Woman's Municipal Platform"; City Club, *Bulletin,* 9 (January 10, 1916): 1–11.

49. This idea was articulated by Samuel Hays in his seminal article "The Politics of Reform," more than two decades ago. See Schiesl, *Politics of Efficiency,* for its application.

50. See Flanagan, *Charter Reform in Chicago,* esp. 22–23, 41–42, 84, 92–93, 114–15. Thus a limited and fragmented geographical view of the city, which may well have existed among women earlier in the nineteenth century, ought not to be applied forward into the next century; see Christine Stansell, *City of Women: Sex and Class in New York, 1789–1860* (New York, 1986).

51. Kathryn Kish Sklar, "Hull House in the 1890s: A Community of Women Reformers," *Signs,* 10 (Summer 1985): 670, 677. Because this activity was happening well in advance of women receiving the vote, the vote should not be seen as propelling women into political activity.

52. While Sklar sees the Hull House women as "advancing political solutions to social problems that were fundamentally ethical or moral, such as the right of workers to a fair return for their labor or the right of children to schooling," I believe that by the 1910s the members of the Woman's City Club see the problems as both ethical and political; *ibid.,* 663. See also Ellen Carol DuBois, "Working Women, Class Relations, and Suffrage Militance: Harriet Stanton Blatch and the New York Woman Suffrage Movement, 1894–1909," *Journal of American History,* 74 (June 1987): 34, for her discussion of political versus social and moral arenas.

53. Baker, "Domestication of Politics," 633, 641–42, gives the basic outlines of the cultural-analysis approach to women's reform agendas. See Philip J. Ethington, "Gender, Class, and Privilege: The Contested Terrain of Political Culture in San Francisco, 1890–1911," paper presented at the 104th meeting of the American Historical Association, December 1989 (copy in my possession), for an additional critique of this analysis when applied to voting on women suffrage.

54. Typescript, undated, in folder 19, Mary McDowell MS Collection, Chicago Historical Society; copy also in Box 1, folder 1, Woman's City Club MS collection.

55. Louise DeKoven Bowen, *The Woman's City Club of Chicago* (Chicago, 1922), 32.

56. For examples, see Hays, "Politics of Reform"; M. McCarthy, "Businessmen and Professionals"; and Schiesl, *Politics of Efficiency.*

57. Many studies explain the attempts of groups such as the City Club to implement business-like efficiency and business-like fiscal responsibility in municipal government, for example, Schiesl, *Politics of Efficiency.* Margaret Marsh's work showing that some suburban males had begun to value spending time at home with their families does not change the fact that a man's primary daily experience remained work outside the home. See Margaret Marsh, "Suburban Men and Masculine Domesticity, 1870–1915," *American Quarterly,* 40 (June 1988): 165–86.

58. McDowell, typescript, folder 19, at Chicago Historical Society; Woman's City Club, *Bulletin,* 3 (April 1915).

59. Bowen, *Speeches,* 1: 107.

60. Membership circular, undated, signed by the founding members, Box 20, folder 1, City Club MS Collection.

61. Walter L. Fisher to Marx and Door, November 16, 1903, Walter L. Fisher Papers, Library of Congress, Washington, D.C. See also City Club, *Yearbook* (1905–06), for details of admission procedures. One could not apply for membership to the City Club without an invitation from the board of directors.

62. Woman's City Club, *Yearbook* (1910).

63. John C. Harding, a member of the Chicago Federation of Labor, belonged to the City Club, but CFL President John Fitzpatrick did not. Possibly, Harding had been invited to join when he was appointed to the board of education.

64. The annual membership fee in the City Club was also set higher than the annual fee for the Woman's City Club.

65. The City Club did not stint on comfortable quarters for itself. In 1905, the club moved to new quarters where, it informed the membership, they would be

"splendidly housed" with private dining rooms; in 1909 the club began sending circulars to the members to raise $75,000 for a new building. Circulars, February 2, 1905, Box 20, folder 1, City Club MS Collection; and June 12, 1909, Box 20, folder 3.

66. Woman's City Club, *Its Book;* Woman's City Club, *Bulletin*, 3 (April 1915); Bowen, *Speeches, Addresses and Letters*, 2: 468–73. The club often found ingenious ways to carry out multiple aims. It investigated various municipal problems by organizing tours of jails, police stations, poor neighborhoods, hospitals, etc. Each woman paid $1 for each trip, and this money was then given to suffrage organizations. Woman's City Club, *Bulletin*, 3 (September 1914). See also Gwendolyn Wright, *Moralism and the Model Home: Domestic Architecture and Cultural Conflict in Chicago, 1873–1913* (Chicago, 1980), 281, for her observations on the different methods of the two clubs.

67. These women were not oblivious to the fact that tax dollars would be needed to pay for municipal ownership and that as wealthier members of the community they, or their families, could be among those hardest hit. One of the reasons wealthier women in Chicago had lobbied hard for the municipal vote was to have a say in their financial interests. But many of them had come to their own conclusions about how they wanted their tax dollars spent, and these conclusions did not necessarily coincide with those of the men of their class; see Jane Addams, *Twenty Years at Hull-House* (New York, 1910), 237.

68. Woman's City Club, *Bulletin*, 2 (July 1913).

69. For example, the City Club urged Mayor Carter Harrison to appoint women to the board of education, saying there was "a peculiar need for the presence on the Board of Education of those who are familiar with social problems and situations, and at the same time are in an intelligent and sympathetic attitude toward the children themselves." However, if the men thought they were advocating women's participation in matters pertaining to children, the women knew that, while serving on the board, they would be making important municipal decisions, such as what manner of vocational education might be introduced into the system. The ideas of the Woman's City Club toward vocational education differed significantly from those of the City Club; thus, if these women had much say in running the schools, the City Club might never see instituted the type of vocational education it wanted. City Club to Mayor Carter Harrison, April 28, 1913, Box 15, folder 6, City Club MS Collection.

70. Helen Lefkowitz Horowitz's comment in *Culture and the City: Cultural Philanthropy in Chicago from the 1880s to 1917* (Chicago, 1976), 144, that "Julius Rosenwald [the head of Sears, Roebuck] would have his chauffeur drive one of the settlement women to join a picket line of workers striking against him, but he did not allow her to influence his negotiations," misses an important point. By moving onto the picket lines and demanding changes for workers, women were in fact influencing Rosenwald's (and every other businessman's) negotiations. By the early twentieth century, men were no longer able to run their affairs and the city's affairs without the "interference" of women.

71. See Ethington, "Gender, Class, and Privilege," for additional insights into the radical implications of "municipal housekeeping" for urban politics.

72. Evidence of this shift is seen in the process of Louise DeKoven Bowen's political growth. While working for the Juvenile Court, she listened to an Illinois legislator telling colleagues to pass the bill providing for probation officers for the

court because "there is nothing in it, but a woman I know wants it passed." She realized, much to her own consternation, that depending on the good will of male politicians was an unsatisfactory means for enacting reform. Louise DeKoven Bowen, *Growing Up with a City* (New York, 1926), 106–07.

73. See Nancy A. Hewitt, "Beyond the Search for Sisterhood: American Women's History in the 1980s," *Social History,* 10 (October 1985): 315, for her cautions against seeing "universal notions of womanhood" or a "single woman's culture sphere" as the cause of women's reform activities; and DuBois, "Working Women, Class Relations, and Suffrage Militance," 57, on tensions over socialist participation in a suffrage movement led largely by middle-class women. But also see John T. Cumbler, "The Politics of Charity: Gender and Class in Late 19th Century Charity Policy," *Journal of Social History,* 14 (Fall 1980): 99–111, for analysis of the differing policies toward charity adopted by men and women of the same class.

Glenda Elizabeth Gilmore

Diplomatic Women

Glenda Elizabeth Gilmore is Professor of History at Yale University. "Diplomatic women" is from her book *Gender and Jim Crow: Women and the Politics of White Supremacy in North Carolina, 1896–1920,* which takes a close look at how African American women in one state maneuvered the rapids of Progressive Era politics.

Part of Progressivism was based on racial, ethnic, and gender hierarchies. This condition was certainly true in North Carolina, where at the turn of the century the state legislature imposed a literacy test and a poll tax that eliminated African American male voters. Many black men could have passed the test and paid the tax, but white registrars administered the test unfairly and mobs attacked black men when they went to vote. Black men had voted and held office in North Carolina at the municipal level, in the state legislature, and in Congress until these laws were passed. After 1902, few black men voted at all, and their former party, the Republican party, declared itself "lily-white." The white Democratic leaders who disfranchised African Americans called themselves Progressives and thought that disfranchisement was a Progressive solution to elevate the nature of the electorate.

With black men out of politics, black women found certain ways to exploit Progressive reform and better their communities, even though they could not vote either. They shared goals with many of the Progressives you have met so far, but their tactics had to be quite different from those of voters or those of white women. Yet they learned to speak the "language" of Progressivism that Connolly illustrates.

To understand this selection, you should think hard about your definition of politics. What is political? Is it voting, holding office, making a campaign speech? Who is in politics? Do you have to vote to be in politics, or can you operate outside the electoral process to influence government?

Questions for a Closer Reading

1. What about the nature of Progressivism made it possible for women to take up its goals? How did women expand the definition of what was political? How did politics differ for white women and black women? Why did the black women featured in this selection want to remain invisible even as they participated in politics?

2. What do these "diplomatic women" have in common with Connolly's ethnic Progressives? What are the main differences in their situations, and how do those differences cause them to take different political tactics?

3. The black women highlighted in this selection draw on Progressive ideas that other authors in this volume put at the core of Progressivism. Imagine a conversation between Lula Kelsey and one of Wiebe's efficient managers. On what would they agree? Now choose another Progressive figure, perhaps one of Hofstadter's Mugwumpian civic leaders or William Jennings Bryan from Sanders's article. What would Lula Kelsey have in common with him or her?

4. How did Lula Kelsey make the Salisbury Civic League a political force? Compare its membership, tactics, and agenda to that of the Woman's City Club in Chicago that Flanagan discusses.

5. Gilmore's discussion of black women in this selection does not apply to all black women. Who is excluded from this analysis? What might Sanders's or Stromquist's article suggest to you about which black women are excluded? How might you go about finding out about the effect that Progressivism had on them and the ways in which they used Progressivism to further their own agendas?

Diplomatic Women

After disfranchisement, "the Negro," white supremacists were fond of saying, was removed from politics. But even as African American men lost their rights, the political sphere underwent a transformation. As state and local governments began to provide social services, an embryonic welfare state emerged. Henceforth, securing teeter-totters and playgrounds, fighting pellagra, or replacing a dusty neighborhood track with an oil-coated road would require political influence. Thus, at the same time that whites restricted the number of voters by excluding African Americans, the state created a new public role: that of the client who drew on its services.[1] Contemporaries and historians named this paradoxical period the Progressive Era.

From the debris of disfranchisement, black women discovered fresh approaches to serving their communities and crafted new tactics designed to dull the blade of white supremacy. The result was a greater role for black women in the interracial public sphere. As long as they could vote, it was black men who had most often brokered official state power and made interracial political contacts. After disfranchisement, however, the political culture black women had created through thirty years of work in temperance organizations, Republican Party aid societies, and churches furnished both an ideological basis and an organizational structure from which black women could take on those tasks. After black men's banishment from politics, North Carolina's black women added a network of women's groups that crossed denominational—and later party—lines and took a multi-issue approach to civic action. In a nonpolitical guise, black women became the black community's diplomats to the white community.

In the first twenty years of the century, the state, counties, and municipalities began to intervene in affairs that had been private in the past. Now, government representatives killed rabid dogs and decided where traffic should stop. They forced bakers to put screens on their windows

Glenda Elizabeth Gilmore, "Diplomatic Women," from *Gender and Jim Crow: Women and the Politics of White Supremacy in North Carolina, 1896–1920* (Chapel Hill: University of North Carolina Press, 1996), 147–75.

and made druggists stop selling morphine. They told parents when their children could work and when their children must go to school. As they regulated, they also dispensed. Public health departments were formed, welfare agencies turned charity into a science, and juvenile court systems began to separate youthful offenders of both sexes from seasoned criminals. Public education expanded exponentially and became increasingly uniform across the state. The intersection of government and individual expanded from the polling place to the street corner, from the party committee meeting to the sickbed.

Black women might not be voters, but they could be clients, and in that role they could become spokespeople for and motivators of black citizens. They could claim a distinctly female moral authority and pretend to eschew any political motivation. The deep camouflage of their leadership style — their womanhood — helped them remain invisible as they worked toward political ends. At the same time, they could deliver not votes but hands and hearts through community organization: willing workers in city cleanup campaigns, orderly children who complied with state educational requirements, and hookworm-infested people eager for treatment at public health fairs.

Southerners at the time called themselves "progressives," but historians have been loath to allow that name to stick. For those who championed a static history of the region, the "Progressive Era" ran counter to their continuity arguments. Moreover, those who found the roots of northern progressivism twining amid urban growth and rapid immigration saw only a stunted transplant on southern soil that remained comparatively rural and isolated. Finally, southern progressive solutions seemed a pale imitation of those in the North. If southerners reformed at all, historians judged their programs to be too little, too late.[2]

Even for those who claimed to locate a southern Progressive Era, the juxtaposition of African Americans losing ground and whites "progressing" remained problematic. In a period when the country moved from an administrative government that maximized free enterprise toward an interventionist state, the white South busily invented and embellished segregation and drove black men away from the polls. White southern Democrats applied a pernicious ingenuity to the task of expanding state services in a society divided by the color line, and they allocated government money in increasingly unequal racial divides. C. Vann Woodward termed it "Progressivism — for Whites Only." J. Morgan Kousser went further, attaching an additional caveat: "Progressivism — for Middle Class Whites Only."[3] Southern progressivism lived but, according to these readings, without the participation of blacks, poor whites, or women.

After Woodward, Anne Firor Scott, searching for southern progressivism, discovered white women at its center. Social reform enabled women to claim a privileged knowledge in civic affairs and to exercise power prior to suffrage, even in the South, where middle-class white women faced a stereotype of helpless gentility. White women fought child labor, ran settlement houses, and assumed responsibility for municipal housekeeping in growing New South cities.[4] Working-class southern white women used progressive ideas and programs to shake the South's confidence in its grossly unfair wage system and to condemn its anti-union virulence, thus challenging the familiar notion that social control was the raison d'etre for reform.[5]

But even if southern progressivism included women, was it reserved for whites? The answer is that whites intended for it to be, and it would have been even more racist, more exclusive, and more oppressive if there had been no black women progressives. Black women fought back after disfranchisement by adapting progressive programs to their own purposes, even while they chose tactics that left them invisible in the political process.[6] As southern African American women began this task, they were further away from southern white women than ever before. Since black men could not vote, white women dropped appeals to black women to influence their male family members. Many white women had chosen race over gender in the white supremacy campaigns and had gained their first electoral experience under a racist banner.

Given the distance between white and black women, the point is not that black women simply contributed to progressive welfare work and the domestication of politics, although, of course, they did. In comparing black women's progressivism to white women's progressivism, one must be cautious at every turn because black and white women had vastly different relationships to power. To cite just one example, white middle-class women lobbied to obtain services *from* their husbands, brothers, and sons; black women lobbied to obtain services *for* their husbands, brothers, and sons.

Black women's task was to try to force those white women who plunged into welfare efforts to recognize class and gender similarities across racial lines. To that end, they surveyed progressive white women's welfare initiatives and political style and found that both afforded black women a chance to enter the political arena. They had two purposes in mind. First, they would try to hold a place for African Americans in the ever-lengthening queue forming to garner state services. Second, they would begin to clear a path for the return of African Americans to the ballot box.

As confused and obfuscating as the term "progressive" is, one might wonder if it even applies to black women activists at all.[7] Considering black women as progressives, however, demonstrates how gender and race as tools of historical analysis can enrich traditional political history. In this case, they lead us to rethink progressivism's periodization, roots, and results. Certainly, one can only apply the term "progressive" to this time and in these circumstances with a profound sense of irony. But it is important to make an explicit attempt to reclaim "progressivism," to stroll among the dismembered corpses of other historians' definitions and gather up some limbs, a hank of hair here, a piece of bone there. Then, like Dr. Frankenstein, perhaps we might build a new progressivism, this one a little less monstrous than some of those other hulks that still walk among us.

Given the expansion of the public sphere and whites' attempts to exclude African Americans from new state and municipal programs, black women's religious work took on new meaning. In the wake of disfranchisement, African American men and women turned to their churches for solace and for political advice.[8] Yet many black men now feared the potentially explosive mixture of politics and religion in turbulent times.[9] Ministers of all denominations began to circumscribe their own discourse and to monitor their flocks' debate. A Baptist minister declared that such "perilous times" made even "preaching of the pure gospel embarrassing, if not dangerous."[10]

Using women's church organizations to press for community improvement incurred less risk than preaching inflammatory sermons on civil rights. The church remained, in the words of John Dancy, "an organized protest," but the nature of that protest transformed itself from arguments at Republican conventions and good turnouts at the ballot box into a flanking movement. While white political leaders kept their eyes on black men's electoral political presence and absence, black women organized and plotted an attack just outside of their field of vision. They began by transforming church missionary societies into social service agencies.

This is not to say that the political intentions of denominational women's groups were apparent to insiders or even omnipresent in the beginning. Initially, the groups did three things: they focused church attention away from spiritual debate and toward social conditions; they taught women to be organized managers; and they offered a slim ray of hope for community improvement in the midst of political disaster. Henry Cheatham, who had been recorder of deeds in Washington, D.C., prior to Dancy's assumption of the post, deplored African Americans' "political misfortunes" and gloomily predicted that civil rights might be lost forever. Cheatham argued that the "one thing" that remained for African Americans was the work women did in Sunday schools to build better homes, to educate the children, and to improve the community in general.[11] In effect, he implored North Carolina Baptist women to use church work as a parapolitical tool.

African American women needed little urging. They understood their new role in community life and their unique ability to execute it. One Baptist home missionary, Sallie Mial of Raleigh, put it this way: "We have a peculiar work to do. We can go where you can not afford to go."[12] Mial's "peculiar work" was social welfare reform. The tasks of black women's home missionary societies read like a Progressive Era primer. They organized mothers' clubs and community cleanup days. They built playgrounds and worked for public health and temperance. Marshaling arguments from the social purity and social hygiene movements, they spoke on sexual dangers outside of marriage. To achieve their goals, southern black women entered political space, appearing before local officials and interacting with white bureaucrats.

Even as they undertook this "peculiar work," black women knew that they must avoid charges of political interference. As a black woman, Mial could go where black men could no longer afford to go—into public space—for two reasons. First, her presence could not be misconstrued as a bid for sexual access to white women, as the Democrats so cunningly characterized black men's exercise of citizenship. Second, Mial could enter the realm of politics as a client, as an interpreter of social needs for families whom she represented to a state that had pledged something to her. Mial and thousands of other southern black women set about expanding on the state's amorphous promise, even as the growing bureaucracy tried to find practical ways to exclude African Americans from its largesse.

Sallie Mial would have never openly characterized her work as political, even though she may have understood it to be. Indeed, her success depended upon remaining invisible in the political process, a posture that contributes to historians' difficulties in recovering her experience. Taking a lesson from the high price of black men's former public presence, capitalizing on the divisions among whites over the allocation of new services to African Americans, and concerned about gender politics among African Americans, black women reformers depended on not being seen at all by whites who would thwart their programs and not being seen as political by whites who would aid them. They used their invisibility to construct a web of social service and civic institutions that remained hidden from and therefore unthreatening to whites.

Women's organizations within religious bodies were not new, but they became more important, expanded, and reordered their priorities after disfranchisement. For example, the Women's Baptist Home Mission Convention of North Carolina began in 1884, primarily as an arm for evangelical work. At the turn of the century, the group employed Mial as a full-time missionary in the state. In this capacity, she organized local women's groups and founded Sunshine Bands and What-I-Can Circles for girls.[13] Mial explained her work to the African American Baptist men this way: "We teach the women to love their husbands, to be better wives and mothers, to make the homes better."[14] At the same time, church workers taught Baptist women lobbying and administrative skills. One woman remembered, "From this organization we learn[ed] what is meant to be united."[15] Another observed, "Many of our women are being strengthened for the Master's use." Along the way, the organization began calling itself the Baptist State Educational Missionary Convention.[16]

Making "the homes better" covered a wide range of community activities. Good homes rhetoric was, of course, promulgated by whites to justify white supremacy; southern educational reformers used depictions of debasement, for example, to justify industrial education.[17] Black women could use this discourse for their own purposes, and they grasped the opportunity it gave them to bargain for the state services that were beginning to improve whites' lives but were denied to African Americans. As Margaret Murray Washington put it, "Where the homes of colored people are comfortable and clean, there is less disease, less sickness, less death, and less danger to others [that is, whites]." Good homes, however, required good government. "We are not likely to [build good homes] if we know that the pavements will be built just within a door of ours and suddenly stop," Washington warned.[18] Turning from the ballot box to the home as the hope of the future was canny political strategy that meshed nicely with the new welfare role of the state, and it explicitly increased women's importance at a time when women across the nation campaigned to extend their influence through volunteer activities and the professionalization of social work.[19]

The elevation of the home to the centerpiece of African American life sprang from several sources. Certainly it resonated with a nationwide Progressive Era movement for better homes, particularly among immigrant enclaves in crowded northern cities. But among North Carolina's African Americans, the movement's roots reached closer to home. Religious convictions that had inspired nineteenth-century black women who did church work continued to serve as moral imperatives to bring families to godly lives. African American women tried to eliminate grist for the white supremacy mill by abolishing the images of the immoral black woman and the barbaric black home. Moreover, now that voting required literacy, education was political, and it began at home. Able to tap into the larger context of rhetoric on better homes and the importance of literacy, black women expanded their roles, first in the church, then in the community as a whole.[20]

Some men felt threatened by this new activity, even though most women made it clear that their goal was not to preach or to rise within the formal church hierarchy, as, for example, Mary Small had done in the African Methodist Episcopal (AME) Zion Church in the 1890s. William F. Fonvielle, a supporter of coeducation at Livingstone College, had called repeatedly on women to work for racial uplift. But in 1900, he complained that there were too many women delegates at the AME Zion general conference. He came away from the experience completely opposed to women representatives, even though "some of them are good friends of mine. . . . It looks like a bad precedent."[21] Many black Baptist men questioned the expenditures for home missions.[22] When Baptist women implored men to "Give us a push," the men wondered if they should not push the women out of the limelight altogether. Unlike the AME Zion convention, by 1900 Baptist men and women met separately, and women often found themselves fending off attempts to abolish the Baptist Educational and Missionary Convention. Even those who did not want to sweep away the women's structure were determined to insure its control by men. They advocated solving the problem "by appointing an advisory committee each year to attend the Women's Convention and to advise with them in their deliberations, and [send] . . . an annual report to this body."[23]

Women did their best to reassure men by stressing their solidarity with them. "We are your sisters, your wives, your mothers. We have not outgrown you. We have been given to you to help you. We dare not leave you. You have opened your hearts, and given us increased privileges in the churches," Sallie Mial told the men's Baptist convention. Roberta Bunn, another paid missionary, said that the women's relationship with the men's convention was "indestructible" but that women had an important place to fill that men could not. She quoted Scripture: "I sought for a man among them that should make up the hedge, and stand in the gap before me." She reminded the brothers that when God could find no man to fill the gap, two women stood in.[24] Over the years, the debate over the power of women's organizations among North Carolina Baptists escalated. By 1917, women insisted that "it behooves us to think of and discuss the great questions confronting us as citizens of this great nation," while the men reiterated that the women needed "intelligent supervision" and directed them to turn their funds over to the men's convention.[25]

The growth of women's organizations in the AME Zion Church demonstrates women's desire to carve out a distinct space for themselves within the denomination. After the turn of the century, AME Zion women created a formal, hierarchical, and separate women's structure and changed the thrust of their work from evangelism to education and social service. When Sarah Dudley Pettey served as treasurer and then secretary of the Woman's Home and Foreign Missionary Society, the organization's primary activity was fund-raising for African missions. She began the "Woman's Column" in the *Star of Zion* during her term as secretary, and her writing revealed her personal concerns more than it represented the society. In the 1890s, society officers met only once every four years at the regular convention, and all were wives of bishops.[26]

The structure of the Woman's Home and Foreign Missionary Society changed radically between 1900 and 1915, and the women moved from integration with the men to performing separate functions within the church. In 1901, while Dudley Pettey still edited the "Woman's Column," the society persuaded the *Star of Zion* to allow Marie Clay Clinton, George Clinton's new wife, to write a "missionary" column.[27] That column eventually grew into a separate women's newspaper, the *Missionary Seer*.[28] At the 1904 convention, Woman's Christian Temperance Union (WCTU) activist Annie Blackwell demanded that women operate the Woman's Home and Foreign Missionary Society autonomously, and a women's convention began meeting the next year.[29] An independent executive board oversaw the society's business, and by 1912, the board dealt with the issue of bishops' wives monopolizing the board by making them nonvoting members.[30] The women's convention began electing the *Star*'s "Woman's Column" editor in 1912.[31] The term "missions" came to be broadly interpreted to mean social service work among African American neighbors.

Two North Carolina women, Marie Clinton and Victoria Richardson, founded youth educational departments within the society. Clinton had arrived in Charlotte in 1901 when she married widower George Clinton, and by the following year, she became fast friends with Victoria Richardson of Livingstone College.[32] Richardson's uncles were the famous Harris brothers who had founded the Fayetteville graded school during Reconstruction. Legend had it that Victoria's parents sent her from Ohio to North Carolina to save her from making an unsuitable early marriage. After a brief stint as Charles Chesnutt's colleague at the Charlotte graded school in the 1870s, Richardson went to teach at Livingstone College when it opened in 1880. She stayed a lifetime, teaching music and building the library. With her warm friend Mary Lynch, Richardson set an example of "finer womanhood" for Livingstone's women students.[33] "Saved" from love, Victoria Richardson never married.

In 1904, Marie Clinton established the Buds of Promise within the Woman's Home and Foreign Missionary Society. "Blooming All for Jesus," the Buds functioned as an educational service club for AME Zion children aged three to twelve.[34] In 1909, Victoria Richardson began the Young Woman's Home and Foreign Missionary Society for teenaged girls. The group took on social service work, nursed the sick, visited the elderly, and presented public health programs.[35] By 1912, the officers of the Woman's Home and Foreign Missionary Society had years of social service experience behind them and an organization that could channel women's energies from the cradle to the grave. Annie Blackwell served as corresponding secretary, and elder Mary Small presided.[36]

These African American women's denominational groups created a vast network throughout the South, virtually invisible to whites. It is helpful to see the groups as cells through which information and ideas could pass quickly. The invisibility of black women's work suited them. They did not want to antagonize their husbands by making a power play within their denominations—the men in the church were already uneasy about their activities. They did not want to endanger their families by drawing attention to themselves. They did not want to risk interference from whites by being overtly political. Better to call social work "missionary work"; better to gather 100,000 Baptist women in a movement to produce good homes. If such activities resulted in organizing the community to lobby for better schools, swamp drainage, or tuberculosis control, no white could accuse them of meddling in politics.

From these bases, women forged interdenominational links. North Carolinian Anna Julia Cooper, by then living in Washington, D.C., was present at the creation of the National Association of Colored Women's Clubs in 1896. Delegates to that first meeting represented a wide range of women's denominational organizations, interdenominational unions such as the WCTU and the King's Daughters, and secular civic leagues. In her capacity as North Carolina's state WCTU president, Mary Lynch attended the first national convention in 1897; she became national corresponding secretary at the second. The Biddle University Club of Charlotte was a charter member.[37] North Carolina black women founded a statewide federation of clubs in 1909 and elected Marie Clinton president.[38]

In addition to the women's clubs, the WCTU survived as an organizational home for black women after the white WCTU women found their work overtaken by the male Anti-Saloon League. By 1901, the national organization was paying a state organizer, and Lucy Thurman, national superintendent of "Colored Work," visited North Carolina regularly.[39] Marie Clinton was an active member, and she helped direct WCTU work toward efforts to help children. Victoria Richardson served as state president of

the Loyal Temperance League, an organization that encouraged young-
sters to sign the temperance pledge and sponsored oratorical contests
denouncing strong drink. Their work left telling memories. At eighty-four,
Abna Aggrey Lancaster recalled her excitement on the day in 1914 when
Mary Lynch visited her Sunday school class. Seven-year-old Lancaster
returned home for Sunday dinner proudly boasting that she would never
allow alcohol or tobacco to touch her lips.[40] Decades later, George Lincoln
Blackwell, Annie Blackwell's nephew, still savored his victory in a Loyal
Temperance League oratorical contest as one of the proudest moments of
his childhood.[41] Almost every large city in the state had a WCTU chapter.
Lynch marveled at the organization's progress: "It seems a long time since
that sultry day in July when in Salisbury we launched our little bark upon
the waves of opposition."[42]

Activist black women also met at frequent regional sociological conferences. The Progressive Era trend toward organization, discussion, and
investigation blossomed in these huge confabulations. Mary Lynch went to
the Negro Young People's Christian and Educational Congress in Atlanta
in 1902, where she delivered the address, "The Woman's Part in the Battle
against Drink."[43] There she met Charlotte Hawkins, a young Boston student who had just moved to Sedalia, North Carolina, and banker Maggie
L. Walker of Richmond. She also renewed ties with Lucy Thurman of the
national WCTU and Josephine Silone-Yates, president of the National
Association of Colored Women's Clubs.[44] The Woman's Day theme was
"No race can rise higher than its women."[45]

As women were building vast voluntary networks, public school teaching
was becoming an increasingly feminized profession. In 1902, the number
of black women teachers and black men teachers was almost the same:
1,325 women and 1,190 men. The percentage of black women teachers
exactly matched that of white women teachers: 52 percent.[46] By 1919, 78
percent of black teachers were women, and 83 percent of the white teachers were women.[47] The growing number of black women teachers did not
escape notice. At the 1903 meeting of the Negro State Teachers Association, more than half of the delegates were women, including Sarah
Dudley Pettey's sisters, Nannie and Catherine. Men had abandoned the
profession, one speaker complained, because "they cannot compete with
[women] teachers who are willing to work for low wages."[48]

But that analysis leaves black women taking the rap for the white
supremacists. White women flocked to public teaching at the same time as
black women, yet their salaries rose because politics determined educational allocations on the state level. It was black men's exclusion from the
political sphere, not black women's willingness to work for low wages, that

caused African American teachers to be poorly compensated. In some counties, salaries for black teachers actually declined after the fusion government* ended.[49] Generally, however, throughout the state in the first two decades of the century, black teachers' wages crept upward, even as they continued to fall further behind white teachers' salaries. The statewide average salary in 1905 was $156 for whites and $107 for African Americans. Fourteen years later, whites averaged $353 and blacks $197.[50] The increasing number of black women teachers was a result, not a cause, of declining wages. In addition to driving black men from the profession, low wages contributed to a difference in the marital status of white and black women teachers. White women teachers were almost always single. Many black women teachers were married women who remained partially dependent upon their husbands' income.

The most staggering statistic was the growth in the number of white teachers: from a total of 5,472 in 1902 to 11,730 in 1919, a 214 percent increase. During the same period, the number of black teachers rose from 2,515 to 3,511, a 139 percent increase.[51] White teachers' numbers grew at the expense of black education. The white North Carolina Normal and Industrial College at Greensboro graduated large numbers of white women teachers at the same time that the state eliminated four black normal schools and banned women from the North Carolina Agricultural and Technical College.[52] Black women had a much harder time than white women formally preparing to teach, and fewer jobs awaited them after they graduated.[53]

Those who did succeed were likely to be active members of church women's organizations, involved in the WCTU, and participants in their city's literary societies and civic leagues. The black woman teacher had to withstand the scrutiny of white superintendents on the lookout for moral failings at the same time that she had to vanquish intense competition among dozens of aspirants for a single position. She had to be so unselfish, so dedicated, and so above reproach that no gossip could touch her.[54] Teachers' organizational connections protected and nurtured them. Conversely, they took their organizations' goals into their classrooms.

Even without their own progressive agenda, African American women teachers would have found schools to be an increasingly politicized setting. After 1900, the importance of literacy for voting and the movement toward industrial education commanded the attention of both the black and white community, and perennial battles over allocating taxes for education turned the black schoolhouse into a lightning rod, propelling

---

Fusion government was the term given to those elected as a result of the political alliance between the Republican and Populist parties.

female teachers into the political sphere, for better or for worse. The disfranchisers split among themselves over black public education after the amendment passed. Alfred Moore Waddell, ever the bumbling misanthrope, once chose a commencement address as a platform for condemning universal education: "There are thousands of enlightened persons who do not subscribe to the belief . . . that in popular education alone is to be found the panacea for all social political evils." Waddell added that education is even less useful when "applied to both races indiscriminately."[55] But other whites, notably Charles B. Aycock, saw universal education as the South's salvation. As far as they were concerned, even African Americans could participate in the forthcoming redemption, though not in equal measure.[56] Charles D. McIver, president of the North Carolina Normal and Industrial College for white women, tried to convince African Americans that disfranchisement would boost black education by encouraging parents to send their children to school, stating that "temporary disfranchisement . . . is a much less evil than permanent ignorance."[57] Aycock, who had threatened to refuse the Democratic Party's gubernatorial nomination if the time limit on the grandfather clause was extended, later threatened to resign the governorship if the state legislature allowed whites to tax themselves separately for the benefit of their own children.[58] His threat sprang partly from compassion—"Let us not be the first state . . . to make the weak man helpless"—but partly from his concern that such a move would encourage the U.S. Supreme Court to find the amendment unconstitutional.

The racial inequities of school funding have been well documented, but the efforts of black students and teachers to keep their schools from starving cannot be celebrated enough. Even in the best black schools, for example, the Charlotte graded school, there were few desks and "two and sometimes three small pupils sat crowded in a wide seat." The state gave so little—inadequate furniture, a meager library—but teachers made so little go so far. "There was much blackboard space in a room which was a good thing," Rose Leary Love recalled. "At the time, blackboards were not termed visual aids, but they really were the most important available ones." The teachers used them to explain lessons; the pupils used them in lieu of paper. In the state's eyes, African Americans were not training to be full citizens; they needed no civics classes, no maps, no copy of the Constitution, no charts on "How a Bill Becomes a Law." That left teachers on their own to define citizenship. Somehow they did. Teachers chose talented students to "draw the National Flag or the State Flag on the blackboard," Love remembered. "These flags were assigned a place of honor on the board and they became a permanent fixture in the room for the year. Pupils were careful not to erase the flags when they cleaned the blackboards."[60] Despite whites' efforts to rob African Americans of their country, black teachers taught each day under the flag.

A centralized state bureaucracy grew to oversee the curriculum in African American schools. In 1905, Charles L. Coon, a white man who had recently been superintendent of Salisbury's schools and secretary of the General Education Board, accepted the newly created position of superintendent of the state colored normal schools.[61] According to his boss, Coon's oversight would "send out into the counties each a larger number of negro teachers, equipped with the knowledge and the training, and filled with the right ideals necessary for the . . . most practical, sensible and useful education of the negro race."[62] By putting African American normal schools under the control of a white man, the state hoped to produce teachers who embraced industrial education and to force the private African American normal schools out of business.

Ironically, state oversight created controversy rather than quelling it primarily because of Coon's independent personality. An amateur statistician who often challenged authority, Coon created a furor by proving that the state spent less on African American education than the taxes blacks paid in. In fact, Coon produced figures to prove that black tax dollars educated white children. Coon's boss, James Y. Joyner, distanced himself from Coon's argument and decried him to Josephus Daniels.[63] But Aycock admitted that Coon spoke the truth, and one white lawyer observed, "Our attempts to oppress the negro's mind are enslaving us just as bad as slavery did."[64]

By the time Coon addressed the predominately female Negro State Teachers Association in 1909, his trial by fire had turned him into a political agitator. He argued that the tide had turned against white supremacy. "I do not believe we need to spend much more time upon that species of the white race who would doom any other race to mental slavery," he commented, "anymore than we should spend time fighting over again the battles of whether a man has the right to hold in bodily servitude another man of another race." He suggested that the teachers unite to work for better instruction, longer school terms, and improved school facilities in the next decade. Furthermore, he recommended that blacks "interest the white people in your schools. . . . Then get your churches, lodges, and societies to help. . . . We must see to it that we interest the local communities, white and black."[65] Coon's prescription for African American education fit perfectly into black women's organizational missions and pointed up the political nature of black women teachers' jobs.

Whites quarreled a great deal more over funding black education than they did over its content, which white educators overwhelmingly agreed should be based on the Hampton model. Very little industrial training could begin, however, without spending dollars on equipment and tools. Ironically, it proved more expensive to build a bookcase than to explain an algebra problem on a broken piece of slate. Outside help would be critical. As a few dollars began to trickle down, black women teachers learned to exploit whites' support of industrial education. The Negro State Teachers Association recognized in 1903 that "the industrial and manual idea . . . is a much felt need in our public and private schools, since the development of negro womanhood is one of its immediate results." At the same time that black women recognized the potential of industrial education to improve home life, they began to clamor for a greater voice in its administration. When officials from the Rockefeller-funded General Education Board and local white educators met with black teachers in 1913, Charlotte Hawkins Brown told the group flatly that since women made up the majority of rural teachers, industrial education would fail unless philanthropists and white educators listened more closely to black women's suggestions and rewarded them for their efforts.[66] African American women's tilting of the industrial education ideology was slight but important. While paying lip service to the ideal of producing servants for white people, black women quietly turned the philosophy into a self-help endeavor and the public schools into institutions resembling social settlement houses. Cooking courses became not only vocational classes but also nutrition courses where students could eat hot meals. Sewing classes may have turned out some dressmakers and cobbling classes some cobblers, but they had the added advantage of clothing poor pupils so that they could attend school more regularly.

The Negro Rural School Fund, a philanthropy administered by the Rockefeller Foundation's General Education Board, gave the state's black women teachers the basic tools they needed to incorporate social work into the public school system. Begun in 1909 as the Anna T. Jeanes Fund, it paid more than half of the salary of one industrial supervising teacher on the county level. County boards of education paid the rest.[67] The Jeanes supervisor traveled to all of the African American schools in a county, ostensibly to teach industrial education. In 1913, the General Education Board offered to pay the salary of a state supervisor of rural elementary schools in North Carolina to oversee the thirteen Jeanes teachers already in place and to expand the work to other counties. In naming the supervisor, the board had a hidden agenda: northern philanthropists did not trust southern state administrators to allocate and spend their grants wisely. They wanted a white man loyal to them in state government, a professional who could walk the tightwire of interracial relations, placating obstreperous legislators at the same time that he kept a keen eye on black industrial curricula. They found their man in Nathan C. Newbold, who had been superintendent of public schools in Washington, North Carolina.[68]

In his first report, Newbold displayed his facility for straddling the color line. He condemned white injustice to African Americans at the same time that he explained it away as a reasonable vestige of the past, now, fortunately, antiquated. "The average negro rural schoolhouse is really a disgrace to an independent, civilized people," Newbold wrote as he surveyed his new field. "To one who does not know our history, these schoolhouses, though mute, would tell in unmistaken terms a story of injustice, inhumanity and neglect on the part of our white people," he observed. If someone unfamiliar with the South's history stumbled upon such buildings, the newcomer would surely think North Carolina's whites "unchristian." But the stranger would be wrong, he explained, since the black schools were no worse than white schools had been twenty-five years ago. Now that whites had remedied their own situation, he was sure they would eagerly set about improving black schools. Newbold always offered whites a face-saving excuse for past inaction at the same time that he spurred them to action.[69]

Nonconfrontational and optimistic, as state agent for the Negro Rural School Fund Newbold became an extraordinary voice for African American education. He quickly persuaded more county boards of education to fund half of a Jeanes teacher's salary at the same time that he forged strong alliances with the incumbent Jeanes teachers. By the end of his first year, twenty-two counties employed Jeanes teachers, who found themselves in the often awkward position of having to report to both Newbold and the county superintendent.[70] Newbold appointed a black woman, Annie Wealthy Holland, as his assistant.[71] The Jeanes board's initial expenditure of $2,144 in the state in 1909 grew to $12,728 by 1921.[72]

Most women who became Jeanes teachers came to social service work through their own organizations. For example, the Jeanes teacher in Rowan County was Rose Douglass Aggrey, a Shaw University graduate, poet, and classical scholar. Her husband, J. E. Kwegyir Aggrey, was born in the Gold Coast, Africa, was educated by British missionaries, and came to the United States to attend Livingstone College. He taught at Livingstone until the Phelps-Stokes Association sent him back to Africa as a missionary in 1920.[73] Staying behind in Salisbury, Rose Aggrey was active in the Woman's Home and Foreign Missionary Society of the AME Zion Church, forging close friendships with Mary Lynch and Victoria Richardson. Aggrey later became president of the statewide federation of black women's clubs.[74] Aggrey's daughter remembered that her mother often appeared before the school board and the county commissioners to plead for money for school improvements, to lobby for a longer school year, or to facilitate consolidation of one-room schools into graded structures.[75] Aggrey was extremely well connected within the Jeanes structure; in 1919, her friend Marie Clinton's husband, George, served on the national board of the Negro Rural School Fund.[76]

Faced with local white administrators' neglect, Jeanes teachers had an enormous amount of responsibility. Sarah Delany, the Jeanes supervisor in Wake County, recalled, "I was just supposed to be in charge of domestic science, but they made me do the county superintendent's work. So, I ended up actually in charge of all the colored schools in Wake County, North Carolina, although they didn't pay me to do that or give me any credit."[77] Delany, raised as a "child of privilege" on the Saint Augustine's College campus, stayed overnight with parents in rural areas, where she encountered not just a lack of indoor plumbing but a condition even more appalling to a citified house guest: no outhouse. Delany went to her pupils' homes to teach their parents how to "cook, clean, [and] eat properly," and when General Education Board officials visited North Carolina in 1913, she agreed to serve on the statewide committee to establish a cooking curriculum. She painted schoolrooms, taught children to bake cakes, raised money to improve buildings, and organized Parent Unions.[78] Jeanes teachers also transformed their students into entrepreneurs.[79] In 1915, their Home-Makers Clubs, Corn Clubs, and Pig Clubs involved over 4,000 boys and girls and 2,000 adults in 32 counties. The clubs were intended to teach farming, of course, but they also enabled poor rural African Americans to make money on their produce. The students raised more than $6,000 selling fruits and vegetables that year.[80]

Jeanes teachers saw themselves as agents of progressivism, and they combined public health work with their visits to schools and homes. Unlike Rose Aggrey and Sarah Delany, Carrie Battle, the Jeanes supervisor in Edgecombe County, had grown up desperately poor. Her mother worked at two domestic jobs and Battle went hungry to save money for tuition at Elizabeth City State Normal School. After she began teaching, Battle visited the homes of pupils across the county to organize a Modern Health Crusade against tuberculosis in the schools. Moving from school to school with a set of scales, she would not weigh ill-groomed boys and girls, nor would she weigh anyone in a dirty schoolroom. She made the children promise to clean up the room, bathe, use individual drinking cups, and sleep with the windows open. One boy reported, "Pa said that was too foolish — I would catch cold and die if I slept with the windows up." Another outmaneuvered his father by waiting to raise the window until the man was snoring. Soon Battle had established Modern Health Clubs in every school and a total of 4,029 children enrolled as Crusaders. Her work attracted attention from the white community, and she began to cooperate with the white Red Cross nurse to produce public health programs. Many of Battle's students had never been farther than ten miles from their homes. She brought the world to them through regularly scheduled visits of the "Moving Picture Car," a truck equipped with projection equipment used to screen films on health education.[81]

Jeanes teachers also built schools across the state—schools for which the state took credit and of which the counties took possession. Weary of asking for their fair share of tax dollars, black communities simply built their own schools and gave them to the county. For example, in the academic year 1915–16, thirty-two black schools were built and thirty improved at a total cost of $29,000. African Americans contributed over $21,000 of the total: $15,293 in cash and the equivalent of $5,856 in labor.[82] The school at Chadbourn represents a typical case. Local African Americans deeded to the county "a large building nearly completed to contain four class rooms, and nine acres of land." Moreover, they pledged more than $850 the next year to pay additional teachers and make further improvements to the building.[83] In Mecklenburg County, the white chairman of the school board told African Americans that the board was "willing to help those people who would help themselves" and that if African Americans "could pay half of the expense in as far as the board was able it would pay the other half." Amazingly, the black community was "encouraged" by this offer, built six schools, and forced the board to make good on its promise.[84]

The next year, the Julius Rosenwald Committee, a Chicago-based philanthropy, appropriated $6,000 to stimulate public school building in rural areas of North Carolina. Although this amount was a great deal less than African Americans were already raising annually to build their own schools, Rosenwald grants often embarrassed state and county officials into contributing funds for building black schools. The Rosenwald grants would provide a third of the cost of schools, local African American communities would raise a third, and tax dollars would account for a third. The Jeanes teachers organized teachers, parents, and students to support school-building projects by raffling box lunches, setting aside part of a field to grow a crop for the school, or providing the building materials for the structure from their own lands.[85] Their efforts made the Rosenwald seed money flower. For example, the first "Rosenwald" school built in North Carolina cost $1,473, of which the fund contributed $300.[86] By 1917, Jeanes teachers saw to it that the state's twenty-one Rosenwald schools teemed with activity night and day. Parent Unions met there, and teachers returned in the evenings to conduct "moonlight schools" where adults could learn to read.[87]

The unique role of the Jeanes teacher points up the distinctiveness of southern progressivism and provides clues to the reasons for historians' difficulties in finding and understanding it. The Jeanes teacher had no counterpart in the North. She did social work on the fly, leaving neither permanent settlement houses nor case files behind through which one might capture her experience. She understood the latest public health measures and passed them along even in the most remote areas. She fought to obtain Rosenwald school money to build schools that were airy and modern, then turned them into clubhouses in the evenings. By establishing Parent Unions, she provided a new organizational center for black communities. She lobbied school boards and county commissions for supplies and support. And she accomplished all of this while trying to remain invisible to the white community at large. To locate the progressive South, one must not just visit New South booster Henry Grady in Atlanta but find as well a schoolroom full of cleanly scrubbed Modern Health Crusaders, lined up for hot cereal cooked by the older girls in Rosenwald kitchens, each Crusader clutching the jelly jar that served as his or her very own glass.

By 1910, African American women in the state realized the need to create a united front to lobby local governmental officials and to improve civic life. Connected on the state level through the North Carolina Association of Colored Women's Clubs, these organizations would have to bring together on the local level denominational women's groups, interface with public school programs, and marshal all of the experience and resources that women had acquired in the past decade. The Salisbury Colored Women's Civic League exemplifies such an organization, and it brought together women who have appeared often in these pages: Mary Lynch, Victoria Richardson, and Rose Aggrey.

It took a strong leader to inspire such accomplished women, and the Civic League found such a leader in its president, Lula Spaulding Kelsey, the daughter of Lucy Sampson and John Spaulding. Lucy, a Lumbee Indian, had met John when he came to teach her class at the State Croatan Normal School in Pembroke. Both of their families were "freeish," the eastern North Carolina term for those blacks and mixed-race people whose ancestors had never been slaves.[88] Their daughter Lula attended normal school in Wilmington and then went on to Scotia Seminary* for two more years. Upon graduation from Scotia, Lula Spaulding began teaching there, probably in home economics since her son recalls that she taught "finer womanhood." About the time that Lula began teaching in Concord, her father, a cousin of C. C. Spaulding, founder of North Carolina Mutual Life Insurance Company, moved to nearby Salisbury to estab-

---

*In the nineteenth century, *seminary* often referred to a school on the secondary level, especially institutions for girls.

lish an office of North Carolina Mutual.[89] Lula visited her family often and soon became friendly with Rose Aggrey.[90] Sometime around 1909, her mother's health failed and her father began to go blind. The young teacher determined that she had no choice but to move to Salisbury and take over her father's business.

The North Carolina Mutual agent held a privileged place in black communities, and the job involved traveling around the county every week "managing the debit": collecting money from customers for premiums. It was so rare for a woman to do this job that the incumbent was known as the "debit man." Lula Spaulding became the debit man in Salisbury. She took over her father's office and went about supporting herself and her parents. Soon she attracted the attention of William Kelsey, the strikingly handsome barber who owned the shop below her office. William, much older than Lula, began courting her with rides in his buggy and promises to build a house for her mother and father beside the house that would be theirs. After their marriage in 1911, Lula always honored William not only for marrying her but also for taking on support of her sick mother and blind father. Repaying this symbolic debt may have been one reason that Lula Kelsey was driven to work so hard as the years went by.

A decade before their marriage, William Kelsey had started a funeral business with Stephen Noble, who had a team of horses and a wagon. Noble was contracting to carry African American bodies for the white funeral home, and Kelsey saw the potential of keeping the business within the black community if he and Noble joined to bury the dead. When Kelsey and Noble began, there was no embalming. Relatives laid out the deceased on a "cooling board," the barber "dressed" the body, and the burial took place the same afternoon or the next morning, with the dead wrapped in a cloth. Eula Dunlap recalled that the first metal coffin she ever saw at Lincoln Academy in Kings Mountain was brought there by "Billy" Kelsey for burying his sister around 1910.[91]

William Kelsey enjoyed barbering and wanted to maintain the undertaking business as a sideline. But Lula Kelsey realized that funeral homes represented the wave of the future, especially since a 1909 law required filing an official death certificate within three days of death, a requirement that prevented families from burying their own dead relatives.[92] Shortly after her marriage, Lula Kelsey went to Raleigh to embalming school and became one of the first licensed female morticians in the state. Thereafter, Lula, not William, went with Noble in his wagon to the homes of the deceased, where she made an incision under the corpse's arm, drained all the blood from the body, and injected embalming fluid in the vein. She brought cosmetics, clothing, and tables on which to display the body. If the minister did not show up at graveside, she preached the funeral. By 1923,

Lula Kelsey purchased a large building for the Kelsey and Noble Funeral Home and drove a big black Dodge hearse.[93] Her insurance background led her to found the Kelsey Mutual Burial Association, in which she served as an agent for a fire insurance company and sold life insurance and bonding services through another. She became a notary public in 1917, and later in life, she founded two other funeral homes in nearby towns. William Kelsey helped in the funeral home, but Lula Kelsey ran it, and he kept his barbering business. On Saturday nights when the barber shop got crowded, Lula would come down from her office and commandeer the system, rotating clients through the chairs more quickly by lathering one while William cut and shaved another.

Throughout all of this activity, William and Lula Kelsey loved one another. Kelsey was proud of his wife's entrepreneurial spirit and progressive attitudes. His job, as he saw it, was to let her "go ahead." They had eight children, most born during the first decade of their marriage, seven of whom lived, and they raised a foster child. Lula and William Kelsey managed their household with the same organization that they applied to their businesses and kept their children busy with chores. At home, Lula Kelsey depended upon Lillie Boger, who served as cook and nanny, and at work upon her lifelong secretary, Annie Hauser.[94]

No woman or man in Salisbury had been in as many homes as Lula Kelsey in her roles as debit man and embalmer. She saw cases of need first-hand, and she knew everyone. Moreover, in both of her occupations, she functioned completely independently of whites. Unlike a public school teacher or even a tradesperson with a biracial clientele, Lula Kelsey did not have to calculate white reaction to her every move. At the same time, she did not have to worry about what African American men thought of her. Her husband supported her career completely, and as one of the city's leading businesspeople, she could not be accused of sticking her nose into men's domain when she proposed reforms. To these advantages Lula Kelsey added supreme self-confidence, organizational genius, enormous energy, and faith in the future. In the middle of this frenetic activity, Lula Kelsey founded the Salisbury Colored Women's Civic League in 1913. She presided over the group for at least two decades, throughout the birth of her eight children and the growth of her companies. The league's constitution stated that "its object shall be the general civic interest of our people." Group goals included increased homeownership, better education, and improved public health. It aimed also to "stimulate a desire for the beautiful" by promoting public cleanup campaigns. Membership was open to any woman who met those challenges and paid ten cents a month. Forty to fifty women regularly attended monthly meetings.[95]

Women from all walks of life joined the Civic League. As Rose Aggrey's daughter recalled, "There wasn't poor and rich . . . not a rigid difference between people. The difference between people was those who had training and those who didn't."[96] Her mother, an active Civic Leaguer, had a knack for getting "women of all backgrounds together." The league's rolls included the wife of an AME Zion bishop, a dressmaker, a teacher, a laundress, a domestic worker, and a woman "from the other side of town—not trained, whose husband was in trouble, but a fine Christian woman."[97] Members embraced a wide range of religious denominations—Mrs. A. Croom was a Baptist minister's wife, Lizzie Crittendon an Episcopalian, Lucy Spaulding a Presbyterian, and Mary Lynch and Victoria Richardson members of the AME Zion Church—and they put the agendas of their women's missionary societies into action in the Civic League.[98] Those with "training" dominated the officers' ranks. Kelsey served as president, Mary Lynch and Victoria Richardson as vice presidents, and Kelsey's business secretary, Annie Hauser, as secretary. In addition to the general officers, the league divided the city into four sections, each of which had a female ward boss.[99] In turn, ward bosses chose block chairwomen and held them responsible for organizing every household.[100]

Many of the Civic League's projects involved interaction with white women. In fact, the impetus for the league's formation appears to have been an interracial community cleanup day, a project initiated by white club women throughout the state. Whites had tried to organize cleanup efforts before 1913, but "the most vigorous urging failed to stir the Negroes to action." It was not until they recruited Lula Kelsey to meet with a white male civic leader that plans for a joint cleanup day went forward. White Salisbury citizens finally realized that they could not coerce civic action among African Americans and that "without a Negro leader it is probable that the movement would have been a flat failure."[101] The city donated twelve barrels of lime, a disinfectant, and the Civic League supervised its distribution. The city's two African American doctors spoke to the women on sanitation and disease.[102]

Cleanup days evoked images of African Americans in the traditional role of servants, but they also put white people to work at servants' tasks: raking yards, whitewashing fences, carting trash, and improving housing. This made them a perfect place for black women to launch interracial forays. Moreover, on cleanup days, the entire community expected white landlords to improve their rental houses in black neighborhoods. As segregation rigidified, even the most prosperous black families found it difficult to buy decent housing, and they often had to tolerate living in neglected white-owned rental housing at close quarters. In the absence of building standards and housing laws, community cleanup days focused white attention on slumlords while also organizing black neighbors around a positive self-help project.[103]

As knowledge of disease transmission grew, whites initiated cleanup days to protect themselves from the peril they imagined they were in due to their poor black neighbors' lack of sanitary measures. Typhoid spread by flies and tuberculosis by uncleanliness, and both represented public health emergencies in the South in the 1910s. It is difficult to imagine just how prevalent and problematic flies were in urban areas with poor sanitation or how thoroughly they invaded homes before screening. In a sketch entitled, "You better eat before you read this," Eula Dunlap recalled that people sold the contents of their privies for fertilizer, and it was spread on fields and gardens, with dire consequences. The flies were so thick inside homes that if someone was sick in the summer, a family member had to fan constantly. Babies wore fly netting draped around them as they played outdoors in the summertime.[104] The death rate during "fly season" soared dramatically in the black community and increased modestly in the white community.[105] In reality, germs traveled to both communities, but better health care for whites limited their mortality rate.

The fly carried more than disease; it also carried the germ of interracial cooperation. Since flies knew nothing about the color line, they flew back and forth across it with no regard for class standing or race. As white interracialist Lily Hammond put it in her essay, "The Democracy of the Microbe," "The [white] club women came upon Christian principles of racial adjustment without realizing that they were dealing with racial problems at all. They simply started out with common sense as their guide and cleanliness as their goal."[106] In order to eradicate flies, one had to pick up garbage and extend sanitary sewage treatment to both the white and the black community. Such a cause fit perfectly into African American women's better homes movement.

As we have seen, interracial contact between women had existed since Reconstruction. The chief vehicle in the 1880s and 1890s was the WCTU. Religious white women from the North consistently worked as social service missionaries to the black community—women such as Lillian Cathcart, the American Missionary Association teacher who headed Lincoln Academy. By the turn of the century, southern white women occasionally worked in charitable causes directed at aiding African Americans. For example, Mary De Bardeleben, a Southern Methodist woman, began the black settlement houses known as Bethlehem Houses that flourished by 1914.[107] A group of white Episcopal women had managed Charlotte's Good Samaritan Hospital for African Americans since the 1890s.[108] Among North Carolina Baptists, white women spent the year of 1906 exploring "Daybreak in the Dark Continent, a Study of Africa" and gave "short but pointed talks" at the black women's missionary societies. White women took up collections for African American home mission work within the state, and at church conferences, black women heard "how the dear white ladies denied themselves to help us."[109] These contacts, well meaning as they were, were fraught with white ignorance about black life and exuded white superiority and privilege.

Interracial cooperation in public health campaigns coupled this missionary tradition with Progressive Era confidence in science and efficiency. No doubt some white women actually cared about African Americans' well-being, but most did not set out to eliminate flies in order to convert the heathen or to forge the ties of interracial cooperation or even to improve the health of the black community. They perceived their domestic servants as sources of disease and saw cleanup days as an attempt to solve this problem by enlisting the aid of black women leaders. As progressive public health campaigns made it apparent that germs spread throughout the entire community, African Americans seized upon white fears as a way to turn attention to their neighborhoods. George Clinton warned, "I am very much afraid that the average [white] Church member knows a great deal more about China than he does of the section of his city where the colored people live; his good wife can tell you more about the children of India than she can about the children of the woman who washes her clothes. In all conscience there can be no apology for this kind of ignorance."[110] In Clinton's Charlotte, when white women heard a program entitled, "Preventable Diseases: Where Does Your Servant Live?," they immediately hatched plans for a citywide cleanup day.[111] When they called a meeting with the mayor and city health officers to launch the work, they invited "the women of the colored missionary societies" to be present.[112] The white Charlotte women included black women not out of a spirit of interracial concern but out of a drive for self-preservation. Still, they were doing something controversial.

The minutes of the Charlotte Woman's Club do not record black women's attendance at the meeting that kicked off the cleanup day. The white women did not want their efforts publicized, and they used coded phrases and silence within their internal records as safeguards. White women operated in the civic sphere without the protection of the ballot and crossing racial lines could fuel the argument that introducing white women to politics would undermine racial segregation. Yet from these feeble beginnings, white women eventually grew bolder as they coupled their original narrow self-interest with a growing concern for the general social welfare. By 1920, the white Charlotte Woman's Club had set up clinics that employed black and white nurses, whose salaries were partly paid by the club.[113] Slowly, a pattern of contact emerged from public health campaigns that led to the institutionalization of interracial work within the social welfare context.[114]

The minutes of the Salisbury Civic League indicate that in Salisbury, as in Charlotte, public health work led to increased interracial contact. Mary Lynch headed a committee that visited "some of the white civic league ladies" and reported that the black women delegates had been cordially treated.[115] This initial visit prompted continuing contact. White women made cash donations and distributed flower seeds and plants to the Civic League, and the two groups cooperated each year in the cleanup campaigns.[116]

These efforts, begun through voluntary club work, aided the institutionalization of charity after 1910. In the following decade, large cities in North Carolina established Associated Charities branches to formalize and coordinate social service casework. In cities that were large enough, as in Charlotte, African Americans formed auxiliaries of the Associated Charities, presided over by leading black club women.[117] In Salisbury, the relationship was more informal, and Lula Kelsey became an unpaid social worker for the Associated Charities. The Civic League joined the Associated Charities in 1917. Soon Civic Leaguers passed out pledge cards for the Associated Charities' annual find-raising campaign throughout the African American community.[118] Thereafter, when a needy case came to the attention of the Civic League, they referred it to the Associated Charities.[119] The Associated Charities used the league to determine whether a person seeking help really needed it and asked Kelsey to perform home studies on applicants. Kelsey's son recalled that whenever an African American came for help to the Associated Charities office, the white social worker there would telephone Lula Kelsey before she acted.[120]

With disfranchisement, African American women became diplomats to the white community, and contact with white women represented a vital, though difficult, part of that mission. As white women gained more power in social service organizations and public education during the first two decades of the century, they began to exercise growing influence in the public sector.[121] Contact between black and white women came about not because the two groups felt gender solidarity but because white women controlled the resources that black women needed to improve their communities. What interracial contact meant to white club women is more confusing, as it must have been to the white club women themselves. Just as their mothers had met educated, middle-class black women for the first time in the 1880s in the Woman's Christian Temperance Union, after the white supremacy campaign, many white club women got their first glimpse of organized African American women when they planned cleanup days together. Such meetings may have been the first time a white woman had ever spoken to black woman who was not a servant. From these contacts, a handful of white and black women formed cooperative working partnerships to further mutual goals, as did Lula Kelsey and the white Associated Charities social worker. But those partnerships were rare. To some, they represented a necessary step toward accomplishing their own civic goals; to others, they offered some fulfillment of religious imperatives. Beyond that, most white women probably did not give much thought to the meaning of their contacts with black women.

Yet however sporadic and confusing women's interracial contacts were, they represented a crack in the mortar of the foundation of white supremacy. White club women came to know more about the black community and its women leaders and became less pliant in the hands of male politicians who attempted to manipulate them to further the gendered rhetoric of white supremacy. The same process had taken place in the 1880s when white temperance women ignored the dire warnings of men and planned local-option campaigns together with black women. But imperialist rhetoric, scientific racism, the Democrats' white supremacy campaign, and women's lack of direct access to the political process had ended those contacts. This time, things would be different. This time, the local contacts between black and white club women had a chance to take root and grow.

In addition to fostering useful contact between women of both races, community cleanup work earned certain black women power within their neighborhoods and brought them into contact with city officials. The Civic League did not just hold cleanup days; it inspected homes afterward, counseled residents who did not follow sanitary practices, and reported them to the city if they did not comply with sanitary guidelines.[122] The membership card of the Civic League required the bearer to pledge to "improve the sanitary condition of the home in which I live" and to use "lime to disinfect and whitewash." Upon presentation, the bearer of the card could claim one gallon of lime, "Given by City; distributed by COL-ORED WOMEN'S CIVIC LEAGUE."[123] This public/private partnership across racial lines was a shaky one, but organized African American women quickly capitalized on it.

White men in local government came to know Lula Kelsey, Rose Aggrey, Mary Lynch, and the other leaguers as spokespeople for the black community—as women who could get things done. The women proceeded as if the city owed them a fair hearing in return for their civic work. Shortly after the first cleanup day, the league voted to send a representative to speak with the city administration about "helping with the cemetery," and by the next month, Lula Kelsey announced to the group that she had met with the mayor and he had "promised that it would be taken care of better in the future."[124] When a disorderly woman came to the attention of the leaguers, a mysterious blind white girl who apparently disturbed the peace of the community, Kelsey reported that she had "discussed her with the mayor and he says that he 'will take her in hand.' "[125]

In the first few months of league activism, contacts with city officials seemed to be limited to Lula Kelsey's privileged relationship with the mayor, but by the next year, the league had appointed a committee to appear before the board of aldermen to urge the passage of an ordinance requiring "sanitary privies" in the city.[126] The city lacked a public playground for its African American children, and the Civic League lobbied city officials to provide one. The league's attempts to win support from local government did not always succeed. Victoria Richardson suggested that a committee appear before the county commissioners to request permission to use the public schools "to give lessons on different subjects" in the evenings.[127] Apparently the commissioners tied African American adult education to literacy and voting and denied the league use of the buildings, but "moonlight schools" began meeting the next month in Lula Kelsey's living room. Within a short time, the moonlight school teachers reported that two men had made "wonderful progress."[128]

The league's projects read like a checklist for Progressive Era reform. Its work to establish playgrounds, for example, reflected two concerns: to provide supervision for children's play and move it from "the neighbor's back yard" to venues where sanitation and activities could be controlled. Both goals meshed with the "play movement" that swept the nation at the turn of the century.[129] Likewise, the women participated in "maternalist politics" by sponsoring "baby day," when mothers could bring their babies to a meeting for a doctor's advice.[130] Civic League women centered much of their effort around the public schools. They held fairs and paper drives to raise money for the industrial department of the graded schools, and a teacher who was a member of the league organized a Junior Civic League at her school.[131] The women visited the city jail regularly, ministered to a chain gang, and began an outreach program at the county home for the indigent.[132]

By 1917, Salisbury's African American women had two mechanisms in place to gain a hearing before both private and public manifestations of the state. First, contacts with white club women provided entry into the growing private social welfare system. Since black club women had met the white club women involved in social service, the Civic League could join the Associated Charities and then use that membership to direct the flow of aid to the African American community. Second, with husbands and brothers virtually disfranchised, diplomatic women could go in their places to the mayor and county commissioners to lobby for city services and, once there, cast their mission in female-coded, and unthreatening, terms.

As much as southern whites plotted to reserve progressivism for themselves, and as much as they schemed to alter the ill-fitting northern version accordingly, they failed. African American women embraced southern white progressivism, reshaped it, and sent back a new model that included black power brokers and grass roots activists. Evidence of southern African American progressivism is not to be found in public laws, electoral politics, or the establishment of mothers' aid programs at the state level. It rarely appears in documents that white progressives, male or female, left behind. Since black men could not speak out in politics and black women did not want to be seen, it has remained invisible in virtually every discussion of southern progressivism. Nonetheless, southern black women initiated every progressive reform that southern white women initiated, a feat they accomplished without financial resources, without the civic protection of their husbands, and without publicity.

At the same time that black women used progressivism to reshape black life and race relations, an organizational approach slowly began to replace racial "paternalism." The black community in Salisbury would not listen to influential whites who told them to clean up their communities. Nothing happened until whites recognized black women leaders, met with them publicly, and gave them authority. Then the city was "completely transformed."[133] Despite whites' extensive efforts to undermine black education by imposing a nineteenth-century version of industrial education, black women's progressive ideas made industrial education modern and useful by linking it to the sanitary science movement. Contacts between white and black women with progressive agendas set the groundwork for inclusion of African Americans in formal social service structures. Her desire to help solve civic problems gave Lula Kelsey the right to appear before city officials during a period when black men risked their lives if they registered to vote for those officials.

This is certainly not to argue that disfranchisement was a positive good or that African Americans were better off with limited social services than they would have been with full civil rights. It means that black women were given straw and they made bricks. Outward cooperation with an agenda designed to oppress them masked a subversive twist. Black women capitalized upon the new role of the state to capture a share of the meager resources and proceeded to effect real social change with tools designed to maintain the status quo.

Notes

1. My conception of the expansion of the public sphere and the growth of an interactive state draws heavily on Jurgen Habermas's work and his redefinition of the term "citizen" and on Nancy Fraser's argument that this movement from citizen to state client was gendered, at least in the United States, since it brought the state into matters that were heretofore in the private, or woman's, sphere. See Habermas, *The Structural Transformation of the Public Sphere: An Inquiry into a Category of Bourgeois Society* (Cambridge: MIT Press, 1989), and Nancy Fraser, "Rethinking the Public Sphere: A Contribution to the Critique of an Actually Existing Democracy," in *Habermas and the Public Sphere,* ed. Craig Calhoun (Cambridge: MIT Press, 1992), 109–42.

2. Richard L. Watson surveys the historiography of southern progressivism in his essay "From Populism through the New Deal" in *Interpreting Southern History: Essays in Honor of Sanford W. Higginbotham,* ed. John Boles and Evelyn Thomas Nolen (Baton Rouge: Louisiana State University Press, 1987), 329–56.

3. Because of southern racial dynamics and arguments regarding change versus continuity, the southern progressive movement remains even less understood than the national progressive movement, if that is possible. See Jacquelyn Hall, "O. Delight Smith's Progressive Era: Labor, Feminism, and Reform in the Urban South—Atlanta, Georgia, 1907–1915," in *Visible Women: New Essays on American Activism,* ed. Nancy Hewitt and Suzanne Lebsock (Urbana: University of Illinois Press, 1993), 166–98; William A. Link, *The Paradox of Southern Progressivism, 1880–1930* (Chapel Hill: University of North Carolina Press, 1992); and Edward Ayers, *The Promise of the New South: Life after Reconstruction* (New York: Oxford University Press, 1992). The classic treatments include Arthur S. Link, "The Progressive Movement in the South, 1870–1914," *North Carolina Historical Review* 23 (April 1946): 172–95; C. Vann Woodward, *Origins of the New South, 1877–1913* (Baton Rouge: Louisiana State University Press, 1951); and Dewey Grantham, *Southern Progressivism: The Reconciliation of Progress and Tradition* (Knoxville: University of Tennessee Press, 1983). For attention to race, see Woodward, *Origins of the New South,* 369–95; J. Morgan Kousser, "Progressivism—For Middle-Class Whites Only: North Carolina Education, 1880–1919," *Journal of Southern History* 46 (May 1980), 168–94; John Dittmer, *Black Georgia during the Progressive Era, 1900–1920* (Urbana: University of Illinois Press, 1977); and Nell Irvin Painter, *Standing at Armageddon: The United States, 1877–1919* (New York: W. W. Norton, 1987), 253–82. On southern white women and progressivism, see Anne Firor Scott, "The 'New Woman' in the New South," *South Atlantic Quarterly* 61 (August 1962): 473–83, and Scott, *The Southern Lady: From Pedestal to Politics, 1830–1930* (Chicago: University of Chicago Press, 1970). On North Carolina, see James Leloudis, "School Reform in the New South: The Woman's Association for the Betterment of Public School Houses in North Carolina, 1902–1919," *Journal of American History* 69 (March 1983): 886–909, and Anastasia Sims, *The Power of Femininity in the New South: Women's Organizations and Politics in North Carolina, 1880–1930* (Columbia: University of South Carolina Press, 1997). For a review of the literature on women and progressivism in the South, see Jacquelyn Hall and Anne Firor Scott, "Women in the South," in *Interpreting Southern History,* 454–509.

4. Scott, *Southern Lady,* pt. 2, and "The 'New Woman' in the New South." For the political dynamics on a national scale, see Paula Baker, "The Domestication of

Politics: Women and American Political Society, 1780–1920," *American Historical Review* 89 (June 1984): 620–47, and William H. Chafe, "Women's History and Political History: Some Thoughts on Progressivism and the New Deal," in *Visible Women*, 101–18. For an argument that women's work in social welfare and politics did not "change the fundamental nature of the state itself or alter the character of the male-dominated polity," see Katherine Kish Sklar, "The Historical Foundations of Women's Power in the Creation of the American Welfare State, 1830–1930," in *Mothers of a New World: Maternalist Politics and the Origins of the Welfare State,* ed. Sonya Michel and Seth Koven (New York: Routledge, 1993), 43–93, and Eileen Boris, "The Power of Motherhood: Black and White Activist Women Redefine the 'Political,'" *Radical History Review* 5 (Spring 1991): 191–203.

5. Hall, "O. Delight Smith's Progressive Era."

6. Anne Firor Scott, "Most Invisible of All: Black Women's Voluntary Associations, *Journal of Southern History* 56 (February 1990): 3–22, suggests that black club women participated in southern progressivism but that their past had been lost, hence they were invisible. I, of course, concur but would add that their invisibility was often deliberate. For a reconceptualization of black women's work in the context of progressivism, see Elizabeth Lasch-Quinn, *Black Neighbors: Race and the Limits of Reform in the American Settlement House Movement, 1890–1945* (Chapel Hill: University of North Carolina Press, 1993).

7. Authors of three works on African American women's voluntary activities during the period chose not to use the framework of progressivism. See Cynthia Neverdon-Morton, *Afro-American Women of the South and the Advancement of the Race, 1895–1925* (Knoxville: University of Tennessee Press, 1989); Jacqueline Anne Rouse, *Lugenia Burns Hope: Black Southern Reformer* (Athens: University of Georgia Press, 1989); Dorothy Salem, *To Better Our World: Black Women in Organized Reform, 1890–1920* (New York: Carlson, 1990).

8. Evelyn Brooks Higginbotham, *Righteous Discontent: The Women's Movement in the Black Baptist Church, 1880–1920* (Cambridge: Harvard University Press, 1993); Jualynne E. Dodson, "Power and Surrogate Leadership: Black Women and Organized Religion," *Sage* 2 (Fall 1988): 40; Cheryl Townsend Gilkes, "'Together and in Harness': Women's Traditions in the Sanctified Church," *Signs* 10 (Summer 1985): 678–99.

9. *A.M.E. Zion Quarterly Review* (Third quarter, July–Aug.–Sept. 1906): 106; E. Franklin Frazier, *The Negro Church in America.* 1964. Reprint (New York: Schocken Books, 1974).

10. *Proceedings of the Thirty-sixth Annual Session of the Baptist Educational and Missionary Convention,* 11.

11. *Minutes of the Thirty-first Annual Session of the Halifax County Sunday School Convention,* 4.

12. *Proceedings of the Thirty-second Annual Session of the Baptist State Educational and Missionary Convention,* 17. This convention was held in New Bern in 1899, and Sarah Dudley and Charles Pettey attended as emissaries from the AME Zion Church (ibid., 9).

13. *Centennial Year, Woman's Baptist Home and Foreign Missionary Convention of North Carolina.*

14. *Proceedings of the Thirty-second Annual Session of the Baptist State Educational and Missionary Convention,* 17.

15. *Yearbook of the East Cedar Grove Missionary Baptist Association,* 9.

16. *Proceedings of the Thirty-second Annual Session of the Baptist State Educational and Missionary Convention,* 17.

17. Even the most sympathetic whites called for home improvement, as did Joanna Moore, a white woman and editor of the widely read journal *Hope,* when she spoke to black Baptist women. Ibid., 9.

18. Mrs. Booker T. Washington, "The Negro Home and the Future of the Race," in *Democracy in Earnest: The Southern Sociological Congress, 1916–1918,* ed. James McCulloch (Washington, D.C.: Southern Sociological Congress, 1918), 334–41.

19. On black women and welfare, see Linda Gordon, "Black and White Visions of Welfare: Women's Welfare Activism, 1890–1945," *Journal of American History* 78 (September 1991): 559–90; Edith L. Ross, ed., *Black Heritage in Social Welfare, 1860–1930* (Metuchen, N.J.: Scarecrow Press, 1987); Gerda Lerner, *Black Women in White America: A Documentary History* (New York: Vintage Books, 1972), 437–520. On the professionalization of social work, see Ellen Fitzpatrick, *Endless Crusade: Women Social Scientists and Progressive Reform* (New York: Oxford University Press, 1990); and Daniel J. Walkowitz, "The Making of a Feminine Professional Identity: Social Workers in the 1920s," *American Historical Review* 95 (October 1990): 1051–75.

20. The argument that the literacy requirement for voting increased the importance of black women as teachers recalls Linda Kerber's argument regarding the importance of the American Revolution and the founding of the republic to women. See Kerber, "The Republican Mother: Women and the Enlightenment— An American Perspective," *American Quarterly* 28 (1976): 187–205, and Mary Beth Norton, *Liberty's Daughters: The Revolutionary Experience of American Women, 1750–1800* (Glenview, Ill.: Scott, Foresman, 1980), 272. The Progressive Era rhetoric on good homes drew on an older Victorian construction of the purity of the home and female moral authority. For a sensitive untangling of this language and its meaning, see Peggy Pascoe, *Relations of Rescue: The Search for Female Moral Authority in the American West, 1874–1939* (New York: Oxford University Press, 1990).

21. *Star of Zion,* 18 Oct. 1900, 5.

22. Mrs. J. J. Lassiter, *Mount Zion Woman's Missionary Union History, 1906–1956.* N.p., [1956].

23. *Proceedings of the Thirty-ninth Annual Session of the Baptist Educational and Missionary Convention,* 49.

24. *Proceedings of the Thirty-seventh Annual Session of the Baptist Educational and Missionary Convention.*

25. *Proceedings of the Third Annual Session of the Union Baptist State Convention,* 27, 55.

26. There were more than 500,000 AME Zion Church members in 1909, according to Mary Helm, *The Upward Path: The Evolution of a Race* (New York: Young People's Missionary Movement of the United States and Canada, 1909), 243.

27. *Star of Zion,* 14 Feb. 1901, 4.

28. Only scattered issues of the *Missionary Seer* exist in the Carnegie Library, Livingstone College, Salisbury, N.C.

29. Mattie W. Taylor, ed., *Celebrating One Hundred Ten Years of Winning "The World for Christ," 1880–1990* (New York: Mission Education Committee, [1990]), 13.

30. Ibid., 15.

31. Ibid., 28.

32. A. B. Caldwell, *History of the American Negro* (Atlanta: A. B. Caldwell, 1921).

33. Taylor, *Celebrating One Hundred Ten Years,* 39; Victoria Richardson personnel folder, William Trent Collection, Livingstone College, Salisbury, N.C.; Hildred Henry Wactor, *Miscellany: A Manual for the Young Woman's Home and Foreign Missionary Society* (Fayetteville, N.C.: Worth Printing Company, 1975), 2; William Frank Fonvielle, *Some Reminiscences of College Days* (Raleigh: Privately published, 1904), 45–46. The characterization of Richardson and Lynch as teaching Livingstone's women students "finer womanhood" is A. R. Kelsey's, a Livingstone student who knew them both (A. R. Kelsey, interview with author, Salisbury, N.C., 14 May 1991).

34. Taylor, *Celebrating One Hundred Ten Years,* 43.

35. Wactor, *Miscellany,* 3.

36. *Star of Zion,* 22 August 1912, 7; Jacob W. Powell, *Bird's Eye View of the General Conference of the African Methodist Episcopal Zion Church* (Boston: Lavalle Press, 1918); David Henry Bradley, Sr., *A History of the A.M.E. Zion Church, Part II, 1872–1968* (Nashville: Parthenon Press, 1970), 237; William Jacob Walls, *The African Methodist Episcopal Zion Church: The Reality of the Black Church* (Charlotte: African Methodist Episcopal Zion Publishing House, 1974), 413–16.

37. For overviews of the beginnings of black women's clubs, see Elizabeth L. Davis, *Lifting As They Climb: The National Association of Colored Women* (Washington, D.C.: National Association of Colored Women, 1933); Charles Harris Wesley, *The History of the National Association of Colored Women's Clubs: A Legacy of Service* (Washington, D.C.: The Association, 1984); Addie Hunton, "Women's Clubs," *Crisis* 2 (September 1911): 210–2; Maude Thomas Jenkins, "The History of the Black Woman's Club Movement in America," Ed.D. dissertation, Columbia University Teachers College, 1984; Gerda Lerner, "Community Work of Black Club Women," *Journal of Negro History* 59 (1974): 158–67; Neverdon-Morton, *Afro-American Women of the South,* 190–201; Salem, *To Better Our World,* 29–63; Stephanie J. Shaw, "Black Club Women and the Creation of the National Association of Colored Women," *Journal of Women's History* 3 (Fall 1991): 10–25.

38. At the eighth convention, Marie Clinton sang to the assembled delegates, Mary Lynch introduced a motion praising Madame C. J. Walker, and Charlotte Hawkins, now Brown, spoke on the "lone woman." See *National Association of Colored Women, Eighth Biennial Session* ([1912]) and *Seventh Biennial Convention of the National Association of Colored Women* ([1910]), both on microfilm in *Records of the National Association of Colored Women's Clubs.*

39. *Star of Zion,* 13 June 1901, 8; 2 Apr. 1903, 8; *Daily Charlotte Observer,* 17 June 1901, 8.

40. Abna Aggrey Lancaster, interview with author, Salisbury, N.C., 25 June 1991.

41. George Lincoln Blackwell, telephone interview with author, 13 Jan. 1991.

42. *Daily Charlotte Observer,* 17 June 1901, 8.

43. *Star of Zion,* 11 Sept. 1902, 5.

44. *Souvenir and Official Program: The Negro Young People's Christian and Educational Congress* (Nashville: National Baptist Publishing Board, 1902).

45. *Star of Zion,* 11 Sept. 1902, 5.

46. *Biennial Report of the Superintendent of Public Instruction of North Carolina for the Scholastic Years 1900–1901 and 1901–1902* (Raleigh: Edwards and Broughton, 1902), 111.

47. *Biennial Report of the Superintendent of Public Instruction of North Carolina for the Scholastic Years 1916–1917 and 1917–1918* (Raleigh: Edwards and Broughton, 1919), 42.

48. Clipping from *Morning Post* (Raleigh, N.C.), 14 June 1903, file 1903-14, box 14, Charles Hunter Collection, Duke University, Durham, N.C.

49. In Wake County, for example, the average annual salary in 1899 for black men was $127; for black women, it was $107. But by 1910, black men's salaries averaged only $105, and black women's annual compensation fell to $90. The gap between white and black teachers' earnings, roughly $20 per year in 1899, increased to more than $200 by 1910. See clipping from *News and Observer,* 28 Oct. 1910, file 1903–14, box 14, ibid.

50. *Biennial Report of the Superintendent of Public Instruction of North Carolina for the Scholastic Years 1904–1905 and 1905–1906* (Raleigh: E. M. Uzzell, 1907), 243, and *Biennial Report of the Superintendent of Public Instruction of North Carolina for the Scholastic Years 1918–1919 and 1919–1920* (Raleigh: Edwards and Broughton, 1921), 97. Lewis R. Harlan, *Separate and Unequal: Public School Campaigns in the Southern Seaboard States, 1901–1915* (New York: Atheneum, 1968), paints a grim picture of the unfair allocations of resources for black education after Aycock's election, including teachers' salaries (106–10). Kousser, in "Progressivism," corroborates Harlan's evidence statistically and focuses on how the taxation system worked to privilege rich counties in the east.

51. *Biennial Report of the Superintendent of Public Instruction . . . 1900–1901 and 1901–1902,* 111, and *Biennial Report of the Superintendent of Public Instruction . . . 1916–1917 and 1917–1918,* 42.

52. On the mission of the Greensboro school, see Pamela Dean, "Covert Curriculum: Class and Gender in a New South College," Ph.D. dissertation, University of North Carolina at Chapel Hill, 1995.

53. For an overview of teacher-training institutions in the state, see "Report and Recommendations of the 'Statewide Committee of Ten Superintendents'" ([1916]), folder 1038, box 115, series 1, subseries 1, General Education Board Collection, Rockefeller Archive Center (RAC), Tarrytown, N.Y.

54. Valinda Rogers Littlefield, "After Teacher Training, What?" Unpublished paper in author's possession, notes the high number of married female teachers in a sample of applications of Durham public school teachers and explores the culture in which black women taught.

55. Clipping from *The State* (Columbia, S.C.), 15 June 1905, 6, and A. M. Waddell to E. A. Alderman, 31 Jan. 1903, both in folder 3, box 1, Coon Papers, Southern Historical Collection, Wilson Library, University of North Carolina, Chapel Hill, N.C.

56. On the educational movement in North Carolina during this period, and McIver and Aycock, see James Leloudis, *Schooling the New South: Pedagogy, Self, and Society in North Carolina, 1880–1920* (Chapel Hill: University of North Carolina Press, 1996). In addition to Harlan, *Separate and Unequal,* and Kousser, "Progressivism," see Henry Leon Prather, *Resurgent Politics and Educational Progressivism in the New South: North Carolina, 1890–1913* (Rutherford, N.J.: Associated Universities Press, 1979); M. C. S. Noble, *A History of the Public Schools in North Carolina* (Chapel Hill: University of North Carolina Press, 1930); Edgar W. Knight, *Public School Education in North Carolina.* 1916. Reprint (New York: Negro Universities Press, 1969).

57. Charles Duncan McIver, "Disfranchisement and Education," *Southern Workman* (February 1901) 189–90.

58. Josiah W. Bailey, "Popular Education and the Race Problem in North Carolina, *Outlook* 68 (May 1901): 114–6.

59. Charles B. Aycock, "Letter to the Legislature," 1901, Governor's Letter Book #109, 141, Charles Brantley Aycock, Governor's Papers and Letter Books, North Carolina Department of Archives and History.

60. Rose Leary Love, *Plum Thickets and Field Daisies* (Charlotte: Public Library of Charlotte and Mecklenburg County, 1996).

61. Leloudis, " 'A More Certain Means of Grace,' " 243; George-Anne Willard, "Charles L. Coon: Crusader for Educational Reform," Ph.D. dissertation, University of North Carolina at Chapel Hill, 1974; J. Y. Joyner to Charles L. Coon, [1904], folder 26, box 2, Charles L. Coon Papers, Southern Historical Collection (SHC), Wilson Library, University of North Carolina, Chapel Hill, N.C.

62. J. Y. Joyner to Charles L. Coon, [1904], folder 26, box 2, Coon Papers, SHC.

63. Summary of Coon's 1909 Atlanta speech for *World's Work;* J. Y. Joyner to Charles L. Coon, 27 Sept. 1909; F. S. Hargrave to Charles Coon, 28 Sept. 1909 (for black reaction); and R. D. W. Connor to Charles L. Coon, 29 Sept. 1909; W. T. Lyon to Charles L. Coon, 30 Sept. 1909; and Charles B. Aycock to Charles L. Coon, 28 Oct. 1909 (for white support), all in folder 28, box 2, ibid.

64. Thurston T. Hicks to Charles L. Coon, 17 Oct. 1909, folder 18, box 2, ibid.

65. Charles Lee Coon, "How to Better the Negro County Schools," folder 28, box 2, ibid.

66. Clipping from *Morning Post* (Raleigh, N.C.), 14 June 1903, file 1903–14, box 14, Hunter Collection, DU; "Minutes First North Carolina Conference for Negro Education," 5, folder 1042, box 115, series 1, subseries 1, General Education Board Collection, RAC.

67. N. C. Newbold, "Supervising Industrial Teachers: Some Things They Helped to Do Last School Year, 1916–1917," folder 1044, box 115, series 1, subseries 1, General Education Board Collection, RAC.

68. N. C. Newbold to Wallace Buttrick, 27 Feb. 1913, folder 1038, and "Report of N. C. Newbold, State Supervisor Negro Elementary Schools for North Carolina, for the Month of June 1913," folder 1042, both in box 115, ibid.

69. "Report of N. C. Newbold, . . . June 1913," 3, folder 1042, box 115, ibid.

70. Ibid., 15. On the work of other philanthropies and the growth of the Jeanes teaching force in the South, see General Education Board, *Report of the Secretary, 1914–1915* (New York, n.d.), 35–9; *Report of the Secretary, 1916–17* (New York, n.d.), 41–4; *Report of the Secretary, 1917–1918* (New York, n.d.), 51–5; *Annual Report of the General Education Board, 1918–19* (New York, n.d.), 53–6; and "North Carolina School Survey," in *Annual Report of the General Education Board, 1920–1921* (New York, n.d.), 39–42; Phelps-Stokes Fund, *Negro Status and Race Relations in the United States, 1911–1946* (New York, 1948), 17–20; Lance G. E. Jones, *The Jeanes Teacher in the United States, 1908–1933* (Chapel Hill: University of North Carolina Press, 1937), 59; James D. Anderson, *The Education of Blacks in the South, 1860–1935* (Chapel Hill: University of North Carolina Press, 1988), 135–47; and Thomas W. Hanchett, "The Rosenwald Schools and Black Education in North Carolina," *North Carolina Historical Review* 64 (October 1988): 387–427. For an analysis of African American education in North Carolina during this period, see U.S. Department of the Interior,

Negro Education: A Study of the Private and Higher Schools for Colored People in the United States, Bulletin no. 38 (Washington, D.C.: Government Printing Office, 1917), 55–83. For an overview of programs available, see Ullin W. Leavell, "Trends of Philanthropy in Negro Education: A Survey," *Journal of Negro Education* 2 (January 1933): 38–52, and Link, *Paradox of Southern Progressivism,* 243–57.

71. Nathan C. Newbold, "Annie Wealthy Holland," in *Five North Carolina Negro Educators* (Chapel Hill: University of North Carolina Press, 1939), 61–85.

72. Arthur D. Wright, *The Negro Rural School Fund, Inc. (Anna T. Jeanes Foundation), 1907–1933* (Washington, D.C.: Negro Rural School Fund, 1933), 171.

73. For the extraordinary story of the Aggrey family, see Edwin W. Smith, *Aggrey of Africa.* On the Aggreys' courtship and marriage, see folder 7, box 147.2, and clipping from *Lodge Journal and Guide* (Norfolk-Portsmouth, Va.), 18 Nov. 1905, 1, folder 35, box 147.1, both in Aggrey Papers, Moreland-Spingarn Research Center, Howard University, Washington, D.C. Aggrey spent most of the 1920s in Africa, returning to New York City in 1927 to defend his doctoral dissertation at Columbia University. He caught a fever and died before his defense. His daughter, Abna Aggrey Lancaster, recalls that the dissertation manuscript was never seen again.

74. Abna Aggrey Lancaster, interview with author, Salisbury, N.C., 25 June 1991; J. R. Larkins, "Testimonial in Honor of Mrs. Rose Douglass Aggrey," 15 Dec. 1957, in author's possession; "Noted Negro Teacher Retires," in author's possession; Louise Marie Rountree, comp. *A Brief Chronology of Black Salisbury-Rowan* ([Salisbury, N.C.], 1976), 16.

75. Abna Aggrey Lancaster, interview with author, Salisbury, N.C., 25 June 1991.

76. Arthur D. Wright, *Negro Rural School Fund.*

77. Sarah Delany and A. Elizabeth Delany, with Amy Hill Hearth, *Having Our Say: The Delany Sisters' First 100 Years* (New York: Kodansha International, 1993), 79–80.

78. Miss S. L. Delany, "Monthly Progress Letter for December 1913," in "Schedule of Educational Work and Progress Letter"; "Minutes First North Carolina Conference for Negro Education," 2; and "Reports of Progress for January, 1914," all in folder 1042, box 115, series 1, subseries 1, General Education Board Collection, RAC.

79. Lance G. E. Jones, *Jeanes Teacher,* 48–52; Neverdon-Morton, *Afro-American Women of the South,* 89–93; James D. Anderson, *Education of Blacks,* 135–47.

80. "Report of N. C. Newbold, . . . June 1913," 6, folder 1042, box 115; N. C. Newbold, "Supervising Industrial Teachers: Some Things They Helped to Do Last School Year, 1916–1917," 2, 6, folder 1044, box 115; and N. C. Newbold, *Summary of Reports of Home-Makers Club Agents, North Carolina, 1915,* folder 1048, box 116, all in series 1, subseries 1, General Education Board Collection, RAC.

81. Mrs. C. L. Battle, "The Effects of the Modern Health Crusade in the Rural Negro Schools of Edgecombe County," paper presented at the Second Annual Conference on Tuberculosis, Goldsboro, N.C., 3 Oct. 1922, reprinted in George E. Pankey, "Life Histories of Rural Negro Teachers in the South," M.A. thesis, University of North Carolina at Chapel Hill, 1927, 77–81. On Battle's background, see ibid., 28, 36–7, 41–2, 49, 58. For similar campaigns held in white schools, see George M. Cooper, "Medical Inspections of Schools in North Carolina," *Southern Medical Journal* 2 (February 1918): 112–5. On motion pictures, see "The American Sociological Congress and Its Plan for the Extension Campaign," folder 909, box 87, series 3, Laura Spellman Rockefeller Collection, RAC.

82. "Summary of Reports of N. C. Newbold, State Agent Negro Rural Schools for North Carolina, July 1, 1915–June 30, 1916," 2, folder 1043, box 115, series 1, subseries 1, General Education Board Collection, RAC. Aycock reported with pride that during his administration (1901–5), 700 schools were built for whites and 100 for blacks. The figures on black contributions to school building cited above call into question whether the state built those 100 black schools or whether African Americans built them. See Harlan, *Separate and Unequal,* 102.

83. "Report of N. C. Newbold, State Supervisor Rural Schools for Negroes for North Carolina, for the Month of March, 1914," 3–4, folder 1042, box 115, series 1, subseries 1, General Education Board Collection, RAC.

84. "Colored Teachers Endorse the County Board of Education," *Charlotte Chronicle,* 6 May 1914, microfiche 255, Hampton University Newspaper Clipping Files.

85. N. C. Newbold, "Supervising Industrial Teachers: Some Things They Helped to Do Last School Year, 1916–1917," folder 1044, box 115, series 1, subseries 1, General Education Board Collection, RAC. On the campaign to build Rosenwald schools in North Carolina, see Hanchett, "Rosenwald Schools." Hanchett deals primarily with school building in the 1920s and 1930s.

86. "Summary of Reports of N. C. Newbold, State Agent Negro Rural Schools for North Carolina, July 1, 1915–June 30, 1916," 4, folder 1043, box 115, series 1, subseries 1, General Education Board Collection, RAC.

87. N. C. Newbold, "Supervising Industrial Teachers: Some Things They Helped to Do Last School Year, 1916–1917," folder 1044; "Summary of Reports of N. C. Newbold, State Agent Negro Rural Schools for North Carolina, July 1, 1915–June 30, 1916," folder 1043; and "Summary of Reports of Mr. N. C. Newbold, State Agent for Negro Rural Schools of North Carolina, January 1, 1916, to December 31, 1916," folder 1044, all in box 115, series 1, subseries 1, General Education Board Collection, RAC.

88. Lumbee Indians and African Americans intermarried, and North Carolina folklore holds that the Lumbee are descendants of English members of the Lost Colony and Croatan Indians. John Spaulding was African American. The Spaulding family regarded themselves, in the words of their grandson, Aaron R. Kelsey, as "Negroes." Kelsey also called his family "freeish," a term that probably came from the expression "free issue" used to describe African Americans born free during slavery. See A. R. Kelsey, interview with author, Salisbury, N.C., 14 May 1991. I am indebted to Kelsey for sharing with me his memories of his mother, his encyclopedic knowledge of racial politics in Rowan County, and his keen sense of place and time.

89. On the founding and growth of the North Carolina Mutual Life Insurance Company, see Walter B. Weare, *Black Business in the New South: A Social History of the North Carolina Mutual Life Insurance Company* (Urbana: University of Illinois Press, 1973).

90. L. M. Spaulding to Prof. and Mrs. J. E. Aggrey, 26 May 1906, folder 6, box 147.3, Aggrey Papers, MSRC.

91. Eula Wellmon Dunlap, "Reminiscences," Lincoln Academy Papers, Amistad Research Center, New Orleans, La.

92. Mable Parker Massey, "Vital Statistics in North Carolina," *South Atlantic Quarterly* 13 (April 1914): 129–33.

93. A. R. Kelsey, interview with author, Salisbury, N.C., 14 May 1991.

94. Ibid.

95. Constitution, in Minutes of the Salisbury Colored Women's Civic League, Livingstone College. The league changed its name from "Colored" to "Negro" in 1920, although Mary Lynch began suggesting the name change in 1916. The information on members is taken from rolls and dues lists throughout the minutes.

96. Abna Aggrey Lancaster, interview with author, Salisbury, N.C., 25 June 1991.

97. Ibid.; A. R. Kelsey, interview with author, Salisbury, N.C., 14 May 1991. Lancaster and Kelsey went over the rolls and told me stories about the women they remembered from their childhood.

98. Lizzie Crittendon was the wife of W. B. Crittendon, who formed the Colored Voters' League of North Carolina.

99. Minutes of the Salisbury Colored Women's Civic League, 28 July 1913, 28 June 1916, LC.

100. *Outlook* 106 (4 Apr. 1914): 742.

101. Ibid.

102. Minutes of the Salisbury Colored Women's Civic League, 28 July 1913, LC.

103. "The Negro Problem: How It Appears to a Southern Colored Woman," *Independent* 54 (18 September 1902): 2221–28. Black families began developing their own suburban neighborhoods in order to exclude white landlords and control housing standards. McCrorey Heights was such a neighborhood in Charlotte. See Mamie Garvin Fields, with Karen Fields, *Lemon Swamp and Other Places: A Carolina Memoir* (New York: Free Press, 1983), 162–79, and C. H. Watson, ed., *Colored Charlotte* (Charlotte, n.p. [1915]).

104. Eula Wellmon Dunlap, "Reminiscences," Lincoln Academy Papers, ARC. Typhoid can be spread by flies, but tuberculosis cannot. William A. Link argues, "None of the southern social reforms of the Progressive Era were individually more important or together more coherent than the modernization of public health and public education" ("Privies, Progressivism, and Public Schools").

105. Mable Parker Massey, "Vital Statistics in North Carolina," 131.

106. Lilly Hammond, *Southern Women and Racial Adjustment* (Lynchburg, Va.: J.P. Bell, 1917).

107. On Cathcart, see Dunlap, "Reminiscences." On De Bardeleben and the Bethlehem Houses, see Jacquelyn Dowd Hall, *Revolt against Chivalry: Jessie Daniel Ames and the Women's Campaign against Lynching.* Rev. ed. (New York: Columbia University Press, 1993).

108. Good Samaritan Hospital Collection, North Carolina Department of Archives and History; uncatalogued material in the Jane Renwick Wilkes Papers, Charlotte Public Library, Charlotte, N.C.

109. *Minutes of the Fifteenth Annual Meeting of the Woman's Missionary Societies,* 52; *Minutes of the Twenty-third Annual Session of the Women's Baptist Home Mission Convention,* 5, 13. See also Mary Helm, *From Darkness to Light* (New York: Fleming H. Revell, 1909), 209, 211, 215, 217, and Hammond, *Southern Women and Racial Adjustment.*

110. Bishop George W. Clinton, "What Can the Church Do to Promote Good Will between the Races," in *Democracy in Earnest.*

111. Minutes of the Charlotte Woman's Club, 1910–11, 20, 21, Charlotte Woman's Club Papers, Special Collections, Atkins Library, University of North Carolina, Charlotte, N.C. On white women and the "servant problem," see W. D. Weatherford, *Negro Life in the South: Present Conditions and Needs* (New York: Association Press, 1918), 37–8.

112. Hammond, *Southern Women and Racial Adjustment,* 16.

113. During an undocumented period of the association's history, it appears that the board was interracial in 1910, including North Carolina Agricultural and Technical College president James Dudley and Charles McIver's widow, Lula McIver. See James B. Dudley to Charles N. Hunter, 22 Mar. 1910, file 1910–12, box 4, Hunter Collection, DU. By 1920, a new board, made up of white club women and one white male physician, had institutionalized the effort across the state. See *The First 50 Years* (N.p.: North Carolina Tuberculosis Association, [1956]), 4–6, pamphlet, American Lung Association of North Carolina Records, Raleigh, N.C. Despite the lack of documentation on the effort to eradicate tuberculosis, it is clear that in North Carolina, white club women seized the public health initiative and, working through state educational officials, solicited help from the Rockefeller Sanitary Commission to eradicate hookworm, build sanitary privies, and establish county health departments. See James Y. Joyner to F. T. Gates, 23 Dec. 1909, folder 114, box 5; [?] to Mrs. Eugene Reilley, president of the North Carolina Federation of Women's Clubs, 8 Feb. 1910, folder 114, box 5; Wickliffe Rose to Dr. John A. Ferrell, 17 Oct. 1910, folder 114, box 5; and John A. Ferrell to Wickliffe Rose, 12 Oct. 1919, folder 115, box 5, all in series 2, Rockefeller Sanitary Commission Collection, RAC. For the best account of public health reform, see William A. Link, *Paradox of Southern Progressivism,* 142–49.

114. The minutes of the Atlanta Anti-Tuberculosis Association emphasize interracial cooperation. See Mary Dickinson, "Report of Race Relationship as Illustrated by the Atlanta Anti-Tuberculosis Association—Presented at the Conference at the Southern Methodist Church at Memphis, Tenn., Oct. 6–7, 1920," and report of Rosa Lowe, Anti-Tuberculosis and Visiting Nurse Association, both in scrapbook, folder 21, box 8, Atlanta Lung Association Collection, Atlanta History Center, Atlanta, Ga.; Mary Ellen Kidd Parsons, "White Plague and the Double-Barred Cross in Atlanta, 1894–1945," Ph.D. dissertation, Emory University, 1985; Tera Hunter, *To 'Joy My Freedom': Southern Black Women's Lives and Labors after the Civil War* (Cambridge: Harvard University Press, 1997); Rouse, *Lugenia Burns Hope,* 71–2, 80–2; and Louise Shivery, "The History of Organized Social Work among Atlanta Negroes, 1890–1935," M.A. thesis, Atlanta University, 1946.

115. Minutes of the Salisbury Colored Women's Civic League, 26 Aug. 1913, LC.

116. Ibid., 27 Jan. 1914, 24 Mar. 1913, 26 Jan. 1915.

117. In Charlotte, Mary Jackson McCrorey became president of the Associated Charities Auxiliary in 1916.

118. Minutes of the Salisbury Colored Women's Civic League, 7 Jan. 1917, and City-Wide Associated Charities Campaign Card in Minute Book, LC.

119. Ibid., 4 Sept. 1917.

120. A. R. Kelsey, interview with author, Salisbury, N.C., 14 May 1991. The social worker was Mrs. Linton.

121. Nancy Fraser, *Unruly Practices: Power, Discourse, and Gender in Contemporary Social Theory* (Minneapolis: University of Minnesota Press, 1989).

122. Minutes of the Salisbury Colored Women's Civic League, 30 Sept., 28 Oct. 1913, LC.

123. Membership card of the Salisbury Colored Women's Civic League, in ibid.

124. Ibid., 30 Sept., 28 Oct. 1913. The mayor was Walter H. Woodson, who served from 1913 to 1919. See *Salisbury Evening Post,* Bicentennial Edition, 29 Apr. 1975, 12.

125. Minutes of the Salisbury Colored Women's Civic League, 25 Nov. 1913, LC.

126. Ibid., 1 Sept. 1914.

127. Ibid., 28 Jan. 1916.

128. A. R. Kelsey, interview with author, Salisbury, N.C., 14 May 1991; Minutes of the Salisbury Colored Women's Civic League, 26 Feb., 11 Apr. 1916, LC.

129. Minutes of the Salisbury Colored Women's Civic League, 28 Apr., 29 Sept. 1914, 26 Feb., 8 Aug. 1916, LC. On directed play and controlled recreation, see Dominick Cavallo, *Muscles and Morals: Organized Playgrounds and Urban Reform, 1880–1920* (Philadelphia: University of Pennsylvania Press, 1981); John F. Kasson, *Amusing the Million: Coney Island at the Turn of the Century* (New York: Hill and Wang, 1978), 102–4; and A. W. Traywick, "The Play Life of Negro Boys and Girls," in *Democracy in Earnest.*

130. Minutes of the Salisbury Colored Women's Civic League, 30 Sept. 1913, LC. For mothers' aid and the welfare state, see Sonya Michel and Seth Koven, "Womanly Duties: Maternalist Politics and the Origins of Welfare States in France, Germany, Great Britain, and the United States, 1880–1920," *American Historical Review* 94 (October 1990): 1076–1108.

131. Minutes of the Salisbury Colored Women's Civic League, 27 Jan., 30 June, 24 Nov. 1914, LC.

132. Ibid., 28 Mar. 1915, 3 Nov. 1914, 28 Jan. 1916.

133. *Outlook* 106 (4 Apr. 1914): 742.

Suggestions for Further Reading

The literature on Progressivism is vast, much of it in useful articles beyond the scope of this bibliography. The suggested readings that follow touch on general themes in the introduction or try to answer the question "Who were the Progressives?"

What were the intellectual, religious, and scientific catalysts that inspired people to set about changing their society? For those who see Progressivism as an ideology—a coherent cluster of ideas—that transcended politics-as-usual or mere economic necessity, this is the most important question to ask. Many historians, including Richard Hofstadter in this volume, argued that the idea that Christianity should be useful in society—the Social Gospel—inspired much of the Progressive fervor. Robert M. Crunden's *Ministers of Reform: The Progressives' Achievement in American Civilization, 1889–1920* illuminates how the Social Gospelers took their ministries to city streets to solve problems caused by urbanization and industrialization. In his 1981 work, *The Progressive Mind, 1890–1917,* David Noble links these Social Gospel thinkers, people such as the prolific Progressive writer and minister Walter Rauschenbusch, with educators and sociologists. All were trying to understand what Noble calls the "social nature of natural man" and to reorganize society according to a set of natural principles that made progress possible. Some intellectual historians, for example, Morton White, *Social Thought in America: The Revolt Against Formalism,* look even deeper for the new ways of thinking that converged in the 1890s, and they find intellectuals in revolt against tradition and received wisdom and eager for experimentation and rigorous proof of lived experience.

Historians have attempted to link intellectual leaders to the participatory democracy they hoped to create, exploring how those intellectuals saw the American public. Recent work in this vein includes Kevin Mattson, *Creating a Democratic Public: The Struggle for Urban Participatory Democracy during the Progressive Era,* and Leon Fink, *Progressive Intellectuals and the Dilemmas of Democratic Commitment.* Fink describes particularly well how

Progressive experts conceptualized the masses and public opinion. Matt-son explores the ways in which those experts attempted to deliver their messages to various groups of average people. Although Progressives envi-sioned experts in a conversation with the people, they also believed that participatory democracy came about by excluding the poorest and least educated "whites" and most of the African Americans who lived in the South, according to J. Morgan Kousser in *The Shaping of Southern Politics and the Emergence of the One-Party South, 1880–1910,* and Alexander Keyssar in *The Right to Vote: The Contested History of Democracy in the United States.*

Recently some historians have been pointing out that Progressivism did not necessarily grow out of strictly American concerns and ideas, but had close connections to international thought and social change. Two books make these connections in different ways: James Kloppenberg's *Uncertain Victory: Social Democracy and Progressivism in European and American Thought, 1870–1920* and Daniel Rodgers's *Atlantic Crossings: Social Politics in a Progres-sive Age.* These international perspectives not only connect the origins of Progressivism with the rest of the world, but they also give us a way to measure what was particularly American about the reforms that the U.S. Progressives accomplished.

Still other historians argue that Progressivism sprang in part from changes in gender roles that brought women into public space, a problem we touch on in the readings. From the 1970s onward, as historians began to uncover women's history, they found that, across the country, women had been Progressive Era reformers in areas as divergent as prisons, labor legislation, direct democracy, mental health, vice, protection against con-tamination, and many others. Anne Scott recalled as she set out to study the Progressive Era in the South that she "kept stumbling over the women." The result was her *Southern Lady: From Pedestal to Politics.* Across the country, as evidenced by Maureen A. Flanagan's article in this volume about Chicago, historians are restoring women to the Progressive ranks and asking what difference their presence and leadership made to the shape and outcome of Progressive reform.

Some approaches to women Progressives have been biographical, such as Ellen Fitzpatrick's *Endless Crusade: Women Social Scientists and Progressive Reform* and Kathryn Kish Sklar's *Florence Kelley and the Nation's Work: The Rise of Women's Political Culture, 1830–1900.* Others have centered on the fight for the passage of the Nineteenth Amendment that gave women the right to vote. Aileen Kraditor's 1965 book, *Ideas of the Woman Suffrage Movement,* connects suffrage to Progressive reform, and Nancy F. Cott's 1987 work, *The Grounding of Modern Feminism,* sets an entire range of women's re-forms in the context of the suffrage fight. In the South, Marjorie Spruill

Wheeler's *New Women of the New South: The Leaders of the Woman Suffrage Movement in the Southern States* offers a regional analysis. Knowing that women wanted to extend social housekeeping into the public sphere gives us another wellspring for Progressivism.

Where Progressives effected reform has also engaged historians: Their gaze has moved from high to low, from the federal government to neighborhood settlement houses. For example, Martin J. Sklar looks at the governmental business regulation in *The Corporate Reconstruction of American Capitalism, 1890–1916: The Market, the Law, and Politics.* Numerous state studies abounded in the 1960s and 1970s, for example, David P. Thelen, *The New Citizenship: Origins of Progressivism in Wisconsin, 1885–1900.* Allen F. Davis, in *Spearheads of Reform,* offers the best overview of the settlement house movement, and many studies on individual cities have followed John Buenker's 1973 work, *Urban Liberalism and Progressive Reform.* Elizabeth Lasch-Quinn's *Black Neighbors: Race and the Limits of Reform in the American Settlement House Movement, 1890–1945* takes a close look at settlement work among black Progressives that escapes restriction to a single city and emphasizes the national network of African American women.

Most agree that one of the Progressives' goals was regulation of certain aspects of the economy and urban life. Some historians also argue that Progressives built a larger state apparatus to enact that regulation. The goal may have been to protect people or to protect capital. The growing state did both very imperfectly. Representative overviews that capture both the laudable reforms and imperfections of Progressivism include John W. Chambers II, *The Tyranny of Change: America in the Progressive Era,* Arthur S. Link and Richard L. McCormick, *Progressivism,* and John Milton Cooper, *Pivotal Decades: The United States, 1900–1920.* It was during the Progressive Era that the regulatory state with which we are familiar today began to grow. Lately, historians have examined the administrative functions of that larger state; a good example is Stephen Skowronek's *Building a New American State.* A vigorous debate on the origins of welfare and the growth of the state has included a debate about the role of women. Although not included in this volume, this debate demonstrates the importance of Progressivism to current U.S. politics. For divergent views, see Linda Gordon, *Pitied but Not Entitled: Single Mothers and the History of Welfare, 1890–1935,* Theda Skocpol, *Protecting Soldiers and Mothers: The Political Origins of Social Policy in the United States,* and Kathryn Kish Sklar, *Florence Kelley and the Nation's Work: The Rise of Women's Political Culture, 1830–1900.*

Similarly missing from this volume, but important to Progressivism as a whole, is the link between domestic reform and imperialism. For a wonderful treatment of domestic reform, vigorous manhood, and imperialistic designs, see Gail Bederman, *Manliness and Civilization: A Cultural History of Gender and Race in the United States.* On overseas markets and domestic ideology, see Emily S. Rosenberg, *Spreading the American Dream: American Economic and Cultural Expansion, 1890–1945,* and Matthew Frye Jacobson, *Barbarian Virtues: The United States Encounters Foreign Peoples at Home and Abroad, 1876–1917.* For a brief and entertaining survey of how Americans linked foreign policy and domestic Progressivism, see Michael H. Hunt, *Ideology and U.S. Foreign Policy.*

Progressive solutions at the beginning of the twentieth century sparked the growth of an activist government in mid-century, and the Progressive Era cast a shadow far past its chronological boundaries. Alan Dawley's synthesis, *Struggles for Justice: Social Responsibility and the Liberal State,* puts the Progressive Era in historical context, relates it to the 1920s and the New Deal, and evaluates its importance. Historians have long debated when Progressivism died. Some argued that Wilson's antidemocratic measures in World War I ended Progressivism, since many Progressives, including Jane Addams, experienced the gathering of experts, the growth of governmental power, and the masterful manipulation of the press during the war as a threat to liberty. Others have seen in World War I an ironic flowering of Progressive methods—for example, in the propaganda machine George Creel created to produce patriotism or in the high point of organization we find in Herbert Hoover's campaign to harness volunteers to forestall famine in Europe. William E. Leuchtenburg has argued that the concentration of talent in government during World War I served as an "analogue" for the New Deal, which realized many Progressive Era dreams, including mothers' pensions, in the Social Security Act of 1937.

Ironically, as past historians overlooked women, they generally regarded Progressivism as over by 1920, the date that woman suffrage became law. Historians of women argue about how suffrage affected Progressive women's power to effect reform. Historian Suzanne Lebsock has even argued that women may have had more political power in the Progressive Era years that preceded their right to vote than they did in the 1920s after suffrage, when they became a splintered group.[1] Historian William Chafe has suggested that we might reconsider the period spanned by Progressivism by looking at the involvement of women in social causes. Many of the women Progressives who advocated solutions through voluntary associations in the 1910s entered politics in the 1920s, and entered the federal government itself in the New Deal.[2] Foregrounding women, as Chafe does, suggests more continuity between Progressivism and the New Deal than other historians have recognized.

The Progressive Era shaped the way we experience our freedom and our responsibility to government into the twenty-first century. It is a period from which we have an enormous amount of data, articulate voices telling us how they felt about change, and passionate movements springing up to reorder individual lives. For those who care about the possibilities of social change, the Progressive Era is a laboratory in which to test their hypotheses.

Notes

1. Suzanne Lebsock, "Women and American Politics, 1880–1920," in Louise Tilly and Patricia Guin, eds., *Women, Politics, and Change* (New York: Russell Sage Foundation, 1990), 35–62; Nancy Cott, "Across the Great Divide: Women in Politics Before and After 1920," in *Women, Politics, and Change,* 153–76.

2. William Chafe, "Women's History and Political History: Some Thoughts on Progressivism and the New Deal," in Nancy A. Hewitt and Suzanne Lebscock, eds., *Visible Women: New Essays on American Activism* (Urbana: University of Illinois Press, 1993), 101–18.

Acknowledgments (continued from p. iv)

GLENDA ELIZABETH GILMORE. "Diplomatic Women." From *Gender and Jim Crow: Women and the Politics of White Supremacy in North Carolina 1896–1920* by Glenda Elizabeth Gilmore. Copyright © 1996 by the University of North Carolina Press. Reprinted by permission of the Publisher.

RICHARD HOFSTADTER. "The Status Revolution and Progressive Leaders." From *The Age of Reform: From Byran to F.D.R.* Copyright © 1955 by Richard Hofstadter. Reprinted by permission of Alfred A. Knopf, a division of Random House, Inc.

RICHARD L. McCORMICK. "The Discovery That Business Corrupts Politics: A Reappraisal of the Origins of Progressivism." From *American Historical Review*, Volume 86, No. 2, April 1981. Copyright © 1981. Reprinted by permission.

ELIZABETH SANDERS. "Agrarian Politics and Parties after 1896." From *Roots of Reform: Farmers, Workers, and the American State, 1877–1917.* Copyright © 1999 by Elizabeth Sanders. Reprinted by permission of the University of Chicago Press.

SHELTON STROMQUIST. "The Crucible of Class: Cleveland Politics and the Origins of Municipal Reform in the Progressive Era." From the *Journal of Urban History*, Volume 23, January 1997. Copyright © 1997. Reprinted by permission.

ROBERT H. WIEBE. "Progressivism Arrives." From *The Search for Order: 1877–1920.* Copyright © 1967 by Robert H. Wiebe. Reprinted by permission of Hill and Wang, a division of Farrar, Straus & Giroux LLC.